AF477529

CONRAD: EASTERN AND WESTERN PERSPECTIVES

General Editor: Wiesław Krajka

VOLUME VIII

JOSEPH CONRAD: EAST EUROPEAN, POLISH AND WORLDWIDE

Edited with an Introduction by
WIESŁAW KRAJKA

EAST EUROPEAN MONOGRAPHS, BOULDER
MARIA CURIE-SKŁODOWSKA UNIVERSITY, LUBLIN
DISTRIBUTED BY COLUMBIA UNIVERSITY PRESS, NEW YORK

1999

EAST EUROPEAN MONOGRAPHS, NO. DXLVII

TABLE OF CONTENTS

ABBREVIATIONS

I. Conrad's Works

AF	*Almayer's Folly*
Ch	*Chance*
LJ	*Lord Jim*
MS	*The Mirror of the Sea*
N	*Nostromo*
NLL	*Notes on Life and Letters*
NN	*The Nigger of the "Narcissus"*
OI	*An Outcast of the Islands*
PR	*A Personal Record*
SA	*The Secret Agent*
SL	*The Shadow-Line*
TLS	*'Twixt Land and Sea*
TS	*Typhoon and Other Stories*
TU	*Tales of Unrest*
UWE	*Under Western Eyes*
V	*Victory*
WT	*Within the Tides*
YS	*Youth: A Narrative, and Two Other Stories*

All references to Conrad's works in the following essays are to the Dent Uniform Edition (1923-28) or to its reprints and other editions with identical pagination (the Doubleday editions of the 1920s and the Oxford University Press's World's Classics edition).

II. Conrad's Letters

CL   *The Collected Letters of Joseph Conrad.*
Ed. Frederick R. Karl and Laurence Davies. 5 vols. to date. Cambridge: Cambridge U. P., 1983- .

DEDICATION

This volume is dedicated to professor Stephen Fischer-Galati, the Editor of *East European Monographs* and *Social Science Monographs*, Columbia University Press, New York, which host the series *Conrad: Eastern and Western Perspectives*. I (the general editor of this series), and the editors, authors and contributors to all the 8 volumes of the series are grateful for the opportunity to publish with these prestigious and internationally esteemed publishers. Professor Fischer-Galati's professorial wisdom, his understanding of the value of publishing high quality academic books and his dedication to worldwide dissemination of academic ideas is preeminent and exemplary. It is owing to him that our series *Conrad: Eastern and Western Perspectives,* a truly international joint enterprise of Conradians, has become what it is.

Ad multos annos professor Fischer-Galati.

Wiesław Krajka

Wiesław Krajka,
Maria Curie-Skłodowska University/University of Wrocław,
Lublin/Wrocław, Poland

Introduction

The present volume consists of selected papers from the proceedings of the II International Joseph Conrad Conference at Maria Curie-Skłodowska University, Lublin, Poland, which took place between 1st-4th September 1996 in Lublin-Kazimierz Dolny, Poland. The conference was organized by the Conrad Studies Section of the English Department at Maria Curie--Skłodowska University within the East European Monographs – Maria Curie-Skłodowska University Conrad Project. It was held in honor of professor Stephen Fischer-Galati, the Editor of East European Monographs and Social Science Monographs (Columbia University Press).

The volume is a collection of essays written by eminent and emerging Conrad scholars from all the continents, from various corners of the world: USA, Poland, Germany, Spain, Turkey, Australia, South Africa, Brazil and India. It addresses a spectrum of themes and aspects of the literary output of Joseph Conrad: from ethical-axiological issues to those of ideology and politics; from mythical organization of the sea universe to archetypal studies in the subconscious; from philosophy to gender hybridism and other elements of the colonial encounter; from artistic methods of character creation to psychology; from rhetoric and narrative strategies to symbolism and irony; from parallels with Whitman and Turgenev to the influence of Dostoevsky and Polish romantic literature; from the application of elements of Polish/East European ethnos and culture to those of Jewish folklore; from parallels with South American colonial experience to Conradian inspirations in Dutch-Indonesian post-colonial literature; from tracing parallels with Western romantic idealism to an examination in terms of Indian mystical philosophy; and others. The present volume highlights Conrad's position as the second (after Shakespeare) most international writer in the history of English literature. It is hoped that it also contributes to strengthening mutual understanding among scholars from such diverse intellectual traditions and cultural backgrounds.

The volume also displays a broad scope of methodological approaches to Joseph Conrad's oeuvre, of both established and original literary theoretical and philosophical perspectives: the history of literature, the history of ideas, critical reception, various strategies of close reading and interpretation of a literary text, comparative studies (conducted in terms of both parallels and influences), editorial investigations, mythographic and archetypal criticism, psychoanalytic and feminist approaches, cross-cultural and postcolonial studies, and various other kinds of interdisciplinary research. Some essays are rooted in Western literary theory and Conrad scholarship, whereas others introduce fresh theoretical-interpretative visions or approach Conrad's oeuvre from remote intellectual positions, broadening the possibilities of their interpretation. The essays bring considerations of new issues and reinterpretations of old ones in Conrad studies in illuminating and original presentations. Some of them cover a large area of the Conrad canon, whereas others penetrate his single literary texts: mostly "Heart of Darkness", *Under Western Eyes* and *Lord Jim*, but also "Amy Foster," "Karain: A Memory," "The Secret Sharer," *Almayer's Folly* and *The Secret Agent*.

The volume is divided into two parts, reflecting two principal dimensions of Joseph Conrad's works: East European/Polish and Worldwide. The article by İçöz, commencing part I, considers certain principal characteristics of Conradian ethics and outlook: ego-ideal and identity, private vision vs public action, self-interest vs social duty, solidarity and fidelity vs betrayal – in both general terms and in *Lord Jim* and *Under Western Eyes*. Her interpretation of the latter novel (constituting a major part of her argument) is focused on the interplay of West European rationality and Russian irrationality in the actions of Razumov and other characters. Immersion into the Russian mind is continued by Toy who examines the interrelationship between narrative strategies, rhetoric and the multivocal, ambiguous presentation of ideological conceptualizations and political systems of thought in *Under Western Eyes*. She treats narrative unreliability as a means of testing and evaluating various culturally accepted ideologies and political dogmas.

Içöz's and Toy's inquiries into ethics and politics in *Under Western Eyes* form a general introduction to the following comparative studies of Conrad and Dostoevsky by Andersen and Majewska. Among numerous juxtapositions of *Under Western Eyes* and *Crime and Punishment,* Andersen's is distinguished by focusing on the presence/absence of elements of the genre of tragedy, responsible for different delineations of Russian psychology. Her comparison is concentrated on various conceptions of Fate, spirituality and morality, on conventions of ancient Greek and Elizabethan tragedy, as well as on different aspects of man's existential situation. Majewska takes up a neglected area of Dostoevskian elements in Conrad's *The Secret Agent*. She interprets Stevie as a Christ-figure, as a firework of sophisticated allusions to various aspects of the personality and spirituality of Prince Myshkin from *The Idiot*, and as a vehicle of Conrad's ideological polemic with Dostoevsky (especially with his conceptions of holy idiocy, Christian virtues and his vision and interpretation of Christ s crucifixion). The vein of comparison of Conrad with great masters of Russian literature is continued by Sokołowska who brings together *Lord Jim* and Turgenev's *Rudin*. She traces similarities between both novels in the realms of social vs universal implications of character creation, complex and ambiguous conception and depiction of fictional personalities, the method of narration and its epistemological consequences, and both writers' objective/subjective, univocal/multivocal presentation of characters vis-à-vis the literary conventions of realism.

The articles by Krajka and Brzozowska-Krajka compose the Polish cluster in the volume. They oppose Busza's thesis about the Young Poland (modernist) "Tatromania" as inspiring and influencing the creation of Yanko Goorall in "Amy Foster."

Krajka surveys multiple interpretations of the protagonist of
"Amy Foster": autobiographical, archetypal/universalizing,
cross-cultural, colonial, Polish/East European. He corrects
many misinterpretations of various aspects of the protagonist's
East Carpathian/Polish ethnos and ethos, and makes a plea for
regarding his complex and multilayered ethnic-cultural substance in explications of this short story. Brzozowska-Krajka
views the figure of Yanko Goorall as an embodiment of the
poetics, axiology and ideology of Polish romanticism, his outfit
as being determined by his geographical-cultural location and by
the ideologies of romantic Polonophilism and Messianism. Her
essay sheds light on the personality and life choice of Joseph
Conrad himself, on the hidden dialogue between his first and
second homelands, on his attitude to the romantic outlook.

The first three papers of part II of the volume ("...and
Worldwide") – Kozak's, Schaffer's and Seeber's – form a sequence of mythological/archetypal/psychoanalytical interpretations. Kozak illuminates the spatial organization of the Conradian sea universe in terms of mythical axiology and worldview:
of the binary oppositions of myths of creation, and especially of
the concepts of the sacred and the profane; Cosmos, "our"
world, light and Chaos, the dark domain of malevolent demons;
imago mundi. He also discusses semantic tensions arising from
interrelationships of the ship, the land and the sea, and from the
axiological statuses of these elements. A related interpretation of
Conrad's sea fiction is presented by Schaffer who views the
character of Leggatt in "The Secret Sharer" in terms of the
archetypal/mythical figure of Golem in Jewish folk culture – an
offspring of elemental forces, a variation of the doppelgänger, an
original formulation of the emanation of the dark, instinctive,
primordial, irrational side of the human psyche, of the dark
underworld. He discusses symbolic, psychoanalytical and moral
aspects of the parallel and the common function of these figures.
Seeber elucidates the psychoanalytical, semantic, aesthetic,
anthropological and epistemological implications of the categories of fascination and voice in "Heart of Darkness," of the
chain of fascinations achieved through the medium of voices and

sounds, of the kind of experience conveyed through Marlow's language. He examines the moral, aesthetic, religious and nonlogical aspects of fascination, as well as various meanings, functions and implications of Kurtz's voice.

A set of four subsequent papers constitutes the postcolonial section in the second part of the volume. Brown and Sant apply conceptualizations of postcolonial literary theory to their interpretation of "Karain: A Memory," which defines the construction of the identities of Karain and of the Orient as an exotic Other by the West. In particular, they focus upon the problematics of sexualization and gender identification of racial individuals in terms of the theory of the gaze, pertaining to white male constructions of othered subjectivities. The key postcolonial category of gender hybridism (as related to Western ethnocentric thought and hegemonic culture) is applied in de Oliveira's interpretation of Nina in *Almayer's Folly* and the harlequin in "Heart of Darkness." In particular, she ponders the interlocking concepts of race and gender, transcultural relationships and problematic construction of cultural selves, the possibility/impossibility of discovering one's right and pure culture, and the conjunction between discourse and the wielding of power. Colonial racial-cultural hybridism/purity appears in Trout's examination of the idiosyncratic language of two episodic half-caste characters in *Lord Jim* who occupy a gray area (racially, culturally and linguistically) between the colonizer and the colonized, between the white colonial elite and the marginalized half-castes, between self and Other. Their presentation by Marlow, their imperial editor, is pregnant with implications concerning the spread of European culture among nonwhites, the stability and nature of his outlook, and especially his view upon racial equality/superiority/inferiority, as well as the use of humor in *Lord Jim*. The spectrum of colonial/postcolonial considerations in the volume is broadened by Poniatowska's discussion of the use of "Heart of Darkness" in "Full of Sound and Fury" by Beb Vuyk (a Dutch-Indonesian writer) – a fictional representation of some aspects of the Indonesian war for independence. She traces Conradian inspirations in the realms of narrative technique, symbolism, cross-racial transfer of ideology and values, in the modeling of the protagonist of this short story upon the character of Kurtz, as well as in its colonial/post-colonial and universal message.

The next two essays – by Mathew and Fraustino – present respectively Eastern and Western idealistic frames for Conrad's visions and outlook, and especially for the notions of the ultimate truth, meaning, values and the perfectibility of man, in opposition to Western economic barbarism. Mathew examines the notion of evil in "Heart of Darkness" and *Under Western Eyes* in terms of the philosophy of Indian mystic-philosopher Sri Aurobindo. She focuses on ways of opposing rational ethics and overcoming fragmented consciousness, of achieving moral re-generation, self-perfection and spiritual progress through evol-ution of consciousness, harmony with nature and fellow beings; it is within the scheme of Sri Aurobindo's Integral Philosophy that she places evil and its attendant concepts of pain, suffering and death. Fraustino, on the other hand, traces parallels with and a possible influence upon "Heart of Darkness" of American romanticism, and in particular of W. Whitman's "Passage to India." His comparative study is focused on the concepts of civilization, superman, the role of nature, man's relationship with his inner world, his subconscious and the past, and on possibilities of self-discovery and spiritual unification and regeneration in the materialistic world of hypocritical and false Western civilization.

The volume closes on a note of Western pragmatism in the essay by Sacido-Romero. His presentation of the editorial history and clarification of some circumstances of publication of the posthumous anthology *The Shorter Tales of Joseph Conrad* sheds light upon Conrad's publishing intentions and policies in the last year of his life. The paper especially answers the intriguing question of what made Conrad accept the publication of such a volume despite his initial opposition to it and despite his concern not to be considered a writer of the sea.

The present, 8th volume of the series *Conrad: Eastern and Western Perspectives* marks an important change in the direction of its development. The primary intention of the founding fathers of the series (on its "birth" during the I International Joseph Conrad Conference organized by Maria Curie-Skłodowska University, Lublin, in Baranów Sandomierski, Poland, in September 1991) was to stimulate and internationally promote both East-Central European aspects of Conrad's oeuvre and East-Central European contribution to world Conrad studies. And this East-Central European focus was dominant in the first five volumes of the series. On the other hand, volumes 6 and 7 significantly broadened its scope by including some essential American and English perspectives. And the present volume continues this tendency by making the series truly worldwide, which hopefully will be the dominant direction in its further development. This additionally justifies the title of the present volume – *Joseph Conrad: East European, Polish and Worldwide* – which seems to be an adequate summary of both the history of the series and of the chronology of Conrad's life and work.

(kol 8 – vacat)

Part I

Joseph Conrad: East European, Polish

Nursel İçöz,
Middle East Technical University,
Ankara, Turkey

Commitment to the Ego-Ideal and Betrayal

Conrad's oscillation between endorsing and rejecting individualism has led critics like C. Watts to call him "a janiform writer" (Watts, 46). A continuous fluctuation between belief in social values and destructive withdrawal can be seen in almost all his works. This is dramatized in the contradiction between private vision and public action: the test of what a man really is is not what he thinks he is, but what he does – not his individual consciousness, but his public role (Berthoud, 191). The predicament of Conrad's protagonists is often a consequence of their response to the claims of the ideal and self-interest or of social duty and common humanity. Conrad's interest in betrayal, an act counter to the principles of solidarity and fidelity to a social code of conduct, is an indication of his belief in the necessity of commitment to society. This belief is based on his distrust of the individual and his awareness that it is impossible for a man to succeed and to be happy in isolation. Nonetheless, Conrad also advocates the romantic view that one must try to actualize one's idealized conception of oneself and that there is much to be admired in characters who choose to do so. If the term "modern" as applied to the English literature of the early twentieth century is taken to suggest an intense preoccupation by the writer with the inner world of the individual rather than with large social issues, then Conrad may be considered a "modern" writer. At the same time, the emphasis Conrad has laid on society distinguishes him from the other "modernist" novelists of the early part of this century who reject society and the notion that man is a social being, and who endorse alienation.

In short, the Moderns' interest in subjectivity and individualism is found in Conrad side by side with an affirmation of the values of solidarity and fidelity. The reason for this seems to be that Conrad's faith in the reality of the inner world is in conflict with his scepticism about it. Moreover, the inner world is challenged by and ruled out by the outer. As Berthoud points out, he knows the inner world must exist, but he does not know how it can. As a result, Conrad's protagonists often discover the reality of their own values through defeat or contradiction (189).

L. F. Seltzer remarks that Conrad's fiction "repeatedly suggests that 'the way to be' is to commit oneself to upholding these values essential both to self-realization and to the survival and moral well-being of society" (Seltzer, 122). Seltzer also states that "the greatest paradox in Conrad's work is that it simultaneously discloses the ultimate irrelevance of moral ideas and provides eloquent – and morally meaningful – arguments for their acceptance" (97).

A prevalent theme in Conrad's fiction is the exploration of the nature of identity and this is dealt with through analyses of incidents of betrayal, both of one's self and of others. In *Almayer's Folly* and *An Outcast of the Islands* the untalented and irresponsible Almayer's and Willems' dreams of identity are disclosed. In *The Nigger of the "Narcissus"* an ideal code of conduct is established and that is set against the instinctive self in "Heart of Darkness," and against the ideal of self in *Lord Jim*. In *Nostromo* the ideal code of conduct and the organicist model (on which that code is based) are brought up against a society dominated by "material interests"; in *The Secret Agent* the collapse of Conrad's model in a society characterized by conflicting self-interests is expressed. *Under Western Eyes* presents a search for identity through acts of betrayal in a corrupt society, whose corruption influences and limits the search (Hampson, 8-9).

In both *Lord Jim* and *Under Western Eyes* it is suggested that individuality and the community can have equally valid claims to make in the life of man; hence, however valuable individual freedom may be, the individual cannot properly exist independently. The desire for a free individuality leads both Jim and Razumov first to solitude and then to self-destruction because they cannot find a way of meaningfully relating themselves to the human community. Jim's early heroic achievements in Patusan are a consequence of his involvement in the political and social life of the native community, and Razumov's confession, which saves him from self-torture and enables him to have peace, is wrung out of his heart after he establishes a kind of relationship with Nathalie Haldin.

Conrad affirms the necessity of fidelity and solidarity indirectly, that is to say, by showing how acts of infidelity, such as Jim's desertion of the *Patna* and Razumov's betrayal of Haldin, lead to the undoing of his major characters. Marlow states the case for solidarity in the strongest terms by "We exist only in so far as we hang together" (*LJ*, 164). Solidarity in Conrad is a means of escape from existential meaninglessness and something necessary for the survival of humanity and the individual. The alienated man is redeemed only if he is "able to identify his personal career with the life of a community" (Fleishman, 71). Berthoud remarks that most major works of Conrad, including *Lord Jim* and *Under Western Eyes*, "rest on a common assumption, namely that the real is to be found not in the sphere of the inner and the private, but in that of the outer and the public" (Berthoud, 187).

In both *Lord Jim* and *Under Western Eyes* Conrad presents a search for identity explored through acts of betrayal. In *Lord Jim* the ideal code of conduct is separated from the self-ideal to examine the deception of the self-ideal (Hampson, 116). Jim has been taught a code of seamanship. At the same time he has a romantic vision of himself as "always an example of devotion to duty and as unflinching as a hero in a book" (*LJ*, 5). In the first half of the novel Jim is judged in terms of the ideal code of conduct he has betrayed. But he is also being judged by himself in terms of his self-ideal. In the second half of the novel, in Patusan, he is apparently allowed to redeem himself and to realize his self-ideal; but, as Hampson points out (Hampson, 116-17), this ideal itself is judged and evaluated in the final pages.

The action in *Lord Jim* is focused on a universal conflict which centers on the question of individual responsibility with respect to a social code of conduct. Jim, who wants to live up to an idealized notion of himself, is incapacitated for practical action by his powerful imagination. Marlow and Stein, two evaluators of Jim's personality, espouse respectively a realist and a romantic concept of self. Marlow speaks for human solidarity while Stein advises following the dream in order to actualize one's idealized conception of oneself. Yet Marlow's stand is by no means so clear-cut. Although he mentions his membership in a body of men held together by a "certain standard of conduct" (*LJ*, 37), he at the same time talks about "the doubt of the sovereign power enthroned in a fixed standard of conduct" (37). The fixed standard of conduct is of social origin, the result of mankind's need to find protective solidarity in an unknowable world. But the code implies men are free to act according to its command whereas it is never clear to man whether he has the free will necessary to carry out its imperatives. That is what Marlow's doubt refers to and that is why Jim's predicament seems to Marlow to involve an "obscure truth...momentous enough to affect mankind's conception of itself" (69). Jim's commitment to his ego-ideal requires that he rise above his natural self, and as he does not, it causes him to betray those whom he has undertaken to protect two times.

D. van Ghent claims that in his dealings with Jim "Marlow is unofficial attorney both for the defense and the prosecution" (Van Ghent, 383-4). Therefore, Marlow's response to Jim's individualism reflects both the realism of the French lieutenant and the romanticism of Stein. When Marlow takes over the job of narrating the story in Chapter 5, it is obvious that he is not eager to accept the court's verdict of guilty as final and he is at once critical of and sympathetic to Jim. He is convinced that "we are snared into doing things for which we get hanged and yet the spirit may well survive" (*LJ*, 32). Even though Marlow does his best to understand Jim so that he can put his case clearly to the reader, all he can say at the end is that Jim has remained an enigma to him: "I don't pretend I understood him. The views he let me have of himself were like those glimpses through the shifting rents in a thick fog" (56). Not relying completely on his own intellectual capacity to understand Jim, Marlow refers his problem to experts who bring in their own verdicts. The French lieutenant's verdict embodies an aspect of Marlow's point of view, moral judgment, while Stein's embodies imaginative sympathy, another aspect of Marlow. Thus these two referees serve the purpose of objectifying the contradictions in Marlow's understanding of Jim.

Marlow meets the French lieutenant when our sympathies are directed toward Jim. He is the man who remained on board the *Patna* for thirty hours while it was being towed to Aden after Jim deserted the same ship of which he was chief mate and left eight-hundred passengers to their fate. Marlow's opinion of the Frenchman is ambiguous. At first, as he watches the lieutenant who has been tried and tested – the evidence of which is the scar on his hand and the seam at the side of his temple – he has a sudden awareness of the worth of this steady, reliable man (Cox, 34). Yet at the same time the man's dispassionate manner and the lack of any sign of pride in his achievement cause Marlow to think that he merely was performing a duty while towing the *Patna* without being personally involved in this humane task. The Frenchman admits, "Man is born a coward" (*LJ*, 108), "One is always afraid" (107). His statement of the code of conduct is clear: "One's courage does not come of itself" (108); courage is grounded in habit, which is learned in the community of other men and it implies a restraint on fear. Marlow's response to the effect that those in charge of the ship set a bad example by abandoning the ship first when it collided with a floating derelict and for this reason a more lenient view of Jim's action should be taken only leads to the lieutenant's stressing Marlow's mistaken view. According to P. Kirschner, the lieutenant's statement reveals that "courage is a social function" (Kirschner, 53), and according to Berthoud, "courage is the product of necessity" (Berthoud, 70) and the code of conduct is "essentially social both in its origins and purposes" (71). Consequently, it is Jim's failure to appreciate the import- ance of social relatedness, or his determination to live by a code of his own that is responsible for his failure. The lieutenant derives his strength from a sense of solidarity with men of his own vocation whereas Jim spends his time dreaming of performing heroic deeds on his own. The lieutenant implies that life is worth nothing without honor and he knows "nothing of it" (*LJ*, 109). His code of honor rejects Jim. Marlow is so irritated by his rigidity that he ventures, "But couldn't it reduce itself to not being found out?" (109) and this brings the conversation between the two to an end. Cox claims that the Frenchman is like an executioner "taking away Jim's last hope of a reprieve" (Cox, 34). He seems to have sacrificed his imaginative life to a fixed standard of conduct and his dullness invalidates his verdict.

At the end of his conversation with the lieutenant Marlow feels "discouraged about Jim's case" (*LJ*, 109) and is convinced that whatever good dispositions Jim may have had, he has committed a moral crime, and affirms Jim was "guilty and done for" (111). Marlow firmly asserts "the real significance of crime is in its being a breach of faith with the community of mankind and from that point of view he was no mean traitor" (115). Still wishing "to spare him the mere detail of a formal execution" (111), Marlow lays before Jim Brierly's plan of escape, but Jim refuses it in scorn, despair and resolution.

The story of Bob Stanton, who was drowned in the *Sephora* disaster while trying to save an hysterical lady's maid that refused to leave the sinking ship, seems to establish Jim's cowardice firmly. However, the description of Bob wrestling with the lady's maid who "held to the rail like grim death" (110) makes us wonder if Bob "had not carried altruism beyond the limits of good sense" (Cox, 35).

Chester's opinion of Jim is also used to objectify Marlow's judgment of Jim. Chester represents realism and amoral selfishness (Hampson, 127). As his values are in contrast with those of the French lieutenant and those of Jim, he provides a different perspective on Jim's position. The fact that Jim has taken "to heart" (*LJ*, 119) his disgrace in the Inquiry is, for Chester, a failing on Jim's part and he is "no good" (119) whereas for Marlow, Jim's decision to face the Inquiry demonstrates a kind of courage.

Brierly, who is driven to suicide by the mere notion of failing like Jim, voices his disappointment with Jim's betrayal as follows: "We are trusted...a decent man would not have behaved like this to a full cargo of old rags in bales. We aren't an organized body of men, and the only thing that holds us together is just the name for that kind of decency" (50). Brierly has done the kinds of things that Jim dreams of doing. He is successful and aware of his merits. Brierly, like Marlow, experiences Jim's failure both as a threat to the brotherhood of the sea and as a threat to his own self-confidence. He wants Jim to run away because then Jim will have renounced his fidelity to the code of merchant marine and will no longer constitute a danger to those faithful to the code. Jim forces Brierly, for the first time in his life, to face the possibility of inadequacy. Brierly, who seems to be one of those lucky fellows who know "nothing of indecision, much less of self-mistrust" (43), commits suicide by jumping overboard a week after the Inquiry. The fear of failing like Jim and losing his honor in an unexpected and dangerous situation seems to be the only explanation of his suicide. Apparently, Jim's case leads Brierly to understand what Marlow tells Jewel later: "Nobody, nobody is good enough" (234). His mate's comment after his death , "Maybe his confidence in himself was just shook a bit at the last" (46), again points to the influence of Jim's case upon him and reveals that Brierly's suicide is a refusal to confront and grasp the implications for human existence of Jim's jump (Raval, 48). Raval argues that Brierly's trust in the code has not been tested until Jim's jump, and Brierly's egotism is too fragile to sustain itself in the face of any evidence against the code's sovereignty (56).

One of the helmsmen testifies that the reason why he did not leave the helm was because there had been no order to that effect (*LJ*, 72) thus displaying an admirable sense of duty but at the same time an unthinking rigidity similar to that of the lieutenant.

Even in the training ship Jim looks down from his station in the fore-top "with the contempt of a man destined to shine in the midst of dangers" (5).Yet his active imagination makes him extremely conscious of the dangers involved in the heroic role he projects for himself and paralyzes him by fear when there is an emergency. His failure to act in the training ship, from which incident he fails to draw any lessons, is a prelude to the *Patna* incident two years later. On the *Patna* Jim continues "contemplating his own superiority" (17) and spends his time in daydreams of heroism. The narrator remarks, "he loved...the success of his imaginary achievements. They were the best parts of life, its secret truth, its hidden reality" (15). Hence when the *Patna* strikes a floating derelict, Jim is once more paralyzed and feels threatened by natural phenomena. After some hesitation he jumps from the ship and becomes a traitor. He tells Marlow that he was prepared perfectly for everything except the "inconceivable" (69). What happens, in fact, is not the "inconceivable" but merely the unexpected. However, since his imagination carries him away from the reality and magnifies the horror, he becomes afraid of the emergency, even though, as he claims, he is not afraid of death.

One reason why Marlow takes such an interest in Jim, who has betrayed a code of conduct which Marlow values so highly, is that unlike the other officers of the *Patna* Jim stays to confront the trial and to bear the consequences of his act of desertion. What Marlow does not realize at first is that Jim's courage in facing the trial is the result of a defiant mood and a commitment to a personal creed rather than a submission to the claims of a personal morality. As I. Watt remarks, "What really matters to Jim is his personal failure to live up to his ego-ideal" (Watt, 62) and that is why he regards the *Patna* affair as "a chance missed" and decides to wait for "another chance" (*LJ*, 97). Later he becomes more hopeful and exclaims, "Someday one's bound to come upon some sort of chance to get it all back again" (132). He is so convinced of his superiority that he never loses his self-respect. This is another reason why Marlow believes in Jim's worth and sympathizes with his idealism despite the fact that he is a defender of traditional morality. In Marlow's opinion Jim makes too much of his disgrace while it is the guilt that matters. Since Jim cannot accept he is guilty, he spends the rest of his life striving to prove to himself that the common view of him as a coward is untrue; furthermore, he never abandons his dream of the heroic ideal.

What bothers Marlow is not simply the fact that Jim has committed a serious crime but that his appearance belies his conduct. He reveals his painful dilemma by the utterance, "I would have trusted the deck to that youngster on the strength of a single glance...and by Jove! – it wouldn't have been safe" (34). Marlow eventually acknowledges, "Nobody, nobody is good enough!" (234) and no "fixed standard of conduct" can be upheld unquestioningly. In fact, as M. Ray remarks, Jim is contagious, shattering the confidence of even the most assured and self-possessed of men, like Brierly (Ray, 43). Jim appeals to common humanity, but to admit the force of such an appeal is to risk the infection of his "subtle unsoundness" (*LJ*, 66). When Jim asks Marlow what he himself would have done in the same position, Marlow feels he must not speak a word lest "I should be drawn into a fatal admission about myself" (79). As he begins to think that a human being had better be judged by the quality of his consciousness than by the propriety of his behavior, he is estranged from the characters with a fixed opinion. Marlow's position as the defender of fidelity becomes rather ambivalent when he comes to see the inadequacy of the rigid realism advocated by the French lieutenant, which requires a selfless commitment to society at the expense of individuality. The lieutenant's heroism is unconscious, a simple performance of duty. Ironically, as Van Ghent points out (Van Ghent, 388), it is this heroism which Jim has made into a conscious ideal. The lieutenant fails to see, as Berthoud remarks, "there is more to human life than the demands of the code" (Berthoud, 71). The lieutenant's verdict on Jim is uttered, Marlow thinks, in a machine-like manner, and Marlow refuses to accept it as final. We can infer that despite the pervasive ambiguity in his narrative, Marlow has judged Jim positively and wants to rescue him from the kind of fate that awaits such failures. Thus he refers Jim's problem to Stein, who is antithetical to the Frenchman.

The question Marlow puts to Stein is "How to be!" (*LJ*, 155). Stein's proposed solution has proved to be problematic and critics have come up with diametrically opposed interpretations. Stein understands what Jim's problem is because he himself is romantic. His response to Marlow is, "The question is not how to get cured, but how to live" (155). Stein, unlike Jim, is aware that man "is not a masterpiece" (152). Moreover, there is no place for man on earth. His existence is not wanted, but unaware of this, man wants to dominate nature and ends up disturbing it. As a romantic idealist, Stein conceives of existence as "the destructive element" (156), a medium hostile to humanity, which can keep itself alive only through a constant struggle (Raval, 52). This struggle enables human beings to generate ideals and aspirations with which to transform the hostility of natural existence into a means for the realization of their own goals. Stein also insists on the inevitability of failure of all aspirations which lead to "the heart pain – the world pain" (*LJ*, 156). The reason for failure is our inability to subdue either the natural world or our own ideals.

In his youth Stein had followed his dreams and realized them. Unlike Jim, his imagination had not prevented him from making use of the opportunities that came his way. He has lived a life that combines idealism and practical action. He has learned to survive the mutability of his dreams and to be contented with the day-to-day affairs of a less than ideal present with the aid of his butterflies. The butterfly, the emblem of ideal beauty, symbolizes Stein's dreams. Yet the butterfly has to die first to defy destruction. Moreover, in nature, the butterfly and the insect, the beautiful and the ugly, the good and the bad exist side by side. Stein himself had not been afraid of getting into dirt in order to catch what he wanted in the same way that the perfect butterfly cannot avoid touching dirt. Although Stein has isolated himself for the sake of his dreams, he has not cut off his ties with the world. He has continued "corresponding with entomologists in Europe, writing up a descriptive catalogue of his treasures" (151). Jim, in contrast, is unable to own his weakness, and consequently suffers so much. Accepting his fear would imply giving up his dreams of heroism and he cannot do that. Stein knows how dull it is to live without dreams and recommends that we strive to realize our dreams by adopting ourselves to circumstances, to the nature of the destructive element in which we must live (Cox, 39). Since Stein's utterance ends with, "That was the way. To follow the dream, and again to follow the dream – and so – *ewig – usque ad finem...*" (*LJ*, 157) and since he offers to send Jim to Patusan as a practical remedy, he appears to be suggesting that it is not good for men to discover that they lack the power to live up to an ideal of conduct with which they have identified themselves (Rader, 232) and that men should not resign themselves to their limitations, but should rather commit themselves to making their dreams come true however destructive they may be but they should also be ready to adapt themselves to life and make the most of what it offers. Thus his words do not allow us to settle for either affirmation or negation. In Stein's opinion, the reason why man cannot actualize his dreams is that he is imperfect and restless, yet if one is born a romantic like Jim there is no cure for that. Hence the best way to help Jim is to enable him to follow his dream in Patusan, a place where "the haggard utilitarian lies of our civilization wither and die, to be replaced by pure excesses of imagination" (*LJ*, 206).

The remote community of Patusan offers Jim a totally new set of conditions in which he may try to actualize his idealized conception of himself as a hero by committing himself to action. Jim succeeds in becoming the leader of an entire community of natives by feats of daring and in establishing peace and order. Marlow suggests that Jim comes to symbolize civilization in a primitive community and is psychologically satisfied because the conditions of "utter insecurity for life and property" (167) give him the chance to fulfil his dreams of heroism. Yet he remains utterly isolated from the natives he serves. Moreover, unlike Stein, he cuts off all his ties with the outside world.

During his visit to Patusan Marlow becomes convinced that Jim has "achieved greatness" (165) and "at last mastered his fate" (238). However, as the two of them watch the moon floating away above the split summits of the two separated hills, the split seems to be a reminder of the gap between ideal human code and human capability. Moreover, Marlow is aware of the illusory quality of Jim's success. Still, his remark, "it is respectable to have no illusions – and safe – and profitable – and dull" (165) seems to imply that he fears that because he has risked nothing, he has achieved nothing, and by leading a sheltered life and by acting according to the marine code of conduct, he has missed the excitement and pleasures of a life of subjective experience. He feels sterile and insincere. Nonetheless, he cannot endorse Jim's idealism wholeheartedly because he is aware that Jim seems "to love the land and the people with a sort of fierce egoism, with a contemptuous tenderness" (182). Since Jim does all he does more by a desire to convince himself of his superiority than by a sense of duty and social responsibility, he remains an outsider in Patusan.

Jim's failure to take action against Gentleman Brown makes him a betrayer for the second time, and from being the protector of Patusan he is reduced to becoming its destroyer when Brown kills the native leader Doramin's son, Dain Waris, and a number of his followers. The reason why Jim insists on giving Brown permission to leave unharmed may be the result of his identification with Brown, who claims he is not responsible for his past and blames the circumstances, and Jim accepts the claim from his own conviction of having once been the victim of circumstances.

After this event Jim is seen as the enemy of Patusan. There are two practical courses of action open to him: to flee or to fight. Since proving his worth is more important for Jim than remaining alive, he cannot make a choice; he is chosen by the ideal he has lived by (Raval, 64). He says there is nothing "to fight for" and "no escape" (*LJ*, 302); he is determined to "conquer the fatal destiny itself" (302). Having become fearless, he is willing to die in order to be true to his idealistic conception of himself and lets Doramin shoot him, dying with "a proud and unflinching glance" (306). He will not allow the dark powers to "rob him twice of his peace" (301). As Rader maintains, he chooses honor over a love meaningless without honor and leaves Jewel grief-stricken (Rader, 234). To Raval, Jim is so thoroughly entrapped within his ideal that "he continues to defend it even when it has become severed from the context in which it possessed its significance" (Raval, 62). Jim's failure to understand Brown and himself is rooted in this entrapment. Jim admits to Marlow that he is convinced that the people of Patusan trust him with their safety. Then how can he endanger this trust first by promising a clear road to Brown despite the natives' opposition, and second, by laying these people open to external threats in the future after his death? Jim's ideals are a product of the community in which he was brought up. Cut off from his community, Jim has nonetheless organized his life in order to represent these ideals and does not see that martyrdom and courage of his sort have little significance in Patusan.

Does Jim's "heroic" death show he has accepted or escaped from his responsibility for the catastrophy? Marlow's words to the "privileged man" (*LJ*, 248) sound like an admission that Jim's individualist faith is "mightier" than publicly accepted truths and that his subjectivism is preferable to "laws of order." Marlow says, "of all mankind Jim had no dealings but with himself and the question is whether at last he had not confessed to a faith mightier than the laws of order and progress" (249); for, continues Marlow, "is not mankind itself driven by a dream of its greatness and power upon the dark paths of excessive cruelty and excessive devotion?" (257). Marlow also strives to persuade the reader that Jim's "spirit seemed to rise above the ruins of his existence" (302). Yet Marlow's romantic affirmations of the value of individual experience are balanced by realist ethical judgment: "The imprudence of our thoughts recoils upon our heads, who toys with the sword shall perish by the sword" (252). Moreover, he cannot forgive Jim for leaving Jewel; in Marlow's words, "He goes away from a living woman to celebrate his pitiless wedding with a shadowy ideal of conduct. Is he satisfied – quite, now, I wonder?" (306-7).

The question is how far can one justifiably go to realize a dream? Is the realization of the dream its own justification? Jim's character is summed up as "a sort of sublimated, idealized selfishness" (130). Does the sublimation make up for the selfishness? The final judgment on Jim is suspended and, as Armstrong remarks, ambiguity remains the main theme of the novel (Armstrong, 139). One message of the novel is "We must fight in the ranks or our lives don't count" (*LJ*, 249) while another is "Those who do not feel do not count" (163). The novel's answer to the question of "How to be" is complicated. On one hand, *Lord Jim* suggests the safest way is to live like or with the others; on the other hand, it suggests that to do this is to become unthinking, to "go through life with eyes half-shut, with dull ears, with dormant thoughts" (105). Conrad seems to be suggesting that the honor Jim seeks is always beyond his grasp, and therefore, always has an aspect of illusion; nonetheless, it is implied that the pursuit of the ideal of honor is a supreme good (Rader, 232). Conrad's affirmations and denials are inseparable and that is why he is considered "a janiform writer" (Watts, 46).

Under Western Eyes like *Lord Jim*, explores the consequences of an act of betrayal. The two novels are similar in form as well: an elderly narrator's examination of the motives of a young protagonist over two locations and two periods; but both the nature of the betrayal and the nature of the relationship between the narrator and the protagonist are quite different. The narrator in *Under Western Eyes*, an English teacher of languages, dislikes Razumov and claims to be incapable of understanding his conduct and attitudes whereas Marlow in *Lord Jim* makes Jim his protégé, sees him as "one of us" and is deeply concerned in the ambiguities and contradictions of Jim's career.

The stance of the language teacher as a serious representative of rationality expresses the main dilemma on which the narrative is based: the problem of how far rationality is dependent on the existence of a viable public realm. Razumov also stands for rationality. His name connotes the Russian word *razum* – reason (Raval, 133). The narrator and Razumov share an identical conception of reason. The difference between their predicaments has to do with the difference in their nationalities. The narrator being from a liberal society that respects individual thought may assume he is self-sufficient and lead his life in detachment and disengagement. Razumov, in contrast, is cut off from all possibility of retreat living as he does in the absolutist Russia, and demonstrates that "in its relation to the public realm, the life of reason has to be, paradoxically, at once autonomous and dependent" (Berthoud, 185). The narrator's insight and failure are necessary to an examination of the relation between self and community in the context of ideological conflicts and of the interdependence of political and moral questions (Raval, 127). As Berthoud states,

> For the narrator of *Under Western Eyes*, rationality is a function of the interdependence of the individual and the community. Such interdependence pre-supposes that the individual should be free to commit himself to his community in the expectation that the community will respect his freedom. Under Russian autocracy, however, the state and the people draw apart, as a consequence of which the state is deprived of the service of the majority of its citizens and the citizens are deprived of the possibility of rational political action and of serious political thought because they are inhibited from developing into responsible citizens. (Berthoud, 169)

Since in Nathalie's words, "There is no legality, there are no institutions" (*UWE*, 135) in Russia, the citizens either sink into submission or throw themselves desperately into revolt. This is what Sophia Antonovna seems to imply by "Life, Razumov, not to be vile must be a revolt – a pitiless protest – all the time" (260).

In the novel the rational West Europeans and Razumov are set against the irrational Russians. Although the rational narrator may try to persuade us of the undesirability of the Russian way of living, the depth of feeling and the degree of enthusiasm and idealism he observes in Nathalie, Victor, Tekla and Sophia Antonovna rather convince us of the inadequacy of the narrator's complacency. Moreover, the liberal narrator is intelligent enough to deplore the "perfection of mediocrity" (203) which characterizes Geneva and repeatedly expresses his disdain for the average Swiss citizen "whose fate is made secure from the cradle to the grave by the perfected mechanism of democratic institutions" (175). As Cox observes, we feel that the Russians, like Jim, "achieve a kind of superiority by their submission to the truths of extreme experience" (Cox, 104). Like Kurtz in "Heart of Darkness" they have looked into the abyss of which the Swiss are ignorant. The contempt Razumov feels for Geneva is similar to the narrator's and is best expressed in the description of the isle named after Jean Jacques Rousseau as "naive, odious and inane" (*UWE*, 290).

Razumov leads an isolated, withdrawn life before Victor Haldin's visit: "He was as lonely in the world as a man swimming in the deep sea" (10). In a period of political and mental unrest in a society where students in particular are liable to be suspected of subversion, he remains distant from the political conflicts and maintains his balance of mind by keeping a "hold on normal, practical everyday life" (10) and by hard work. He is looked upon as a "strong nature – an altogether trustworthy man" (6). He has conceived for himself a linear kind of development proceeding via the silver medal for the prize essay to the role of celebrated professor. He hopes to overcome his namelessness by intellectual effort and make his name an honored one by distinction. Deprived of all family relationships, Razumov has no alternative but to look to the state for recognition and advancement. Nothing intervenes between himself and his country. He thinks he owes all his loyalty to Russia, which is his only parentage and the source of all his expectations in life. He trusts in institutions, which seem to him "rational and inde-structible" (21). They express "a force of harmony" (21) which he appreciates because it opposes both the anarchy of the revolutionaries and the emptiness of his alienated life. Razumov is proud of his mental capacity and hopes to create his own future by the free use of his intelligence, not perceiving that individual freedom is incompatible with an autocratic system since an honorable identity is maintained there by supporting or serving the institutions of the autocracy, and that the critical intelligence which he upholds can flourish only under conditions guaranteeing the individual a certain degree of independence whereas in an autocratic state, as Mikulin tells Razumov, one is free to think as long as one knows it is permissible.

Razumov's rational existence and dream of distinction are destroyed by the sudden appearance of Victor in his room demanding help after assassinating the Minister of State. Haldin represents the forces of irrationality and absurdity often found in Conrad's fiction, such as Gentleman Brown's appearance in Patusan. Razumov's powerful imagination, like Jim's on the *Patna*, magnifies the terrors awaiting him if his involvement with Haldin is discovered. All he wants to do is to go back to his stance of non-commitment, which is impossible in an autocratic state.

Ironically, Razumov's rational existence is responsible for Haldin's appeal to him. Razumov's reputation for trustworthiness, a product of his sanity and sobriety, is what draws the ardent idealist to him. Moreover, Victor's nobility of mind makes him seek the help of a man who has no family to implicate, but who, unfortunately, for that very reason, is excessively dependent on the institutions of the state.

Razumov's visit to the low eating-house in search of Ziemianitch, the driver of horses whom Haldin expects to help him escape, takes Razumov away from his isolated and sheltered existence into contact with suffering humanity "on the verge of starvation and despair" (28). Finding the driver, Victor's "bright spirit" (18) dead drunk, Razumov is so frustrated that he beats the man frantically with a stable-fork, yet is still unable to bring him to his senses. Razumov feels trapped between "the irrational drunkenness of the peasant incapable of action and the dream-intoxication of the idealist incapable of perceiving the reason of things and the true character of men" (31). Razumov does not see that it is the lack of legality and rationality under the repressive autocracy which has led the idealistic Haldin to commit an act of crime. What is more, instead of sympathizing with the misery of the poor people he meets there, motivated by the instinct of self-preservation, he takes refuge in his own superiority and wilfully blinds himself to the reasons for their suffering. He converts his frustration into a political analysis and asserts his commitment to autocracy from a desire for self-preservation. He hates Haldin and Ziemianitch because they endanger him. Accordingly his thought processes lead him toward the decision to betray Haldin as the only way out of the situation. Saying, "If I must suffer let me at least suffer for my convictions, not for a crime, my reason – my cool superior reason – rejects" (35), he convinces himself that he will betray Haldin, not out of selfishness but in order to maintain his independence. Razumov is filled with self-pity because he has no one to go to to ask for advice as to how he should act at this crucial moment, and conveniently disregards the fact that he is acting against the claims of hospitality by deciding to betray Haldin. Here once more we notice a similarity with Jim, who cites the lack of exemplary behavior on the part of the other officers of the ship to exonerate himself from his act of betrayal. Jim has betrayed both his social responsibility and his own self-ideal by jumping from the *Patna*. He feels no guilt at his failure to live up to the code of the sea, but shame at failing to live up to his own ideal. At the same time he is unwilling to give up that self-ideal by allowing it to be challenged by facts. As Hampson points out, Razumov's lack of family has led him to construct a self-identity which does not exist in the present but is projected on to the future (Hampson, 169). In this he resembles Willems of *An Outcast of the Islands* as well as Jim. Razumov's immediate goal is the silver medal, a step to his long-term goal: "to become a celebrated old professor...one of the glories of Russia" (*UWE*, 13). He pursues this identity due to insecurity in the oppressive conditions of the society he lives in. It is because Haldin's entry into his life endangers his position in society and thus threatens his future-projected self-identity that he betrays Haldin. In fact, Haldin's first speech with Razumov dramatizes the gap between Razumov's self-identity and public identity, and Haldin's claim for help is a fact that threatens his steady progress to the fulfilment of his self-ideal and is like the derelict that strikes the *Patna*, leading to Jim's jump and betrayal.

Berthoud, who endorses this view claims that Razumov's recoil from Haldin is not cowardice but a despairing resentment that the prospect of a sane, normal future is being taken away from him (Berthoud, 173). He fails to realize that the community on which he relies for the fulfilment of his aspirations is incapable of sustaining rational life because it denies inner loyalties. In his dependence on the public realm Razumov has no alternative but to choose Russia and to take refuge in the ideology of Holy Russia. He commits himself to the reactionary dogma that "absolute power should be preserved...for the great autocrat of the future" (*UWE*, 35). Even as he plans to betray Haldin, Razumov is taken by the idea of confessing to Haldin. Razumov's desire to confess signifies his need to reduce the gap between his self-identity and public identity. Yet his first attempt to align the two identities turns out to be his betrayal of Haldin to the authorities.

Razumov's appeal to Prince K– shows he has chosen the so-called institutions of law and order with which he has always associated himself. Prince K–, extremely pleased with Razumov's "patriotic" behavior, takes him to General T– to tell his story. Razumov loathes the general, who gazes at him with unbelieving and suspicious eyes and he is shocked by the evil he discerns in the "goggle-eyed imbecile" (45). General T– is the guardian of autocracy and his defense of autocracy is unthinking. His ironical claim that his existence has been built on fidelity (51) is a perversion of Conrad's highly valued moral concept. Razumov's perception of the fact that General T–'s use of the concept of fidelity to the state enables him to prohibit every vestige of independent life within his area of influence destroys his self-respect and plunges him into despair and anguish because he can no longer justify his crime against Haldin. He finds himself defending Haldin and feeling remorse toward Ziemianitch. He tries to find another justification for his conduct by saying to himself he believes in the organic growth of institutions, which anarchism is sure to destroy. Like Jim, who blames his companions on the ship as well as the "Dark Powers" (96) for his jump, Razumov shifts the responsibility for his betrayal to others, the revolutionaries who create anarchy. He realizes, however, that under an autocracy every citizen is an automatic suspect including the servants of the autocracy itself and that his betrayal of Haldin will not clear his name.

When Razumov returns to Haldin, he has an urge to make a second confession and tell Haldin that he has given him up to the police. It is in this scene that Razumov begins the ironic double-talk that becomes his characteristic mode and signals his uneasy sense of the falseness of his position and of the gap between his two identities. It also expresses the simultaneous desire to reveal himself and to conceal himself. One result of this conflict is Razumov's disguised confession to Haldin: "There are secret motives of conduct. A man's most open actions have a secret side to them" (59). And before Haldin leaves, Razumov feels a compulsion to clarify his political position also and does so.

From this moment on Razumov cannot keep himself sane by appeal to the familiar or by involvement in daily routine. He awakens into a world that seems "without significance or interest" (68). He feels dull, lifeless, inert, and "mortally ill" (68). He tries to convince himself that now he can return to his former peaceful existence: "Extraordinary things do happen. But when they have happened they are done with.... Life is a public thing" (54). However, the pangs of conscience he suffers from demonstrate how mistaken he is in this thought. If life were a public thing, as he asserts, then the fact that no one concerned knows about his betrayal should be enough to make him feel at peace and contented. But Razumov's private knowledge continues to haunt him, isolating him utterly from both the autocrats and the revolutionaries. He cannot communicate what really counts in his life to anybody. Berthoud sees this moral isolation as "a kind of non-being" (Berthoud, 179). The stopping of his watch after Haldin leaves his room symbolizes the stopping of his existence as attested by the state of aimless passivity into which he sinks where even his senses do not perform their normal functions.

Haldin's appeal to Razumov makes it clear to him that his pose of non-commitment is impractical and human beings will make claims on his moral allegiance, and eventually he is forced to acknowledge that his prized freedom of mind is at the mercy of the irrationality which governs others. With his fellow students taking it for granted that he is a revolutionary and with the authorities imposing upon him the role of secret agent, he can no longer control his identity or keep his independence of mind. After his room is searched by the police, he feels that his old identity created out of discipline and routine is destroyed forever. He blames the "lawlessness of autocracy" together with the "lawlessness of revolution" (*UWE*, 77) for preventing him from exercising his intellectual freedom. He has become, Raval notes, mere ideological raw material for both groups (Raval, 131).

Although Razumov tries to convince himself he is not guilty of Haldin's death, he knows perfectly well that the responsibility is his alone. General T– makes it clear that had Haldin "not come with his tale to such a staunch and loyal Russian as you [Razumov], he would have disappeared like a stone in the water" (*UWE*, 47). Haldin's confidence in Razumov may have been misplaced but Razumov had at first acted as if he justified this confidence. Moreover, Haldin leaves Razumov's room as soon as he senses that Razumov does not seem to approve of his conduct and ideas. Furthermore, Razumov has not been under any external pressure to betray him. He is entirely guilty. In betraying Haldin, Razumov has not only broken a human law but also resisted the appeal of virtue. As Razumov is later informed by Mikulin, Haldin refuses, even at the point of death, to implicate the man who betrayed him. Razumov's illness at this stage of his life is apparently an outcome of his desire to escape from these disturbing actualities.

In the course of the novel, Razumov progresses from his initial position of isolation to making a choice of sides. The first step in his progress is the discovery that he makes that his apparent aloofness from the political conflicts of his society is an illusion. Razumov's self-interest, at the start of the novel, directs him toward conservatism and the autocratic institutions "which give rewards and appointments" (11). With Haldin's entry, the self-interest that had dictated an unacknowledged support for the autocracy now directs Razumov to help Haldin escape in an attempt to recover the conditions upon which his future--projected identity depends for its fulfilment. He is at the same time made aware of political uncertainties in the outside world which he had been ignoring and is forced to realize that his future is menaced by the lawlessness of autocracy as well as of the revolution, which makes it impossible for him to realize his self-ideal. He feels himself misunderstood by the revolutionists and mistrusted by the authorities. This leads to a fear at the power of these forces over him, especially after his rooms are ransacked by the police. He is caught between two sides to neither of which he belongs. At the same time, he is under pressure to align himself clearly with one or the other. What is more, since his original self-ideal – projected into the future – is no longer viable, he also has to forge a new identity for himself and find a new basis for that identity (Hampson, 176).

Since the task of a spy is to exploit the confidence of others, it is only appropriate that Razumov should become a counter--revolutionary secret agent under Mikulin's half-persuasive, half-threatening arguments. His betrayal has not brought him either the independence or the peace of mind he expected to get; rather it has changed his existence into a never-ending cycle of repetitive effort to repress his conscience. His cruel treatment of Kostia, as Cox remarks, is another attempt to confirm in himself his contempt and hatred for what he has betrayed and his feeling that moral obligations are preposterous (Cox, 111). In Geneva the way for Razumov's acceptance is prepared by Haldin's misreading of Razumov's character combined with Nathalie's ignorance and trust. The misinterpretation that had created Razumov's false identity is at work again. Razumov has replaced the false identity and the betrayal imposed upon him by Haldin with a consciously adopted false-identity and a second, open-eyed betrayal (Hampson, 178). Consequently, the sense of isolation and the burden of guilt have increased immeasurably. This subjection to authority undermines his moral conscious-ness, and to regain some measure of integrity he writes his secret diary, and paradoxically, the diary enables him to live with duplicity (Raval, 134). In Geneva he is seen to draw a satanic enjoyment from mocking the greatness of Peter Ivanovitch and from observing Sophia Antonovna's deception concerning

Haldin's betrayer after the suicide of Ziemianitch. His isolation has made him unfit for human communication. The Razumov who declared "Life is a public thing" (*UWE*, 54) has been transformed into the Razumov who sees life as "a dream and a fear" (316).

In Geneva Razumov recovers from his inertia but now he finds that his concept of reality has entirely changed. Everything has lost its significance and he strives to exist in a state of angry, mocking aloofness. Yet the strain of this new role of detachment causes his personality to split. He tries to preserve his precious freedom of mind by manipulating other people and by resisting their attempts to understand him. Once more his bodily functions are disturbed by his continual hypocrisy. He cannot sleep, his voice becomes extinct, dried up in his throat, and his lips are parched. On the isle where he goes to write his first report to Mikulin as a spy, his identity appears close to extinction. He sits "motionless, without thought and sight and hearing, almost without life" (290).

In fact, Razumov's feeling of shame and guilt can be traced back to the time of his actual betrayal, and even prior to it. After beating Ziemianitch, he has a vision of rushing home and flinging himself on his knees before Haldin and confessing, because the idea of betrayal has subconsciously planted itself in him (39-40). Immediately after Haldin leaves his room, unaware of the police trap awaiting him, Razumov feels like a man undergoing torture on a rack and longs to admit his guilt: "He heard himself suddenly saying, 'I confess'" (65). Next, he wants to confess to Councillor Mikulin. References to his feeling of being tortured occur again and again. The fact that he fails to recognize the face of the man being tortured on the rack demonstrates, according to Cox, his unwillingness to recognize his own guilty self and to acknowledge the consequences of his guilt (Cox, 113), and to Hampson, this pale figure on the rack could be either himself or Haldin (Hampson, 176). When his fear for himself is mixed with his sense of guilt, this is expressed through an identification with Haldin. His body and mind are dislocated as he perceives after his visit to Egeria: "he felt...as though another self, an independent sharer of his mind, had been able to view his whole person very distinctly indeed" (*UWE*, 230). His split personality can only be healed by confession. In Geneva, he turns to writing down his thoughts and memories in his journal despite the risk involved because he is unable to speak openly with anyone. The narrator thinks that writing proves to be a "formula of peace" (5). "Is it possible that I have a conventional conscience?" (288) he asks himself when his feeling of remorse becomes unbearable. Razumov's awareness of his emotional needs comes to the surface only after meeting Nathalie. Her faith in him intensifies his guilt although at the beginning he desires to conquer her soul. Nathalie is to exorcise Haldin and to reestablish his own control over his life. Razumov's anguished response to the mention of Haldin's name by Nathalie is misunderstood by her. The language teacher, after his first meeting with Razumov, likens his appearance to that of a revolutionist "everlastingly on his guard against self-betrayal" (187). Razumov is indeed "on his guard" against "self-betrayal," but the betrayal he fears is the disclosure of his "true" identity to the revolutionists, that is, identity as the betrayer of Haldin and as the intended betrayer of the Geneva group. He records in his diary, "You [Nathalie] were appointed to undo the evil by making me betray myself back into truth and peace" (358) just before he goes out to make his confession to the revolutionaries.

Razumov also discovers that the mind and what it perceives are inextricably bound together, and that sanity, or moral health, depends on a true relationship between the inner and the outer life. It is the lack of such a relationship which disables his mind from controlling the objective world and from functioning independently, and which causes him to act irrationally at times as demonstrated by his beating of Ziemianitch, his verbal duels with Sophia Antonovna, and his cruelty to Kostia, as well as writing down his memories in his journal.

At the moment when he is freed from all suspicion in Geneva by the suicide of Ziemianitch, which is interpreted by Sophia Antonovna as evidence of his remorse for having betrayed

Haldin, Razumov is driven further to cynicism and isolation because he feels surrounded by "the choking fumes of falsehood" without the possibility of "a breath of fresh air" (269). In deceiving others, he has become alienated from any clear understanding of himself. At the very moment when Razumov seems to have succeeded in establishing his false identity, he undergoes an apprehension of self-division. Sophia Antonovna noticing his disturbed state warns him: "Take care, Razumov, my good friend. If you carry on like this you will go mad. You are angry with everybody and bitter with yourself" (269). The narrator's earlier remark had a similar implication: "No human being could bear a steady view of moral solitude without going mad" (39). It is to escape such loneliness and madness that Razumov confesses his crime and re-establishes himself in society.

While telling Mrs. Haldin his concocted but coherent story of Haldin's betrayal, he experiences a recognition of the essential falsehood of his constructed identity and begins to yearn for integration into the community of human beings, which his betrayal and rationalization have made impossible. Just before he flees from Mrs. Haldin's room he meets Nathalie, who has returned home. Razumov is so unnerved by his experience in Mrs. Haldin's room that he cannot bring himself to repeat that "silly story" (341) to Nathalie. He is not in control of himself. The confession that follows is an oblique expression of his guilt and moral responsibility. After his confession to Nathalie, Razumov loses her forever, yet he feels "washed clean" (357) and can once more breathe freely. He then departs to make his confession to the revolutionaries.

His confession is an attempt to end his self-alienation and self-betrayal, both of which are consequences of his betrayal of Haldin and the revolutionaries. Razumov's experience of love allows him to speak without irony or dissimulation (Raval, 137). This is a kind of suicide, like Jim's facing Doramin's pistol. The false-self Jim has built in Patusan, like Razumov's in Geneva, is an obstacle to his feeling fully satisfied despite the fact that Patusan has given him the chance to realize his heroic self-image.

His sense of guilt at his own inauthenticity becomes unbearable after the treachery of Gentleman Brown. When Jim faces Doramin, he is still caught up in the drama of his self-ideal. Razumov's confession, in contrast, is not ambivalent and he is integrated into the community of the revolutionists. Jim sacrifices Jewel to his self-ideal and Razumov sacrifices Nathalie, but Razumov could not have regained and retained his "true" identity without confessing to Nathalie the fact that he is the betrayer of her brother. Love brings Razumov to a full consciousness of his guilt so that he can affirm his love only through renunciation. Thus for Razumov to love Nathalie is to disclose those secrets which would make impossible her reciprocation of his love. To love her genuinely is to be deprived of her love forever (137) while Jim dies without confessing to Jewel his past betrayal from which springs his need to feel trusted, as a consequence of which he cannot conceive of a life after betraying the trust of the inhabitants of Patusan and he dies unaware of the fact that he is betraying Jewel as well. Unlike Razumov, Jim dies maintaining his silence. After the Brown mishap he is unable to write a letter home because his ideal has no relation to human affairs. Raval rightly claims that "his ideals were manifestations of egoistic self-entrapment that deprived him of ordinary human language, of its imperfect, provisional and necessary concepts" (139). Razumov, in Bergson's words, becomes the "author of his own condemnation" (cited in Berthoud, 181). The writing down of his confession is a disclosure of the truth to Nathalie and is unlike his earlier writing in his diary to regain his composure. His first attempt at communication ironically cuts him off from his fellows. He gains his independence of mind but he is condemned to a blankness reminiscent of his earlier vision of the immense Russian soil under a heavy blanket of snow (*UWE*, 32-3). Earlier, his crime cut him off morally from his fellows, now his confession cuts him off physically. In reassuming his independence by relinquishing his role as a spy, he has simultaneously antagonized those who have employed him and those against whom he has been employed. Appropriately, he is mutiliated by another double agent, Necator. The confession may heal his split personality but at the cost of deafness. As Cox points out, in *Under Western Eyes* and the other later novels, commitment to human relationships is inevitably associated with an act of self-immolation (Cox, 103). The predicament of Heyst in *Victory*, Decoud in *Nostromo*, and Peyrol in *The Rover* may be cited to support Cox's view.

Under Western Eyes confirms the concept of revolutionary hope and looks forward to a period of concord and justice (*UWE*, 104) which will end the anguish of the Russians. Under autocracy, each ideology – Ivanovitch's nihilism, Haldin's populism, General T–'s extreme rightist position – sacrifices the present to the future, a future that depends on the removal of social and ideological contradictions (Raval, 140). It is implied that the alternative to both autocracy and terrorism is the concord and justice which will be achieved through the universal values of compassion, love and charity as well as through the reconciliation of the Russians from all levels of society. Thus, after the confession, the crippled Razumov survives largely with the selfless devotion and compassion of Tekla; back in Russia, he is visited by the revolutionaries, who have forgiven him and who want to benefit from his intelligence; in short, his confession actually brings him into relation with others. Nathalie goes back to Russia as well and devotes herself to helping the poor and the sick. Even Peter Ivanovitch marries a peasant girl for the sheer love of her after Mme de S– dies.

The question is can the example of Tekla, Nathalie, and Sophia Antonovna, who sacrifice their lives and chances of happiness to be of use to the miserable Russian people be regarded as an alternative to Razumov's extreme egoism? The narrator's liberal conservatism is shown to be inadequate to grasp either the aspirations or the confession of Razumov (132). In the words of the narrator, "There was no longer any Nathalie Haldin, because she had completely ceased to think of herself" (*UWE*, 375). Can her choice of the renounciation of her identity in favor of society be seen as an alternative to Razumov's attempts to assert his individuality to maintain his freedom of mind? Although Razumov breaks the shell of his solipsism after he confesses to Nathalie and makes his diary a means of communication, his last entry is, "After all, it is they [the revolutionaries] and not I who have the right on their side! – theirs is the strength of invisible powers.... I am independent – and therefore perdition is my lot" (362). He can confront the revolutionaries but will not join them. This declaration of moral and intellectual freedom, like Jim's final defiant gaze, does not resolve his tragic dilemma, but rather constitutes it since from the General to Ivanovitch to Victor and Nathalie Haldin, all Russians seem to hold views that require a total subordination of the individual to the state or a collectivist dream (Raval, 140).

Razumov at the end escapes from solitude into community. As Hampson remarks, through the assertion of his independence from others he finds an integrity that becomes the basis for a true relation to others (Hampson, 190). What makes the assertion significant is his initial identification with an altered or false identity, which made him suffer so much. In contrast, Jim is still trying to stick to his self-ideal when he faces Doramin. Razumov frees himself from dependence on others' opinion of him, which was responsible for his isolation. Yet, in doing so, he becomes dependent on others physically. Thus, it can be asserted that through Razumov Conrad reaffirms the need for a concept of community and human solidarity. In fact, the narrative from the very beginning assumes bonds of human solidarity and that is why Razumov is tormented by his decision to betray Haldin to the authorities. In *Lord Jim*, however, the issue is not so clear-cut. In Patusan Jim has made "a jump into the unknown" (*LJ*, 168) and has been given "a refuge at the cost of danger" (169), which is in contrast to his sense of security on the *Patna*. His life of risks in Patusan allows him to fulfil his dreams, but despite his regained self-confidence, the concealed past remains as a potential source of guilt and insecurity, which prevents him from becoming a part of the community of Patusan. His solitude is in no way lessened. Gentleman Brown acts as a catalyst whose presence precipitates Jim's unresolved conflicts. Jim betrays his eastern commitments at the call of the white world and loses all men's confidence by being once more unfaithful to his trust.

Although Jim accepts responsibility for the deaths that result from his misjudgment, he is determined to "prove his power in another way and to conquer the fatal destiny itself" (302). His acceptance of responsibility is, at the same time, an assertion of his heroic self-image. While Razumov's betrayal can be traced to the oppressive conditions of the autocratic state, the deeper reason for Jim's fall lies within Jim himself. It is Jim's ignorance of both himself and the world in which as a human being he must live that has put in motion the process of self-destruction from the beginning. Since Jim does not recognize the power of the contingent to subvert human intentions, he fails to understand Brown's intention and loses all he has. Jim's final posture embodies his insistence on affirming the truth and justice of his essential self. This self-assertion cannot be separated from self-glorification and it is this which has alienated him from those in relation to whom his values make human sense, but Jim is unable to realize this. The interpretation of the meaning of his death is also ambiguous. Either he has found the opportunity for complete self-realization or he has made a romantic gesture that saves him from confronting himself. However, even if his way of dying has redeemed his betrayal of the trust of the people in Patusan, the same action deepens his betrayal of Jewel's trust in him. In Marlow's words, he has betrayed the "living woman" for a "shadowy ideal" (306-7).

Thus the contradiction in Conrad's work between private vision and public action is once more dramatized. A sense of the value of individuality is again at war with a sense of the value of society because Conrad sees man as a free agent as well as a social animal. Although he is aware of the "priority of the social unit to the individual self" (Fleishman, 56-7), he seeks for a way of being for the individual that frees him from the determinism of society. As J. Baines points out, the tragedy or misfortune of Conrad's characters is invariably the consequence of isolation and of their failure to abide by the principle of solidarity (Baines, 441). Jim's desire to be a hero and Razumov's hope to become a celebrated professor lead them to such introspectiveness that they are deprived of the possibility of communion and sympathy with other men and lose the ability to act purposefully. Yet since Conrad also recognizes the value of subjectivity and independence, he suggests that capitulation to the demands of society can only be at the cost of authenticity and sincerity, that is, by becoming unthinking and by losing one's singularity. To conclude, Conrad's fluctuations between endorsing and rejecting individualism appear to be unresolvable although in the later novels a tendency more in favor of commitment to society whatever the cost to the individual is observable.

WORKS CITED

Armstrong Paul B. *The Challenge of Bewilderment: Understanding and Representation in James, Conrad and Ford.* London: Cornell U.P., 1987.

Baines Jocelyn. *Joseph Conrad: A Critical Biography.* London: Weidenfield and Nicolson, 1967.

Berthoud Jacques. *Joseph Conrad: The Major Phase.* Cambridge: Cambridge U.P., 1967.

Cox C. B. *Joseph Conrad: The Modern Imagination.* London: Dent, 1974.

Fleishman Avrom. *Conrad's Politics: Community and Anarchy in the Fiction of Joseph Conrad.* Baltimore: The Johns Hopkins U.P., 1967.

Ghent Dorothy Van. "On *Lord Jim,*" in "*Lord Jim,*" ed. Thomas C. Moser. London: W. W. Norton, 1968.

Hampson Robert. *Joseph Conrad: Betrayal and Identity.* New York: St. Martin's, 1992.

Kirschner Paul. *Conrad: The Psychologist as Artist.* Edinburgh: Oliver and Boyd, 1968.

Rader Ralph W. "*Lord Jim* and the Formal Development of the Novel," in *Reading Narrative: Form, Ethics, Ideology,* ed. James Phetan. Columbus: Ohio State U.P., 1989.

Raval Suresh. *The Art of Failure: Conrad's Fiction.* Boston: Allen & Unwin, 1986.

Ray Martin. *Joseph Conrad.* London: Edward Arnold, 1993.

Seltzer Leon F. *The Vision of Melville and Conrad: A Comparative Study.* Athens: Ohio State U.P., 1970.

Watt Ian. "The Ending," in *Joseph Conrad's "Lord Jim": Modern Critical Interpretations,* ed. Harold Bloom. New York: Chelsea House Publishers, 1987.

Watts Cedric. *A Preface to Conrad.* Harlow: Longman, 1982.

Phyllis Toy,
University of Southern Indiana,
Evansville, USA

Joseph Conrad's *Under Western Eyes*:
The Language of Politics and the Politics of Language

> To render a crucial point of feelings in terms of human speech is really
> an impossible task. Written words can only form a sort of translation.
> ("Author's Note," *WT*, x)

It is precisely his steadfast, skeptical refusal to accede to any immutable truth of things that distinguishes Joseph Conrad from most of his nineteenth century precursors and places him solidly in the modernist tradition.[1] Hence, according to A. Guerard, Conrad's complex narratives mark a strategic fault line in the emergence of contemporary modernist discourse (Guerard, *Conrad the Novelist*, 11). F. Jameson pushes the point even further when he suggests that "a case could be made for reading Conrad not as an early modernist, but rather an anticipation of that later and quite different thing we have come to call variously textuality, *écriture*, postmodernism, or schizophrenic writing" (Jameson, 219). Clearly, from differing critical orientations, Conrad's texts can readily accommodate an extraordinarily wide variety of readings. For this reason, any attempt to contain his works by imposing a unitary critical perspective is disturbed by lingering traces of the metaphysics of Schopenhauer, the evolving goals of modernism, and the nascent "schizophrenia" of postmodernism. Such complexity of thought, such determined reluctance to say things simply and unambiguously, resists facile classification and marks Conrad as the oblique and intriguing writer that he is acknowledged to be.

Conrad's typical protagonist, for example, is impelled by irrational impulses to commit a catastrophic and irreversible action – Kurtz's fall, Jim's jump, Nostromo's fraud, Razumov's betrayal – which results in his alienation from the larger community. Yet as each plot progresses, it becomes increasingly obvious to the reader that the human fallibility at issue is hardly in itself necessary and sufficient cause for the prolonged suffering the protagonist endures. In fact, what finally appears to motivate the tragic action is frequently less individual impulse than already existing cultural dynamic, often economic in nature, in which the central character is unknowingly implicated: the imperialist motives of "the Company of Light"; the greedy indifference to human life of the *Patna*'s owners; the material and political interests generated by the San Tomé silver mine, for instance.

That the individual affected is unwittingly entrapped within these cultural formations sets into motion the moral ambiguity that disturbs Conrad's works and that demands his narrator's full engagement. The narrator's sympathetic identification with the protagonist's uncertain moral position leads finally to the extended scrutiny of legitimized but ethically suspect cultural forces that is characteristic of Conrad's narratives. Paradoxically, then, cause and motivation become curiously obscured. Either individual impulse or culturally generated ideology – each standing in apparent contradiction to the other – is arguably the determining ground for personal crisis, or for human action generally. With the status of causation thus compromised, Conrad's plots militate against any attempt to retrieve an original principle "that can stand at the beginning of things and look confidently to the end."[2]

For Conrad this inability to retrieve fully extends to language as well. As he wrote in his "Author's Note" to *Within the Tides*, "To render a crucial point of feelings in terms of human speech is really an impossible task." Curiously, however, Conrad also suggests in a letter to Hugh Clifford that "things 'as they are' exist in words, therefore words should be handled with care lest the picture, the image of truth abiding in facts should become distorted – or blurred" (Jean-Aubry, I, 280). What seems most significant in these two seemingly paradoxical statements is Conrad's firm assumption that, even in language, complete, unmediated access to any original ground of meaning is an impossibility. Not only does language impede us from ever recovering the full truth of the past in its original form (or formlessness). It also provides us with the only possible access to the past, to "the image of truth abiding in facts," which remains to us, and it is precisely the necessity for "translating" and transmitting that past that is repeatedly highlighted in Conrad's works.

Underscoring the importance Conrad places on narrative transmission, one of the most striking features of his work, apparent in "Heart of Darkness" (1898), as well as in *Lord Jim* (1900), "Youth" (1902), and *Chance* (1913), is the added presence of an anonymous narrative voice that provides the prologue and epilogue which frame these tales. Conrad's repeated foregrounding of such a framing device may in fact indicate a major focus of his work; for, as W. Benjamin reminds us, story-telling itself serves to remind us that the retrieval of an original essence is an illusion, that "what is at stake" in such an embedded discourse "is often less the 'message' of the story than its reception, less what it says than how it communicates" (Benjamin, 83). With Conrad's insistent foregrounding of repeated transmission, the need to articulate is shown to expand outward; the "message" is caught in a process of continuous deferral and restructuring. Such repeated retellings foreground too the very inadequacy of language that necessitates our continuing effort to reexamine and rearticulate. It is for these reasons that some critics note the futility of "truth-seeking" in Conrad's works.[3]

The narrative refraction produced by Conrad's distinctive "framing device" in other works is accomplished in *Under Western Eyes* by assigning the burden of narrative recovery to the rather questionable "translation" provided by the bland and anonymous professor of languages, who translates from the Russian and recasts for us (with at times hostile commentary) the contents of Razumov's journal, which in turn interprets the significance of the young man's life. Even as this summary account makes clear, *Under Western Eyes* is thoroughly cognizant of its status as a *text* – as a "translation" or approximation which shapes and structures its view of events. And in changing the title of the work from "Razumov" to *Under Western Eyes*, Conrad was announcing the theme of perspectivism; instead of focusing on a locatable, definable character – Razumov – we are invited by the new title to notice instead the refracted interpretation imposed by the "western eyes" of the work's narrator, and, by implication, those of the work's readers. Such a change of focus surely assumes that audience reception shapes and even informs significance, that meanings are culturally generated, and that knowledge is continuously mediated.

Reminiscent of the African interior in "Heart of Darkness," one of the "many blank spaces on the earth," we are informed in *Under Western Eyes* that Russia exists as "a monstrous blank page awaiting the record of an inconceivable history" (*UWE*, 33). This condition of blankness, which could be described as potential meaning – semantically void until predicated – initiates a logic of desire that demands interpretation, for we can come to comprehend such an "insubstantiality" only after it has been assigned cultural and linguistic significance (Brooks, 238-63). The process of defining such a "blank page" thus depends to a great extent on meaning attributed within the assumptions of a specific cultural schema: in the case of *Under Western Eyes*, the liberal democratic values privileged by the "western eyes" of its narrator and translator, the old professor of languages.

When compared to the measured restraint of Marlow's narration in "Heart of Darkness," especially, the old professor's rendering seems most unreliable, seriously qualified by his obvious imperceptiveness as well as by his automatic imposition of normative Western values. His too insistent claim to full recuperation would be suspect in the case of any translation; in addition, as many critics have noted,[4] this narrator's persistent and strenuously self-deprecating denials of both imagination and invention finally ring false:

> But this is not a work of imagination; I have no talent; my excuse for this undertaking lies not in its art, but in its artlessness. Aware of my limitations and strong in the sincerity of my purpose, I would not try (were I able) to invent anything. I push my scruples so far that *I would not even invent a transition*. (*UWE*, 100, emphasis mine)

Although the old professor offers what purports to be a self-effacing, undistorted reiteration of past events, his is not at all the simple retrieval of a seamlessly coherent story.

Instead, it becomes increasingly obvious that his narrative is a patently textualized reconstruction: Razumov's recollections, "something in the nature of a journal, a diary, yet not exactly that in its actual form" (4) (which it must be noted contains Razumov's own retrospective entries as well as numerous temporal gaps); a series of reconstructed conversations; an unconfirmed newspaper account; and hearsay provided by casual acquaintances and unnamed "informants" – all of which are interspersed with the speculative intrusions, dubious opinions, and facile moralisms contained in the narrator's numerous digressions. It is notable, too, that his attempt to create a summarizing overview is continuously agitated and disrupted by precisely those other voices that his recounting appropriates. When reported by the old professor, for example, the speech of the other characters – Razumov, Nathalie, Haldin, Kostia, etc. – is moved from its independent existence into a new and alien context, one moreover that is constrained by the narrator's own rather limited and prejudiced vision.

For example, the professor informs us that immediately following his betrayal of Haldin, Razumov lies in his room and broods on the violent convulsions that the "lawless forces" of both autocracy and revolution have introduced into his life:

> "A common thief," he said to himself, "finds more guarantees in the law he is breaking, and even a brute like Ziemianitch has his consolation." Razumov envied the materialism of the thief and the passion of the incorrigible lover. The consequences of their actions were always clear and their lives remained their own. (78)

Because the structuring strategy used in his recounting is that of an embedded dialogue, Razumov's own speech is reported in such a way as to retain significant traces of his earlier utterance, but at the same time it reflects the narrator's very different manner of observing, depicting, and evaluating. Thus, on the one hand, the professor's recitation always includes his own subjective responses, responses that infiltrate and contaminate the other characters' discourses, thematizing their views in subtle ways with his own intonations and prejudices. Clearly, the old professor's need to create a coherent "translation" thus attempts to incorporate and appropriate all of the text's discordant voices, orchestrating and thus mediating his "Russian story for Western ears" (163).

On the other hand, however, the narrator's attempt to create a single-visioned overview, rendered to his audience in a "normative" English that reflects its own overarching ideological conceptualization of the world – the tenets of western liberal democracy – is continually called into question. To an extent his account is even discredited, not only by the alien voices and intentions inhabiting his text, but also by their opposing ideologies – totalitarianism and revolutionism – which inject his western narrative with the competing viewpoints and valuations of what M. Bakhtin calls a "hidden polemic."[5] In addition to the conflict created by the inclusion of other voices, we find in *Under Western Eyes* the infusion of competing "languages" – English, French, and translated Russian – each freighted with its own self-regulating and self-perpetuating view of the world. (In this regard, the fact that critical opinion is so divided on the significance in *Under Western Eyes* of allusions to Rousseau's *The Social Contract* only intensifies its disruptive power.)

By placing these differing voices, languages, and political allegiances in critical confrontation, Conrad sets into motion the dynamic of continuously competing "truths," each of which reveals a drive toward mastery. At the same time, however, each also serves to transgress and decentralize the stabilizing centers of the others. Despite his establishment of spurious "transitions," his sequencing of events, his arrangement of scenes, his speculations about relationships – as well as his many other efforts to dominate the mutinous voices in his narrative – the professor's attempt to stabilize and totalize his Russian text finally fails. Yet his very failure to master his material serves to bring into sharper focus the capricious indeterminacy that agitates within Conrad's text. In this way his unreliability itself becomes a prominent element of Conrad's dynamic: a strategy which makes possible the testing and exposure of all culturally accepted ideas and ideologies, including those of western liberal democracy. And the reader is again reminded that, given Conrad's determinedly skeptical approach, his insistence that "my thinking is always multiple" (Jean-Aubry, II, 59), no single interpretation or evaluation can ever be definitive or final.

In a letter to Olivia Garnett, Conrad confided that *Under Western Eyes* is a text "exclusively concerned with ideas" (Garnett, 233). It is hardly surprising, therefore, that his characters function to some extent as allegorical figures engaged in an endless debate over various orders of signification. As T. Tanner observes, a self-critical interrogation of any fixed or inherent idea is "characteristic of Conradian strategy"; his ironic juxtaposition of "opposed realms, or more exactly segments of the world in which life in all its cultural aspects – linguistic, religious, ethical, etc. – is structured differently" (Tannner, 18) – serves to remind us of the sheer contextuality of human judgment and of the ultimate arbitrariness of all cultural constructions. Ultimately, then, it is precisely these cultural formations – expressions of what Ian Watt calls our "collective conditioning force" (Watt, 45) – that are called into question by the irrational actions of Conrad's protagonists.

Individual perception is thus revealed to be the product, too, of culturally shared assumptions, of inherited ideologies that can both create and destroy. In *Under Western Eyes* the speech of each character, as well as its reception, is designed to reveal a political ideology which contests the governing assumptions or "languages" of the other characters. In this way linguistic categories that are too facilely accepted as the norm, as natural or essential, are exposed as strange and sometimes monstrously self-deceptive rationalizations fostered by egoism, fear, or greed. This kind of semiotic enslavement, one which ignores transform-ing nuances, may give the impression that a concept is self--contained and strictly delimited, that it exists independently of its context. Conrad challenges this assumption by demonstrating that rigid definitions and fixed ideas ultimately fail as absolute or unchanging concepts; they can in fact suppress or distort "the image of truth abiding in facts" (Jean-Aubry, I, 280).

Similarly, in his "Preface" to *The Nigger of the "Narcissus"* Conrad complains of "the old, old words, *worn thin*, defaced by ages of careless usage" ("Preface," *NN*, ix). The most serious liability of such mechanical linguistic habit is that it sustains the outworn ideologies of an age or culture, and so remains closed to new experience. Used in this way, language, much like autocratic tyranny, replicates continually the coercive power of prevailing norms and paradigms. Yet, by placing such "authorized" or "official" versions in ironic confrontation with each other, Conrad produces ideological ruptures and displacements that call into question all preconceived, normative views. So organized, the text becomes in a sense closed in on itself: an autonomous system or self-contained world that refuses customary, hierarchical order. And Conrad's reader, who both participates in and stands outside the prevailing paradigms that the text contests, cannot avoid implication in the ethical readjustment and political reassessment demanded by such continuously shifting perspectives. Thus, while Conrad's dynamic strategy cannot engender an entirely new language, it does serve to expose the sterility of "the old, old words," creating a linguistic fluidity that reveals fresh connotations and new relationships.

There is no doubt that the primary focus of concern in *Under Western Eyes* is the looming shadow of Russian autocracy. As Conrad asserts elsewhere: "From the very first ghostly dawn of her [Russia's] existence as a State she had to breathe the atmosphere of despotism; she found nothing but the arbitrary will of an obscure autocrat at the beginning and end of her organization" (Jean-Aubry, II, 98-9). Possible responses to entrapment within such an inherently totalitarian force would seem to be limited to either revolt or submission. Razumov's choice of action, for example, forces him to confront a moral dilemma: fidelity to an individual, the revolutionist Haldin; or loyalty to a group, the authoritarian Russian State.

Initially, then, like so many of Conrad's other protagonists, Razumov embodies a dangerously unaware "innocence" that is threatened by external forces. The alleged but unacknowledged son of an Archpriest's daughter and a certain Prince K–, Razumov is described as one whose imagination, whose constitution as a person, whose identity are shaped, for better or worse, by the history of a nation. As he informs Haldin, "I haven't inherited a revolutionary inspiration together with a resemblance from an uncle"; to the contrary, he continues, "I have nothing to think against. My tradition is historical" (*UWE*, 61). Since his only parentage is purely historical – the history of Russia itself – his conditioning is one that demands subordination of the individual and tacit allegiance to the authority of the State. And it is into this unquestioning and uncomplicated existence that Haldin appears, introducing the subversive ideas that initiate Razumov's confrontation with both political power and moral responsibility. Caught as he is between the demonic mirror images of autocracy and revolution, Razumov seems to have no really clear moral alternatives. That Haldin himself could as easily be seen as bearing responsibility for both the crime and the ensuing catastrophe, as having compromised or betrayed Razumov, only complicates the issue further.

And it is of course Haldin and the other revolutionists who oppose Russia's tyrannous tradition and seek to abolish its monstrous power. Nevertheless, despite the revolutionists' own heroic self-portrait – always regarding their rebellion in the context of an altruistic struggle for the good of the whole – Conrad allows few if any genuine distinctions between "the assertion of the divine right of autocracy" and the revolutionists' struggle for unrestrained freedom. In the world of *Under Western Eyes*, revolution cannot even mitigate, much less eradicate, autocracy's poisonous oppression. Instead, Conrad insists, such revolutionary overturning is "merely a change of names" ("Author's Note," *UWE*, x). As the narrator informs the elderly Mrs. Haldin, the pernicious results of rebellion are disconcertingly similar to those of its arch-enemy:

> A violent revolution falls into the hands of narrow-minded fanatics and of tyrannical hypocrites at first. Afterwards comes the turn of all the pretentious intellectual failures of the time. Such are the chiefs and

> the leaders. You will notice that I have left out the mere rogues. The
> scrupulous and the just, the noble, humane, and devoted natures; the
> unselfish and the intelligent may begin a movement – but it passes
> away from them. They are not the leaders of a revolution. They are its
> victims: the victims of disgust, of disenchantment – often of remorse.
> Hopes grotesquely betrayed, ideals caricatured – that is the definition
> of revolutionary success. (*UWE*, 134-5)

Rebellion, no less than autocratic oppression, is here portrayed as a pernicious weapon of human enslavement. Its
doctrines and its rhetoric seduce, deceive, and even coerce those
who seek political change into the illusion that they are ending
their own oppression and creating a more humane world. The
text of *Under Western Eyes* discloses that, to the contrary, both
groups share a self-delusive intoxication which allows them to
assassinate opponents and purge colleagues in the elevated name
of an abstract "idea." So the relationship that actually exists
between the two ideologies is not one of stark opposition, as is so
commonly supposed. It reveals itself instead to be a polarity that
J. Mukařovský terms a "dialectic antinomy," a reciprocal
relation that simultaneously holds each concept as both com-
plicitous and distinct (Mukařovský, 213). This dynamic reci-
procity is perhaps best exemplified in *Under Western Eyes* by the
figure of the sinister Nikita, nicknamed Necator, who "was
supposed to have killed more gendarmes and police agents than
any revolutionist living" (*UWE*, 266). Yet it is later revealed
that, simultaneously acting as both executioner for the revolutionists and secret agent for the State police, the General
Secretariat, Necator kills with relish for either group.

Similarly, Nathalie Haldin's firmly held faith in a transcendent, redemptive grace initially inspires in many readers (and
many critics) a sense of her deeper compassion and profounder
knowledge:

> "Yes." She bowed her head in assent, and hesitated for a moment. "I
> must own to you that I shall never give up looking forward to the day
> when all discord shall be silenced...the weary men united at last, taking
> count in their conscience of the ended contest feel saddened by their
> victory, because so many ideas have perished for the triumph of one,
> so many beliefs have abandoned them without support.... But at last
> the anguish of hearts shall be extinguished in love." (376-7)

Yet Nathalie's vision is born of a revolutionary urge clearly associated with the inherently Russian tendency toward mysticism reflected in Madame de S–'s shrill revolutionary cry for a "spiritualization of our discontent." Such compulsory conformity, despite its self-avowed "spiritualization," represents an impulse toward ideological totalitarianism in which no protest and no exit is possible. And so even Nathalie's ardent, idealist faith in Utopian revolutionism, her adamant rejection of the world as it is in the name of a transcendent alternative, cannot escape Conrad's skeptical examination. Indeed, while asserting the humanitarian triumph of spiritual love and political liberty, Miss Haldin's words, to western ears, reveal instead a spiritual absolutism, a world in which "all discord shall be silenced," that is equally as insidious as any autocratic political rule.

Conrad's skeptical examination thus exposes not so much the assumed antipathy as the actual similarities that exist between the obverse and inverse of imposed power. The western reader, in response, may be tempted to dismiss these disturbing correspondences by a smug retreat into a third alternative: western liberal democracy. But even in this, Conrad less obviously but characteristically challenges his readers' complacent acceptance of any unexamined ideology. In response to the professor's thinly veiled disapproval of her brother's self-sacrifice for the revolutionary cause, for example, Nathalie counters with a censure of her own: "You belong to a people which has made a bargain with fate and wouldn't like to be rude to it. But we have made no bargain. It was never offered to us – so much liberty for so much hard cash" (134). Here Nathalie simply restates a position that Conrad himself articulates in his 1905 essay, "Autocracy and War." Western democracy, while claiming to found itself on individual freedom, in actual practice fosters a corrupting self-interest, a self-interest that leads to a militant assertion of power. As Conrad observes in "Autocracy and War," its supremacy of material interests, of progress and empire, stand ready, almost eager, to appeal to the sword.

Even the old professor, contrary to his expected valorization of western values, later remarks on the "terribly heavy sentence" imposed for unknown reasons on Privy-Councillor Mikulin by the Russian State: "It seems that the savage autocracy, no more than the divine democracy, does not limit its diet exclusively to the bodies of its enemies. It devours its friends and servants as well" (306). The text of *Under Western Eyes* repeatedly, and from diverse points of view, exposes the bland mediocrity and blind indifference of bourgeois Geneva. His portrayal of Geneva, at the very least, demonstrates Conrad's own ambivalence toward some of the deeper implications – the materialism and moral complacency – of the liberal democratic system: what would become the western nations' silent indifference to Russia's seizure of Poland, for example.

In this way Conrad calls into question the efficacy of "the old, old words," of such presumably transparent terms as "autocracy," "revolution," and "democracy," exposing each as masking fixed dogma, questionable values, and self-delusive attitudes. Unquestioned acceptance and proliferation of such abstract language and ideas, Conrad implies, promote disaster by concealing the disparity that exists between linguistic categorization and actual experience or historical fact. Moreover, these inherited ideologies display their deficiencies by the consequent misfortunes of the characters who try to live by them. Haldin, for instance, tries to justify his execution of the State Minister as an act of higher patriotic duty: "He [de P–] had to be stopped. He was a dangerous man – a convinced man" (16). Yet the irony of Haldin's indictment of de P– is not lost on the reader. In fact, it offers another of Conrad's dramatic reversals of perspective: as fully dedicated to his own anarchic cause as de P– is to that of the despotic monarchy, Haldin embodies that same single-minded pursuit of his own ends that Conrad, throughout *Under Western Eyes*, repeatedly challenges and contests. Both men, autocrat and revolutionary, are profoundly committed believers; as a result, each suffers from a blind imperviousness to any other point of view.

Thus compromised by both "the lawlessness of autocracy – for autocracy knows no law – and the lawlessness of revolution," Razumov is unwillingly catapulted from his "unstained, lofty and solitary existence" into the chaos of competing "truths" and dubious "moralities." Convinced he is acting rationally, he gives Haldin up to the State, which summarily executes the revolutionist. Razumov, in turn, experiences unrelenting guilt for his betrayal, and Haldin's image is quickly internalized by Razumov as "a moral spectre infinitely more effective than any visible apparition of the dead" (299-300). Yet Haldin's image is only the first of the ghosts of the past that comes to haunt Razumov's consciousness. The eyes of both General T– and Privy-Councillor Mikulin, representing of course the potent and antithetical claims of the State, become resident phantoms of his mind as well. Razumov, it becomes clear, has internalized the power commanded by these mortally opposed ideologies along with their spectral representations. These opposing systems of belief begin to impinge upon and influence his thought subtly from within. Razumov's own discourse, much like that of the old professor, has been inhabited by "alien" voices and points of view.

Prior to his betrayal of Haldin, Razumov's thought mechanically replicated and reinforced the prevailing norms of a repressive Russian autocracy; now, however, he is forced to participate in an active (internal) dialogue and to mediate his intentions through the intentions of others. Razumov, however painfully, now has something "to think against." And it is finally these internalized, conflicting points of view that lead to his overwhelming struggle of conscience in Geneva, where he now operates as a double agent living in duplicity and self-betrayal. Even on the personal level, then, an act of revision, of entering an old text from a new critical perspective, is a prerequisite to the rethinking of value systems – and so of learning "how to live." While Razumov was earlier portrayed as an uncritical replica of received dogma, he has now assumed individual responsibility. Having accepted responsibility, he can experience guilt, and can therefore be punished – and perhaps redeemed.

Yet it is important to note that while Haldin's – and Nathalie's – internalized point of view have provided a corrective to Razumov's unthinking allegiance to the State, his written confession to her, although clearly remorseful, is certainly not a simple reversal of hierarchical positions or what Conrad refers to as a mere "changing of names." To the contrary, he concludes his letter to Nathalie by rejecting both blind allegiance to authority as well as the rival claims of the revolutionists. Thus, rather than offering any resolvable dialectic, the conflict among the novel's different ideologies finally breaks down all single-voiced, totalizing discourses. And it is precisely in this strategy that Conrad's skepticism becomes most apparent; he is much too honest a thinker to offer serene utopian hopes for a future mystically "silenced of discord." In point of fact, the only silence Razumov will be allowed is that of permanent physical deafness. Now assuming responsibility for his betrayal of Haldin, Razumov risks everything in his final confession to the high-ranking revolutionaries assembled at the house of Julius Laspara. His contrition elicits only retribution, however, and he is deafened by the fist of his own secret sharer, the double agent Nikita-Necator.

Having turned his back on all totalizing systems of thought – autocratic, revolutionary, or utopian – Razumov is compelled to experience the ultimate groundlessness of all value systems, the radical loss of certainty that, for Conrad, lies at the very heart of the human condition. Razumov's rejection of the distorting political fictions that have hitherto marked his life, and the resulting breakdown of all of his interpretive systems, both reminds us of the limits of our own knowledge and promotes an extended reexamination of all single-minded political commitment. That Conrad's text refuses to endorse for Razumov a transcendent, utopian reality – or any other viable, reclaimable political reality for that matter – further serves to underscore the facticity as well as the exhaustion of our available political models. (Razumov does not, it must be noted, seek "safe haven" in the West.) Read in this way, Razumov's rejection of all external definition seems to be nothing less than a desperate attempt toward personal emancipation, a freedom from the false positions inherent in all rigidly defined belief systems – as well as from the lexical distortions promoted by blind adherence to ideology.

Yet things are never quite so simple in Conrad's view of the world. Razumov's anarchic rejection of all human contact, his demand to be "independent of every single human being on the earth," seems also to enact a skepticism so powerfully disintegrative of all signifying systems that it finally fills him with the urge to move beyond the boundaries of human society altogether. His personal identity, cultural assumptions, and ordering principles have been thrown into chaotic turmoil. As a result, Razumov teeters on the edge of meaninglessness, retaining no clear models for appropriate living or for purposeful future action.[6] On the one hand, then, *Under Western Eyes* seems to offer an incontestable judgment on all fixed values – linguistic and conceptual as well as political; on the other hand, the text is marked with a profound ambivalence toward the final destruction of these values. That is, Razumov's rejection of all "falsehoods" has plunged him into a dangerously phantasmagoric present where liberation seems indistinguishable from a wish for annihilation.

Finally, then, Razumov's assertion of an inviolable freedom is shown to be both psychically intolerable as well as physically impossible. And we find that the external world of physical fact quickly reasserts its inevitability in the guise of a south-shore tramcar. Permanently deafened by Necator's blow and temporarily blinded by lightning, Razumov steps helplessly in front of the tramcar. Suffering two broken limbs and a crushed side in the accident, he is left permanently disabled. As a result, instead of achieving the radical independence he had so hopefully envisioned as his future, Razumov sinks into abject helplessness. Significantly, it is in response to a promise made in the very past that he has rejected that "the Samaritan" Tekla appears to care for him. Fleeing the political violence in Geneva, both retire to an isolated region of southern Russia where Razumov's health continues to worsen. Here Tekla tends him "unweariedly with the pure joy of unselfish devotion. There was nothing in that task to become disillusioned about" (379).

On the one hand, we could impute to Razumov's and Tekla's mutual dependence Conrad's continued adherence to the communal, compensatory virtues he has always held dear: human sympathy, solidarity, restraint, honor, and duty. In short, in the final pages of *Under Western Eyes* Razumov does succeed in severing himself from the false positions embodied by the text's other characters. A reading so focused would highlight Razumov's increased self-awareness, his psychic reintegration, and his rejection of both totalizing hierarchies and conceptual chaos. In A. Fleishman's reading of the novel as an extended search for genuine community, for example, Razumov does finally achieve both self and community. Accordingly, Fleishman finds that with Razumov, as with "Jim and Nostromo, the extreme individualist becomes integrated with a group at last" (Fleishman, 237).

Still, since the text so determinedly withholds the vitalizing promise of a new beginning, Razumov's and Tekla's retreat hardly resembles a utopian escape; rather, it appears to be little more than an exhausted and skeptical withdrawal from the disillusioning political systems that motivate the earlier text. From this perspective, *Under Western Eyes* can easily accommodate a much darker interpretation: Razumov's rapidly deteriorating physical health as well as his isolated physical environment are as important for what they deny as for what they affirm. In his retreat to provincial Russia, then, he is even more a victim of alienation and paralysis than he was earlier. Razumov's position thus remains uncertain despite the visits by the revolutionaries – who, it could be argued, are only once again appropriating his experiences for their own political motives. From this critical perspective, Fleishman's generally optimistic reading is ironically undercut by the realization that Razumov has even fewer options for the future, is perhaps even more mired in the past than ever before. Finally, because the text has exhausted its viable political models, Razumov's efforts could be seen as little more than retreat from a world that is inherently and unremittingly political.

Although these alternate interpretations in no way exhaust the range of possible readings offered by Conrad's work, they do suggest that *Under Western Eyes* so complicates *any* univocal judgment that even Razumov's condition at the end of the novel finally becomes an undecidable issue. Nor can it be otherwise. For, as K. Carabine informs us, Conrad, in composing *Under Western Eyes*, maintained a close personal identification with Razumov's predicament. Thus what Carabine calls perhaps the most autobiographical of Conrad's fictions is also perhaps the most political; as a child, Conrad endured the devastation of both his own family and his Polish homeland by political strife (Carabine, "'The Figure...'," 1-37).[7] That Conrad refuses to endorse any of the self-contradictory political alternatives examined in *Under Western Eyes* is hardly surprising. That his novel refuses to offer any viable alternative to these destructive ideologies is even less surprising. For Conrad, it is enough if he can make us "see."

In a work that so resolutely qualifies and contests the authority of all symbolic readings, no single interpretation can fully displace any other. Rather than imposing an either/or logic, then, the text of *Under Western Eyes* finally allows no stable vantage point from which to evaluate conclusively. So, despite Razumov's and Tekla's mutual affection at the end, their relation in no way resembles the typical modernist attempt to recuperate a lost past or origin. Rather, it seems indicative of a quite different modernist sense that the past can never be escaped. Indeed, like many postmodern works, *Under Western Eyes* exhibits an ironic uncertainty whether human liberation is ever fully possible. And it is precisely its resistance to full resolution that leaves each reader to formulate his or her own understanding of the text, to translate the tale into his or her own language.

NOTES

1. For differing evaluations of Conrad's skepticism, see J. M. Kertzer (121-40), J. H. Miller (13-39), W. W. Bonney (8-30), and R. Davis (155-73).

2. After returning from his dispiriting journey into the African interior, Conrad wrote: "The only indisputable truth of life is our ignorance. Besides this there is nothing evident, nothing absolute, nothing uncon-

tradicted; there is no principle, no instinct, no impulse that can stand alone at the beginning of things and look confidently to the end."

3. In this connection, see especially J. H. Miller (20-6), J. Guetti (58-67), and A. Krupat (63-85).

4. While many critics have commented on the old professor's unreliability, A. Guerard ("The Conradian Voice," 105-18), D. L. Higdon (39-54), E. K. Hay (121-51), and P. R. Szittya (817-40) are especially illuminating on this point.

5. Concerning the "hidden polemic," M. Bakhtin observes: "Besides its referential meaning, the author's discourse brings a polemical attack to bear against another speech act.... The other's discourse is not reproduced; it is merely implied; but the entire structure of speech would be completely different if there were not this reaction to another person's implied words" (Bakhtin, 195).

6. M. Levenson notes that "the fragility of identity, the barriers to knowledge, the groundlessness of value – these great Conradian motifs appear most often in terms of a sensory derangement that casts the individual into unarticulated space, a space with no markers and no boundaries, with nothing behind, nothing above, nothing below" (Levenson, 5). For another discussion of this sense of psychic dislocation in Conrad's work, see J. H. Miller.

7. For a most suggestive and thoroughly cogent discussion of the relationship between Conrad's personal concerns and his novel, also see Keith Carabine, *The Life and the Art: A Study of Conrad's "Under Western Eyes."*

WORKS CITED

Bakhtin Mikhail. *Problems of Dostoevsky's Poetics*, trans. Caryl Emerson. Minneapolis: U. of Minnesota P., 1984.

Benjamin Walter. "The Storyteller: Reflections on the Works of Nikolai Leskov," in Benjamin Walter. *Illuminations.* New York: Schocken Books, 1969, 83-107.

Bonney William W. *Thorns & Arabesques: Contexts for Conrad's Fiction.* Baltimore: Johns Hopkins U. P., 1980, 8-20.

Brooks Peter. "An Unreadable Report: Conrad's 'Heart of Darkness'," in Brooks Peter. *Reading for the Plot: Design and Intention in Narrative.* New York: Alfred A. Knopf, 1984, 238-63.

Carabine Keith. "'The Figure behind the Veil': Conrad and Razumov in *Under Western Eyes*," in *Joseph Conrad's "Under Western Eyes": Beginnings, Revisions, Final Forms,* ed. David Smith. Hamden, Conn.: Archon Books, 1991, 1-37.

Carabine Keith. *The Life and the Art: A Study of Conrad's "Under Western Eyes."* Amsterdam–Atlanta: Rodopi, 1996.

Davis Roderick. "Crossing the Dark Roadway: Razumov on the *Boulevard des Philosophes,*" in *Joseph Conrad's "Under Western Eyes": Beginnings, Revisions, Final Forms,* ed. David Smith. Hamden, Conn.: Archon Books, 1991, 155-73.

Fleishman A. *Conrad's Politics: Community and Anarchy in the Fiction of Joseph Conrad.* Baltimore: Johns Hopkins U.P., 1967.

Garnett Edward, ed. *Letters from Joseph Conrad, 1895-1924.* Indianapolis: Bobbs-Merrill, 1928.

Guerard Albert. "The Conradian Voice," in *Joseph Conrad: A Commemoration,* ed. Norman Sherry. London: Macmillan, 1977.

Guerard Albert. *Conrad the Novelist.* Cambridge, Mass.: Harvard U.P., 1958.

Guetti James. *The Limits of Metaphor: A Study of Melville, Conrad and Faulkner.* Ithaca, N.Y.: Cornell U.P., 1967, 58-67.

Hay Eloise Knapp. "*Under Western Eyes* and the Missing Center," in *Joseph Conrad's "Under Western Eyes": Beginnings, Revisions, Final Forms,* ed. David Smith. Hamden, Conn.: Archon Books, 1991, 121-51.

Higdon David Leon. "Conrad, *Under Western Eyes,* and the Mysteries of Revision," *Review of English Studies,* 39, 39-54.

Jameson Fredric. "Romance and Reification: Plot Construction and Ideological Closure in Joseph Conrad," in Jameson Fredric. *The Political Unconscious: Narrative as a Socially Symbolic Act.* Ithaca, N.Y.: Cornell U.P., 1981, 206-80.

Jean-Aubry Gérard. *Joseph Conrad: Life and Letters,* vols. 1-2. London: Heinemann. 1927.

Kertzer J. M. "'The Bitterness of Our Wisdom': Cynicism, Skepticism and Joseph Conrad," *Novel,* 16: 2 (Winter 1983), 121-40.

Krupat Arnold. "Antonymy, Language, and Value in Conrad's 'Heart of Darkness'," *The Missouri Review,* 3 (Fall 1979), 63-85.

Levenson Michael. *Modernism and the Fate of Individuality: Character and Novelistic Form from Conrad to Woolf.* Cambridge: Cambridge U.P., 1992.

Miller J. Hillis. *Poets of Reality: Six Twentieth-Century Writers.* Cambridge, Mass.: Harvard U.P., 1966, 13-39.

Mukařovský Jan. "The Esthetics of Language," in *A Prague School Reader on Esthetics, Literary Structure, and Style.* Washington D.C.: Georgetown U.P., 1964.

Szittya Penn R. "Metafiction: The Double Narration in *Under Western Eyes,*" *English Literary History,* 48 (1981), 817-40.

Tanner Tony. "Eating and Narrative in Conrad," in *Joseph Conrad: A Commemoration,* ed. Norman Sherry. London: Macmillan, 1977.

Watt Ian. *Conrad in the Nineteenth Century.* Berkeley: U. of California P., 1979.

Mildred C. Andersen,
University of South Africa,
Pretoria, South Africa

Conrad's Perspectives on Dostoyevsky's
Crime and Punishment: An Examination of
Under Western Eyes[1]

It is inevitable that the writing of two such profound thinkers as
Conrad and Dostoyevsky should have provoked critical reaction from the time their first works came into being. Conrad's
productions coincided with the early twentieth-century British
enthusiasm for things Russian, and the Russian elements in *The
Secret Agent* and *Under Western Eyes* predictably prompted
a comparison of Conrad with Russian writers in general and
with Dostoyevsky in particular. In describing the kind of
criticism Conrad encountered, T. S. Eliot writes of a "tendency,"
at the time,

> to insist, when we praise a poet, upon those aspects of his work in
> which he least resembles anyone else.... We dwell with satisfaction
> upon the poet's difference from his predecessors...we endeavour to
> find something that can be isolated in order to be enjoyed. (Eliot, 48)

Those who saw in Dostoyevsky an obvious source for
Razumov lent force to Eliot's charge that that which manifestly
emanated from a recognizable line of art was all too often
greeted with a "phrase of censure." They did not merely
judge Conrad "by the standards of the past" but instead,
to continue with Eliot's flow of thought, they "amputated"
him (47, 50). Conrad himself was resigned to such critical
slings and arrows:

> [Books] have their fate...and it is very much like the destiny of man.
> They share with us the great incertitude of ignominy or glory – of
> severe justice and senseless persecution – of calumny and misunder-
> standing – the shame of undeserved success. ("Books," *NLL*, 4-5)

61

In its discussion of Conrad's indebtedness to Dostoyevsky, much of the criticism of the time[2] drew attention also to a related denial by Conrad of any knowledge of either Russia or the Russian language. Wheeler mentions Najder's suggestion that Conrad's "alleged 'anti-Russianness' became a 'fashionable theme' in particular after the Second World War for political reasons'" (Wheeler, 34, fn. 6). Whatever its parentage, the subject certainly exercised the critics' minds, many of whom regarded Conrad's attitude as a pose, since he clearly had much in common with Dostoyevsky; there was even (some of them claimed) an affinity, whether unconscious or conscious – and thus fervently suppressed by the anti-Russian Pole. This is not as surprising at it may seem. While Conrad was heir, by adoption, to the Western tradition, he was also heir, by birth (however much he might protest),[3] to the Slavonic line of literature to which Dostoyevsky belongs. Both writers, moreover, were subjected by the Russian Government to several years in exile; and surely it was the enforced period of isolation that prompted in each an existential awareness that was to manifest itself in a regard for solidarity or brotherhood. This is a subject to which I shall return.

Conrad's recorded comments on Dostoyevsky are limited mainly to comparison with Turgenev and to a response to Constance Garnett's 1912 translation of *The Brothers Karamazov*, which was printed a year after *Under Western Eyes*. Vizetelly had published a translation of *Crime and Punishment* in 1886 which by 1906, according to Garnett, was no longer obtainable.[4] Despite Wheeler's claim that *Everyman* had brought out a translation of the work in 1911 (31), some critics believed Conrad's access to it was through the earlier French version. He was not in France, however, at the time of its publication. Moreover, notwithstanding Conrad's denials that he could read Russian (Karl, 78fn), there are also assertions that he had read it in its original language.

All this is speculation but, although Conrad does not mention *Crime and Punishment* in his formal writings, there can be no doubt he had read it and had it in mind when creating his

Russian novel. The two works share a great deal. Each protagonist, for instance, is a student with no regular family ties. He lives alone in a rented room, access to which is gained by means of a frequently mentioned staircase. Each entertains a fixed idea resulting in some loss of life;[5] each experiences a reversal of a significant intention and, in consequence of an act of betrayal, experiences hallucinations, physical illness, fever and mental confusion. Both novels feature a mother's anxiety about her son, with consequent derangement and death. Many verbal parallels also exist.[6] It is significant, however, that, like Dostoyevsky, who seemed to have no qualms about borrowing,[7] Conrad made no attempt to disguise the borrowed material. "Imagination, not invention," according to Conrad, "is the supreme master of art as of life" (*PR*, 25).

The question of literary influences is a complex one. *The Book of Ecclesiastes* asserts that there is nothing new under the sun. This does not mean death to art; that nothing remains but to present a colorless variation of the same ideas. The consciousness of history which, according to Eliot, is present in all great artists, not only brings back what has gone before but it also unites with the writer's different perspective and his "great labour" to give new color to the faded stuff of life. Originality stems, if I may take Coleridge's words out of context, from the "interfusion...of the different throughout a base radically the same" (Coleridge, 212). Originality emanates, too, to borrow a philosophic term, from the "lived-experience" of the artist who resets the old jewel. The use of old material is appropriately justified by Conrad through the will to "present it in a fresh way" (*CL*, I, 381); so that, although (in his words) he "picked up" his Dostoyevskian subject from among those that "lay about for anybody to pick-up"[sic] (IV, 488), the topic suffers a seachange when aspects of the Polish expatriate, the mariner and the writer merge with it in an esemplastic embrace.

Today, it is not necessary for a writer to defend himself against the charges described by Eliot. Bakhtin claims, in *The Dialogic Imagination*, that

> in the makeup of almost every utterance spoken by a social person
> – from a brief response in a casual dialogue to major verbal-
> -ideological works (literary, scholarly and others) – a significant
> number of words can be identified that are implicitly or explicitly
> admitted as someone else's, and that are transmitted by a variety of
> different means. (Bakhtin, 354)

Similarly, Foucault acknowledges that the "frontiers of a book are never clear-cut; beyond the title, the first lines, and the last full-stop...it is caught up in a system of references to other books, other texts, other sentences: it is a node within a network" (Foucault, 23); and, in a discussion of poetic discourse, Riffaterre defines it as not only "the equivalence established between a word and a text" but, more significantly, between "a text and another text" (Riffaterre, 19).

All these comments are relevant to my concern with the repetition of identifiable utterances in a major literary work and point to the concept of intertextuality, which has its name from J. Kristeva. In "Word, Dialogue, and Novel" which is reproduced in *Desire in Language...*, Kristeva attributes to Bakhtin the insight that "any text is constructed as a mosaic of quotations; any text is the absorption and transformation of another." "The notion of *intertextuality*," she continues, "replaces that of intersubjectivity, and poetic language is read as at least *double*" (Kristeva, *Desire in Language...*, 66). Roudiez stresses, however, that Kristeva's term "intertextuality" has been inaccurately used: in her understanding the word applies, in fact, to "the transposition of one or more *systems* of signs into another, accompanied by a new articulation of the enunciative and denotative position"; it has "nothing to do with matters of influence by one writer upon another, or with the sources of a literary work" (15). This is a point Kristeva herself makes in her *Revolution in Poetic Language*, where she mentions that the word "inter-textuality" "has often been understood in the banal sense of 'study of sources'" (Kristeva, *Revolution...*, 59-60).[8] Nonetheless, in the commonly (if erroneously) accepted sense of the term as implied above, the concept has been widely recognized and justified in the latter half of this century.

I return to Bakhtin, focusing more especially on his comments on the novel and its writer. "For the novelist working in prose, the object is always entangled in someone else's discourse about it," he says, expanding this by-now-familiar claim with the assertion that such discourse "is already present with qualifications, an object of dispute that is conceptualized and evaluated variously" (Bakhtin, *The Dialogic Imagination*, 330). Moreover, for Bakhtin "the novel" is "a dialogized representation of an ideologically freighted discourse" (333). My aims in this paper are, accordingly, not only to examine the ways in which Conrad's work is influenced by and departs from Dostoyevsky's, but also to reveal why Conrad transformed what he found in his predecessor and made it his own. I shall contemplate the ideological distance between them and show how this prompts a comparison of the texts in broadly generic terms.[9]

In *A Personal Record*, Conrad asserts

> that a novelist lives in his work. He stands there, the only reality in an invented world, among imaginary things, happenings, and people. Writing about them, he is only writing about himself. ("A Familiar Preface," *PR*, xv)

In order to understand Conrad's enduring preoccupations it is necessary to know something about this "only reality" of which he writes, and about the origins of his ideas, many of which gave rise to the tragic vision encountered throughout his writing and, therefore, in *Under Western Eyes*. The world into which Józef Teodor Konrad Korzeniowski was born in 1857 was characterized by division. The third partition of 1795, which carved what remained of Poland into portions that increased the shares of Russia, Prussia and Austria, ended Poland's autonomy. In addition to its geographical fission, Poland was split internally into three political groups: the Appeasers, the Whites and the Reds, or Radicals. Added to this, there was division, politically, among members of Conrad's family.[10] Divided loyalty brought about much conflict within the boy, and it is not surprising that his life and his literature reveal a continuing search for stability and order.

It was the idealistic nature of Conrad's father, Apollo, that led him to work towards a better future for Poland. His ideals cost him, his wife Ewa, and his four-year-old son a term of exile in Vologda, Siberia. Only the child survived the experience. Apollo and Ewa contracted, and died from, tuberculosis. During their illness the young Conrad spent long, solitary hours. Karl notes a "sense of isolation and marginality" in the boy, stemming also from sporadic attendance at school and a consequent "failure to find where he fitted and what he belonged to" (Karl, 93). The effects are apparent in the novels: many characters are orphans or have not led a normal family life. Razumov, the illegitimate son of a prince, is described as "nobody's child" ("Author's Note," *UWE*, ix). It is easy to comprehend, moreover, why the adult Conrad had difficulty in overcoming an inherent reserve – which his wife sensed even as "a prospective bride" (Jessie Conrad, 3) – so that he could not openly show his affection (Stoler, 80). This is a problem which is mirrored in *Chance*, in the portrayal of the courtship and the early months of Flora and Captain Anthony's marriage.

The inability to communicate fully surely contributed to Conrad's consideration of isolation from all angles. Such isolation is frequently accompanied by fear, as the teacher of languages concludes from his perception of Razumov's existential situatedness: "Who knows what true loneliness is – not the conventional word, but the naked terror?" (*UWE*, 39). Conrad examines the physical aspects of isolation, as in Heyst's retirement to his island, and those which are psychological, as when Winnie and Verloc are divided by "his habits of mind" which are "indolent and secret" and her "philosophical, almost disdainful incuriosity" (*SA*, 237, 245). Even in the most successful attempts at coexistence, Conrad concludes, man's condition is essentially separate. This is what Marlow means when he says that "we live, as we dream – alone" ("Heart of Darkness," *YS*, 82).

Possibly the greatest dividing gulf occurs when an act of betrayal drives one spiritually or physically from others, as Jim is driven when he abandons the damaged *Patna* and its passengers. Jim's life-saving jump suggests self-interest but not the kind of self-interest that is allied to materialism. While it is Jim's dereliction of duty that obliterates his inner calm, for Dr. Monygham it is the pursuit of material interests that denies us peace and rest, even when they are directed to progress. For Conrad, dreams and visions associated with money and power are bound to fail. In fact, Conrad's attitude towards dreams and ideals in general is little better. This does not imply that he sees nothing praiseworthy in them. We should indeed "believe and hope" but we should also "preserv[e] in our activity the consoling illusion of power and intelligent purpose" ("Anatole France," *NLL*, 34). Having seen what blinding ideals, coupled to a fixed idea and relentlessly pursued, can do to family and to national life, he himself chose a life far removed from Poland's destructive – and for him, tragic – influence. He chose the sea.

Conrad's imagery constantly contrasts "the incorruptible ocean" (*NN*, 6) with the land, which he associates with squalor; and, not surprisingly therefore, he portrays life at sea as superior to a shore-bound existence. The reason for this is not that those who choose the sea have an unusually high sense of morality but because life on board ship makes claims that "are simple and cannot be evaded" (*Ch*, 32). Fidelity to its demands, which include hard work and endurance, can mean the difference between life and death. Significantly, Conrad's family emblem represents fidelity: to country, to religion, and to God (Karl, 17n). For Conrad, fidelity is among the few fundamental ideas upon which the temporal world rests ("A Familiar Preface," *PR*, xxi) and he includes, here, fidelity to one's fellows.

"We exist only in so far as we hang together." The words are Marlow's and he is speaking about what he calls the "solidarity of our lives" (*LJ*, 224). A ship is a microcosm of society. Conrad explains that, through dependence on cooperation, the unity which life at sea commands raises a group of men, "so to speak, above the frailties of their dead selves" ("Well Done," *NLL*, 183) and creates what he calls "the brotherhood of the sea" (*NN*, 30). In the "Preface" to *The Nigger of the "Narcissus,"* Conrad uses the word "solidarity" to indicate this binding principle that unites "all humanity" ("Preface," *NN*, viii). So important to

Conrad is the idea of brotherhood that the themes which constantly recur in his work are merely positive or negative aspects of the concept, the antithesis of which is isolation. Compassion, law and order, work, and fidelity, all of which comprise solidarity, are opposed by self-interest and materialism, anarchy and revolution, indolence, and betrayal.

Conrad himself was charged with betrayal for leaving Poland and, like Captain Anthony, for throwing himself "figuratively speaking, into the sea" (*Ch*, 39). He did so in order to survive, yet speaks of having suffered "a storm of blame from every quarter," ("A Familiar Preface," *PR*, xvi) of having "been charged with the want of patriotism,...of sense, and...of heart," so that he endured "agonies of self-conflict and shed secret tears not a few" (*PR*, 110). Pride in Apollo's exploit combined with Conrad's attitude towards destructive idealism to induce irreconcilable "guilt and remorse" with their attendant suffering. This is a point made by Karl in his biography of Conrad (Karl, 94) and by Carabine in his recent, detailed examination of the relationship between Conrad, his father and Dostoyevsky (Carabine, 8). Although guilt and suffering are recognized components of Dostoyevsky's writing, appearing throughout his works and especially in *Crime and Punishment*, Conrad clearly used these two themes because they were close to his heart. As he wrote to Pinker, the subject of *Under Western Eyes* had haunted him for some time and had to come out (Karl, 636).

I have mentioned Conrad's belief that a novelist's world "cannot be made otherwise than in his own image." *Under Western Eyes* testifies to this.[11] Conrad not only imaginatively converts his factual material; he also incorporates his own attitudes. All the favored themes are there: the self-interest as represented in Peter Ivanovitch and Nikita; the fidelity and compassion of solidarity as embodied in Tekla; the negative effects of idealistic pursuits as seen in the disruption of Razumov's life, in the deaths of the Minister de P–, Victor and Mrs Haldin; and, of course, the betrayal by Razumov and the accompanying isolation. No wonder Karl views the work as "that shadow novel of so much in Conrad's life, perhaps more an autobiography than *A Personal Record*" (102). Indeed, there is obviously much in *Under Western Eyes* that departs from Dostoyevsky.

I have suggested that Conrad's early experiences were responsible for a view of life that, for him, was closely allied to tragedy. It is in keeping with this vision (so remote from Dostoyevsky's as I shall illustrate) that after completing the first part of the novel "the whole story revealed itself to [him] in its tragic character and in the march of its events as unavoidable" ("Author's Note," *UWE*, vii). The point at which this revelation came to him is immaterial, for it seems that, in having taken up the challenge of the Dostoyevskian topic, unconsciously or consciously Conrad intended to show how it should have been handled.[12] "Discourse lives, as it were, on the boundary between its own context and another, alien, context" (Bakhtin, *The Dialogic Imagination*, 284) and, indeed, the Conradian discourse thus impelled into life provides ample evidence of what Riffaterre refers to as "intertextual incompatibilities" (Riffaterre, 128). Their presence is confirmed in Phelps's contention that *Under Western Eyes* is "an *exposé* of the kind of Russian psychology that Dostoyevsky represented, and a vigorous assertion of a very different point of view" (Phelps, 179). I propose to show, as indicated earlier, that the changed perspective produces a work that is, in broad terms, generically distinct from Dostoyevsky's.

The different treatment is immediately apparent in Conrad's presentation of his hero. Unlike Raskolnikov who has the affectionate support of his family, Razumov is alone. In contrast to the idle Raskolnikov, Razumov has worked hard at his studies to give his life meaning; and whereas Raskolnikov has not earned a good name among his fellows, Razumov has a high reputation at the St. Petersburg University, where he is regarded as "a strong nature – an altogether trustworthy man" (*UWE*, 6); one of those rare beings, according to Haldin, who lead "[u]nstained, lofty, and solitary existences" (137). While Raskolnikov's murderous act is premeditated and the ensuing distress is his due, Razumov is the victim of Haldin's "visitation" (32) and does not deserve his misfortune. He acts merely in an attempt to save himself: it is the "blind rage of self-preservation" that "possesse[s]" him (30) when he realizes that the drunken Ziemianitch will not rid him of Haldin's incriminating presence.

The word "visitation" quoted above suggests the complicity of that once much-feared being, Fate. The implication is appropriate, since, as previously indicated, the "character" of *Under Western Eyes* is "tragic"; and where tragedy exists, there dwells Fate. The demeanor of Fate in the Conradian scheme has much in common with what he observed in nature around him. Big trees bend "before a brutal and merciless force" (*AF*, 19) and the wilderness shows in its "playful paw-strokes...the preliminary trifling before the more serious onslaught" ("Heart of Darkness," *YS*, 105). In *The Shadow-Line*, the captain feels that the "perfect silence" which surrounds his becalmed ship, and which is "joined to perfect immobility, proclaimed the yet unbroken spell of our helplessness, poised on the edge of some violent issue, lurking in the dark" (*SL*, 115).

Perhaps, as suggested by the captain's element, this idea of Fate is conveyed most readily by the sea – "the sea that plays with men till their hearts are broken, and wears stout ships to death" (*MS*, 148). The sailors on the *Narcissus* survey "the weather and the ship as men on shore watch the momentous chances of fortune"(*NN*, 50); and, in the same vessel, Singleton regards "the immortal sea with the awakened and groping perception of its heartless might"; he perceives it "unchanged, black and foaming under the eternal scrutiny of the stars" and hears "its impatient voice calling for him out of a pitiless vastness full of unrest, of turmoil, and of terror" (99).

If Conrad's Fate resembles nature in its brutal heartlessness, however, the two are clearly not identical. His figure of Fate owes nothing to the features of the Greek gods but wears a twentieth-century countenance: humanity is destroyed by its own creations and institutions.[13] "Nations it may be have fashioned their Governments," says the narrator in *Under Western Eyes*, "but the Governments have paid them back in the same coin" (*UWE*, 25). A "despotic Government" (25) "envelops and crushes" Razumov ("Author's Note," *UWE*, ix). The word "envelops" recalls the engulfing power of the sea – aptly, because Conrad sees the ocean not only in terms of its incorruptibility, as I have illustrated. In its "murderous innocence" (to borrow a pair of words from Yeats), it is, according to Conrad, also capable of displaying the "conscienceless temper of a savage autocrat" (*MS*, 137). It is not surprising, then, that in *Under Western Eyes* Fate emerges as the tyrannous specter of autocracy. Razumov senses that he is "being crushed – and...can't even run away" (*UWE*, 32); the "shadow of autocracy" lies upon him and upon "Russian lives in their submission or their revolt" (109). To make the analogy between autocracy and Fate more complete, the narrator describes Razumov's "record" as being "like the open book of fate" (105). This the servants of autocracy peruse "with the full sense of their unbounded power over all the lives in Russia, with cursory disdain, like...Olympians glancing at a worm" (306).

From the moment the champions and the opponents of autocracy fix their gaze upon Razumov, he is in its toils, and the element of tragic inevitability is manifest. Agamemnon will die. Oedipus will kill his father. Razumov will betray Haldin: the story "in the march of its events," writes Conrad, is "unavoidable" ("Author's Note," *UWE*, vii).[14] Razumov forfeits his hearing. Oedipus loses his sight. At this point in the latter's history, his blindness, like Whalley's in "The End of the Tether," is physical. Yet Conrad is as concerned as Sophocles with mental or spiritual blindness. In the "Author's Note" to *Nostromo*, Conrad attributes the disastrous events in the novel to "the passions of men short-sighted in good and evil" ("Author's Note," *N*, ix). Kayerts and Carlier, in "An Outpost of Progress," live "like blind men," "understanding nothing"(*TU*, 92-3). Like Razumov initially, countless of Conrad's characters are spiritually myopic; and not only do they fail to see clearly, but they are also exposed to testing existential situations,[15] requiring a difficult choice of some kind. Jim must weigh the consequences of giving or of failing to give Brown his freedom; the captain in "The Secret Sharer" must decide whether or not to hide his stowaway at great personal risk. Razumov is also faced with a delicate choice. His failure to "cut short" the talk with Haldin and tell him "to go away" is no "sound instinct" (*UWE*, 20), as the hero believes, but is an error in judgement leading ineluctably to his fall.

This error of judgement and its effect recall the *hamartia* and the *peripeteia* which Aristotle locates in tragedy and in the tragic hero. Conrad's tragic vision and his portrayal of it are related to the way in which he experienced life and art. An examination of the tragic situatedness of existential man was Conrad's immediate response to contemporary life;[16] his artistic development was fostered, *inter alia*, by an encounter with Shakespeare, whose works Apollo translated into his native tongue. Although Conrad tells of his early encounter with Apollo's manuscripts, I can find in his writings no significant concern with Aristotle and the Greeks. Hay however, asserts that Conrad knew the writings of Plato and Aristotle "directly or indirectly through his Catholic background or his school reading" (Hay, 15); and she quotes a letter in which he says that "as a boy in a great public school" he was "steeped in classicism to the lips."[17] Yet, while there is much in Conrad to suggest an affinity with Greek writers, possibly this derives from his independent perception of the efficacy in tragedy of a number of features we have come to associate with Aristotle:[18] Razumov's "high reputation" (he is, too, the son of a prince), the "fall into misery" and the "undeserved misfortune" are in accord with Aristotle's pronouncements (Aristotle, 48).

Dostoyevsky's concern is with the "fall into misery" of mankind, with the anxiety engendered in society through the loss of God. Without "faith in one's soul and its immortality," he claims, "existence is unnatural, unthinkable, impossible," so that one is led "to the inevitable conviction of the utter absurdity of...existence on earth" (Dostoyevsky, *The Diary...*, 538). Dostoyevsky favored Orthodox Christianity under the Russian Czar, an implied regard for autocracy which, in addition to his Russian identity, plainly augmented the Polish Conrad's dislike of him.[19] Since in Dostoyevsky's stand there is obviously little place for tragedy, it is not surprising to find that the latter's writing and Aristotle's Poetics have nothing in common. For Aristotle, the protagonist's fall should be due not "to vice and depravity" but, as seen, "rather to some error" (Aristotle, 48). An error in Raskolnikov's judgment there certainly is, but the decision to kill an old moneylender for the sake of an idea is indeed "vice and depravity." His situation has "nothing in it," therefore, that would promote pity or fear in the Aristotelian sense: "our pity is awakened," he says, only "by *undeserved* misfortune, and our fear by that of someone just like ourselves" (48, my emphasis). Obviously the average reader of *Crime and Punishment* is not fearful that, "just like" Raskolnikov, she or he may become a murderer, nor does any pity emanate from the perception that Raskolnikov's adversity is unmerited. We are a long way from catharsis here.

I wish to return to Conrad's focus on spiritual blindness. He presents the acquisition of insight, of vision, as something achieved at great price. Kurtz acquires knowledge "only at the very last," Marlow tells us; after "the wilderness had found him out early, and had taken on him a terrible vengeance for the fantastic invasion," "it had whispered to him things about himself which he did not know" ("Heart of Darkness," *YS*, 131). "Out of a tried heart," Alvan, in "The Return," stands in a paradoxically "revealing night" ("The Return," *TU*, 183); and Razumov passes through his own "revealing night," meeting with great pain the cost of the significantly "dropped black veil." Indeed, the old teacher of languages describes him as looking as if "he [has] stabbed himself...and more than that – as though he were turning the knife in the wound and watching the effect" (*UWE*, 350-1). In *Crime and Punishment* Raskolnikov does suffer, but his vision is something vouchsafed, doubtless through the intercession of Sonia as mediatrix. Until liberated by his dream, he continues to see his ill-conceived theory as right and, afterwards, thinks no more of the crime it prompted. The young deviant's payment for his new life is what Dostoyevsky's narrator calls "the beginning of a new story" (Dostoyevsky, *Crime and Punishment*, 559) which is not the reader's concern. In tragedy (and in Conrad) we would witness the transaction; and to eyes attuned to tragedy, Raskolnikov's saving dream possibly smacks of intervention by some *Deus ex Somno.*

Tragic insight yields to redemption. As seen, Conrad gives Razumov the dimensions of a tragic hero who grows in insight, while the unheroic Raskolnikov fails to recognize his error. Conrad's idea and treatment of redemption point to yet another instance of a departure from Dostoyevsky's handling of a common theme. Like insight, redemption implies a purchase. In the tragic view, some mental distress and a prison sentence of eight years are a relatively low return for Raskolnikov's two murders, at least one of which is calculated. In Dostoyevsky, Christ has paid all and for all men. It is the favorable disposition towards God that counts and the "Epilogue" to *Crime and Punishment* suggests that Raskolnikov is on the way to such an attitude.

While I am supported by a number of adherents to the gospel of Razumov's full payment and release – Baines (397, 441, 447) and Guerard (252) among them – there are some critics who feel that he does not redeem himself or that he achieves, at best, a qualified redemption. Hay is one of these, despite her claim that Conrad's novels resemble "the classical tragedies...so closely" (Hay, 308). The novel must speak for itself: Razumov turns his back on spiritual death, and makes himself "free from falsehood, from remorse – independent of every single human being on this earth" (*UWE*, 368) on the very day that Sophia Antonovna's announcement to the revolutionaries ensures his security. Heedless of his personal safety, he confesses his perfidy, feeling afterwards that he has been "washed clean" (357). Surely he is punished well beyond his deserts. For "the safety of his lonely existence" (21) and for displaying a natural reserve, Razumov's life is in ruins: he is stone deaf, "crippled, ill, [and] getting weaker every day" (379). Redemption has cost him "not less than everything," to use a phrase from Eliot's "Little Gidding." Sophia Antonovna, whose first name means wisdom, assesses Razumov's sacrifice and his accomplishment. She perceives the "character" in his "discovery" – the word recalls Aristotle's term *anagnorisis* – that authentic life and the "ignominy" of a sullied "existence" (380) cannot be reconciled. In contrast, Raskolnikov succumbs to illness when life becomes insupportable, because Dostoevsky aims to show what happens when we reject God. In the case of Razumov and those like him, their stalwart choosing to face the worst that life can do to them,[20] their tragic stoicism, "that fine [and Senecan] attitude before the universally irremediable" ("Author's Note," *V*, x) ennobles them in our eyes.

At this point I wish to emphasize that, although *Under Western Eyes* is a novel, it is essentially tragedy of a kind. Life is characterized by flux, and in art, which is a reflection of life, little remains static. In tragedy, therefore (since it is as dynamic and organic a thing as any literary genre), circumstances – to borrow Crichton's admirable epigram – alter cases. After the term "tragedy" has served us for approximately two and a half thousand years, it is comprehensible that, while some of its elements remain fixed, one man's understanding of the concept may vary significantly from another's. Conrad's idea of tragedy, as we have seen, shares certain features with the Greek and, therefore, with the Elizabethan models, and it claims kinship with existentialism.

I wish to dwell a little longer on Conrad's affinity with tragedy in the classical sense. As shown, *Under Western Eyes* inclines towards the tragic in its vision and in its Aristotelian structure. It thus accords with two out of the three elements Aristotle distinguishes in generic classification, namely content (that which is imitated) and form.[21] Obviously, hovever, the medium of narration in Conrad's work departs from Aristotle's third category – the mode of enunciation which, in tragedy, is mimetic; and for Aristotle, *mimesis* is direct representation "as it functions on the stage," comprising "gestures and speech" (Genette, *Figures...*, 130), a view that contends with the opinion, in Plato's *Republic* Book III, that dialogic elements in narrative (or *diegesis*) are mimetic. Plato's view was based on a consideration of the combined narrative and dialogue in Homeric epic. That this combination is present also in *Under Western Eyes* implies (but only from the Platonic perspective, of course) that mimetic elements do exist in Conrad's text. An interesting addition to the argument is Batchelor's claim that "there is a good deal of emphasis on gesture" in *Under Western Eyes* and that Conrad was "thinking in terms of the theatre" when writing the novel (Batchelor, 178).

The generic aspect of *Crime and Punishment* is not as easily determined, particularly if we take into account Steiner's view that a novel is in essence a secular vehicle (Steiner, 28ff, 239). Indeed, for many years Dostoyevsky's multifaceted work eluded attempts at classification, containing, as it does, elements of tragedy, comedy (the progress of the Marmeladov funeral meal is Dickensian comedy in a Russian setting), and melodrama, as in the street scene where Mrs Marmeladov urges her children into song and dance. With the possible exception of the pastoral, Dostoyevsky offers the reader everything that Polonius claims for the repertoire of the actors who appear in Elsinore for Hamlet's diversion; and even in this category the description of the countryside in *The Little Hero* throws some doubt on the idea that its writer is capable only of an urban focus.

The difficulties of categorization can be readily appreciated. As is common in writing of a religious nature, there are elements of allegory in Dostoyevsky, not least of which is that names were frequently chosen to illustrate aspects of the characters concerned.[22] *Crime and Punishment* has much in common with Dante's allegory, *The Divine Comedy*, tracing, as it does, Raskolnikov's taking a wrong path, his purgatorial journey and, ultimately, the view of the celestial kingdom with Sonia in the role of Beatrice. An early definition has it that comedy is the kind of literary work that records progress from misfortune to happiness. Despite its predominantly heavy shadows, therefore, *Crime and Punishment* may be viewed as following the kind of course that prompted Dante to classify his poem as comedic. With its perilous approach to the abyss and, ultimately, the rescue through reconciliation, forgiveness and love, the work can also be likened in structure to Shakespeare's final romances where joy at the close is an essential ingredient.[23]

Yet apart from its ending and a number of lesser passages, *Crime and Punishment*, as suggested above, is indubitably composed in a minor key. The resolution, which resembles a literary *Tierce de Picardy*, has proved troublesome to critics bent on placing the work generically. In his *Problems of Dostoevsky's Poetics*, however, Bakhtin presents a convincing case for the rebirth, in Dostoyevsky's writing, of menippean characteristics.[24] Bakhtin's work has done much to resolve the critical diffculties inherent in *Crime and Punishment* not only because of its conclusion but also because of the presence of seemingly incompatible features such as its "free fantastic, symbolic...[and] mystical-religious element," the "extraordinary philosophical universalism" and "ultimate questions," the focus on "abnormal moral and psychic states of man," the well-known "scandal scenes" and the "elements of *social utopia*" (Bakhtin, *Problems of Dostoevsky's Poetics*, 115-18). Moreover, the problem raised by Steiner's view that a novel is essentially secular is resolved by Bakhtin's assertion that the menippea have long been associated with Christian literature (113, 135-6).[25] "Does this mean," asks Bakhtin, "that Dostoevsky proceeded *directly* and *consciously* from the ancient menippea?"

> Of course not. In no sense was he a *stylizer* of ancient genres. Dostoevsky linked up with the chain of a given generic tradition at that point where it passed through his own time, although the past links in this chain, including the ancient link, were to a greater or lesser degree familiar and close to him.... Speaking somewhat paradoxically, one could say that it was not Dostoevsky's subjective memory, but the objective memory of the very genre in which he worked, that preserved the peculiar features of the ancient menippea. (121)

No doubt, bearing in mind, *inter alia*, what he calls the "polyphonic" nature of Dostoyevsky's writing, Bakhtin continues:

> The generic characteristics of the menippea were not simply reborn, but also *renewed*, in Dostoevsky's work. In his creative utilization of this generic potential, Dostoevsky departed widely from the authors of the ancient menippea. In its posing of philosophical and social problems, in its artistic qualities, the ancient menippea seems in comparison with Dostoevsky primitive and pale. (121)

Having said this, Bakhtin makes a point similar to mine in my consideration of the generic characteristics of *Under Western Eyes*: "we consider it necessary to emphasize that the generic label 'menippea,' like all other generic labels – 'epic,' 'tragedy,' 'idyll,' etc. – is, when applied to the literature of modern times, a means of designating the *essence of a genre*, and not any specific genre canon (as in antiquity)" (137).

I return, now, to Conrad's attitude towards Dostoyevsky and his writing. Doubtless, Conrad would have rejected the size of and the preponderance of detail in Dostoyevsky's menippean canvas. Although the intensity of Conrad's feelings towards the Russians played its part in the manner in which he received Constance Garnett's translations of Dostoyevsky's work, Conrad was too much an artist not to have recognized merit where it exists. If we accept this – he did call *The Brothers Karamazov* "an impossible lump[?] of valuable matter...impressive and exasperating" (*CL*, V, 70, editors' square brackets) – then we shall accept, too, that his protests about "the grimacing haunted creature" (Garnett, 249) were directed more at Dostoyevsky the poet than at Dostoyevsky the man. In the first place, Conrad, with his seaman's reliance on order, does not portray the world as a place where, as in Dostoyevsky's writing, madness is an everyday occurrence. Perhaps the evidence of a didactic approach in the Russian's work was even more distasteful to Conrad. As early as 1896, the narrator of *An Outcast of the Islands* pronounces words which testify to this standpoint: "if Babalatchi considered it a song, then it was a song with a purpose and, perhaps for that reason, artistically defective" (*OI*, 138), and over twenty years later, in 1920, he maintains that to "charg[e] a single one of [his] pages with didactic purpose" would amount to nothing less than an injury: "I don't mean insult, I mean injury" ("Author's Note," *Ch*, ix). Possibly these emphatic words constitute Conrad's conscious view of his approach to art. All the same, and despite similar claims to "detachment" in portraying the Russians in *Under Western Eyes* ("Author's Note," *UWE*, vii), it is ironic that Carabine can detect here, as with "Autocracy and War," "a public and a private face"; Conrad, says Carabine, draws upon the "passions and prejudices" of his father and race to demonstrate his "fidelity to a lost cause"...by attacking Poland's great enemies...and by conducting a savage assault upon Dostoevsky's political principles and vision of Russia. (Carabine, 11)

Dostoyevsky himself saw propaganda in art as evidence of an "unworthy purpose" but could openly overrule his own strong feelings:

I am anxious to express certain ideas, even if it ruins my novel as a work of art, for I am entirely carried away by the things that have accumulated in my heart and mind. Let it turn out to be only a pamphlet, but I shall say everything to the last word. (Dostoyevsky, *The Devils*, ix)

The message he was anxious to give the world was, as indicated earlier, the Gospel of peace through the fellowship of souls under both the guidance of the Russian Orthodox Church and the patronage of the autocratic Czar. I have mentioned Conrad's abhorrence of autocracy; however, it was possibly the recourse to religion that rankled most. Experience had led him not to rely on divine intervention as a way out of his own and his family's troubles. The correspondence with Edward Garnett explains his feelings about Christianity:

It's strange how I always...disliked the Christian religion, its doctrines, ceremonies and festivals. (*CL*, II, 468)
Christianity – is distasteful to me. I am not blind to its services but the absurd oriental fable from which it starts irritates me. Great, improving, softening, compassionate it may be but it has lent itself with amazing facility to cruel distortion and is the only religion which, with its impossible standards, has brought an infinity of anguish to innumerable souls – on this earth. (V, 358)

Yet, even in this aspect of Dostoyevsky's writing, Conrad's objection can be viewed as intrinsically artistic rather than personal. "Inspiration [Conrad maintains], comes from the earth, which has a past, a history, a future, not from the cold and immutable heaven" (*PR*, 95). No doubt, to his way of thinking, Dostoyevsky and his book end, like Ziemianitch in *Under*

Western Eyes, "by falling into mysticism. So many of our true Russian souls end in that way!," Conrad has Razumov exclaim: "Very characteristic" (*UWE*, 283).[26]

I have indicated that a recognition of man's existential situatedness is shared by the two writers. Among the existential elements in Dostoyevsky's writing are the spiritual isolation of his characters (Raskolnikov is but one of a host of similarly afflicted fellows) and the demand for freedom of choice: Raskolnikov's decision to pursue his Napoleonic dream is an instance of this. Obviously, Conrad's existentialism differs from Dostoyevsky's in some respects, however:[27] Dostoyevsky makes a Kierkegaardian leap of faith to "something" – Christ – "by which he is prepared to live, and to which he has a non-rational commitment" (Warnock, 7). Not surprisingly, it is in the quest for God that Dostoyevsky's characters find their authenticity and, thus, their identity. Conrad, on the other hand, belongs to that secular brand of existentialism which has to seek its meaning in a Godless world and which regards with indifference man's unceasing travail. Conrad's writing reflects this. It also reflects the courage in such a stance. I make this claim in defiance of many accusations that he was a pessimist.[28]

In concluding this paper, I wish to turn to H. Bloom who, although writing about poetry, has much to say that is relevant to authors of prose fiction in general and to Conrad in particular; in the words that follow, the affinities with both intertextual theory and Eliot are patent:

> You cannot write or teach or think or even read without imitation, and what you imitate is what another person has done, that person's writing or teaching or thinking or reading. Your relation to what informs that person is tradition, for tradition is influence that extends past one generation, a carrying over of influence. (Bloom, 32)

"Poetic *strength*," Bloom continues (and for these words, substitute "literary strength"), "comes only from a triumphant wrestling with the greatest of the dead *and from an even more triumphant solipsism*" (9, my emphases). Contemplating this triumph, he quotes the existentialist, Kierkegaard, who always insisted that "We become great...in proportion to the greatness we fight against, whether that greatness belong to a man, an idea, a system or a poem" (108). In *Under Western Eyes*, Conrad fights against all four – a man, Dostoyevsky; an idea, Russian Orthodox Christianity; a system, Russian autocracy; and a novel, *Crime and Punishment*.

NOTES

1. The presentation of this paper at the II International Joseph Conrad Conference at Maria Curie-Skłodowska University, Lublin, Poland, was made possible by means of travel grants from the Centre for Science Development and the University of South Africa, to whom I express my appreciation.

2. I am referring to response in the West.

3. I am aware that, in his youth, Conrad was temporarily attracted to the idea of Pan-Slavism. See F. R. Karl, 210 and K. Carabine, 7.

4. The "present generation of English readers," Garnett declared, "knows not Dostoyevsky" (Berman & Van Wagenen, 272).

5. Raskolnikov would prove himself as daring as a Napoleon figure; Razumov's thoughts are dominated by the silver medal in an essay competition.

6. Some of these verbal similarities are that the protagonists' names commence with and end with common syllables and that the names "Razumikhin" and "Razumov" are both prefaced with the equivalent of the Russian word (*razum*) for "reason." Marmeladov's asking if Raskolnikov realizes "what it means when you have nowhere to go to" (Dostoyevsky, *Crime and Punishment*, 33) is echoed in Razumov's words to Nathalie: "Do you know why I came to you? It is simply because there is no one anywhere in the whole great world I could go to" (*UWE*, 353-4); and Mikulin's "Where to?" in response to Razumov's wish "simply to retire" (99) recalls Porfiry's "And where, pray, can he escape to" (Dostoyevsky, *Crime and Punishment*, 355)? In his suffering, Raskolnikov comments on the need for air and Razumov experiences an equal lack of ventilation until his last confession brings him "air to breathe at last – air!" (*UWE*, 361).

7. *Crime and Punishment* owes much to Balzac's *Père Goriot* and something to Pushkin's *The Queen of Spades*; and, as Lary illustrates in *Dostoyevsky and Dickens*, Dostoyevsky's liability to Dickens manifests itself in verbal likenesses. Also, the darkness and the grotesque horror condemned by some readers are easily traced to Ann Radcliffe's influence (Magarshack, 40).

8. G. Genette (81-2) refers to "*textual transcendence* – namely, everything that brings it into relation (manifest or hidden) with other texts. I call that *transtextuality*, and I include under it *intertextuality* in the strict (and, since Julia Kristeva, the "classical") sense – that is, the literal presence (more or less literal, whether integral or not) of one text within another.

9. Some of my argument is drawn from aspects of my unpublished Master's dissertation, "The Transformation of Dostoyevskian Themes in Conrad with Special Reference to *Crime and Punishment* and *Under Western Eyes*." The University of South Africa holds the copyright.

10. See F. R. Karl, 25-6.

11. Ibid., 18, 23, 34, 102 and 103, for instance, demonstrates that the revolutionary, idealistic Haldin has much in common with Apollo; that Razumov betrays Haldin as, in deserting Poland and its cause, Conrad betrays his father; and that Razumov is the typically isolated character.

12. This view is corroborated by a number of critics, among them J. Baines, 360-1 and G. Phelps, 178-9.

13. In its absence of religious faith for the most part, such a world is indifferent to human travail. In this respect, it is a world inhabited by the kind of Fate that stalks the pages of Hardy's 19th-century Wessex novels. Unlike Conrad's 20th-century figure, however, Hardy's Fate is unrelated to the destructive influence of "man's creations and his institutions." D. D. McElroy in his *Existentialism and Modern Literature* describes present-day man as prey to "economic crises, unemployment, and war." "The world he has built has become his own master; the work of his own hands has become a god before whom he bows down" (McElroy, 8).

14. The certainty of a fall is implied in the image of Razumov at the Château Borel, where he feels "the ungravelled ground of the deeply shaded walk damp and as if slippery under his feet" (*UWE*, 207).

15. The tragic sense of life is familiar to the existentialist. See O. Bohlmann, 19, for instance.

16. Briefly, existential philosophy confronts the problem and the meaning of existence: the problem because the dread of death promotes anxiety; the meaning because in a modern world devoid of God life appears to be absurd. Moreover, despite an overpopulated world, human-beings are not only essentially alone but they lose all sense of uniqueness. Individuality and associated authenticity are achieved only through the exercise of free-will. Existentialists, however, recognize no universal moral law, no absolutes. Each person has to choose how to live; yet such freedom augments anxiety, as choice is coupled with responsibility.

17. See the letter of 14 December 1922 to George T. Keating in G. Jean-Aubry, II, 289.

18. J. Batchelor (177-8) says that Conrad borrowed "Bradley's hugely influential *Shakespearean Tragedy*" from Richard Curle in 1913 or 1914 but thinks that Conrad may have read it when it was first published in 1904.

"Bradley takes Aristotle as the model on which Shakespeare is building," Batchelor continues, and "Conrad would have been aware of this." Batchelor does not, however, take into account the presence of elements resembling Aristotle's *hamartia, peripeteia* and *anagnorisis* elsewhere in Conrad, even before *Under Western Eyes* was published. *Lord Jim* is an example. See fn. 17.

19. Among other personal reasons for Conrad's dislike of Dostoyevsky was, possibly, the animosity towards Poles in his writing: for him, Poles were ingrates who were unable to appreciate the call to Pan-Slavism. In *The Brothers Karamazov*, Rakitin expresses a belief in the "inferiority" of Poles, referring to Grushenka's erstwhile lover as a "dirty little Pole" (Dostoyevsky, *The Brothers Karamazov*, 422); and, in *Crime and Punishment*, Porfiry, in testifying to his high opinion of Raskolnikov's honor, claims that "a Pole will escape abroad, but not *he*" (Dostoyevsky, *Crime and Punishment*, 355).

20. In contrast, consider how, in *Death of a Salesman*, Willie Loman takes his life. Miller paints a man who, determined by his environment, has no choice. In traditional tragedy, the hero responds to the dispensations of fate by choosing, at least, to act stoically and in defiance of fortune. In Conrad, Jim, for instance, will "conquer the fatal destiny itself."

21. G. Genette points out that form – the third "type of differentiation among the arts of imitation" – receives "no real attention in the *Poetics*, whose system of genres comprises by and large only objects and modes" (Genette, 12).

22. Raskolnikov's name derives from the Russian word (*raskol'nik*) for a heretic or a schismatic; the name of the rational Razumikhin stems from *razum* which means reason; and the word *lebezyat* is clearly related to the fawning Lebezyatnikov (Peace, 21, 29, 45). See, too, C. E. Passage who, in relating Dostoyevsky's "nomenclature" to an expansion and adaptation of the "Comedy of Manners," acknowledges Dostoyevsky's awareness of the relationship between allegory and "names [that] have a meaning." This consciousness is given voice through Maximov in Dostoyevsky's *The Brothers Karamazov* (16-17).

23. That the close of its "Epilogue" resounds like Schiller's hymn is probably not fortuitous. Dostoyevsky told his brother that he loved Schiller, and it is doubtless a consciousness of the German poet that was also responsible for Dostoyevsky's having Dmitry in *The Brothers Karamazov* tell Alyosha how he wishes "to begin [his] confession with...Schiller's Hymn to Joy. *An die Freude*" (121).

24. I shall not touch on Bakhtin's discussion of carnivalization in Dostoyevsky except to mention its compatibility with the menippea. Menippus of Gadara was a slave who lived during the third century B. C. and who "purchased his freedom, settled in Thebes, and proceeded to satirize all formal schools of philosophy and all philosophical elites." Briefly, Menippean satire is "characterized by its mockery of serious forms,

its digression and exaggeration, and its mixture of prose and verse"
(Bakhtin, *The Dialogic Imagination*, 316).

25. This is despite the fact that the "carnivalesque structure" (see note
24) is, in Kristeva's words, "anti-Christian." A "carnivalesque genre," the
menippea, in addition to influencing "Christian and Byzantine literature,"
"had an enormous influence on the development of English literature and
especially the formation of the novel"; however, "only modernity – when
freed of 'God' – releases the Menippean force of the novel" (Kristeva,
Desire in Language..., 79, 82, 85). While Dostoyevsky's *Crime and
Punishment* does, indeed, describe increasing Godlessness in his world, my
argument shows that he himself does not identify himself with such
developments.

26. K. Carabine points out that such mysticism was shared by Apollo
and Poland. Although, in taking up Poland's cause against Russia, Conrad
attempted in *Under Western Eyes* to lessen the perception of his betrayal of
his father, the rejection of Russian mysticism is ironically a rejection of an
essential aspect of Poland's, and thus his father's, psyche (Carabine, 11, 16).

27. J. Batchelor, 178, ignoring the existentialist essence of Dostoyevsky's *Crime and Punishment*, calls it "Christian, broadly, in its outer
assumptions and in its frame of reference, while Conrad's novel is wholly
secular – indeed existentialist – in its frame of reference." As Kierkegaard,
Marcel and Berdyaev show (and my continuing argument implies),
Christianity and existentialism are not incompatible. See Bohlmann, 53,
104-5, inter alia.

28. Tadeusz Bobrowski, who greatly influenced his nephew, wrote to
him that pessimism is "aridity of soul and action" (Najder, 155), an idea
that recurs in the novels: even the psychologically disabled Karl Yundt in
The Secret Agent has enough sanity left to perceive that pessimism "rots the
world" (*SA*, 42). "Pessimism," Bobrowski explains, "ruins the individual
and his life and stultifies his actions." Between the extremes of pessimism
and "excessive optimism," however, "is the 'golden mean' which contains...the basic truth of life" (Najder, 152). Despite the well-known
"knitting machine" letter to Edward Garnett (its negative effect is, in fact,
mitigated by wry amusement), Conrad recognized and depicted the world's
virtues. While also acknowledging and describing its ills, he was not
defeated by them.

WORKS CITED

Aristotle. "On the Art of Poetry," in *Classical Literary Criticism: Aristotle;
     Horace; Longinus*, trans. and Intro. T. S. Dorsch. Harmondsworth:
     Penguin, 1977.

Baines Jocelyn. *Joseph Conrad: A Critical Biography*. Westport, Conn.:
     Greenwood Press, 1975.

Bakhtin Mikhail. *Problems of Dostoevsky's Poetics*, ed. and trans. Caryl Emerson, Intro. Wayne C. Booth. Manchester: Manchester U.P., 1984; *Theory and History of Literature*, vol. 8.

Bakhtin Mikhail. *The Dialogic Imagination*, ed. Michael Holquist, trans. Caryl Emerson and Michael Holquist. Austin: U. of Texas P., 1988.

Batchelor John. *The Life of Joseph Conrad: A Critical Biography*. Oxford: Blackwell, 1994.

Berman Jeffrey and Van Wagenen Donna. "*Under Western Eyes*: Conrad's Diary of a Writer?," *Conradiana*, 9: 3 (1977), 269-74.

Bloom Harold. *A Map of Misreading*. New York: Oxford U.P., 1975.

Bohlmann Otto. *Conrad's Existentialism*. London: Macmillan, 1991.

Carabine Keith. "Conrad, Apollo Korzeniowski, and Dostoevsky," *Conradiana*, 28: 1 (1996), 3-25.

Coleridge Samuel Taylor. *Biographia Literaria*, ed. and Intro. George Watson. London: J. M. Dent, 1975.

Conrad Jessie. *Joseph Conrad as I Knew Him*. Garden City, N.Y.: Doubleday, 1972.

Dostoyevsky Fyodor. *The Diary of a Writer*, trans. (with annotations) Boris Brasol. New York: George Braziller, 1954.

Dostoyevsky Fyodor. *Crime and Punishment*, trans. and Intro. David Magarshack. Harmondsworth: Penguin, 1975.

Dostoyevsky Fyodor. *The Brothers Karamazov*, vol. 1, trans. and Intro. David Magarshack. Harmondsworth: Penguin, 1976.

Dostoyevsky Fyodor. *The Devils*, trans. and Intro. David Magarshack. Harmondsworth: Penguin, 1979.

Eliot Thomas Stearns. *The Sacred Wood: Essays on Poetry and Criticism*. London: Methuen, 1953.

Foucault Michel. *The Archaeology of Knowledge*, trans. A. M. Sheridan Smith. London: Routledge, 1994.

Garnett Edward, ed. and Intro. *Letters from Joseph Conrad. 1895-1924*. Indianapolis: Bobbs-Merrill, 1928.

Genette Gerard. *Figures of Literary Discourse*, trans. Alan Sheridan, Intro. Marie-Rose Logan. New York: Columbia U.P., 1992.

Genette Gerard. *The Architext: an Introduction*. Berkeley: U. of California P., 1992.

Guerard Albert J. *Conrad the Novelist*. Cambridge, Mass.: Harvard U.P., 1969.

Hay Eloise Knapp. *The Political Novels of Joseph Conrad: A Critical Study*. Chicago: U. of Chicago P., 1963.

Jean-Aubry Gérard. *Joseph Conrad: Life and Letters*, vol. 2. Garden City, N.Y.: Doubleday, Page, 1927.

Karl Frederick R. *Joseph Conrad: The Three Lives. A Biography*. London: Faber & Faber, 1979.

Kristeva Julia. *Revolution in Poetic Language,* trans. Margaret Waller, Intro. Leon S. Roudiez. New York: Columbia U.P., 1984.

Kristeva Julia. *Desire in Language: A Semiotic Approach to Literature and Art,* ed. Leon S. Roudiez, trans. Thomas Gora, Alice Jardine and Leon S. Roudiez. Oxford: Blackwell, 1987.

Lary N. M. *Dostoevsky and Dickens: A Study of Literary Influence.* London: Routledge and Kegan Paul, 1973.

Magarshack David. *Dostoevsky.* London: Secker and Warburg, 1962.

McElroy Davis Dunbar. *Existentialism and Modern Literature.* Secaucus, N.J.: The Citadel Press, 1972.

Najder Zdzisław, ed. *Conrad's Polish Background: Letters to and from Polish Friends,* trans. Halina Carroll. London: Oxford U.P., 1964.

Passage Charles E. *Character Names in Dostoevsky's Fiction.* Ardis: Ann Arbor, 1982.

Peace Richard. *Dostoyevsky: An Examination of the Major Novels.* Cambridge: Cambridge U.P., 1971.

Phelps Gilbert. *The Russian Novel in English Fiction.* London: Hutchinson University Library, 1956.

Riffaterre Michael. *Semiotics of Poetry.* Bloomington: Indiana U.P., 1984.

Steiner George. *Tolstoy or Dostoevsky: An Essay in Contrast.* London: Faber & Faber, 1959.

Stoler Peter. "Sea Changes," *Time,* 118: 80-4 (24 August 1981).

Warnock Mary. *Existentialism.* Oxford: Oxford U.P., 1979.

Wheeler Marcus. "Russia and Russians in the Works of Conrad," *Conradiana,* 12: 1 (1980), 23-36.

Monika Majewska,
Maria Curie-Skłodowska University,
Lublin, Poland

Stevie: Conrad's Christ?

Whereas one would hardly dispute Dostoevsky's literary presence on the pages of *Under Western Eyes,* very little has been written so far about Dostoevskian elements in Conrad's earlier novel, *The Secret Agent.* The vast majority of critical comments on the subject under discussion are but occasional remarks on the margins of critical works devoted to various aspects of Conrad's novel. Many of them point to the affinity between Conrad's Stevie and Prince Myshkin, the main protagonist of Dostoevsky's *The Idiot.*

Thus, examining the character of Stevie, F. R. Karl remarked that his beauty of soul, like Myshkin's in *The Idiot,* makes it extremely difficult for the "poor boy" to cope with the demands of the materialistic world of realities (Karl, 197). The critic's observation brings to mind Thomas Mann's much earlier assertion (expressed in his introduction to the German edition of *The Secret Agent*) that it is inconceivable that Conrad could have created the character of Stevie without being acquainted with the above-mentioned novel by Dostoevsky (Mann, 23). I. Howe, too, indicated a connection between Stevie and Prince Myshkin. He called Conrad's character a "literary cousin of Myshkin" but, at the same time, pointed to an important difference between the two: whereas Dostoevsky's prince occasionally approaches the sublime, Stevie "never emerges from the pitiable," having been cast in the novel in the role of a "prepared victim" (Howe, 96-7). A. Fogel, in turn, commented on the intensity of Winnie's sisterly devotion to Stevie which was "not quite like anything else in English fiction" and reminded him of "some domestic bond in Dostoevsky" (Fogel, 161). In his analysis of the destructive force of sympathy the critic focused on Inspector Heat's "compassionate" thoughts produced over

Stevie's remains, and observed that in *The Idiot* there can be found a similar compassionate meditation: Prince Myshkin pondering over the instant death by guillotining (169).

A special place among critical comments on the subject under discussion should be assigned to E. K. Hay. Although she does not explicitly point to Myshkin as the "prototype" of Stevie, she singles out *The Idiot* as one of the three novels by Dostoevsky (*The Devils* and *Crime and Punishment* are the remaining two) which, "had [Conrad] wanted to rewrite [them] all in one, he could not have succeeded better than with this story [i.e. *The Secret Agent*]" (Hay, 235). Her more specific opinion concerns the figures of the Verlocs. She considers the "Simple Tale" (as Conrad subtitled his novel) to be "almost a parody of Dostoevsky in that Winnie and Adolf Verloc are...heavily disinclined to explore moral and political questions – any kind of questions for that matter" (235).

All the observations represent a high level of generality, which arises from their status of marginal remarks. I would like to look closer at the possibilities of comparison between Stevie and Myshkin signalled by the critics and consider the question of whether Conrad's creation of Stevie might, too, be viewed as influenced by his intention to parody the hated Dostoevsky.[1]

A depiction of a "positively beautiful man"[2] was Dostoevsky's primary objective during his work on *The Idiot*. And since the author believed firmly that "nothing is more beautiful, profound, sympathetic, reasonable, manly and more perfect than Christ,"[3] the story of the main protagonist's life reads like an allegorical reworking of biblical tales, with Prince Myshkin cast in the role of Jesus. The crazed but saintly figure of the Russian *yurodivy*, or God's fool, whose path to salvation led through meekness and self-abasement, was another source of inspiration for Dostoevsky.[4]

But the idiocy of Myshkin is not solely an expression of a religious concept dear to the Russian people. It is also, as R. Peace demonstrates, the writer's solution to a difficult artistic problem of how to make the presentation of such an ideal credible (Peace, 60). Dostoevsky's close examination of other virtuous heroes in European literature made him realize that readers would accept an embodiment of virtue only if some device, such as laughter or pity, allowed them to establish their own sense of superiority over it. Therefore, he decided to employ Myshkin's idiocy as some sort of a periscope – to enable his readers to look down on an image which, in fact, was far above them (60).

While discussing the figure of Myshkin, it is almost impossible not to mention the place this character occupies in the Bakhtinian analysis of the carnivalistic-fantastic atmosphere that, according to the critic, permeates the entire novel (Bakhtin, 173). The Russian scholar views the prince as the major Dostoevskian hero closest to the Ridiculous Man, the central protagonist of "The Dream of a Ridiculous Man," who, in turn, displays many features of the ambivalent, i.e. serio-comical, image of the "wise fool" and "tragic clown" of carnivalized literature (150). The carnivalizing function of the image of Prince Myshkin, on which the critic comments at length, consists in the ability to "'penetrate' through the life-flesh of other characters and reach their deepest 'I'" (173). Wherever the eccentric prince appears, his incongruous behavior (from the point of view of ordinary logic) and inappropriate gestures make hierarchical barriers between people penetrable and cause "false seriousness" to give way to "carnival frankness" (174).

Sometimes perceived as "a sort of [the author's] idealized self-projection," this particular hero held for the writer a special significance (Leatherbarrow, viii).[5] The views on beauty, Catholicism, socialism and spiritual vacuum at the heart of the contemporary society the prince articulates can be found in Dostoevsky's journalistic articles and on the pages of his personal correspondence. Myshkin's epilepsy, interest in calligraphy, fascination with certain paintings, are just some out of many autobiographical traits present in the delineation of Dostoevsky's prince. In addition, the prince's strong preoccupation with the fate of a man about to be executed has been traditionally traced back to Dostoevsky's own experience in 1849 when, convicted of participation in a plot against the regime of Nicholas I, he himself faced a firing squad for several terrifying minutes before being informed that his sentence had been changed for that of hard labor in Siberia.

The same can hardly be said about Conrad's Stevie. Nothing is known about the writer's particular attachment to this character and, with regard to autobiographical influences, it is not Conrad but Martial Bourdin, the young anarchist sympathizer who blew himself up in the actual Greenwich Bomb Outrage of 1894 that has usually been suggested as the prototype of Stevie (Baines, 330). Like Bourdin, Conrad's character does not damage the observatory, but gets killed by the bomb he carries. What is more, Stevie and Bourdin resemble each other physically: Stevie is slight and fair, while the actual perpetrator was described as a "remarkably short man...well-nourished and proportioned, but inadequately developed"; his hair and moustache "silky and fair."[6] But whether Stevie inherited from Bourdin certain features of his outward appearance is a minor issue here. It seems more important that although the young anarchist and his fate might have provided Conrad with inspiration for *The Secret Agent*, they can hardly account for all complexities of the character of Stevie – perhaps Conrad's version of Dostoevsky's favorite hero.

Myshkin's Christian virtues of meekness and compassion are tested in the apocalyptic world of nineteenth-century Russia. Apocalyptic themes are introduced overtly and explicitly into the novel by one of the minor characters, Lebedev, who has set himself up as an interpreter of the Apocalypse. According to him, the "star Wormwood" that appears in Revelation denotes the network of railroads spreading over Russia (Dostoevsky, 391). He hastens to reassure his listeners that he does not mean so much the railways themselves as the spirit of self-seeking, capitalist enterprise behind them, that has already managed to penetrate the minds of many of his compatriots (393-400). In his interpretations, often viewed as a key to the reality presented in the novel, Lebedev points to the commercialism of the age and to the seduction of his contemporaries by the power of finance. And, indeed, the society depicted in *The Idiot* is corrupted by the market place and mesmerized by money. It is hardly surprising, then, that in such a society a very important (from Dostoevsky's perspective) social virtue – the spirit of community – has long been lost.

Conrad's Stevie is cast in the no less threatening "spiritual Babylon" of London at the turn of this century (Tennant, xi). The society – atomized, infected with moral nihilism – of which Stevie is a member, reveals close resemblance to that portrayed in *The Idiot*, since it suffers from the same disease: lack of organic unity, which for Conrad was an important value.

But although both Dostoevsky and Conrad place their heroes in the social surroundings sharply contrasted to the two writers' ideals,[7] it should be noted that Myshkin is far better equipped to face the world he enters than Stevie, who is of little value to the money-oriented society. Shortly after his arrival in Russia the prince inherits a fortune, from which point he is regarded as a man of substance (Dostoevsky, 175). Furthermore, Stevie's mental potential does not compare with that of Myshkin, who is relatively outspoken, sufficiently educated and fully aware of his illness. In the course of the novel other characters come to realize that despite his proclaimed idiocy, the prince is intelligent enough to notice things others cannot see. All these advantages of Myshkin over Stevie notwithstanding, both characters share a similar plight. Myshkin's passage through people's lives can, at best, be said to fail to improve them, if not provoke destruction,[8] and terminates in his relapse into mindlessness. Stevie's very existence in such an imperfect form pushes Winnie into a loveless marriage, prompts his mother to leave for an almshouse, while his death by explosion unleashes destructive forces latent in his sister. In the case of Myshkin the Christlike beauty of the soul manifests itself in altruism and a compassionate attitude towards suffering humanity and, in Stevie's case – in sympathy with suffering mankind and some representatives of the animal world (see his being struck by the "dramas of fallen horses" – *SA*, 9).[9] All in all, both Myshkin and Stevie display an essential lack of ability for "worldly accommodation," which has serious, ultimately lethal, consequences.

But the character of Stevie seems to have been conceived as far from a mere fairly faithful copy of Dostoevsky's prince. He is not simply a secularized Myshkin – more generously endowed with idiocy and lowered in social status. Several traits of Stevie make it possible to view him as a firework of more sophisticated allusions to various aspects of his Russian counterpart's personality.

Thus, Stevie's favorite occupation of drawing circles may be related to Myshkin's fascination with calligraphy. In the course of the two novels both characters are put into parallel situations. The specimens of their art/"art" are closely examined. On being shown a number of sentences written by the prince in different scripts General Yepanchin praises him as not simply a calligrapher but an artist (Dostoevsky, 35). Stevie's drawings attract the attention of Ossipon. With the help of Lombroso's theories, the anarchist classifies them as a perfect symptom of their author's degeneracy. Interestingly enough, in the light of the popular view of Lombroso's disciple, Max Nordau, whose *Degeneration* has been said to exert influence upon the psychology of the characters that appear in *The Secret Agent* (Ray, 126), the judgements passed by General Yepanchin and Comrade Ossipon are in essence the same. It is due to the fact that Nordau's simplifiers viewed him as claiming that "artist" was synonymous with "degenerate" (129). The two words are used in reference to Stevie interchangeably; classified by Ossipon as a degenerate, he is at the same time described by the narrator as an artist (*SA*, 45). Conrad's playing in the novel with the notion of artistic inclinations as closely linked to degeneracy makes the possibility of an intertextual reading of this device even more appealing. Perhaps Ossipon's "degenerate" is in some way a response to General Yepanchin's "artist."

In addition to calligraphic skills (reduced in Stevie's case to drawing circles), Myshkin is endowed with another ability (partly supernatural) which Stevie lacks: he can read minds and faces. Faces figure prominently, especially in the first part of *The Idiot*. In his conversation with Madame Yepanchina and her three daughters the prince tells Adelaida how to paint the face of a man about to be executed (Dostoevsky, 67-9), declares his ability to read the girls' faces (70), to "look closely at faces now" (80) and, finally, guesses the personality of each of them from the evidence of her outward appearance (80-1). But, as far as his uncanny gift is concerned, Myshkin displays the real acme of perfection in his analysis of the portrait of Nastasya Filippovna. He not only intuits her suffering and pride, but also prophesies her death – remarking that Rogozhin, if married to Nastasya, might murder her a week later (37). Myshkin's paramystical practices seem to be ridiculed in Conrad's novel where, for the sake of parody, the whole situation is reversed. Stevie, instead of reading into others intuitively, is himself being read into "scientifically" by Comrade Ossipon, who on the evidence of the lobs of the boy's ears calls him again a perfect example of some form of degeneracy (*SA*, 46-7).

The prince's speaking strategies and concern for his own speech might have also attracted Conrad's attention. Unlike Stevie, who finds it extremely difficult to produce a well--constructed sentence, Myshkin seems to be quite an articulate person, although his linguistic behavior is a bit on the eccentric side. Already in the opening scene of *The Idiot* the prince is shockingly guileless in his answers to Rogozhin, who is being informed about the most intimate details of Myshkin's life. Next, he violates social conventions by starting a conversation with General Yepanchin's footman, to whom he delivers a short lecture on guillotining (Dostoevsky, 21-3). During his first meeting with Madame Yepanchina and her daughters he mentions the braying of an ass he heard in Switzerland (59) and makes long speeches on such inappropriate subjects as capital punishment and the young Swiss girl Marie, who was seduced by a travelling salesman, ostracized from the society, and whom he befriended shortly before her death (72-8). Whereas in the first part of the novel Myshkin impresses the people he meets with his amazing readiness to open himself up, in parts two and three he appears as a man of relatively few words. At the evening gathering at the Yepanchins' villa in the fourth part he goes into rapturous emotion for no apparent reason, and a remark implying a connection between his late benefactor Pavlischev and the Jesuits provokes his violent and unstoppable attack on Roman Catholicism, which culminates in an epileptic fit.[10] Like his literary father who, occasionally, commented on his own lack of verbal facility (Peace, 316), Myshkin is aware of the peculiarities of his linguistic behavior. He expresses his deep dissatisfaction with his oral performance, stating that the words he chooses do not correspond to the lofty ideas he wants to propagate. The prince articulates his fear of being laughed at, complains about his own oversensitivity, lack of fitting gestures and sense of proportion, and concludes by saying that he would rather abstain from speaking than debase his thought by expounding it himself (Dostoyevsky, 359; see also 547, 583).

Provided his mental competence were satisfactory enough to make him realize his limitations, Conrad's character would have far more reasons to despair of his lack of verbal facility. The problems Myshkin has with his own speech are experienced by Stevie on a larger scale. Being "no master of phrases" (*SA*, 171), he finds it difficult to render not only "lofty ideas," but even the simplest messages. He stutters and mutters or, occasionally, produces monosyllabic cries that are not immediately comprehensible. At the same time, the boy's lack of verbal articulateness, which may be viewed as a part of his Myshkinian heritage, seems to be employed in the novel as a means of emphasizing the distance separating him from other characters (Schwarz, 170). Stevie's silence contrasts sharply with the anarchists' verbosity, conveying nonsensical messages. From this perspective his lack of speech means lack of nonsense. In the character of Stevie Myshkin's amazing straightforwardness and insufficient conformity to the established social rules governing the use of language (i.e. the traits in the prince's personality which, according to M. Bakhtin, help him perform the function of destroying the "false seriousness" – Bakhtin, 174-5) are brought to their extremes, for the boy, unlike the anarchists, takes everything for truth, not for pretence. This literalization of the others' discourse makes him, for instance, misinterpret Ossipon's metaphoric remark concerning the "cannibalistic" nature of the contemporary economic conditions and "get into passions" over the poor whose flesh is eaten and blood drunk (*SA*, 51). Like Myshkin, who is oversensitive and tends to react too emotionally to certain issues, Stevie displays hypersensitivity to suffering of others, gets easily impressed by "tales of injustice and oppression" (9). But whereas the prince can, at worst, shock his bemused listeners with a sudden outburst of verbal violence, hardly consonant with his own teachings on humility and compassion, Stevie's excitability finds more dangerous manifestations, for it culminates in violent actions. The boy touches off a set of fireworks (9), or even resorts to a carving knife in his revengeful rage at the German officer guilty of tearing off half of the ear of a recruit (60).

Their difficulty in expressing themselves notwithstanding, both Myshkin and his less articulate but more aggressive English counterpart are vehicles for spreading certain truths which are summed up in very few words. Thus, clues to Myshkin's philosophy may be found in the two aphoristic sayings attributed to him by other characters, i.e. "meekness is a mighty force" (Dostoevsky, 417)[11] and "beauty will save the world" (555), while Stevie's worldview is presented in his "[b]ad world for poor people" (*SA*, 171), which he manages to produce when deeply moved by the plight of the cabman and his horse. These phrases point to an important contrast between the two characters: whereas Stevie focuses on the outside world, defines its victims, the only thing that can be inferred from the above-mentioned sayings about the Myshkinian outside world is that it needs saving. Unlike Conrad's hero, the prince is not so much concerned with the diagnosis of the world's disease, as with the cure for it, which is to be sought in redeeming one's spiritual inside. The contrast of the outside vs spiritual inside is further enhanced when Stevie thinks of the police as a force able to counteract the evil, and has to be cured of this mistaken belief by Winnie (in *The Secret Agent* Conrad undermines the salvation-bringing role of this particular and other institutions). On the other hand, Myshkin makes it explicit time and again in the novel that salvation could be reached within, since each human being carries in himself a seed of his future renewal, and it is to this seed of "goodness" in everyone that the prince appeals.

All these potentially good men should follow the example set by the embodiment of the idea of the Russian Christ (according to the writer, it is Russia alone which has preserved the only true image of Christ – Peace, 70), i.e. Myshkin himself. At the time of his work on *The Idiot* Dostoevsky was already familiar with *The Life of Jesus* by Ernest Renan – one of the most hotly discussed books of the nineteenth century, presenting Jesus not as the Son of God but as the most perfect of mortals. It helped the Russian writer to cope with the difficult task of portraying his Christlike hero. Thus, the story of Myshkin's life absorbed many details of the French author's account of Christ's ministry (Leatherbarrow, xviii).[12] Like Christ, Myshkin enters the world from the other, very different one (i.e. from the perfect world of Switzerland), with the intention of propagating his ideals. He confesses the aim of his mission to the Yepanchin sisters: he regards himself as a philosopher who has come to teach (Dostoevsky, 62). In his recollections Switzerland appears as a sort of paradise: it was there that his Christian virtues of meekness, truth and compassion won him the trust of those he met, and it is also to this country that he longs to retreat when he feels completely shattered by the pressures of Russian reality. The anecdotes Myshkin tells about the period he spent in Switzerland, too, offer parallels between his life and that of the founder of Christian religion. Thus, the story of Marie recalls the tale of Jesus and the fallen woman, Mary Magdalene, whereas the account of his friendship with the children of the Swiss village evokes another biblical image – that of Christ surrounded by children. What is more, some circumstances of the prince's stay in his native land, too, invite the reader to connect Jesus and Myshkin. The merchants and moneylenders on the steps of the Temple were the first people Christ encountered after his entry into Jerusalem, and on his arrival in Russia Myshkin immediately strikes an acquaintance with the representatives of these two professions: the merchants Rogozhin and Totsky and the moneylender Ptitsyn. Like Jesus, who in the course of his mission abandoned his disciples and retreated into wilderness for some time, the prince leaves St. Petersburg for six months in order to collect his thoughts. Parallels between various events from the lives of Myshkin and Jesus could be drawn almost endlessly. In addition, on many occasions other characters speak about the prince's Christlike qualities and point to his heavenly descent. "You're an out-and-out holy fool and God loves the likes of you," exclaims Rogozhin in his conversation with Myshkin (14), and Madame Yepanchina expresses her belief that it was God who sent the prince from Switzerland to Petersburg just for her sake (87).

In contrast to Dostoevsky's hero, who has been cast in the role of the religious pivot of *The Idiot* and whose resemblance to Jesus and associations with God are so strongly emphasized, Stevie recalls Christ only faintly, due to the beauty of his soul. There is no aura of saintliness around him, there is nothing holy about his idiocy. Quite often perceived by other characters as a fool, he is nonetheless never viewed as a "holy fool." In the novel by Conrad this character serves as an index of the modern world's departure from the foundations of more universal, not strictly religious, morality; his life can hardly be seen as an allegorical reworking of biblical tales.

But, as M. Holquist has observed, the significance of Christ's story in *The Idiot* does not boil down to "mere characterological parallels between the saintly progress of Jesus and Myshkin" (Holquist, 104). The critic views the plot of the novel as "a series of narrative turns on the structure of the execution of Jesus and its relation to time before and after his death on the cross" (103). He also pays a lot of attention to the role played in *The Idiot* by Hans Holbein's painting of *Christ in the Tomb*, which Dostoevsky saw in the Basel Museum in 1867, at the time he was trying hard to formulate the conceptual framework of his new novel.

The painting depicts with harrowing realism the body of Christ just after he was taken down from the cross. A "good" copy of it hangs in Rogozhin's gloomy house; Myshkin recalls having been appalled by the original, which he saw abroad, and remarks that such a picture could destroy an onlooker's faith (Dostoevsky, 229). But this terrifying image, serving in the novel as "the symbolic centre of the dilemma: belief or unbelief in God" (Peace, 88), does not function in the consciousness of Myshkin alone. Rogozhin and Ippolit, two other major characters of *The Idiot*, are, too, deeply moved by the idea the painting expresses; their reactions to *Christ in the Tomb* provide clues to their spiritual interior (Stempczyńska, 55-60). A full description of the horrific effect Holbein's work produces on onlookers is given by Ippolit:

> The picture shows Christ, just taken down from the cross. I believe artists usually depict Christ, whether on the cross or taken down from it, as still retaining a trace of extraordinary beauty in the face; they seek to preserve this beauty in him, even during the most terrible agonies. There was no trace of beauty in Rogozhin's picture; it is an out-and-out depiction of the body of a man who has endured endless torments even before the crucifixion – wounds, torture, beatings from the guards, blows from the populace, when he was carrying the cross and fell beneath it, and finally the agony of the cross.... In the picture the face is terribly mangled by blows, swollen, with terrible, swollen, bloody bruises, the eyes open and unfocused; the whites wide open, gleaming with a kind of deathly, glazed lustre. But it's odd; as you look at this corpse of a tortured man a most curious question comes to mind; if a corpse like that (and it must certainly have been exactly like that) was seen by all his disciples, his future chief apostles, and seen by the women who followed him and stood by the cross, by all in fact who believed in and worshipped him, how could they have believed, looking at such a corpse, that the martyr would rise again? The compulsion would be to think that if death was so dreadful, and nature's laws so powerful, how could they possibly be overcome? How could they be overcome when even he had failed, he who had vanquished even nature during his lifetime, he whom nature obeyed, who said "*Talitha cumi!*" and the girl arose, who cried "Lazarus come forth!" and the dead man came forth? Looking at that picture, one has the impression of nature as some enormous, implacable, dumb beast, or more precisely, much more precisely, strange as it may seem – in the guise of a vast modern machine which has pointlessly seized, dismembered, and devoured, in its blind and insensible fashion, a great and priceless being, a being worth all of nature and all her laws, worth the entire earth – which indeed was perhaps created solely to prepare for the advent of that being! The picture is, as it were, the medium through which this notion of some dark, insolent, senselessly infinite force to which everything is subordinated is unwittingly conveyed. (Dostoevsky, 429-31)

This strongly naturalistic picture of the defeated Christ resonates throughout *The Idiot*: R. Peace calls it the novel's symbolic heart (Peace, 97). According to M. Holquist, the painting may be viewed as the major structural metaphor for the failure of Myshkin's mission in Russia; the prince's activities in his native land in the six months' interval between the long years spent in the Swiss asylum, which constitute the novel's major plot, do not change anything, they fail to establish an expected new order (Holquist, 104). The lives of other major characters are also marked by the failure of an inspired moment to bring about any change or, in other words, the failure of *kairos* to effect *chronos* (104).

In Conrad's novel there is an analogous scene involving no less strikingly naturalistic image of a human corpse: Inspector Heat examining the results of the Greenwich explosion. Similarly to Christ's execution in Holquist's analysis, the explosion is frequently perceived by Conrad scholars as the central event of *The Secret Agent*. For example, R. W. Stallman noticed that the first three chapters serve in the book merely as the prologue to the drama proper, and that it is only the Greenwich bombing (which is first made known in the fourth chapter) that initiates all subsequent action (Stallman, 112). J. Wiesenfarth commented on the main time-shift in the novel as pivoting on the day of Stevie's death (Wiesenfarth, 515), and according to J. R. Smitten, all the events in *The Secret Agent* relate back to this particular moment as either a cause or an effect (Smitten, 158-9).

The associations with Christ's sacrifice the circumstances of the Greenwich explosion could evoke seem clear enough. Like Jesus, who, sent by his father, died on the cross to redeem humanity, Stevie, acting at his surrogate father's instigation, takes the bomb in order to right the wrongs of the world and gets killed in the course of his mission. A possibility of biblical interpretation of the situation depicted in the novel is outlined by D. Erdinast-Vulcan. She calls both Jesus and Stevie literalizers of suffering and compassion, and views the boy's "passions" over the sufferings of others as a parody of the passion of Christ (Erdinast-Vulcan, 218). She compares Stevie's death in the explosion to "an unwitting act of *Imitatio Dei*," in which the boy "offers himself up as a human sacrifice" (218). With regard to the results the Greenwich bombing produces, i.e. a heap of Stevie's mangled remains, the critic demonstrates how the narrative literalization deprives the whole act of any redemptive value: Holy Communion, a symbolic partaking of the savior's flesh and blood, turns in Conrad's text into a literal "feast for cannibals" (218).

D. Erdinast-Vulcan focuses primarily on the complex relationship between ethics and aesthetics in the novel and devotes relatively little space to the Christian-oriented connotations evoked by Stevie and his fate. J. Darras, on the other hand, is far more generous with producing statements concerning various religious symbols and motifs which he perceives to appear in abundance on the pages of *The Secret Agent*. Thus, the ironically-minded critic calls the Verlocs "the Holy Verloc Family" (Darras, 103) and "a loveless trinity" (104); he claims they embody degeneration of the Christian family, for their "apparent respectability" serves only as "a cover-up for repressed savagery" (103). He also views Stevie's death as a parody of Christ's sacrifice (104). Unfortunately enough, Darras fails to prove his theses, to argue convincingly for all the interesting religious connotations indicated. It is not surprising, then, that his interpretation of *The Secret Agent* as "a parody of the various trinities consecrated by Western civilisation" (105) has not become popular with Conrad scholars. Darras was criticized for being overly influenced by the "preconceived notions" with which he approached the novel (de Vries, 215).

Nevertheless, since there are very few critical comments suggesting the possibility of reading *The Secret Agent* against the background of the world of Christianity, the question arises of whether more evidence justifying viewing Stevie as a Christ--figure can be found in Conrad's text.

D. Erdinast-Vulcan highlighted "the curious symbiosis and the neat symmetry" between Mr. Verloc and Inspector Heat and viewed both of them as father-figures – the ironical portrait of Mr. Verloc as a protector of society and a noble *pater familias* cultivating his domestic virtues and finding at home "the ease of his body and the peace of his conscience" (*SA*, 5-6, 12; see also Erdinast-Vulcan, 215). Verloc's fatherly image is further enhanced by Winnie's imaginative casting of him in the role of surrogate father to her retarded brother: she watches them leaving for their first walk together and "inspired by the similarity of wearing apparel" (their coats being made of the same material, their hats – of identical color and shape) says to herself: "Might be father and son" (*SA*, 187).

In her attempt to arouse Mr. Verloc's liking for "the poor boy" Winnie tells her husband that Stevie "worships" him (186) and, indeed, Stevie's attitude to his "father" can best be characterized as some sort of quasi-religious admiration. Stevie was taught by his mother and sister to consider Mr. Verloc an object of cult, as a guarantee of his material security. The process of training undergone by Stevie reads like a devastating parody of religious education, with Mr. Verloc occupying the post of the Christian God. The two women instilled into the boy a firm conviction that Mr. Verloc is good, they "had established that ethical fact on an unshakable foundation. They had established, erected, consecrated it behind Mr. Verloc's back, for reasons that had nothing to do with abstract morality.... Mr. Verloc was obviously yet mysteriously *good*" (175-6). As a result, Stevie treats his brother-in-law as some sort of godlike creature. For example, he gapes at Mr. Verloc returned from the Continent with "reverence and awe," flings himself upon Mr. Verloc's bag, seizes it and, finally, bears it off with "triumphant devotion" (182). When Winnie's husband is engrossed in what Stevie interprets as "sorrowful thoughts," the boy even experiences something not unlike a mystical moment, feeling himself "in such close communion with the mystery of that man's goodness" (176).

A triangle, too, could serve as justification for Conrad's intention to treat his secret agent not only as a worshipped *pater familias*, but also as God the Father. As A. Fleishman observed, the triangle appears as Mr. Verloc's attribute quite often: it is the mark of his spy identity (*SA*, 27), the shape of Brett Place, the site of his home (150, 276), the form the tails of his coat assume when he sits down to the table (183) and, finally, the design of the label containing the Verloc address sewn by Winnie under the collar of Stevie's overcoat in case the boy gets lost (Fleishman, 197-8). Traditionally, the triangle has primarily been viewed as the delta of Verloc's code designation pointing to his being a triple secret agent. A. Fleishman interprets it also as a sign of enclosure and secrecy, associates its representation in architecture (the shape of Brett Place) with human solitude, with indifference of the nonhuman world and, on the whole, perceives it as an emblem of social fragmentation (197-8).

But there are also other meanings which can be attached to this geometrical figure. Some religious connotations of the triangle were merely signalled by Darras and, indeed, in the Christian tradition almost from time immemorial the triangle has been used to denote the Holy Trinity, i.e. the union of the three forms of God: the Father, the Son and the Holy Spirit (Kopaliński, 431).[13] Since the seventeenth century the triangle proper has occasionally been modified by addition of other elements, such as, for example, four Hebrew letters JHWH standing for God's name or the monogram of Christ, or some parts of the body, i.e. an eye, a hand or a head. An equilateral triangle, precisely such as Mr. Verloc's, has also been employed to symbolize God the Father; many examples of depictions of God the Father with a triangular halo can be found in fine arts.

If Mr. Verloc stands for God the Father, Stevie, whose attachment to his brother-in-law is so strongly emphasized, could be viewed as the Son. And, indeed, as a member of the Holy Trinity, the boy has every right to wear its emblem. Winnie, perhaps Conrad's version of Virgin Mary, who becomes the mother to Stevie/Jesus, somehow against the laws of nature (neither she/the Virgin nor Mr. Verloc/God the Father are Stevie's/Christ's parents in terms of biology – both in Conrad's book and according to the Christian dogma) is not entitled to be designated by the triangle: she is, of course, a member of, to use Darras's expression, "the Holy Verloc Family," but not of the Holy Trinity.

The circumstances of Stevie's death provide even more evidence to justify its associations with Christ's sacrifice (propounded by both Darras and Erdinast-Vulcan). As the Greenwich bombing is never directly rendered in the novel, the details of the boy's crucible have to be reconstructed on the basis of testimonies provided by two witnesses: the old woman who noticed two men coming out of the railway station (*SA*, 88) and the constable who saw the lightning of the explosion and ran to the spot (87). The woman is a housekeeper to a retired publican and "attends the chapel in Park Place sometimes" (88). The allusion to her religious practices makes her resemble, albeit faintly, the pious women who followed and worshipped Christ, and whose presence at the cross is mentioned in the Bible and in Ippolit's account of the crucifixion. Her testimony strangely admits that although two men were leaving the station, they were hardly together; she took almost no notice of "the big one" (88), i.e. the corpulent Mr. Verloc, but, to the constable's surprise, she was able to pick up such an unimportant detail of "the slight chap" as the velvet collar of his overcoat (89-90), not to mention the tin varnish can the boy was carrying (88). The old woman's account is an open invitation to perceive the death of Stevie through the prism of Christ's sacrifice.

It makes known that unlike in the actual Greenwich incident in which Bourdin went to the area by tram, Conrad made his character appear out of the Maze Hill Station, the first railway stop past Greenwich going eastwards (Tennant, 315). This fact has been regarded as insignificant but perhaps, for some reason, Conrad wanted his hero to start his crucible from the station, not from the tram-stop. In English, like in Polish, the word "station" denotes one of the so-called Stations of the Cross, i.e. a set of fourteen pictures showing events during Christ's last sufferings and death, usually put up in the fixed order round walls inside a Roman Catholic Church. The evidence that the concept of such a Station of the Cross was on Conrad's mind during his work on *The Secret Agent* can be found later in the novel, where it occurs in reference to the alcoholic Mrs. Neale. The narrator calls the pub she frequently attends "the unavoidable station on the *via dolorosa* of her life" (*SA*, 185). The old woman makes it also explicit that the bomb was not handed to Stevie only at the place of explosion: just like Christ, who carried his cross himself,[14] the boy left the station with the instrument of his torture and execution – a tin varnish can – in his hand.

The constable's relation of the moment of bombing – "He had seen something like a heavy flash of lightning in the fog.... The concussion made him tingle all over" (87) – may be, in turn, read as an allusion to the biblical description of certain unusual phenomena which occurred in nature immediately after Christ's death on the cross. They caused fear among those who had crucified him: "And, behold, the veil of the temple was rent in twain from the top to the bottom; and the earth did quake, and the rocks rent" (Matthew 27: 51).

Over the head of crucified Jesus there was an inscription written: "Jesus of Nazareth the King of the Jews" (John 19: 19). The information concerning Stevie's identity, a triangular label classifying him as a member of the Verloc household, although unnoticed, is also present at the place of his death serving as an ironic allusion to Christian imagery. Whereas the triangle, the symbol of the Holy Trinity, was frequently represented with a hand, a head or an eye framed in it, Conrad depicts it with all organs and limbs possible. All of them reached the state of total fragmentation, and the only part of Stevie's body that is mentioned as constituting a separate item or, at least, can be recognized and classified as such, is his foot (*SA*, 89). The choice of this particular limb seems also far from accidental. According to The Bible, Jesus was crucified with two other men. He was the first to die and the only one whose legs were not broken when Pilate, asked by the Jews who did not want the bodies to remain on the crosses on the sabbath day, ordered his soldiers to break the crucified men's legs, to accelerate their death. As Jesus had been already dead before the soldiers came to him, they did not need to break his legs (John 19: 31-3). Thus, Stevie's relatively complete foot is another point of resemblance between him and Jesus Christ.

The partition of Jesus's garments is another detail of the execution of Christ which might have been woven into the fabric of Conrad's novel.[15] After the crucifixion of Christ, the soldiers took his clothes and "made four parts, to every soldier a part; and also his coat" (John 19: 23). As "the coat was without seam, woven from the top throughout" (John 19: 23), they decided not to rip it into four but to cast lots for it. What is left of Stevie are also the bits of his clothes scrupulously collected by the loyal governmental servants, i.e. two policemen. Although the garments do not look extremely promising, to say the least, they still arouse interest. Inspector Heat is especially interested in what has been left of Stevie's coat, staring at "a narrow strip of velvet with a larger triangular piece of dark blue cloth hanging from it" (*SA*, 89). But even though the Inspector does not have to throw dice to obtain the triangular bit, which he finds most attractive and which he tears off showing total disregard for the "narrow strip of velvet" and the "larger triangular piece" as constituting an organic whole, he, "carrying off his spoil hastily," still speculates on the "casual manner" it has come into his possession, and tries to penetrate the mystery of Fate that has "thrust that clue into his hands" (90).

On the whole, it can be said that Conrad's text provides the reader with quite a few clues which enable him/her to view Stevie as a Christ-figure, for even if, unlike Myshkin's, his life cannot be seen as an allegorical reworking of biblical tales, his death by explosion sheds new light on this character. Thus, Stevie seems to have been cast in the role of Christ in Conrad's parodic version of the crucifixion in which, unlike the real founder of the Christian religion, he is completely unaware of the sad end awaiting him and gets killed purely by accident, stumbling against the root of a tree. What is more, his death comes as a real surprise even to his "unloving father" (Darras, 104), by whom he was sent, while his remains are to be used during a literal cannibal feast which, following D. Erdinast-Vulcan's suggestion, seems to replace Holy Communion in the novel by Conrad.

All things considered, in both *The Idiot* and *The Secret Agent* there are accounts of the same event, and they are as different as the two relations of the crucifixion: one created by a highly religious writer, and the other – by a man who, his early upbringing as a Roman Catholic notwithstanding, displayed a rather reserved attitude to religion.[16] But although Conrad's "grotesque parody of Judaic drama" (104) can hardly be said to have anything in common with the Russian writer's very serious treatment of Christ's sacrifice, similarities between the scene in the mortuary and Ippolit's account of Holbein's painting are not difficult to pick up. Whereas in Dostoevsky's novel readers are given a naturalistic description of the terrifying effects crucifixion and the preceding torments produced on Christ's body, Conrad is at pains to render the extent of Stevie's disintegration as effectively as possible. The constable, who was "the first man on the spot" after the explosion, tells the Chief Inspector that he had to use a shovel to collect all the remains (*SA*, 87), and although Heat is "shocked" at the sight of "a heap of rags scorched and bloodstained, half concealing what might have been an accumulation of raw material for a cannibal feast" (86), the author prolongs the scene in the mortuary making his hero contemplate "the nameless fragments" (87) for a longer period of time. The two accounts also share the motif of dismembering and devouring: in Dostoevsky's novel Ippolit compares nature to "a vast modern machine" which has "pointlessly seized, dismembered and devoured...a great and priceless being" (Dostoevsky, 430),[17] and Conrad's Stevie, apart from being dismembered nearly to the point of annihilation, is viewed as an object of, so to speak, gastronomical interest for Heat, who is looking at the table "with a calm face and the slightly anxious attention of an indigent customer bending over what may be called by-products of a butcher's shop with a view to an inexpensive Sunday dinner" (*SA*, 88).

With regard to devouring, the comment made by Conrad's narrator evokes Dostoevsky's Lebedev and his story of a twelfth-century monk-eater. The story proper is followed by his speculations on the advantages of the monkish diet over the secular one, in which he displays a shockingly profane attitude to a human corpse discussing the lay infants' minute nutritiousness, over-sweet and sickly taste, as well as their small size which stand no comparison with those of monks (Dostoevsky, 398-9). Conrad's narrator resembles Lebedev in his profane comments and, like Dostoevsky's character referring to cannibalistic acts in terms of "diet" and "gastronomical variety," he makes his readers see cannibalism in a new light: as a matter of habit and routine.

Conrad's version of the defeated Christ is not based solely on Ippolit's account of Holbein's painting. It might have also absorbed other elements scattered on the pages of *The Idiot*, such as Myshkin's compassionate relations of executions describing in great detail the feelings of the man about to be guillotined (in the first part of the novel). The affinity between Heat's thoughts and the prince's compassionate meditation on the instant death by guillotining was signalled by A. Fogel. And, indeed, the Chief Inspector's posing the question of whether a death so instantaneous was painless, or whether the victim experienced inconceivable pain even in the moment of his violent disintegration (*SA*, 87-8), evokes the prince's brooding over the possibility that a decapitated head might go on thinking for a few moments (Dostoevsky, 69). But since Heat is, as T. B. Gilmore put it, "not ordinarily inclined to impractical speculation" (Gilmore, 48), his banal observations produced after he manages to rise "by the force of sympathy, which is a form of fear, above the vulgar conception of time" (*SA*, 87-8) may well be viewed as Conrad's ironic jibe at Myshkin's sympathetic speeches and obsessive preoccupation with "the last moment."

But, on the whole, Conrad's mortuary scene holds together as a filled with macabre humor mad parody of Ippolit's account of *Christ in the Tomb*. The mutilated corpse of Dostoevsky's Christ is contemplated by a metaphysician and Stevie's remains are scrutinized by "no physiologist, and still less of a metaphysician" (87). Whereas Dostoevsky seems to be at pains to convey the depth of spiritual experience aroused by each contact with the painting, Conrad is at his ironic best to render the absurdity of the whole situation. In both novels examination of the dead body inspires the onlookers with strong sensations: in the case of

Dostoevsky – purely spiritual ones, in Conrad's case – of a physiological, or rather nauseating nature: "the second man on the spot" is "as sick as a dog" (87), and the Chief Inspector fights down "the unpleasant sensation in his throat" (87). While Dostoevsky's Ippolit is appalled at the realization that there is no sense of imminent resurrection or eternal life in Christ's corpse, Conrad seems to imply that it is possible to cope with such a problem: the reduction of Stevie to mere fragments notwithstanding, his "homeless soul" finds its shelter in Winnie's body, which has lethal consequences for Mr. Verloc (262) and totally perverts the very idea of resurrection.

A comparison of Myshkin and Stevie reflects a substantial difference between Dostoevsky and Conrad. Dostoevsky's profound religiosity, fideism, Christianity, impersonated in Myshkin, are merely echoed in the character of Stevie, whose motivation is in the realm of universal morality. Consequently, both characters serve as "moral barometers"[18] indicating their societies' departure from the religious (in the case of Dostoevsky), or from more universal (in Conrad's case) moral foundations. Neither Stevie nor Myshkin should be viewed as his creator's panacea for the evils of modern times. Stevie gets physically destroyed and, what is more, both his life and death become targets for Conrad's irony, which forms a general and overpowering semantic tendency of *The Secret Agent*, sending the author's position on presented issues ambiguous (Hewitt, 88). And Myshkin, no doubt, embodies Dostoevsky's ideal, but the writer was honest enough to allow other characters to laugh at the prince's naïveté and quixotic impulses and, finally, to make the novel end as it does: in the failure of "the positively beautiful man." And if readers are interested in finding out which (if any) of characters offers an efficacious remedy for problems of the modern age, they are free to choose from the whole polyphony of various voices that constitute *The Idiot*, though they can never be sure whether the author himself would approve of their choice.

The fact that Conrad resorts to Dostoevsky's character in order to create his version of the society's "discarded conscience" (Schwarz, 170) does not discourage him from pouring ridicule on various aspects of its Dostoevskian prototype. Thus, Myshkin's (and at the same time Dostoevsky's, although it is not known whether Conrad realized it) fascination with calligraphy, mystical inclinations, problems with and concern for his own speech, find their parodic reflections in the character of Stevie. In addition, the Myshkinian/Dostoevskian obsession with "the last moment" has been ridiculed in Heat's thoughts over Stevie's remains. And although Stevie can by no means be called "Conrad's Christ" in the sense that Myshkin is for Dostoevsky, "the poor boy" seems to have been cast in the role of Jesus in the parody of, first of all, Christ's death on the cross and, then, of Ippolit's account of Christ in the Tomb. Allusions to *The Idiot* not merely help to appreciate the macabre humor of the mortuary scene in *The Secret Agent* but also make it possible to uncover new ironic layers in Conrad's masterpiece.

NOTES

1. A comparison of Stevie and Myshkin has been one of the focuses of my "Dostoevskian Elements in Joseph Conrad's *The Secret Agent*" accepted for publication in *RuBriCa. The Rusian and British Cathedra*, ed. V. Bychenkov, Moskva. The present paper provides a wider perspective on some of the issues discussed in the earlier article, in which the possibility of reading Stevie as a Christlike figure has been merely signalled.

2. Dostoevsky in a letter to his niece, quoted after W. J. Leatherbarrow, xv.

3. Dostoevsky in a letter to Madame Fonvizina, quoted after P. Conradi, 17.

4. For the details of Dostoevsky's work on *The Idiot*, see W. J. Leatherbarrow, xii-xv; R. Peace, 59-60. For a discussion of the figure of *yurodivy* see G. P. Fedotov, 205-19; A. Andrusiewicz, vol. 2, 75-6.

5. For more autobiographical traits present in the delineation of Myshkin see B. Urbankowski, 31, 83-5, 114.

6. *The Times* report of the bombing, quoted after J. Baines, 330.

7. Dostoevsky's ideal of community has been discussed in the second chapter of G. C. Kabat, *Ideology and Imagination. The Image of Society in Dostoevsky*. For a discussion of Conrad's views on social relations as compared to those of Dostoevsky, see K. Sokołowska "The Social Axiology...."

8. Critics vary in their opinions of Myshkin's actual impact on other characters; for a brief discussion of the main critical approaches to this issue see S. Monas, 70-1.

9. I view this trait of Myshkin's personality, which manifests itself very vividly in the cab-ride episode, as an allusion to the Raskolnikov of the marebeating scene in *Crime and Punishment* – see my "Stevie, the Horse, Dostoevsky & Conrad," in *Journeys, Myths and the Age of Travel: Joseph Conrad's Era,* ed. K. Hansson (Karlskrona/Ronneby: U. of Karlskrona/Ronneby, 1998), 144-65.

10. See Conrad's narrator's sarcastic remark concerning Stevie: "However, he never had any fits (which was encouraging)" (*SA*, 9).

11. Sometimes translated as "humility is a mighty force." The combination of humility with power is reflected in the prince's very name: his first name, Lev, means "lion," while the surname, Myshkin, derives from the word *mysh* meaning "mouse." Thus, the prince himself is to embody the power of humility. Interestingly enough, the expression "proud humility" appears in *The Secret Agent*. It is used in reference to Mr. Verloc in the episode of his conversation with Mr. Vladimir. Having raised his voice as a reaction to the Secretary's accusations, Mr. Verloc "with a note of proud humility...apologized for forgetting himself" (23).

12. All the examples of parallels between Christ's ministry and the life of Myshkin that follow are given after W. J. Leatherbarrow, xviii-xix.

13. All the information concerning the triangle that follows is given after W. Kopaliński, 431.

14. Though it is customary for Christ to be depicted in fine arts as bearing his cross himself, the authors of the Gospels (with the sole exception of John) mention Simon of Cyrene whom the soldiers escorting Jesus to Golgotha made at some point carry the cross instead of Jesus (Matthew 27: 32; Mark 15: 21; Luke 23: 26). Besides, like other men condemned to crucifixion in Roman times, Jesus was most probably led to the place of execution carrying only the horizontal pole of the cross (*patibulum*). The upright post (*stipes*), which could be used more than once, was already set into the ground. For the details of the crucifixion of Jesus see, for example, J. Hall, 81-5.

15. John views both the partition of Jesus's garments and the fact that his legs were not broken as a fulfilment of the Old Testament prophecies. For the partition of garments see Psalm 22: 18; for the preservation of the bones – Exodus 12: 46; Numbers 9: 12; Psalm 22: 17; Psalm 34: 20.

16. For a discussion of Conrad's attitude to religion see C. F. Burgess, "Conrad's Catholicism."

17. Interestingly enough, Dostoevsky's image of a "modern machine" evokes associations with Conrad's letter to Cunninghame Graham of 20 December 1897 on the "knitting machine," which, in turn, as E. W. Said

pointed out, recalls the final section of Nietzsche's *The Will to Power* – see
E. W. Said, 73.

18. An expression used by Schwarz in reference to Stevie – see D. R.
Schwarz, 170.

WORKS CITED

Andrusiewicz Andrzej. *Mit Rosji*, 2 vols. Rzeszów: Wyższa Szkoła
Pedagogiczna, 1994.

Baines Jocelyn. *Joseph Conrad: A Critical Biography*. London: Weidenfeld
and Nicolson, 1960.

Bakhtin Mikhail M. *Problems of Dostoevsky's Poetics,* ed. and trans. Caryl
Emerson. Manchester: Manchester U. P., 1984.

Berthoud Jacques. *Joseph Conrad: The Major Phase*. Cambridge: Cambridge U. P., 1978.

Burgess C. F. "Conrad's Catholicism," *Conradiana*, 15: 2 (1983), 111-26.

Conradi Peter. *Fyodor Dostoevsky*. London: MacMillan Press, 1988.

Darras Jacques. *Joseph Conrad and the West. Signs of Empire*, trans. Anne
Luyat, Jacques Darras. London: MacMillan Press, 1982.

Dostoevsky Fyodor M. *The Idiot*, trans. Alan Myers. Oxford: Oxford
U. P., 1992.

Erdinast-Vulcan Daphna. "'Sudden Holes in Space and Time': Conrad's
Anarchist Aesthetics in *The Secret Agent*," in *Conrad's Cities. Essays for
Hans van Marle*, ed. Gene M. Moore. Amsterdam: Rodopi, 1992,
207-21.

Fedotov G. P. *Svyatye Drevney Rusi*. Paris: YMCA Press, 1931.

Fleishman Avrom. *Conrad's Politics. Community and Anarchy in the Fiction
of Joseph Conrad*. Baltimore: Johns Hopkins U. P., 1967.

Fogel Aaron. *Coercion to Speak. Conrad's Poetics of Dialogue*. Cambridge,
Mass.: Harvard U. P., 1985.

Gilmore Thomas B. "Retributive Irony in Conrad's *The Secret Agent*,"
Conradiana, 1: 3 (1969), 41-50.

Hall James. "Crucifixion," in Hall James. *Dictionary of Subjects and
Symbols in Art*. New York: Harper and Row, 1974, 81-6.

Hay Eloise Knapp. *The Political Novels of Joseph Conrad: A Critical Study*.
Chicago: Chicago U. P., 1963.

Hewitt Douglas. *Conrad: A Reassessment*. Cambridge: Bowes and Bowes,
1952.

Holquist Michael. *Dostoevsky and the Novel*. Princeton: Princeton U. P.,
1977.

Howe Irving. *Politics and the Novel*. London: Stevens and Sons, 1961.

Kabat Geoffrey C. *Ideology and Imagination. The Image of Society in
Dostoevsky*. New York: Columbia U. P., 1978.

Karl Frederick R. *A Reader's Guide to Joseph Conrad*. New York: Noonday Press, 1960.

Kopaliński Władysław. "Trójkąt," in Kopaliński Władysław. *Słownik symboli*. Warszawa: "Wiedza Powszechna," 1990, 431.

Leatherbarrow William J. "Introduction," in Fyodor M. Dostoevsky, *The Idiot*, trans. Alan Myers. Oxford: Oxford U.P., 1992, vii-xxii.

Mann Thomas. "Einleitung," in Joseph Conrad. *Der Geheimagent*. Berlin: S. Fischer Verlag, 1927, 9-25.

Monas Sidney. "Across the Threshold: *The Idiot* as a Petersburg Tale," in *New Essays on Dostoevsky*, eds. Malcolm V. Jones, Garth M. Terry. Cambridge: Cambridge U.P., 1983, 67-93.

Peace Richard. *Dostoyevsky: An Examination of the Major Novels*. Cambridge: Cambridge U.P., 1975.

Ray Martin. "Conrad, Nordau, and Other Degenerates: The Psychology of *The Secret Agent*," *Conradiana*, 16: 2 (1984), 125-40.

Said Edward W. "Conrad and Nietzsche," in *Joseph Conrad: A Commemoration*, ed. Norman Sherry. London: MacMillan Press, 1976, 65-76.

Schwarz Daniel R. *Conrad: The Later Fiction*. London: MacMillan Press, 1982.

Smitten Jeffrey R. "Flaubert and the Structure of *The Secret Agent*: A Study in Spatial Form," in *Joseph Conrad: Theory and World Fiction. Proceedings of the Comparative Literature Symposium*, January 23-25, 1974, eds. Wolodymyr T. Zyla, Wendell M. Aycock. Lubbock: Texas Tech U.P., 1974, 151-66.

Sokołowska Katarzyna. "The Social Axiology of *The Secret Agent* by Conrad and *The Devils* by Dostoevsky," *Kwartalnik Neofilologiczny*, 40: 4 (1993), 321-34.

Stallman Robert W. "Time and *The Secret Agent*," *Texas Studies in Literature and Language*, 1: 1 (1959), 101-22.

Stempczyńska Barbara. *Dostojewski a malarstwo*. Katowice: Uniwersytet Śląski, 1980.

Tennant Roger. "Introduction," "Explanatory Notes," in Joseph Conrad. *The Secret Agent*. Oxford: Oxford U.P., vii-xx, 313-17.

The Holy Bible. Authorized King James Version. Collins World.

Urbankowski Bohdan. *Dostojewski: Dramat humanizmów*. Warszawa: "Alfa," 1994.

Vries Jetty de. "Stevie and Recent Criticism," *Conradiana*, 17: 2 (1985), 119-30.

Wiesenfarth Joseph. "Stevie and the Structure of *The Secret Agent*," *Modern Fiction Studies*, 13: 4 (1967), 513-17.

Katarzyna Sokołowska,
Maria Curie-Skłodowska University,
Lublin, Poland

Artistic Aspects of Character Creation
in *Lord Jim* by Conrad and *Rudin* by Turgenev

Conrad admitted intellectual and artistic affinity with only one Russian writer: Turgenev.[1] In the letters to Cunninghame Graham Conrad attests to his familiarity with Turgenev's short stories, among them "Three Portraits" and "Enough," and his essay, "Turgenev," written as a preface to Edward Garnett's study of the Russian reveals Conrad's appreciation of a writer "so independent of the transitory formulas and theories of art" ("Turgenev," *NLL*, 45). Conrad was certainly acquainted with *Notes of a Hunter*; he declared to Colonel Harvey an intention to evoke the spirit of Turgenevyan short stories in his own collection of sea sketches *The Mirror of the Sea*.[2] Close similarities can be detected between Conrad's and Turgenev's views. The two writers share a pessimistic vision of nature, one cruel and indifferent to human suffering, and of man subject to powerful irrational forces at work in the cosmos, forces which are no longer kept in check by Providence.[3] Like Turgenev, Conrad insists on the estrangement and opposition between human consciousness and nature.[4] For both consciousness is to blame for the dramatic condition of man's existence,[5] since it is consciousness which enables him to recognize his precarious position in the universe, helplessness in the confrontation with the overwhelming power of nature: "What makes mankind tragic is not that they are the victims of nature, it is that they are conscious of it. To be part of the animal kingdom...is very well – but as soon as you know of your slavery the pain, the anger, the strife – the tragedy begins" (*Joseph Conrad's Letters...*, 70).[6] Anti-intellectual sentiment informs both Conrad's and Turgenev's anthropology, although Conrad shifts the emphasis from the Turgenevyan belief in the disruptive influence of

113

reflection on man's primeval animal-like unity[7] to the conviction that reason, the source of man's greatness, simultaneously strips him of illusions which guarantee peace of mind, and as such it should be less trusted than instincts.[8] Conrad elucidates his stance in a letter to Cunninghame Graham defending the creation of Singleton as a simple man: "Would you...cultivate in that unconscious man the power to think. Then he would become conscious – and much smaller – and very unhappy. Now he is simple and great like an elemental force" (53).

In his essay "Gamlet i Don-Kikhot [Hamlet and Don Quixote]" (173-6) Turgenev presented a theory of personality, distinguishing two ideal types – Hamlet (i.e. a sceptic committed to analytical thought), and Don Quixote (an enthusiast, a man of strong will and of action).[9] As Turgenev concludes, a pure Hamlet and a pure Don Quixote are only abstractions; they never obtain reality since their features blend in different proportions in every personality (189). Instead, the coexistence of these contradictory features gives rise to inner tension and ultimately to the protagonist's failure. Turgenev maintains that man is unable to reconcile enthusiasm and action with critical faculty. Consequently, Hamlets, endowed with the capacity for reflection, do not possess enough determination to take any action, whereas Don Quixotes, with their minds bent on heroic deeds, lack the guidance of reason (183-4). Almost all the main characters of Turgenev's novels – Rudin, Lavretsky, Bazarov, Litvinov, Nezhdanov – are torn apart by inner contradictions, and fail to integrate the principles of enthusiasm and reflection in their personalities. The Hamlet/Don Quixote dichotomy can be applied to define Conradian characters such as Tom Lingard or Charles Gould who veer towards the Don Quixote extreme, dedicating themselves to idealistic goals and undertaking risky enterprises which either degenerate into obsession or fall through and inflict suffering on others. There is also a Hamlet, Heyst, who, after quixotic attempts to commit himself to some ideals, discards activity and involvement in life, which he perceives to be "universal nothingness." Nevertheless, he is forced out of his seclusion and faces the world only to find out that all his efforts to save Lena have been futile. His final dismissal of scepticism further complicates the interpretation of his personality in terms of one of the extremes.

The Hamlet/Don Quixote dichotomy which underlies the presentation of characters in *Lord Jim* and *Rudin*[10] alerts us to the principle of ambivalence as the one generating both Jim's and Rudin's personalities. Consequently, the two heroes are difficult to label; at no point can the reader claim full knowledge of either Jim or Rudin. They both function as the centers for other characters; they provoke others (like Marlow or Lezhnyov) to ask questions about their identity.[11] However, in *Rudin* the third person narration predominates, and various perspectives of the protagonist (which are furnished by Lasunskaya, Pigasov, Natalya and Lezhnyov) are manipulated by the narrator so as to generate the unequivocal vision of Rudin's personality and to suppress any indications of his ambivalence. In contrast, in *Lord Jim* the multiplicity of points of view on Jim rules out any unambiguous interpretation of his personality. The subjectivity of the first person narration emphasizes that the absolute truth is impossible to reach, bringing into focus the process of perception which takes place in Marlow's consciousness. The mode of narration employed in Conrad's novel poses a question about the reliability of Marlow's presentation of Jim, and, as a result, effects a shift in emphasis from the penetration of Jim's psychology to the understanding of how Marlow's mind works and how his projections distort Jim's image.[12] Thus, the first person narrator whose presence amounts to observing, relating and commenting, and whose involvement in the events is scanty, rises to the status equal to that of Jim. In Turgenev's novel as well, the reliability of certain points of view is questioned, e.g. Pigasov's or Lipina's perception of Rudin. However, these points of view are embedded within the omniscient narration which is dominated by one voice – the narrator's monologic vision of the reality. Yet, the narrator provides clues as to which viewpoints should be interpreted as reliable, thus implying that it is possible to establish the final truth about Rudin.

Turgenev's typical strategy of building up characters is through detailed biographic sketches.[13] Almost all the characters in *Rudin* are supplied with this sort of profile which establishes them as fixed personalities (with the significant exception of Rudin, who receives only cursory description). The lack of a biographic sketch of Rudin signals Turgenev's strategy of constructing a character through the confrontation with other characters[14] who are equipped with unchangeable personalities so that they might function as mirrors for the protagonist. Rudin's interaction with Lezhnyov, Natalya and Pigasov not only sheds light on hidden facets of his personality but also stimulates his self-knowledge. Similarly, Jim's personality emerges as a construct of the multiple viewpoints provided by characters more or less directly involved in his case, such as Marlow, Brierly, the French lieutenant, Stein, Chester, Egström or Brown. Thus, the ambivalence of Rudin's personality, which is conveyed through his association with other characters, relates him to Jim, although Rudin is presented mainly by the third person narrator, in a seemingly objective way, whereas Jim can be reached only through the filter of Marlow's consciousness (excluding the first four chapters). Due to the narrative method, Jim's interaction with others is always related by Marlow whose personality and mode of perception must be taken into consideration.[15] Such an approach is missing from Turgenev's novel, except for Lezhnyov's account which, however, does not subvert the authority of the third person narrator. Thus, in *Lord Jim*, the very strategy of building up the protagonist's image based on subjective presentation is exposed, whereas in *Rudin* the narrative mode implies a clear-cut distinction between those characters whose accounts can be trusted and those whose evaluations should be dismissed as unreliable.

In Turgenev's novel the confrontation with Pigasov offers an initial insight into Rudin's contradictions. Pigasov's attitude towards Rudin in many respects parallels the one of Brierly towards Jim, revealing new aspects of the two protagonists' personalities. Similarly to Brierly who disapproves of Jim, Pigasov evinces animosity towards Rudin who challenges his status in society. Pigasov, disillusioned by a failure to climb up the ladder of the administrative hierarchy, finally rises to prominence in Darya Lasunskaya's household and establishes his reputation as a witty man of sound opinions and deep understanding of life. On his arrival, Rudin easily takes over Pigasov's privileged position focusing everybody's attention while Pigasov almost immediately falls into oblivion. Although Pigasov resents Rudin's show of self-confidence and dismisses his knowledge of philosophy as superficial, he loses confidence and withdraws, accepting a lowered standing in Lasunskaya's household. As a result of this humiliation, he remains hostile towards Rudin. Jim's case has an equally disruptive effect on Brierly's life. His self-confidence verges on complacency and arrogance, similarly to Pigasov. The moment when Jim appears in his life marks the peak of Brierly's career. The result of the confrontation with Jim, Brierly's suicide, shows to what extent Jim's case must have undermined his inner sense of worth, rendering him conscious of some flaw in his personality that nullified all his achievements, the source of his high self--evaluation.

The relationship between Pigasov and Rudin is based on overt conflict and covert affinity, the pattern which can be detected in the Brierly-Jim relationship as well. Pigasov, strongly critical of Rudin, is the first to defy Rudin's philosophy and notice his moral weaknesses. He contests Rudin's conviction that general ideas precede facts and challenges the notion of truth, pointing out the tension between words and reality. Pigasov claims that ideas such as truth exist only as words with no reference to real entities. Rudin opposes this viewpoint, yet, in the course of events, he turns out to be unable to translate words into action, thus corroborating Pigasov's critical remarks.[16] Rudin demands to be in the spotlight,[17] to command admiration, like Pigasov. That is why, when one of them retreats into the background the other enters the scene. Pigasov comes up with a half-jocular classification of people: those who have long tails (i.e. are successful and self-assured) and those who are bob-tailed (i.e. are social failures although often more gifted than the former). He puts both himself and Rudin into the category of the bob-tailed, which reinforces the impression of their affinity. Yet, both Pigasov and Rudin fail to assert themselves as equal partners of women. Pigasov manifests contempt for women even though his social position depends on Lasunskaya's favors. Similarly, Rudin lacks determination to fight for his love and withdraws when Lasunskaya puts pressure on him.

At first sight Brierly seems to stand in total contrast to Jim who committed a transgression against the seaman's code. Yet, Brierly's vulnerability to Jim's case testifies to the existence of a bond between them. Brierly is a Jim who was lucky to be exposed to clear-cut situations which called for no more than a mere show of courage and, that is why, he never lapsed in his fidelity to the seaman's code. Both Jim and Brierly are obsessed with their self-image: Jim dreams of courageous exploits to win admiration for heroism; for Brierly the sense of inner worth is founded on his impeccable reputation. Brierly condemns Jim, finds no extenuating circumstances, but despite that, he offers to help Jim run away. In this way, as a member of the Court of Inquiry which is to decide Jim's guilt, he himself transgresses the law. His readiness to accept complicity with the man whom he despises in order to protect the reputation of the professional group of seamen points to a bond of guilt between them and reveals Brierly's weak spot which makes him so vulnerable. Brierly's suicide, the reenactment of Jim's jump, reinforces the affinity and sheds new light on Jim's inability to face emergency as well as, later, on his motivation to stand trial. The reason for suicide is never stated. Brierly either failed to rise to the occasion while managing to keep it secret or he realized that his reputation was founded on the illusory sense of inner worth since he was never put to real test.[18] Whatever the reason, Brierly is a flawed personality, like Jim, unable to resolve the tension between the outward appearance of a successful seaman and a hidden sense of inadequacy. Thus, both Pigasov and Brierly seem to function as Rudin's and Jim's doubles revealing their inner tension and defining their personalities.

Natalya, Lasunskaya's daughter, is invested with the moral authority to pronounce judgement on Rudin, similarly to the French lieutenant and Stein who, as Marlow believes, possess a deeper insight into Jim's case. Natalya is presented as a sensitive, perceptive girl, able to distinguish between good and bad, eager to commit herself to some great ideals. That is why she is easily fascinated by Rudin who talks with her about important problems or discusses literature and philosophy. But, in fact, Natalya dominates Rudin whose youthful enthusiasm is shown to have given place to fatigue and scepticism. She is strong and determined and embraces idealism, like Rudin, but, unlike him, she is ready to give everything up and follow her ideals.[19] The narration in *Rudin* contains direct comments emphasizing Natalya's high moral status as well as the reliability of her intuition in judging others: "She spoke little, listened and watched attentively...as if she wanted to absorb everything she saw and heard" (Turgenev, *Rudin*, 75), "She could feel profoundly and strongly, but in secret" (75). Consequently, Rudin's attitude towards her is a touchstone of the sincerity of his ideals and the rejection of Natalya's love reveals his weakness.

For Marlow it is the French lieutenant who functions as a moral authority to offer a reliable assessment of Jim. The lieutenant spent several hours on board the *Patna* after it had been found abandoned and towed back to the coast. Thus, he had to face the situation Jim chose to escape from. This fact contributes to the perception of the lieutenant as a man of moral authority.[20] He stands in contrast to Jim as a down-to-earth person who does not get involved in detailed self-analysis and, as a result, seems more trustworthy to Marlow who compares him to a priest and considers him "the raw material of great reputations, one of those uncounted lives that are buried without drums and trumpets under the foundations of monumental successes" (*LJ*, 143-4). Although the lieutenant, unlike Jim, tends to be concise and often falls silent, Marlow interprets even his silence as meaningful: "he, in his occult way, managed to make his immobility...as full of valuable thoughts as an egg is of meat"

(145). In this respect he resembles Natalya who is equally reticent in contrast to eloquent Rudin. Apart from the lieutenant, Stein is also presented as a man of great wisdom who has experienced both happiness and suffering in life. He is an idealist following his dreams and a realist who knows how to achieve success: "His life had begun in sacrifice, in enthusiasm for generous ideas...whatever he followed it had been without faltering, and therefore without shame and without regret" (215). The positive presentation of Natalya, Stein and the French lieutenant adds legitimacy to their assessment of Jim and Rudin. However, Natalya's criticism is meant to be the final indictment of Rudin's weakness. As a result, Rudin emerges as an unambiguous character who deserves contempt, which is in accord with Turgenev's intention to respond to the ideological preoccupations of his times and create a critical portrait of a typical representative of the Russian intelligentsia in the 1840s. The dominant position of Natalya's critical viewpoint is reinforced by Rudin's acceptance of her charges. In a letter to her, Rudin confesses to weakness: "At the first obstacle I will give up completely...I was simply frightened of the responsibility laid upon me and so I proved myself unworthy of you" (Turgenev, *Rudin*, 145). There are no other points of view equally important in the narrative to correct this final impression. Basistov, who remains Rudin's admirer to the end, is a minor character barely sketched in the novel. Only Lezhnyov modifies this thoroughly negative evaluation of Rudin after marrying Lipina, pointing to some positive aspects of his personality,[21] but the main charges against Rudin – weak will and an inability to put his great talents to real use – remain valid.

The assessment offered by the French lieutenant is less definitive than that of Natalya, or even Lezhnyov, and its implications, negative for Jim, are moderated by Marlow. The lieutenant is not willing to utter an outright condemnation of Jim. While talking to Marlow he insists that everybody is a coward and he is no exception, but experience and self--knowledge allow man to recognize his fear, the natural reaction to danger, and overcome it. Jim failed not because he felt fear but because he refused to admit and confront his inborn weakness. The lieutenant invokes the idea of honor which forms the foundation of his moral attitude: "The honour...that is real.... And what life may be worth when...the honour is gone.... I can offer no opinion – because...I know nothing of it" (*LJ*, 148). Although in terms of the code of honor Jim's jump deserves condemnation, the lieutenant refrains from stating it explicitly and Marlow's ambiguous response tones down the severity of judgement. It seems that the lieutenant's evaluation canot aspire to the status of the final truth about Jim, as it is only one of several viewpoints, each of them offering an incomplete, subjective understanding of his case, and each being filtered through Marlow's critical perception, which further enhances the incertitude about the possibility of discovering the truth. In contrast, Natalya does not have any doubts about the rightness of her verdict which is supported by critical opinions voiced by Lezhnyov, Volyntsev and Rudin himself. The cluster of these negative evaluations which are neither undermined nor juxtaposed against positive assessment generates the impression that it is possible to come up with an unequivocal definition of Rudin's personality.

Lezhnyov and Marlow play central role in building up Rudin's and Jim's image. They each have a unique narrative status in the novel: Marlow as the first person narrator who relates the whole of Jim's life, except for the first four chapters, and who brings together all the testimonies provided by other characters to create his version of Jim's story; and Lezhnyov who takes over narration in order to give an account of Rudin's youth.[22] Thus, Rudin's biographic sketch is not an arbitrary presentation of apparently reliable information provided by the omniscient narrator, as in the case of other characters, but an overtly subjective first person narrative, similar to Marlow's narrative in this respect. The relationship between Jim and Marlow bears similarity to the one between Rudin and Lezhnyov. Marlow is involved in the search for the truth about Jim which runs parallel to the investigation of his own moral dilemmas and the reappraisal of his moral assumptions. Lezh-

nyov is also brought to scrutinize the attitudes which determine
the way he assesses his friend, although Marlow's self-awareness
surpasses Lezhnyov's. Right from the beginning, Marlow realizes the moral implications of Jim's case for himself as a representative of the marine profession[23] and, on a more universal
level, as one of the number of ordinary, decent men not
immune-to-weakness: "I see well enough now that I hoped for
the impossible – for the laying of what is the most obstinate ghost
of man's creation, of the uneasy doubt... – the doubt of the
sovereign power enthroned in a fixed standard of conduct" (50).
However, Marlow penetrates deeper into his compulsion to
explore Jim's case and discovers personal motives behind his
interest:[24] "Was it for my own sake that I wished to find some
shadow of an excuse for that young fellow...?" (51). Lezhnyov,
emotionally involved in Rudin's case, does not trace back the
origin of his concern. He remains blind to Rudin's significance
for his moral and emotional growth and blames him for the
decline of their friendship without even looking into his own
attitude. He tries to rationalize his resentment towards Rudin
and it is Lipina who understands that this bitterness stems from
his unresolved dilemmas. Marlow's preoccupation with the
universal aspect of Jim's case does not have an exact counterpart
in Turgenev's novel, whereas Rudin's conduct raises questions
about national identity, like the detachment of the intelligentsia
from the Russian people, which stifles creative impulse and
inhibits development of both individuals and the whole nation.[25] Lezhnyov concludes that "his eloquence isn't Russian"
(Turgenev, *Rudin*, 91) and "Rudin's unhappiness is that he
doesn't know Russia...outside nationality there is no art, no
truth, no life, nothing" (158).

Marlow not only manifests greater knowledge than Lezhnyov
as far as the motives of his interest in Jim's case are concerned
but also greater consciousness of the possible distortions in his
perception which arise when a personal issue is at stake.
Although both Marlow and Lezhnyov are critical of the
protagonists, Marlow recognizes the underlying causes of his
resentment. In contrast to Marlow, Lezhnyov seems unable to

identify distortions in his perception, and Lipina has to assume the task of alerting him to his subjectivity. Both Marlow and Lezhnyov find the confrontation with the protagonists' dilemmas disconcerting. However, Marlow is ready to give a hearing to Jim himself, not only to his critics, and strives to capture all facets of Jim's personality, whereas Lezhnyov manipulates his narrative[26] in order to reduce Rudin's complexities to the weakness of will. Consequently, Lezhnyov obsessively attacks Rudin, refuses to admit any bond between them. His accounts are riddled with vicious remarks and hints at Rudin's moral inadequacy which later turn out to be exaggerated. He accuses Rudin of egoism and incapacity for emotional involvement, of ruining the beauty of his first love through despotic interference. He resents Rudin's coldness, the lack of common sense, the empty eloquence, but he unwillingly admits that Rudin, the soul of the students' circle, infused them with enthusiasm, opened their minds to ideas,[27] brought lucidity into their chaotic knowledge. Thanks to his talent for synthesis, Lezhnyov and other students felt that "well-balanced orderliness was introduced into everything we knew...everything evinced rational necessity and beauty" (96-7). Lezhnyov evaluates his influence as beneficial: "He was the first to take an interest in me and make something of me. I was...fond of Pokorsky...but I was closer to Rudin" (100). Marlow disapproves of Jim's weakness, but, unlike Lezhnyov, he resists the temptation to condemn his young friend because he feels compelled to discover the truth about him first. He seeks to maintain neutrality towards Jim to avoid compassion which would follow the identification with Jim and which might lead to the feeling of complicity. If Marlow succeeds in keeping a distance from Jim and does not indulge self-pity and a desire to justify himself, it is because he never loses sight of his own hidden anxieties stirred by Jim's case. Marlow is disturbed by Jim's deceptive appearance of a young, reliable man whom he would entrust with a ship without hesitation, which calls into question his capability of sound judgement, the very foundation of his trust in people: "I would have trusted the deck to that youngster...it wouldn't have been safe. There are depths of horror in that thought" (*LJ*, 45). Furthermore, Jim's ambivalence raises Marlow's doubts about the reliability of young adepts of the seaman's craft Marlow was preparing for "the service of the Red Rag"[28] and, consequently, shatters his idealized vision of the seamanship.

Both Lezhnyov and Marlow are tainted with ambivalence, which affects the way they perceive Rudin and Jim. Lezhnyov wavers between youthful idealism epitomized by Rudin and present realism reflected in his commitment to hard work and pursuit of material success which brings him closer to Lasunskaya.[29] He even makes a concession to her when a new boundary between their estates is drawn, marking the temporary physical proximity between them.[30] Soon afterwards, he endeavors to suppress ambiguous feelings and severs social links with Lasunskaya. This isolation and outward appearance – seedy clothes reminiscent of the student years – may suggest moving away from "mature" realism back to youthful idealism, all the more conspicuous since he voices unceasing admiration for Pokorsky and his ideals: "Oh, it was a marvellous time...I don't want to believe that it's all gone in vain!" (Turgenev, *Rudin*, 98). Lezhnyov identifies his maturity with sobriety and dismisses enthusiasm as deceptive and useless because of its short-lived nature. That is why he disapproves of Lipina's fascination with fire: "fire isn't good for anything. It flames, smokes, and goes out. – 'And warms,' added Alexandra Pavlovna. – 'Yes – and it can burn you'" (31). At the same time he reproaches Rudin with being cold, the vice he regards as a merit in himself. The ambivalence underlying Lezhnyov's image of himself and attitude towards others alerts us to the unreliability of his judgement of Rudin, and, consequently, subverts the one-sided, apparently complete and objective vision of Rudin's personality.

Marlow is troubled by ambivalence as well, but, contrary to Lezhnyov, he is aware of it and tries to moderate his criticism. Already the way Marlow introduces himself establishes him as a complex personality experiencing tension between contradictory forces personified in the form of a guardian angel and a devil: "each of us has a familiar devil as well. I want you to own up, because I don't like to feel exceptional in any way, and I know I have him" (*LJ*, 34). It seems that Marlow suffers from some sort of unresolved inner tension which brings him closer to men with soft spots, like Jim. He also has to grapple with disappointment caused by the discrepancy between dreams about sea adventures and harsh reality, but, unlike Jim, he succeeds in coming to terms with the exactions of life at sea, although he emerges disillusioned from the struggle: "Hadn't we all commenced with the same desire, ended with the same knowledge" (129), "In no other kind of life...is the begining *all* illusion – the disenchantment more swift – the subjugation more complete" (129). Marlow's ambivalence accounts for the way he approaches Jim, for wavering between compassion and severity in evaluating him. These contradictory emotions arise from awareness that everybody, including himself, has to confront weakness inherent in human nature and the consequence is never certain.[31] Marlow recognizes his affinity with Jim based on common human plight and this makes him sympathetic to Jim's appeal for justification:[32] "in what was I better than the rest of us to refuse him my pity?" (129). However, he is aware that Jim is playing on his emotions and refuses to give in to manipulation, trying to remain as objective as possible and to keep in mind how much he is vulnerable to Jim: "I was being bullied now, and it behoved me to make no sign lest...I should be drawn into a fatal admission about myself which would have had some bearing on the case" (106). As a result, Marlow himself is not sure how to assess Jim and tends to withhold judgement emphasizing his inability to reach any final conclusions in this case.[33] Marlow's account, even to a greater extent than Lezhnyov's, produces a complex and ambiguous vision of the protagonist who remains a mystery to the very end.

Marlow's and Lezhnyov's judgements are also affected by confrontations with other characters whose comments undermine their opinions of Jim and Rudin and expose their subjectivity. Lezhnyov is given an opportunity to respond to an openly formulated statement questioning his truthfulness. Lipina demonstrates that he shows bias against Rudin: "I am sure everything you've said is the truth...and yet you've presented everything in such an unpleasant light!" (Turgenev, *Rudin*, 83). After some time, Lezhnyov's harshness gives way to almost enthusiastic praise, which may be ascribed to the happy marriage to Lipina as well as a sense of stability and emotional balance.[34] However, he does not recount charges against Rudin, merely tones down criticism and, thus, succeeds in balancing the negative sides of Rudin's personality against the positive ones. Lezhnyov's newly achieved maturity is symbolized by Lipina who is always able to reconcile altruism and egoism, reflected in her concern for the poor and friendship with Lasunskaya.[35] Soon, Lezhnyov is mature enough to acknowledge personal motives behind his critical attitude and admits to Lipina: "I was frightened he might turn your head" (159). He is also able to appreciate Rudin's merits: "He has enthusiasm...we should be grateful to anyone who rouses us" (157).

Marlow is aware of the difficulties in assessing Jim unequivocally and, unlike Lezhnyov, he explicitly states his uncertainty. He often remarks that Jim is enveloped in mist, which frustrates every attempt at understanding him: "The views he let me have of himself were like those glimpses through the shifting rents in a thick fog" (*LJ*, 76). At the end of the narrative Marlow admits he has not proceeded far in probing Jim's mystery: "He passes away under a cloud, inscrutable at heart" (416). Indeed, Marlow's confusion about Jim is enhanced by the meetings with Brierly, the French lieutenant and Stein, among others, whose interpretations of Jim's case alter Marlow's point of view. Brierly's critical attitude is crucial in moderating Marlow's severity.[36] Marlow, irritated by Brierly's self-confidence, stands up for Jim and appreciates his courage to face the trial: "on account of that provocation...I became positive in my mind that the inquiry was a severe punishment to that Jim, and that his facing it...was a redeeming feature.... I hadn't been so sure of it before" (68-9). In turn, Marlow's encounter with the lieutenant makes him realize that Jim's transgression, even though it may be psychologically justified by his immaturity, cannot be connived at from the ethical point of view, since he violated the universal code of absolute moral values. Marlow seems annoyed with the outcome of the discussion unfavorable to Jim but the memory of the meeting with the lieutenant brings to his mind Bob Stanton whose unobtrusive heroism stands in contrast to Jim's inability to translate fantasy into action.[37] To Stein, Marlow insists on judging Jim severely. However, Stein tones down Marlow's criticism pointing out that he also failed many times: "And do you know how many opportunities I let escape; how many dreams I had lost.... Everybody knows of one or two like that" (217). Stein refuses to label Jim as blameworthy: "'He is romantic...that is very bad.... Very good, too'" (216). After his conversation with Stein, Marlow gives voice to doubts about the reliability of his judgement and exposes his role in building up Jim's image: "He existed for me, and after all it is only through me that he exists for you.... Were my commonplace fears unjust? I won't say – not even now" (224). Unlike Lezhnyov, Marlow admits the subjective nature of his presentation of Jim, alerts the listeners to a hidden slant in his story, and encourages them to participate in interpreting Jim's case: "You may be able to tell better, since the proverb has it that the onlookers see most of the game" (224). Thus, Marlow turns out to be a storyteller conscious of his creative role, whose comments offer insight into the process of building up the protagonist of the story, whereas Lezhnyov denies his role in creating Rudin's image and insists on being an unbiased intermediary of the objective truth.

In his novel Turgenev employs third person omniscient narration, typical of realism, which enables him to create the illusion of the objective presentation and evaluation of the protagonist. This narrative method enables the author to subordinate all the voices of various characters to the one dominant voice of the third person narrator and, thus, to suggest the only possible interpretation of the protagonist. Conrad, on the contrary, by embedding multiple accounts of Jim within Marlow's first person narration, lays emphasis on the subjectivity of Jim's presentation. Due to this device, all points of view are given an equal narrative status, and, consequently, none of them can aspire to be the vehicle of the final and only truth.

Nevertheless, some elements of Conrad's method of presenting the protagonist can be found in Turgenev, like the juxtaposition of numerous comments of the characters who serve as mirrors for the protagonists, highlighting hidden conflicts and revealing new aspects of their personalities. Also the function of Lezhnyov, the main commentator of Rudin, is parallel to Marlow's. Both Lezhnyov and Marlow narrate the stories about Rudin's and Jim's lives, and the way they narrate reveals their unreliability as witnesses and judges of the two protagonists. Both Marlow's and Lezhnyov's narratives are influenced by their own moral and emotional dilemmas, but Lezhnyov denies being prejudiced and subjective, whereas Marlow, along with telling Jim's story, gives an account of his inner tensions which surface following the confrontation with Jim and recognizes his unreliability. Finally, Lezhnyov is led to admit his bias against Rudin and, then, he is capable of a more profound evaluation, which produces a more complex, ambiguous vision of the protagonist parallel to the presentation of Jim.

Still, it must be kept in mind that the way the protagonist of *Rudin* is depicted, is related to the ideological preoccupations of Turgenev. Turgenev sets out to convey an ideological message concerning the social problems of Russia, especially her struggle for identity distinct from that of Western Europe. He wrote his novel during a crucial moment in Russian history, the Crimean war, which exposed the weakness of the political and economic system and unleashed the wave of discontent about Russia's backwardness.[38] Russia's defeat in 1855 fuelled discussions about the role of the intelligentsia of the 1830s and 1840s. The critical evaluation of Russia's inability to carry out political, social and economic reforms provoked Turgenev to present his stance in the dispute, to depict the generation of the 1830s and 1840s and its both negative and positive aspects. He modelled Rudin on the most prominent representatives of the gentry intelligentsia – Bakunin, Granovsky, Stankevitch – with such typical attitudes as incapacity for action (reminiscent of Hamlet), idealism, eloquence and enthusiastic support of social reforms.[39] His novel was meant to be a judgement of the protagonist and of the whole social group he represented. Yet, while Turgenev in this way participates in the nationwide discussion about his country, Conrad's novel transcends national and social context concentrating on universal issues. Thus, Rudin typifies Russian intelligentsia, whereas Jim is "one of us" and his predicament is relevant to everybody regardless of national or social commitments, since it involves an experience of flawed human nature, of tensions inherent in the romantic worldview, and the dichotomy between the ideal and the reality. In *Lord Jim* Conrad explores the epistemological problem of establishing the truth about the protagonist who, however, does not lend himself to any final definition. In contrast to Conrad, Turgenev's epistemological certitude is informed by a concrete ideological purpose of depicting the generation responsible for Russia's political and economic failure. Nevertheless, despite the differences arising from the social contexts of the two writers' work, artistic strategies of building up a fictional character employed by Turgenev can be detected in Conrad. Yet, Conrad adapts these strategies to his theory of reality much more sceptical of the human capability for reaching the unquestionable truth.

NOTES

1. Leo Gurko, *Joseph Conrad: Giant in Exile* (New York: Macmillan, 1962), 181.

2. Jocelyn Baines, *Joseph Conrad* (London: Penguin Books, 1971), 391.

3. Yves Hervouet, "Conrad's Relationship with Anatole France," *Conradiana*, 12: 3, (1980), 195; Richard Freeborn, *Turgenev: The Novelist's Novelist* (Oxford: Oxford U.P., 1960), 44-5.

4. Galina Kurlandskaya, *Khudozhestvennyi metod Turgeneva romanista* (Tula: Priokskoe Knizhnoe Izdatelstvo, 1972), 78-9; Torsten Pettersson, *Consciousness and Time. A Study in the Philosophy and Narrative Technique of Joseph Conrad* (Åbo: Åbo Akademi, 1982), 27-8.

5. Yves Hervouet, 209.

6. *Joseph Conrad's Letters to R. B. Cunninghame Graham*, ed. Cedric T. Watts (Cambridge: Cambridge U.P., 1969).

7. Andrzej Walicki, "O 'schopenhaueryzmie' Turgieniewa," in Andrzej Walicki, *Osobowość a historia* (Warszawa: Państwowy Instytut Wydawniczy, 1959), 326-7.

8. Yves Hervouet, 210-12.

9. Ivan Turgenev, "Gamlet i Don-Kikhot [Hamlet and Don Quixote]" (1859), in Ivan Turgenev, *Sochinienia* (Moskva: Izdatelstvo "Nauka," 1964), vol. 8, 171-92.

10. Ivan Turgenev, *Rudin* (London: Penguin Books, 1975).

11. Victor Ripp, *Turgenev's Russia. From "Notes of a Hunter" to "Fathers and Sons"* (Ithaca: Cornell U.P., 1980), 128.

12. Albert Guerard, *Conrad the Novelist* (Cambridge, Mass.: Harvard U.P., 1962), 134-5, 140.

13. Richard Freeborn, 57.

14. Galina Kurlandskaya, 261-2; Stanislav Shatalov, *Khudozhestvennyi mir I. S. Turgeneva* (Moskva: Izdatelstvo "Nauka," 1979), 151.

15. Torsten Pettersson, 93.

16. James Woodward, *Metaphysical Conflict. A Study of the Major Novels of Ivan Turgenev* (München: Verlag Otto Sagner, 1990), 28.

17. Ibid., 17.

18. Jacques Berthoud, *Joseph Conrad. The Major Phase* (Cambridge: Cambridge U.P., 1978), 75.

19. Petr Pustovoyt, *I. S. Turgenev – khudozhnik slova* (Moskva: Izdatelstvo Moskovskogo Universiteta, 1980), 180.

20. Steve Ressler, *Joseph Conrad. Consciousness and Integrity* (New York: New York U.P., 1988), 34.

21. Stanislav Shatalov, 161.

22. Richard Freeborn, 59.

23. Steve Ressler, 26.

24. Daniel Schwarz, *Conrad. "Almayer's Folly" to "Under Western Eyes"* (Ithaca: Cornell U.P., 1980), 85.

25. Petr Pustovoyt, 178.

26. Stanislav Shatalov, 163.

27. Petr Pustovoyt, 177-8.

28. Jocelyn Baines, 297.

29. James Woodward, 34.

30. Ibid., 34-5.

31. Torsten Pettersson, 104.

32. Steve Ressler, 26.

33. Wiesław Krajka, *Isolation and Ethos. A Study of Joseph Conrad* (Boulder – New York: East European Monographs – Columbia U.P., 1992), 104-5.

34. James Woodward, 33.

35. Ibid., 36.

36. Torsten Pettersson, 103.

37. Albert Guerard, 159.

38. Antoni Semczuk, *Iwan Turgieniew* (Warszawa: "Wiedza Powszechna," 1970), 134-5.

39. Ibid., 140, 143-4.

Wiesław Krajka,
Maria Curie-Skłodowska University/University of Wrocław,
Lublin/Wrocław, Poland

The Multiple Identities of Yanko Goorall

"Amy Foster"'s multilayered, densely mediated, polyphonic form matches Bakhtin's definition of the novel "as a diversity of social speech types (sometimes even diversity of languages) and a diversity of individual voices, artistically organized...[of] specific points of view on the world, forms for conceptualizing the world in words, specific world views, each characterized by its own objects, meanings and values. As such they all may be juxtaposed to one another, mutually supplement one another, contradict one another and be interrelated dialogically...." (Carabine, 200)

"Amy Foster" is Conrad's short story masterpiece which has fared quite well with critics. Against the landscape of general critical neglect and underappreciation of Conrad's short stories, "Amy Foster" stands out by having inspired a considerable number of illuminating and interesting interpretations.

The most obvious reading of this short story is autobiographical: Yanko Goorall (the protagonist) as a fictional version of the writer's own self. There are certain general parallels between Yanko Goorall who emigrated from the Carpathian mountains in East-Central Europe, reached England as a castaway, underwent a nightmare of humiliation and ostracism, married an English girl, finally got partly assimilated to his new milieu, but died tragically forlorn, and Conrad, who emigrated from Poland, served in British Merchant Marine, felt alienated and aloof all his life (Gillon, *Joseph Conrad*, 56-7), got English citizenship and married an English woman, settled in England to become an eminent writer known and admired worldwide. Yanko Goorall is "a thinly disguised variant of the immigrant Pole, Konrad Korzeniowski...a figure with whom Konrad Korzeniowski could identify and empathize" (Burgess, 126). It has been generally agreed that "Amy Foster" is Conrad's spiritual autobiography, a representation of the writer's own sense of dislocation, foreignness and exile; indeed "[t]he story is undoubtedly based on Conrad's profound feeling of loneliness and even on his personal experience not unlike that of Yanko himself" (Gillon, *Joseph Conrad*, 56-7).

However, the differences between the writer and his fictional character are even more significant than the similarities. They stem primarily from the social class of origin, inherited tradition and culture, the nature of the career made abroad and the relationship with the new environment, the essence and intensity of tragic experiences. The autobiographical texture of this short story embodies "an emotional truth about Conrad's life without involving specific episodes from his personal history" (Fraser, 181). The artistic organization of Conrad's creations carried them beyond the scope of the merely autobiographical and suggested a most general, cautious and discreet reading of autobiographical correspondences – in terms of echoes from Conrad's own experience (McLauchlan).

Studies of the origins and the creative process of "Amy Foster" have pointed to the deletion of passages which might encourage inferences from and speculations about parallels between the writer himself and Yanko Goorall[1] (Carabine, 202-3). They have also indicated revisions meant to preserve the writer's aesthetic distance from his fictional creation (Fraser, 183, 191), to express his "deepest feelings of loneliness and disorientation...involved in writing the story, where they are revealed as universal truths" (181), or as "some 'particle of general truth'" (McLauchlan, 4).[2]

Besides, the evolution of Conrad's conception of "Amy Foster" – its narrative structure, diction, imagery, and the contrast between Yanko Goorall and the English villagers – magnified his tragic experiences, making them particularly suggestive and poignant, felt acutely and intensely by readers, evoking their profound involvement and sympathetic identification (Fraser).

The universality of Yanko Goorall's plight and identity is emphasized by the frame narrator and, first and foremost, by Dr. Kennedy, a narrator, "an attentive philosophical observer of human nature" (Griem, 132). Yanko Goorall has been viewed as a tragic archetypal-mythical human being (Andreach, "The Two Narrators...," 264-9), an adventurer-castaway ("Amy Foster," *TS*, 113; Yim, 836), a shipwrecked person (D'Elia, 165), an outsider (Pinsker, 182), and a King Lear (D'Elia, 167; Epstein, 229). His plight represents the tragedy of an emigrant, consisting in a sense of outsiderhood and nostalgia (magnified by ethnocentricism) for the native country and its culture (Busza, 227; Nettels, 187). He has also been interpreted as a typical Conradian "isolato": separated from both his Carpathian environment and from the Kentish villagers and Amy Foster, and dramatizing the human condition of isolation (Gillon, *The Eternal Solitary....*, 123; Guerard, 14, 49-51; Krajka, *Isolation and Ethos....*, 51-3, 59-60; Moser, 29-30, 86-7, 109, 127; Urbisz, 302-3). The general significance of such patterns is enhanced by comparative studies, tracing their appearance in "Amy Foster" and other literary works: e.g., Polish emigrant stories of the last decade of the XIXth century (Busza, 224-8), Stephen Crane's "The Monster" (Nettels).

Such multiple universal identities of Yanko Goorall turn him into a kind of everyman. "Amy Foster" has been read, e.g., as "the typical Conradian struggle between the contradictory claims of different human impulses," such as egoism and altruism, love of life and fear of the strange (Graver, 106-7), reflecting the human drama "arising from irreconcilable differences and from that fear of the Incomprehensible that hangs over all our heads" ("Amy Foster," *TS*, 108; see also Andreach, *The Slain...*, 30). Tragedy seems to be the common denominator of all these identities of the protagonist of "Amy Foster." It consists in cruel treatment at the hands of the Brenzett-Colebrook-Darnford villagers, who do not recognize him as a fellow creature (Kaplan, 148): "these people of 'obscure minds'...treat[ed] a gentle Christian [Yanko], craving the most basic human needs, as an animal" (Carabine, 196).

A breakdown of communication results from Yanko's abortive attempts to come into contact with the English villagers, and especially from his exchange with Smith who, addressed as a gracious lord and besought for help, regards him as a dangerous lunatic and locks him in a woodlodge. Amy's compassion and Yanko's gratitude develop into their mutual fascination, love and marriage (despite ostracism by almost all the village community), yet later, their separation from the world evolves into their isolation from each other (a typically Conradian pattern – see Krajka, *Isolation and Ethos....*, 59-60, 66), until she eventually comes to share the community's derogatory opinion of her husband. The final climactic scene between Yanko and Amy crowns the failure of communication between them, as "she misconstrues his urgent pleas and gestures as aggressive threats" (Griem, 132). Her name adds a significant ironic twist to his tragedy, as she neither really loves him ("Amy" connotes French *aimer, ami* and Latin *amor* – Kurczaba, 95; Maisonnat, 122), nor takes care of him (she does not really "foster" him as her surname would imply; she "fails to combine love and fostering into a single whole" – Fogel, 134).[3] Meyer (171-3) emphasizes Amy's victimization of her husband.

On the other hand, a positon in defence of Amy is taken by Hooper. She argues that although Amy and the child provide ontological affirmation and security for Yanko, he is blinded "to a real awareness of Amy's needs, and to the fact that his determination to teach his child his own language is an assertion of difference which divides him from her" (Hooper, 60). Goorall sets in contradiction Amy's roles as mother and child, and forces her to choose one of these. His speech in his native dialect, when directed to their child, poses an ontological threat to Amy, to her maternity: "by speaking to her child in a strange language, Yanko is, in Amy's eyes, trying to turn the child into a stranger, to replicate in the child his own alienness and difference" (60).

The figure of silence seems to dominate Amy's actions and the entire short story (Kurczaba, 100-1; Pinsker, 181). It dramatizes the typically modernist view of the inefficacy of language, its failure to adequately convey both human experiences and reality (Pinsker); in "Amy Foster," as in *Under Western Eyes*, words function as "foes of reality" (Kurczaba, 101), not as a means of but as a barrier to communication (Karl, 514-15).

The depiction of Yanko's tragedy applies three principal generalizing frames: Christian, ancient and existential. Purdy (104-5) points to specific verbal allusions to The Bible used in the scene of Yanko's death. Andreach views him as a Christ-like figure, an element of the Christian bond of all humanity. He reads the message of "Amy Foster" as one of hope for redemption and a divine purpose in life, for preservation of ethical values in the unethical world. He maintains that Yanko could and should have been saved by the Kentish villagers and Kennedy if they had adopted a Christian attitude of compassionate identification with the outcast – as did the admirable captain-narrator in "The Secret Sharer" (Andreach, *The Slain...*, 36-43).

A different perspective upon Yanko-as-Christ is presented by Kurczaba. Though he also views the protagonist as a suffering, tragic replica of crucified Christ, similar to the title heroine of Gombrowicz's play *Ivona, Princess of Burgundia*, he claims that "both [these] texts posit a *mundus inversus* at the center of which stands a parodistic variant of the Christ figure" (Kurczaba, 88). In this topsy turvy reality Yanko Goorall functions as the archetype of Christ as scapegoat (94-9). Amy's actions toward him parody basic Christian symbols: at first she offers him sacramental bread, only to later deny him life-sustaining water (96). The protagonist's arrival in England constitutes an ironic reversal of Christ's story: he travels on the ship *Herzogin Sophia-Dorothea* (the life of Saint Dorothea affirmed the existence of paradise – and Yanko dreams of the paradise of America, which later materializes as his debasement upon his landing in England) and after the catastrophe of the ship he swims to the shore on a hencoop with eleven drowned ducks (an allusion to Christ and his eleven disciples – 97). All this neutralizes the sacred in the presentation of the protagonist and subverts the notion of achieving expiation through suffering (97-9).[4]

Ancient tragedy furnishes another generalizing framework for the interpretation of the plight of the protagonists of "Amy Foster." Dr. Kennedy's classical allusions (mostly to ancient

Greek tragedy) emphasize the supraindividual and timeless significance of this short story. Its protagonists are viewed to be in the hands of inexorable, merciless Fate (Andreach, *The Slain...*, 33, 40-1; Griem, 131).

This sense of tragedy is extended by the frame narrator to comprise also the villagers of the Colebrook-Brenzett-Darnford area, representing all laboring, unhappy people, the "sad music of humanity" (Carabine, 193). They are unsmiling, with downcast eyes, overburdened by their toil and by their heavy natures, placed under a cursed obligation to harrow the land – a curse that loads their heavy hearts with heavy chains ("Amy Foster," *TS*, 110-11; see also Carabine, 190). Such presentation conveys almost Hardyan sense of tragedy and fatalism and anticipates and enhances the protagonists' final tragedy. Thus, in his democratic vision, Dr. Kennedy elevates common people to the status of heroes in a cosmic tragedy arising from irreconcilable antagonisms among people (Carabine, 192); he accords them a mythical stature (D'Elia, 168-9) – very much after the fashion of ancient tragedies. This vision is simultaneously typically Conradian – rendering "the highest kind of justice to all 'of obscure minds, of imperfect speech,' whether natives of regions such as Kent and the Malay archipelago, or strangers in their midst like Yanko and Jim" (Carabine, 192).

Such delineation of the protagonists is enhanced by the frame narrator's melancholic depiction of nature in the initial part of "Amy Foster." His sweeping descriptions/generalizations and brief introduction of the essentials of Amy's biography, along with delaying Yanko's account of his own experiences given by Kennedy, function as a prolepsis and bracket Yanko's story within Amy's and within the expository descriptions/reflections. Accordingly, Yanko's tragic fortunes have become part of and are generated by a "sense of penetrating sadness...[which] disengaged itself from the silence of the fields" ("Amy Foster," *TS*, 110).

The protagonist's plight also acquires a dimension of the existential loneliness of man: it is desperate, emblematic of incommunicability and enmity among people (Gillon, *The*

Eternal Solitary...., 123) and a sense of the absurdity of the universe. According to Andreach's religious reading of "Amy Foster," Dr. Kennedy perceives neither any purpose nor any divine plan in life, he is convinced that the world is a wasteland and that mankind's lot is to perish in loneliness and despair; "since Yanko's suffering had no healing effect on the community, since his experience is incomprehensible and purposeless, Kennedy has no faith in the possibility of redemption on earth" (Andreach, *The Slain*..., 36). This short story applies a typically Conradian pattern of placing man in a brutal universe, amid cosmic indifference, in which there is no place for a human being and his moral values, "where he is not wanted" (Epstein, 222). This seems to be an echo of Conrad's own conviction about an absurd, godless and unethical world, hostile to man (Griem, 130) – a typically modernist outlook originating in his profound pessimism and catastrophism.

These archetypal/universal identities of Yanko Goorall are superimposed upon the basic one, autobiographical, mainly by means of Dr. Kennedy's narration. He provides an aesthetic distance between the writer and his text (very much like Marlow in *Lord Jim* and some other Conradian narrators)[5] and introduces generalizing perspectives of interpretation. Kennedy is a man of unappeasable curiosity, "of impressive scientific achievements and wide-ranging experience, and at the same time a generalist with philosophical propensities" (Griem, 130) who "believes that there is a particle of a general truth in every mystery" ("Amy Foster," *TS*, 106). He is deeply convinced that Yanko Goorall's experiences reflect a mysterious essence of life and persistently views the actions of the characters as strange and inscrutable (Nettels, 185-6). Dr. Kennedy listens to the stranger's confession and gathers all other available versions of his experiences (Hooper, 58; Krajka, *Isolation and Ethos*...., 105-7); he interprets his interaction with the villagers, and tries to fathom the minds of the two protagonists, to formulate the universal significance of the story (largely by means of classical allusions) and attendant evaluations. His narration is detached, his version of events is argued persuasively and makes an impression of being rational, comprehensive and definitive. Griem regards Dr. Kennedy's version as reliable, presenting a fairly adequate understanding of Amy and Yanko's actions and convincing explanations of all enigmas of this short story. He achieves a largely successful penetration into the minds of both the stranger and the Kentish villagers and an adequate rendering of these two contradictory perspectives by means of a mixture of the points of view of an outsider and an insider. His knowledge, experience and intelligence enable him to think in broad terms: to understand the story told by Yanko Goorall and to empathize with him. Enjoying great prestige in the area, he is also able to gain the local people's confidence and is largely successful in understanding their mind and their reactions to the stranger; using a lot of regional language expressions makes him indeed one of the village community (Fraser, 184-5).

On the other hand, a host of critics have emphasized the unreliability of Dr. Kennedy's narration. For example, they have regarded him as unable to arrive at the psychological truth about the protagonists, as viewing them in terms of his preconceptions (Kaplan, 146), or simply failing to fathom their psychology (Kurczaba, 100; Epstein, 229-30). Emphasis has been laid on Kennedy's doubts and reservations, on his version of events being one of many interpretations in the polyphonic multivoicedness of "Amy Foster." Kennedy's narration has been regarded as being permeated with a sense of mystery, as applying a profusion of words denoting the enigmas of the two protagonists and their actions (Andreach, *The Slain...*, 30-3; Andreach, "The Two Narrators...," 262-5). Kennedy suggests two kinds of explanation to all these puzzles: a rational one, and an irrational, supernatural, divine or mythic one (Andreach, *The Slain...*, 31-3; Andreach, "The Two Narrators...," 263-5). However, both of them fail to give answers to the questions posed, fail to unravel the mystery of Yanko and Amy's identity and psychology (Andreach, *The Slain...*, 33-4, 41; Kurczaba, 100). This manner of narration expresses both a matter of mere rhetoric of incomprehension and also a broader epistemological conviction about the impenetrability of a human psyche, about the imperfect and relative nature of all cognition (see Andreach, *The Slain...*, 30; Andreach, "The Two Narrators...," 262) – a consideration both typically Conradian (see *Lord Jim*) and modernist.

An extreme position on Kennedy's unreliability as narrator is taken by Hooper. She regards his perception of Amy as "unpenetrating and erratic," gendered by his inability "to recognise or to interpret her as woman and mother" (Hooper, 60-1). Amy's fear is not unaccountable (as Kennedy maintains): it is justified by her maternal instinct and care for her child. Hooper claims that Kennedy fails to depict Amy adequately and is unfair to her. She is made silent to be prevented from interference with Kennedy's version of the protagonist's tragedy; her inarticulacy should be read as a refusal to corroborate this version. For Kennedy "it is convenient...to render her silence as 'inscrutable mystery,' to allow the story to be foreclosed by the 'black hole' of her silence, rather than to confront and acknowledge his own culpability" (63).[6]

Thus, despite Dr. Kennedy's protestations, his interpretation of Yanko Goorall's story is not definitive, but rather one of a few possible versions. What he says may have been designed for the eyes of Conrad's English readers; he may have presented and endorsed the way the writer wanted his English readers to interpret this short story (Carabine, 189)[7] – i.e. neglecting Yanko's foreign, obscure ethnos and emphasizing the tragic and universal significance of his plight. Perhaps Dr. Kennedy offers a basic, pivotal version of the events (like Marlow in *Lord Jim*), inviting other possible illuminations and evaluations. Carabine points to some un-English features of this narrator – subtlety, sensitivity to human tragedy and irreconcilable differences, curiosity, skepticism, a sense of loneliness (191-2, 199, 202) – to suggest that the natures and visions of Kennedy and Marlow "partake of their creator's Polishness" (191).

As "Amy Foster" uses a typically Conradian Chinese boxes method of narration (the principal narrations are those by Yanko Goorall, Dr. Kennedy, and the frame narrator), a comprehensive definition of the status and roles of Dr. Kennedy as narrator has also to take into account his relationship to the frame narrator. Some hold that the latter's vision of events is identical with Dr. Kennedy's – to endorse or develop the doctor's interpretation, evaluation and generalization of Yanko Goorall's tragic fortunes (Andreach, "The Two Narrators...," 267-9; Griem, 132; Hooper, 55). Others argue that the frame narrator's perspective is significantly different from Dr. Kennedy's: that of an objective, detached commentator (like the chorus in an ancient Greek tragedy), who explains Yanko's distress and formulates a moral judgement (Andreach, *The Slain...*, 36-8; Andreach, "The Two Narrators...," 268-9), and who perceives some subtleties of his plight missed by Kennedy's unreliable narration (Maisonnat, 115). According to Hooper, the principal function of the frame narrator is to impose polyphony upon the text, to qualify Kennedy's narrative, "to enable a questioning of its inclusions and exclusions," and especially to present a perspective upon Amy which is different from Kennedy's (Hooper, 55-6). The frame narrator rules out supernatural explanations and places the source of tragedy in man himself (Andreach, "The Two Narrators...," 269). It is also his principal function to delineate the atmosphere of the short story in its introductory descriptions (Carabine, 189; Schwarz, 106-8; Yim, 829). Maybe the frame narrator's reactions to the experiences reported by Dr. Kennedy are those Conrad intended to elicit from his readers (Carabine, 189).

"Amy Foster" dramatizes a typically Conradian theme of disorientation and displacement, of difficulties in cross-cultural contacts, of cultural conflicts endangering identity (Griffith, 16, 18), of isolation by ethnicity, language, culture and religion. According to Conrad himself, the principal idea of this short story is "the essential difference of the races" (*CL*, II, 399, 402), their cultures, values and languages – a theme predominant in his entire fiction (Carabine, 187-8).

The two sides of this cross-cultural encounter – Yanko Goorall and the villagers of the Brenzett-Colebrook-Darnford area – are sharply contrasted in terms of various aspects of appearance and manners, of multiple features of ethnos (Fraser, 189-90; Krajka, "The Dialogue...," 149; McLauchlan, 5). He is presented largely by means of images of upward verticality, whereas the English villagers by images of downward verticality (Maisonnat, 123). And the evolution of the text of "Amy Foster" in the process of its creation took the direction toward heightening the contrast between the protagonist and the villagers (Fraser, 182, 187, 189-90, 192).

The cultural gap between Yanko Goorall and the English villagers has been interpreted in terms of an opposition between Innocence and Experience (Lupack). He stands for Innocence denoting goodness, purity, juvenile and idyllic perception of the world, spontaneity, strong imagination, noncorruption by social conventions and morality. He is presented within the setting of Arcadian archetypes and lives in harmony with nature. This innocent stranger is plunged into the world of Experience which stands for selfishness, hypocrisy, cruelty, unimaginativeness, a harsh and gloomy view of the world, a sense of fear and corruption by institutions and society. This concept of Experience appears in "Amy Foster" against the background of the grim, real world (out of tune with nature and God) which treats the foreigner like a wild primitive, an animal. And Amy, in a flight of imagination and spontaneity, enters the realm of Innocence to fall in love with Yanko, but ultimately she joins the world of Experience to become a part of the Brenzett-Colebrook-Darnford community, to share its bigotry and narrow-mindedness, its contempt for, hatred and rejection of the intruder (Lupack, 445-7).

Upon landing in England Yanko Goorall faces a tremendous cultural gap; he perceives his new surroundings as totally unlike his familiar East Carpathian milieu (see especially "Amy Foster," *TS*, 129). Under his eyes, the overwhelming reality of the Colebrook-Brenzett-Darnford area acquires the shapes of a counter-world, determined by inversions (Kurczaba, 99). "[F]or him...England was an undiscovered country...no longer in this world" ("Amy Foster," *TS*, 111-12); he was "like a man transplanted into another planet, was separated by an immense space from his past" (132), forced to live among "people from the other world – dead people" (129). The spatial distance between the East Carpathians and Kent enhances the unbridgeable gap between the cultures and ethnoses of the protagonist and the English villagers (Krajka, "The Alien...," 196). The newcomer looks as strange to the Kentish villagers as they look to him: each side in this confrontation regards the Other's behavior as outlandish, inhuman, and inexplicable (Carabine, 196). Even later, his English sounded to them like "an unearthly language" ("Amy Foster," *TS*, 117).

Yanko Goorall's ethnocentricism makes him misinterpret the cultural phenomena taking place outside the realm of his native culture: he views them in terms characteristic of his domestic surroundings (Krajka, "The Dialogue...," 149-50), of defamiliarization (Kaplan, 147; Fraser, 186-7; Maisonnat, 108) or impressionism (Epstein, 227). Yanko Goorall takes the country of his miraculous rescue for America; he addresses Amy (a dull and plain village girl) as a gracious lady, and Smith – as a gracious lord; he is surprised at the barrenness of churches and at their being locked on weekdays (Kaplan, 147), etc. All these perceptions testify to his "difficulties of entering into a new culture and attempting to make sense of it" (147), "to *decode* the strange new world he enters" (Carabine, 194); he is unable to comprehend the villagers' culture and reality, and remains a cultural outsider among them, or rather "an inside-outsider" (Griffith, 17-19). The native language and culture create for him a kind of safe zone amid the hostile space of the alien reality. It is his persistent immersion in his original ethnos which the English villagers find offensive (Carabine, 197; Maisonnat, 113) and which is a major reason of his final tragedy (Epstein, 227; Nettels, 187). On the other hand, the English villagers' narrow-mindedness makes them unable to understand the foreigner's ethnos and ethos, to regard him otherwise than in terms of their limited outlook.

Thus, both sides of this cross-cultural encounter display a universal pattern of ethnocentricity – "a natural, if undesirable condition of humanity" (Griffith, 17); they contemplate their ethnocentricity and lack imaginative insight to understand the

Other. These attitudes lead to a familiar/alien antithesis, to an intercultural conflict.

This conflict has been interpreted by Maisonnat as a failure of Lacanian construction of the subject by the symbolic code of language by means of the Name-of-the-Father. The principal theme of this short story consists in "the painful entry of a subject into a foreign language and identity" (Maisonnat, 104), in a struggle into language (Epstein, 228). Yanko Goorall fails to join the symbolic order of the Kentish villagers' language, the world of their articulation and interaction, and, consequently, fails to be constructed as a subject in their community. He is unable to imbue the new reality around him with symbolic representation, and, consequently, he cannot bear its pressure unmediated by symbolic categories (Maisonnat, 108). For the inhabitants of the Brenzett-Colebrook-Darnford area he never reaches the status of a human being, a subject, a member of their community; he is never allowed by them any kind of sincere recognition, which leads to his symbolic nonexistence there.

The same conflict has been interpreted by Krajka as an aborted, merely potential dialogue of cultures (Krajka, "The Dialogue..."). In this exchange both sides merely articulate their positions, strongly affirm their identities, the fundamental principles of their ethnos and ethos – only to fail to bring them into a slightest interaction. This precludes mutual understanding (even partial), appreciation and assimilation of elements of the partner's ego; the two sides remain in isolated realms of their cultural identities. The initial, informative phase of mutual presentation of identities is not followed by authentic dialogue and exchange of ideas and values. This situation excludes genuine understanding, communication, coexistence and inter-action of elements of the Other's culture. Each side's verbal and nonverbal codes of expression are entirely misapprehended by the potential partner (151-2).

According to both Maisonnat and Krajka, even Amy, Swaffer and Kennedy – sympathetic for Yanko, yet isolated in some way from the villagers – fail to change his plight for the better, fail to help him enter the symbolic order of his new social group.

Maisonnat argues that Amy's initial act of compassion for Yanko was hypocritical as it did not grant him an equal status in the new community: it was not a genuine act of symbolic recognition of him on her part (Maisonnat, 112).[8] Swaffer treats him as a curiosity, and not as a true partner in the structure of this society. Likewise, Kennedy fails to grant Yanko "the symbolic recognition that would have given him the status of a subject" (115). Both of them fail to act as symbolic fathers for Yanko (112-15). According to Krajka, the dialogue of cultures between Amy Foster, Swaffer, Kennedy and Goorall is at best partial, but ultimately failed. The relation between the two protagonists evolves from compassion and gratitude through amorous fascination, marital love to marital disharmony caused by misapprehension of the partner's intentions, fear of the unknown and by the irreconcilable differences between people. The connection with Swaffer starts with his fascination with and acceptance of the newcomer's strangeness and consists in mutual gratitude for the services rendered (Krajka, "The Dialogue...," 152-3). Dr. Kennedy's panoramic position turns him into an observer and commentator upon the interaction between the protagonist and the Kentish villagers; he approves of his strangeness and reveals a fairly great degree of comprehension of his tragedy (153). However, Kennedy's unreliability as narrator (see foregoing comments) precludes his complete understanding of Yanko and dialogue with him.

"Amy Foster" reflects a universal pattern of viewing foreigners with fear, suspicion and enmity (Griffith, 17; Krajka, "The Alien..."). The villagers' treatment of the protagonist as a tramp, lunatic and madman originates in their dread, ignorance, racial prejudice, xenophobia and lack of imaginative insight (Carabine, 189, 195-6; McLauchlan, 4). The newcomer feels acutely the hostility of the local people: he is ostracized, his ethnos and ethos are despised and rejected by them (Krajka, "The Dialogue..."). The general significance of this pattern of an alien rejected by an ethnocentric community has been enhanced by comparative studies. Nettels traced it in both "Amy Foster" and "The Monster" by Stephen Crane. In the latter short story the white community of a small town treat a Negro outcast, who inspires them with fear and disrupts the order of their daily life, "as physically grotesque and mentally abnormal" (Nettels, 182), with repulsion and cruelty. In both "Amy Foster" and "The Monster" the communities are devoid of a spirit of true charity and represent a wide range of feelings of hostility for and fear and rejection of the stranger (185).

According to Krajka ("The Alien..."), the English peasants' ostracism of Yanko Goorall reveals a universal mechanism of relationship between the familiar and the alien – typical of a primitive community which treats its own culture as the only culture, and an alien culture as nonexistent. It regards a foreigner as a source of peril, as an emanation of dangerous forces from the Other World. Under the eyes of the English villagers, the protagonist of "Amy Foster" embodies numerous negative features, an antithesis of all fundamental parameters of the familiar identity. His interference poses a threat of disintegration and destruction of the indigenous community's internal structure and entire conception of the world (203; see also Kurczaba, 88; Maisonnat, 114). He undermines this isolated social group "cemented by a culture that was created in the long-term interaction of its participants and strengthened in long-lasting contacts, common traditions, ideology, values, recollections and interests...[which] determine the mutual familiarity of the community's members" (Krajka, "The Alien...," 203).

Motivated by a collective instinct of self-preservation, they cruelly repudiate the alien and bring about his eventual tragedy, turning him into an object of complete ostracism and hostility (Krajka, "The Alien..."). The group's strong defensive reaction "sternly opposes such a radical questioning of the mental and spiritual foundations of its existence" in order to eliminate the stranger and the patterns of his ethos and ethnos from its social life (203). They affirm and strengthen their roots, collective identity and culture, and totally reject the foreigner (Maisonnat, 114-15). Preservation of the unity and structure of their community, threatened by Yanko's intrusion, turns him into a scapegoat (118). In a way typical of a primitive society, repudiation of

the alien is enhanced by the use of magic: Goorall's communication in his native dialect to his baby-son is perceived by
Amy as incomprehensible, mysterious verbal practices of sorcery (Krajka, "The Alien...," 209) – hence her final action to
prevent the transfer of this evil power onto the child. The
Kentish villagers, like a typical ethnocentric community, evaluate their familiar world, *orbis interior*, entirely positively, and the
unfamiliar world, *orbis exterior*, entirely negatively. They fix
a clear boundary between their *orbis interior* and *orbis exterior*
and ignore and eliminate all external phenomena (209-10).

It seems that the implied author of "Amy Foster" does not
blame the well-meaning protagonist for this tragic situation, but
rather the English villagers who behave cruelly toward him
(Krajka, "The Dialogue...," 153-4), who "treat a gentle Christian, craving the most basic human needs, as an animal"
(Carabine, 196). It is their attitude (including Amy, Swaffer and
Kennedy's) which prevents the protagonist's entrance into the
symbolic order of the community of his immigration (Maisonnat, 110). They persistently indulge in various shades and forms
of "an all-out strategy of denial"; they do not succeed in their
role of parent figures, neglect his needs as well as their deep
kinship with him and fail to cope with his Otherness (110-11).

"Amy Foster" has also been interpreted as an echo of
Conrad's colonial fiction, as a manifestation of his critical stance
on imperialism. It conveys Conrad's strictures on the false
self-approbation of the English, their xenophobia, intolerance,
unwarranted national pride and a sense of cultural superiority
(Kaplan, 136). It paints an emphatically negative portrait of the
English as "a remarkably cruel, suspicious, and mean-spirited
people, utterly unable to sympathize with anyone from another
culture" (148). Yanko Goorall represents the voicelessness and
unrepresentability of the colonial Other, typical of *Lord Jim* and
of the writer's other imperial fiction. The newcomer's language
and culture are totally disregarded by the English villagers; he is
rendered by them as inarticulate and "cultureless" and his
experiences are reported not by himself but, after his death, by

Kennedy (145)."Amy Foster" echoes the power structure of colonialism within which syncretism of the colonizing and the colonized is impossible; it questions "the hegemonic outlook that conceives of the subaltern only as a narcissistic extension of the western subject" (149). This short story reverberates with themes of the abuse of imperial power, a sense of western imperial cultural superiority, arbitrary divisions of human beings into the colonizers and the colonized (149).

However, it seems this censure should not apply directly, as the Kentish villagers in "Amy Foster" – an archetypal ethnocentric, isolated, primitive community – are not directly representative of imperialism, have nothing to do with imperialist ideologies, policies and activities. It rather undermines the sense of pride and superiority of the English people in general, arising from their imperial victories and achievements.

Ruppel interpreted "Amy Foster" as Conrad's "colonialist story in reverse," in which the Kentish villagers correspond to the natives in colonial fiction, Yanko Goorall takes the role of Robinson Crusoe, and Amy Foster is a parodic version of the Exotic Woman. The plot and structure of "Amy Foster" follows many standard devices and episodes of popular colonial fiction of Conrad's time: the hero's emigration to seek fortune in faraway lands, his long-lasting accommodation in a new environment, his falling in love with a native woman-helper, his overcoming numerous obstacles and eventual miscegenation, the evolution of his marriage from love to hatred and eventual failure, the presentation of the story from a largely anthropological-ethnological perspective (Ruppel, 127-8). These reversals of the typical colonial situation turn "Amy Foster" into a parody of the imperial adventure tale: it is England which is an "undiscovered country" and the Kentish villagers who are the barbarous "natives"; the Exotic Woman is the plain English girl Amy Foster; the colonialist is an obscure highlander from the East Carpathians whose true superiority is unrecognized by the "natives" (instead he is treated as a subhuman); it is Yanko and not Amy who represents the indigenous. "Amy Foster"'s "indictment of imperialism is limited to its ironic treatment of

England's xenophobia and cultural chauvinism" (131) – the conclusion which coincides with the tenor of Kaplan's interpretation.

However, it has to be emphasized that the statuses of the protagonists of "Amy Foster" reverse those held by their counterpart characters in popular colonial fiction: Yanko does not arrive in Kent as an imperialist, a conqueror, a representative of a superior civilization – instead he is put in an inferior position, at first brutally rejected and later forced into partial assimilation to the new environment; Amy, unlike the Exotic Woman, is in a position superior to him; it is the attitude of Kentish villagers in "Amy Foster" which turns England into "one of the dark places of the earth" (Carabine, 197).

D'Elia's Marxist interpretation emphasizes some anti-capitalistic implications of "Amy Foster": the swindle and exploitation in the recruitment of the East Carpathians for emigration (D'Elia, 166, 174; see also Carabine, 194); the hard labor of generations of English rustics (D'Elia, 168-70); Yanko's servitude in Kent (167); the society's "attempts to 'convert' the stranger to the religious, social, and economic life of this Western and capitalistic society" – opposed by his defensive endeavors to maintain his identity by persisting in his pre--capitalistic style of life (172). D'Elia's interpretation, especially the latter thesis, is controversial, as the village community in "Amy Foster" definitely is not representative of a capitalistic society, and Yanko's indigenous East Carpathian community is not typical of a pre-capitalistic one. This reading overemphasizes the role of the economic factor in the protagonist's relation to the Kentish villagers and in his tragic experiences and death.

Yanko Goorall's Polish/East Carpathian self has invited a number of interpretations of "Amy Foster." Busza convincingly argued that its plot and characters were modelled upon the emigrant story, popular in Polish literature of the last decade of the XIXth century, about "an impoverished peasant who was seeking better living conditions abroad" (Busza, 224). This type of story was created under the auspices of a very strong anti-emigration propaganda conducted in Poland at that time, involving many notable writers. This *littérature à thèse* was both a warning to Polish peasants against emigration and an expression of despair over their miserable plight which forced them to emigrate (implying dramatically the necessity of changing the economic situation of peasants for the better) – very much in tune with the ideology of Polish positivism (228). Such works could have influenced Conrad's writing of "Amy Foster": the shaping of characters, of plot, the emigré protagonists' profound feelings of isolation and outsiderhood in their new environment and nostalgia for their old homeland, as well as their final tragedy (224-8).

Many critics have erroneously identified the protagonist's ethnos and ethos with that of the Tatra highlanders in West Carpathians (229-30; Goetel, 20; Jasińska, 200-3; Morf, 225-6; Najder, 273; Perłowski, 121; Turno, 7). Busza is right to surmise that the descriptions of Yanko Goorall's outward appearance and manners, as well as of his native milieu, resemble a conventional portrait of the Carpathian folk. However, he is *fundamentally wrong* to conclude that Conrad was influenced by the literary stereotype of a Tatra highlander created and propagated by the Young Poland (modernist) men of letters and artists' fascination with this region and its culture (Busza, 229-30). This enchantment was limited to the Tatra and Podhale area (an ethnically Polish part of West Carpathians), whereas it is obvious that the East Carpathian highlands constituted Yanko Goorall's native realm (the East and West Carpathian folk were substantially different in terms of culture, dialect, religion, etc.): "He was a mountaineer of *the eastern range of the Carpathians*" ("Amy Foster," *TS*, 121); "we could read in the papers the accounts of the bogus 'Emigration Agencies' among *the Sclavonian peasantry in the more remote provinces of Austria*" (121; emphases W. K.). Given the great care with which Conrad distinguished between the Slavic and the Polish, his sensitivity on this point, his deliberate use of the word "Sclavonian" in the latter passage rules out Yanko's ethnic identification as a West Carpathian Pole.[9] Besides, it was not the West Carpathians (the

Tatras) but the East Carpathians which formed "the more remote provinces" of the Austro-Hungarian Empire. Thus, Yanko Goorall's ethnic identity is fundamentally East Carpathian, Slavonic, ethnically non-Polish. And any possible features of the West Carpathian (Tatra) or pan-Carpathian ethnos in Yanko Goorall's appearance and performance (Krajka, "The Dialogue...," 157) would merely enrich his fundamentally East Carpathian identity. Besides, the literary stereotype of the *góral* (Tatra/Carpathian highlander) is outlined by Busza in much too general terms. It definitely was not homogeneous, comprising a variety of types.

To further disprove Busza's thesis let us face biographical facts and chronology. "Amy Foster" was concluded in June 1901 and published in December 1901 (*CL*, II, 330, 360-1, 398, 401-2). This was indeed the time of the Young Poland obsession with the Tatra highlands, but Conrad did not come into contact with this movement until his stay in Cracow and Zakopane between July and October 1914, i.e. 13 years *after* the writing and publication of "Amy Foster." Neither his letters nor any other biographical documents testify to his interest in and understanding of this movement before 1914. Between 1874 (leaving for Marseilles) and 1914 (revisiting Poland) Conrad revealed no interest in his first homeland, he did not make any public statements on it (Hay, 22-4, 31-2, 34). Given this general attitude, it is highly improbable that when writing "Amy Foster" in 1901 he suddenly developed a strong and profound interest in a particular aspect of Polish life – "Tatromania." This phenomenon, if Conrad knew and understood it at all, could at best provide an impulse, an idea for writing "Amy Foster," and nothing more.

A host of critics have erroneously identified the protagonist as a Pole, or one who speaks Polish both to his baby-son and on his death-bed in delirium, whereas the words "Pole" and "Polish" do not appear in this short story at all. He may be called "Polish" only in the sense of belonging to the territory of the former Commonwealth of Poland, multiethnic and multinational. It is an oversimplification even to regard him as representing typical anthropological and ethnic features of Polish highlanders (Krajka, "The Dialogue...," 149; Lupack, 440) as Carpathian folk comprised a variety of groups: from ethnically Polish inhabitants of Podhale to various groups of ethnically non-Polish East Carpathians, and the specific location of Goorall's homeland is not clear. It is also imprecise to identify him, after Conrad himself, as "an Austro-Polish highlander" (*CL*, II, 399, 401), as this denomination refers to the entire Carpathian area in the Austro-Hungarian Empire and mistakenly renders his very problematic Polish ethnos as definite. He is rather "a Slav as well as a Pole" (Gillon, *Joseph Conrad*, 54).

The protagonist's name and surname – Yanko Goorall – is a clear signal of his non-English identity: it sounds ugly, ridiculous and unfamiliar to the English ears (McLauchlan, 7; Carabine, 203). "Goorall" is an English transliteration of the Polish word *góral* denoting a highlander – in the text of "Amy Foster" it is explained as "some word sounding in the dialect of his country like Goorall" ("Amy Foster," *TS*, 133). It is not incorrect to presume that the protagonist's surname "implies a degree of 'savagery' or 'barbarism'" (Griffith, 16) which, however, does not automatically imply lack of culture, as the Carpathian folk, though not quite civilized, had its very rich ethnic culture.

The protagonist's name "Yanko" is explained in the text of this short story as meaning "Little John" ("Amy Foster," *TS*, 133), a diminutive of Polish name *Jan*. It definitely sounds familiar and affectionate to the protagonist and strengthens his ties with his native land and his original identity (Gillon, *The Eternal Solitary....*, 124; Wasiolek, 419). It certainly does not emphasize the protagonist's juvenile nature, as Lupack maintains. "Yanko" definitely is not the vocative case (*Janku*) of the Polish name *Jan* (see Gillon, *The Eternal Solitary....*, 124; Wasiolek, 419) but a dialect form of the nominative of *Jan* (John).

By retaining his original name and surname in Kent the protagonist manifests his desire to preserve his native ethnos (419). The transformation his name undergoes in Kent by losing its familiar and affectionate connotations is symbolic of the loss of his identity there (419).[10] "Goorall is not his father's name, the name of his ancestors, connecting him with his origins" (Maisonnat, 120). Yet it is his tribal denomination, indicating an ethnic group of Carpathian highlanders. In this sense, it does connect the protagonist with his origins – not of his family but of his ethnic group. Thus, indeed, by losing his father's surname Yanko breaks the line of generations (122) – but of his family only; by preserving his tribal identification he does not get disinherited from the culture of his native social group.

Particular elements of the protagonist's ethnos, e.g., his religion, have been underappreciated and misinterpreted. Burgess emphasizes his Roman Catholic practices and faith, evident in his adherence to his morning and evening prayers, and in his making the Sign of the Cross before each meal. These religious habits turn him into the most devout Catholic in Conrad's fiction; they also strongly isolate him among the population of the Kentish villagers (Burgess, 120-1; Lupack, 444-5). His Catholicism identifies him with his original ethnos and is for him "the compass of his whole life" (D'Elia, 171). Conrad's revisions of the text of "Amy Foster" emphasized "the integrative aspect of Yanko's faith," binding an individual to the family, the community, and to the former generations (Fraser, 188-9). Both this integrative function and the customs of celebrating miraculous Holy Images on religious feast-days and meditating at wayside shrines with images of Jesus Christ, as well as "the statuary, the relics, the icons, the color, the lavish trappings of the churches of his homeland" (Burgess, 121) determine the religious culture of Yanko Goorall's native milieu. However, they are characteristic not of Polish religious tradition in general, but rather of the religious practices of Polish peasantry (Carpathian highlanders belonging to this social class); his religious habits shape his ethnic identity as distinctly Polish. The protagonist's conversion in Kent should not be interpreted as one "from his primal innocence to worldly experience" (Lupack, 445) but rather as taking place from one mode of religious culture to another. Similarly, his sincere and simple faith is not a demonstration of his childlike innocence, as Lupack claims (444). His religious habits are not simple but rich and complex – like his entire original culture.

Other elements of the protagonist's ethnos have been misinterpreted as well. Although regarded as "Slavic mannerisms" by the English villagers (Gillon, *Joseph Conrad*, 56), they were natural ways of behavior, in accordance with his original ethos and ethnos. His manner of speech, typical of Carpathian highlanders – agitated, passionate, with a singing and vibrating intonation – definitely is not childlike (as Lupack, 443-4, asserts), is not "an imitation of childish speech" (Morf, quoted after Carabine, 203). Yanko's dance in the village inn is not a "kazatsky" (as Burgess claims, 122) but one of the folk dances of his native Carpathian culture. However, it seems erroneous to conclude (Busza, 229-30; Jasińska, 201) that he performs *zbójnicki*, a folk dance of Tatra highlanders – his dance, way of singing and dress are depicted in terms general enough to relate to the ethnos of many groups of Carpathian highlanders. His way of walking ("the soles of his feet did not seem...to touch the dust of the road" – "Amy Foster," *TS*, 111) is perfectly natural for highlanders and does not necessarily make him similar to Jesus Christ who walked on water (as Kurczaba, 98, claims). Similarly, his outward appearance (tall figure, olive complexion, black eyes, etc.) constitutes natural features of the Carpathian anthropological type and does not necessarily resemble Christ (97-8). Such are also the images of upward verticality in his behavior and way of walking, which certainly do not denote his "struggle into the symbolic order" (as Maisonnat, 123, maintains). His strong love of the land is an integral element of his domestic axiology and not the attitude of a woodland creature (as Lupack, 442, claims). Yanko Goorall is a "child of nature" closely attached to his native Carpathian landscape, of which pine-trees are a crucial element. Hence it is perfectly obvious that, when in Kent, he treats three Norwegian pines as brothers, because they remind him of his native realm. Therefore, it is wrong to conclude, as Maisonnat does, that Yanko's attachment to the pines in Kent denotes a confusion between the vegetal and the human to emphasize the protagonist's lack of humanity (Maisonnat, 118).

Goorall welcomes and understands the bleating of sheep and is good with them. This is treated as an important element of Yanko's association with animal imagery (Pinsker, 182-3), as his turning away from the hostile human surroundings to friendly nature (Carabine, 198). Some explanations of Yanko's familiarity with the sheep reveal how ignorance of his original ethnos may lead to funny and ridiculous, though clever, interpretations. Sheep husbandry played a crucial role in the ethos and economy of the Carpathian folk: the highlanders regularly left their homes for a few months each year to take their flocks to pastures in upper parts of the highlands and to tend them there. Hence, it is obvious that Yanko found the bleating of English sheep a familiar sound. Thus, it is both wrong and offensive to interpret his response to sheep as his emergence from the sea to the level of animal consciousness, to find his place among them (Epstein, 227). Though the narrow-minded Kentish villagers perceive Yanko as equated with animality and disconnected from the world of human beings and human discourse (Maisonnat, 117), their perspective is neither adequate nor reliable. They are completely ignorant of the significance of sheep in his domestic milieu and totally misinterpret his relationship with them – to degrade him as a human being.

The protagonist of "Amy Foster" personifies the rich multi-layered and complex Carpathian folk culture. It consists in his specific outward appearance, movements, behavior, ways of speaking, looking, dancing, singing, his folk dress, religious practices, morality, manners, ideas, values, customs, vitality, instinct of self-preservation – all these features sharply distinguish him from the ethnic-anthropological type represented by the Kentish villagers (Krajka, "The Dialogue...," 149-50). His spirit, piety, "attachment to the language and the traditions of his homeland...attest to the vitality of the culture he struggles to preserve" (Nettels, 187). It seems that any interpretation of "Amy Foster" should not ignore this cultural substance impersonated in the figure of its protagonist.

Some critics have regarded Yanko Goorall as outshining the Kentish villagers. His cultural and physical superiority, buoyant, upright verticality, are the natural features of the Carpathian anthropological type and not those likening him to a white imperialist, a conqueror in a colonial story (as Ruppel, 129-30, claims). However, Conradians have emphasized mostly his moral excellence. "Yanko is in many ways superior to the English – imaginative, graceful, sensitive, loyal, 'innocent of heart, and full of good will'" (Kaplan, 145), though viewed by them as inferior (145; Ruppel, 129-30). His culture, faith and ethos of hospitality[11] are emphasized to be more human than that of the Kentish villagers (Gurko, 211; Maisonnat, 120; Ruppel, 129). Perhaps this forms an antithesis to Conrad's Anglophilia, expressed profusely in his works (Gurko, 211; Krajka, "The Dialogue...," 154).

It is the Protestant villagers who are to be blamed for Yanko's failure to enter the symbolic order of language and for his ultimate tragedy (Maisonnat). They manifest lack of true human and religious feelings and Christian virtues: mean-spiritedness, moral corruption, cruelty, xenophobia, narrow-mindedness, hypocrisy and bigotry (Beidler, 114-15; Carabine, 196-7; Epstein, 228; Fraser, 187-8; Kaplan, 148; Krajka, "The Dialogue...," 153-4; Kurczaba, 91, 93; McLauchlan, 5; Maisonnat, 104; Ruppel 129-31). Ms Swaffer and the rectory ladies represent dogmatic Anglicanism's unconcern for human needs and its inability to understand the protagonist's strange religious customs and practices (Burgess, 122; Carabine, 197; Maisonnat, 111). Perhaps "Amy Foster" really shows "the narrowness and spiritual impoverishment of the Protestant spirit" (Carabine, 197).

In view of all these critical opinions, any negation of the substance of the protagonist's rich original ethnos and culture leads to incorrect, ridiculous and offensive interpretations. For example, according to Graver, "Kennedy likens him to an animal or an object growing freely in a natural landscape, a woodland creature or a tree coming to full strength" (Graver, 105). Pinsker calls Goorall a wild, dumb animal sharply contrasted with the world of humans, a woodland creature surrounded with animal-like imagery and placed in various "cages" (Pinsker, 182-3), which reveals "animal needs for food and shelter" and is "less a man than an oversized household pet" (184); the villagers' treatment of Yanko is shared by Amy to form "the basis of her perverse attraction" (183-4). It seems that the impulsive nature of Yanko's actions upon his landing in England is justified: as a castaway he is motivated by the instinct of self-preservation. His condition is not only to crawl on all fours (as Epstein, 227, asserts) but also to walk impressively and dance gracefully (though the beer-drinking local notables are unable to appreciate the beauty and mastery of his ethnic dance). Yanko's upright stature, customs, ways of singing and dancing do not turn him into a mythical creature (Andreach, "The Two Narrators...," 267) but are immanent features of his anthropology and ethnos.

"Amy Foster," like other masterpieces of Conrad's narrative art, is a polyphonic, complex narrative structure, using many kinds of narrative and points of view, each reinterpreting and undermining the others (Carabine, 200). Any interpretation limited to considering one point of view only leads to impoverished and simplistic reading and to false conclusions. Some critics got enslaved by the vision of the inhabitants of the Brenzett-Colebrook-Darnford region, whose biased perspective is neither comprehensive nor dominant nor reliable, by whom "his native language is considered gibberish; his behavior, madness; his faith, heathenism" (Kaplan, 145). It is only for the ears of the narrow-minded, mean-spirited community of Kentish villagers that the protagonist utters "'human accents'...of no more account than parrotting" and is "[d]eprived of comprehendable language" (see Epstein, 227), that his native speech is perceived in terms of animal sounds (Maisonnat, 117-18). Thus, indeed, he "never fully inhabits language" (Epstein, 228) – the English language, of course. On the other hand, he does consciously "inhabit" his native dialect which organizes his impressions into concepts and categories, but which is completely misapprehended, of no use in Kent (Maisonnat, 116-17), and not articulated at all in the text of "Amy Foster" by its silent protagonist.

In their treatment of Goorall the Kentish villagers follow the patterns of behavior typical of a primitive community: they regard their *orbis interior*, culture and ethnos, as the only existing and valuable one, and the outside world, the *orbis exterior* – as the habitation of devils, demons and other dangerous creatures. Any stranger is viewed as unwelcome visitor and any intervention from outside – as threatening the indigenous people (Krajka, "The Alien...," especiallly 209-10). "[T]his mean-spirited little community can only be maintained by actually locking him [the newcomer] up" (Epstein, 228). On the other hand, the more intelligent villagers, surpassing their dull-spirited mass, recognize Yanko's foreignness, though they are not able to locate it properly: Swaffer considers him an outlandish curiosity and looks upon him with interest; two rectory ladies try German and Italian on him but with no success; Kennedy regards him as an unhappy, lonely stranger personifying a general truth about humanity.

The outcast Goorall's is indeed not a *birth* (see Epstein, Maisonnat) but a *re-birth* to language, culture, humanity and social respectability, to consciousness of man's individual and social plight. In his original East Carpathian milieu he was immersed in the rich culture and ethnos of the region, in its elaborate social framework; both before emigration and in Kent he spoke his native dialect. Hence, his emergence from the sea definitely is not one from zero degree of culture, from an embryo of humanity, to climb up the evolutionary tree. On his landing in Kent his original identity is lost and he has "to be re-constructed as a new subject by the British villagers of his new place of residence" (Maisonnat, 104). Thus, his is not a *birth* (as Maisonnat and Epstein assert) but a *re-birth*, a *re-entry* into the symbolic order of language constructing the subject, which, not helped by the Kentish villagers, he fails to achieve.

Epstein and Maisonnat's interpretations concern only the second half of Yanko's journey (the emergence from the sea and his subsequent ordeal in England) and completely ignore its first half (the departure from his East Carpathian homeland and travel by railway and ship). It seems that the theoretical framework of the rite of passage (Van Gennep, Leach) is more appropriate for reading Yanko's experiences, as it takes into account their totality. His ordeal is indeed one of petrified liminality, with the stage of separation completed and the stage of aggregation unfulfilled. By leaving his homeland he got separated from it, physically and spatially (although he remained deeply rooted in his native culture and persisted in speaking his original dialect). And his minimal degree of assimilation to the English peasant community made his aggregation far from complete. Thus, Goorall is posed in a state of "betwixt and between," neither here nor there, in a dangerous zone – which produces his crisis of identity. He does not emerge from nothingness to culture and language: he rather passes from one culture and language to another; symbolically his journey is "a rebirth into an existence entirely different from his life in the Carpathians" (Lupack, 443).

The protagonist lives in Kent "without the protection of linguistic and social familiarity" (Epstein, 228). His impressionistic account of his journey out of East-Central Europe, revealing his inability to organize impressions "into the ordinary currency of language...to perceive the system behind the event" (227-8), does not testify to his childlike perception of the world but to his ethnocentric outlook – precluding his understanding and conceptualization in English of the phenomena alien to his domestic reality, triggering off his confused reactions to the new realm he enters. They are not those of a new-born baby, unable to identify, conceive and structure the surrounding world, posed "at the outset of the process of his entry into the symbolic order" (Maisonnat, 110). Yanko's is not an entry but a *re-entry* into such symbolic order, as he functioned in the symbolic order of his original East Carpathian community before leaving it. His actions and customs are not those of a child (as Lupack maintains) but closely follow the rules of his original ethnos.

The protagonist's original ethnic identity would enrich the interpretation of this short story in terms of universal archetypes of Innocence and Experience, strongly charged with positive and negative evaluation respectively (presented by Lupack). His is neither only nor principally the archetypal purity of a "child of nature" in general, but rather of a special variant of Rousseauan "noble savage" – of a child of Carpathian nature. Such archetypal features of Yanko, distinguished by Lupack, as noncorruption by social codes, conventions and morality, spontaneity, strong imagination, instinctive love of the native land, an idyllic perception of the world, living in harmony with nature, were especially characteristic of the ethos of Carpathian highlanders, of their inherent virtue. His attitude is not one of pure Innocence (as Lupack maintains) but one very strongly imbued with natural experience, constituted by the rich social, moral and cultural treasury of this folk group. Thus, Yanko Goorall represents a combination of Innocence and Experience: his conversion in Kent is not "from his primal innocence to worldly experience" (as Lupack, 445, claims) but rather from his Carpathian mixture of innocence and experience to a new mode of experience in Kent.

Explanations of the Polish/Carpathian identity of the protagonist of "Amy Foster" illustrate the critical paradigm described aptly by Brodsky: Western critics' ignorance of Conrad's Polish contexts, resulting in incompetent, unfair or even ridiculous interpretations. He points to "a critical imbalance resulting in sheer misunderstanding, which has gone almost unchallenged" (Brodsky, 12), to "the West's vacuum of knowledge about particular cultural background and without a body of accessible Polish scholarship untainted by political ideology" (12), and continues to write:

> Most other critical biographers have acknowledged Conrad's Polish heritage only *passim*, before retreating hastily to familiar ground, as if to avoid the embarrassment of nescience. English criticism too often has been subjectively intuitive, and American critics have fallen back on archetypes, to plunge (as they have thought) into Conrad's psyche as if he were a cultural *tabula rasa*, often with weird results...the New Criticism, and more recently...Deconstructionist and Postmodern

critical theory,...have continued a trend of destructive Conrad criticism. Largely restricted in knowledge and sentiment to their own cultural tradition, western critics have found it mirrored in the Conrad canon against the dark background of a Polish cultural *terra incognita*. This neglect of Conrad's centuries-old heritage has resulted in some grotesque interpretations of his work...a cultural background of an earlier [Conrad's Polish] past...for too long has been a heart of darkness for western scholarship. (12-13, 29)

NOTES

1. Such erroneous or doubtful speculations are exemplified by Retinger, 112; Meyers, 145-7.

2. Apart from Conrad's own experiences, critics have indicated some other sources of the characters and plot of "Amy Foster," especially of Yanko Goorall: the shipwrecked German sailor appearing in a local tale recorded in F. M. Ford's "The Cinque Ports" (Herndon, 550-4); the Polish sailor Conrad met in The Sailor's Home in Saigon (Gillon, *Joseph Conrad*, 2); the protagonist of Stephen Crane's "The Monster" (Nettels). It has been argued that Amy was modelled upon Jessie Conrad (Herndon, 563-6), the Conrads' servant girl (560, 565), the protagonist of Flaubert's story "Un Coeur simple" (550, 559-62, 566), the Prioress from Chaucer's *The Canterbury Tales* (Beidler). "Amy Foster" has been also considered to reflect Conrad's own marital relationship and domestic life (Graver, 105; Herndon, 549, 563-6; Meyers, 145-7), some of his experiences in Congo (Herndon, 556-9), the topography of the environment of the writer's home in Kent mirrored in the depiction of the locale and village atmosphere (555).

3. Her surname also connotes Old English *fostor* (nourishment) and Old Icelandic *fostr* (food) – see Kurczaba, 95; Maisonnat, 123. The episode with the Smiths' parrot, attacked by a cat and shrieking for help, which Amy fails to save, has been generally interpreted as proleptic of Amy's eventual treatment of Yanko.

4. Possibilities of a Christian interpretation of "Amy Foster" were also suggested by Andreach ("The Two Narrators...," 266), Meyer (352), Nettels (185), Pinsker (182).

5. Carabine (191-2, 196, 199-200) calls Kennedy a Marlovian narrator.

6. According to Hooper, Kennedy represents the morality of naturalism which sanctifies Yanko's tragedy (Hooper, 57); he is partly responsible for the protagonist's death, "is guilty at least of a crucial failure of perception and insight, at worst of dereliction of duty" (61), which is however never acknowledged in this short story, as Amy's is.

7. Some have argued that Conrad, intending to help sell the story to the English reading public, entitled it "Amy Foster" (rather than "A Husband"

or "A Castaway"), which made Amy, rather than Yanko, the principal focus of interest (e.g. Graver, 108). Others have claimed that Amy's central importance is justified by the internal semantic organization of this short story (Epstein, 229, 232; Fraser, 190-1) rather than by any reading-market strategies. Still others have argued for Yanko Goorall's central importance (Maisonnat, 104; Krajka, "The Dialogue..."; "The Alien..."). According to Hooper, the title emphasizes Amy's significance and in a way compensates for her inarticulacy (Hooper, 64).

8. However, the majority of critics interpret Amy's action as a true humane gesture: e.g., according to Wasiolek (419), she manages to bridge the gap between the foreigner and the indigenous community "by the universal language of compassion" (Wasiolek, 419).

9. An opposite, erroneous view is conveyed by Morf and Perłowski's implication that Yanko's Slavic ethnos was intended to mask his essentially Polish, Tatra highlander identity, as Conrad avoided Polish themes in his writings published for English readers (Morf, 225-6; Perłowski, 121).

10. Wasiolek's claim that Amy manages to capture the pathos of Yanko's name by calling their son "Johnny, little John" seems wrong: it is this pathos which makes the difference between his original name and its English equivalents.

11. According to the Polish proverb – *Gość w dom, Bóg w dom* (A visitor at home is God at home) – any guest is treated like God, i.e. with open-heartedness, hospitality and eagerness to please.

WORKS CITED

Andreach Robert J. "The Two Narrators of 'Amy Foster'," *Studies in Short Fiction*, 2: 3 (Spring 1965), 262-9.

Andreach Robert. *The Slain and Resurrected God. Conrad, Ford, and the Christian Myth.* New York – London: New York U.P. – U. of London P., 1970.

Beidler Peter G. "Conrad's 'Amy Foster' and Chaucer's Prioress," *Nineteenth Century Fiction*, 30: 1 (June 1975), 111-15.

Brodsky Stephen G. W. "Conrad's Two Polish Pasts: A History of Thirty Years of Critical Misrule," in *Conrad and Poland*, ed. Alex S. Kurczaba. Boulder – Lublin – New York: East European Monographs – Maria Curie-Skłodowska University – Columbia U.P., 1996, 9-31; *Conrad: Eastern and Western Perspectives*, ed. Wiesław Krajka, vol. 5.

Burgess C. F. "Conrad's Catholicism," *Conradiana*, 15: 2 (1983), 111-26.

Busza Andrzej. "Amy Foster," in Busza Andrzej, "Conrad's Polish Literary Background and Some Illustrations of the Influence of Polish Literature on His Work," *Antemurale* (Institutum Historicum Polonicum Romae; Societas Polonica Scientiarum et Litterarum in Exteris Londini; Romae – Londini: 1966), 10, 224-30.

Carabine Keith. "'Irreconcilable Differences': England as an 'Undiscovered Country' in Conrad's 'Amy Foster'," in *The Ends of the Earth*, ed. Simon Gatrell. London: The Ashfield Press, 1992, 187-204.

D'Elia Gaetano. "Yanko, the Man who Came from the Sea: A Note on Conrad's 'Amy Foster'," *Conradiana*, 11: 2 (1979), 165-76.

Epstein Hugh. "'Where He Is not Wanted': Impression and Articulation in 'The Idiots' and 'Amy Foster'," *Conradiana*, 23: 3 (1991), 221-32.

Fogel Aaron. *Coercion to Speak. Conrad's Poetics of Dialogue*. Cambridge, Mass.: Harvard U.P., 1985.

Fraser Gail. "Conrad's Revisions to 'Amy Foster'," *Conradiana*, 20: 3 (1988), 181-93.

Gennep Arnold van. *The Rites of Passage*, trans. M. B. Vizedom, G. L. Caffee. Chicago: U. of Chicago P., 1960.

Gillon Adam. *Joseph Conrad*. Boston: Twayne, 1982.

Gillon Adam. *The Eternal Solitary. A Study of Joseph Conrad*. New York: Bookman, 1960.

Goetel Ferdynand. "Na Podhalu," *Wiadomości Literackie* (Warszawa), 1934: 33 (560), 20.

Graver Lawrence. *Conrad's Short Fiction*. Berkeley – Los Angeles: U. of California P., 1969.

Griem Eberhard. "Physiological Possibility in Joseph Conrad's 'Amy Foster': The Problem of Narrative Technique," *Conradiana*, 24: 2 (1992), 126-34.

Griffith John W. *Joseph Conrad and the Anthropological Dilemma. "Bewildered Traveller."* Oxford: Clarendon Press, 1995.

Guerard Albert J. *Conrad the Novelist*. Cambridge, Mass.: Harvard U.P., 1958.

Gurko Leo. *Joseph Conrad. Giant in Exile*. New York: MacMillan, 1962.

Hay Eloise Knapp. "Reconstructing 'East' and 'West' in Conrad's Eyes," in *Contexts for Conrad*, eds. Keith Carabine, Owen Knowles, Wiesław Krajka. Boulder – Lublin – New York: East European Monographs – Maria Curie-Skłodowska University – Columbia U.P., 1993, 21-40; *Conrad: Eastern and Western Perspectives*, ed. Wiesław Krajka, vol. 2.

Herndon Richard. "The Genesis of Conrad's 'Amy Foster'," *Studies in Philology*, 57: 3 (July 1960), 549-66.

Hooper Myrtle. "'Oh, I Hope He Won't Talk': Narrative and Silence in 'Amy Foster'," *The Conradian*, 21: 2 (Autumn 1996), 51-64.

Jasińska Barbara. "Adresat 'Amy Foster'," in *Studia conradowskie*, ed. Stefan Zabierowski. Katowice: Uniwersytet Śląski, 1976, 199-205.

Kaplan Carola M. "Conrad the Pole: Definitively not 'One of Us'," in *Conrad and Poland*, ed. Alex S. Kurczaba. Boulder – Lublin – New York: East European Monographs – Maria Curie-Skłodowska University – Columbia U.P., 1996, 135-51; *Conrad: Eastern and Western Perspectives*, ed. Wiesław Krajka, vol. 5.

Karl Frederick R. *Joseph Conrad. The Three Lives. A Biography*. London: Faber and Faber, 1979.

Krajka Wiesław. *Isolation and Ethos. A Study of Joseph Conrad*. Boulder – New York: East European Monographs – Columbia U. P., 1992.

Krajka Wiesław. "The Alien in Joseph Conrad's 'Amy Foster' and Jerzy Kosiński's *The Painted Bird*," in *Conrad and Poland*, ed. Alex S. Kurczaba. Boulder – Lublin – New York: East European Monographs – Maria Curie-Skłodowska University – Columbia U. P., 1996, 195-215; *Conrad: Eastern and Western Perspectives*, ed. Wiesław Krajka, vol. 5.

Krajka Wiesław. "The Dialogue of Cultures in Joseph Conrad's 'Amy Foster'," *New Comparison*, 9 (Spring 1990), 149-57.

Kurczaba Alex. "Witold Gombrowicz's 'Princess Ivona' and Joseph Conrad's 'Amy Foster'," *L'Epoque Conradianne*, 19 (1993), 85-105.

Leach Edmund. *Culture and Communication. The Logic by which Symbols Are Connected*. Cambridge: Cambridge U. P., 1976.

Lupack Barbara Tepa. "Conrad's 'Amy Foster': A Study of Innocence and Experience," *Études Anglaises*, 36: 4 (octobre-décembre 1983), 440-7.

Maisonnat Claude. "Exile, Betrayal and the Foreclosure of the Name-of--the-Father in 'Amy Foster'," *L'Epoque Conradienne*, 18 (1992), 103-24.

McLauchlan Juliet. "'Amy Foster' – Echoes from Conrad's Own Experience?," *The Polish Review*, 23: 3 (1978), 3-8.

Meyer Bernard C. *Joseph Conrad. A Psychoanalytic Biography*. Princeton, N.J.: Princeton U. P., 1967.

Meyers Jeffrey. *Joseph Conrad. A Biography*. New York: Charles Scribner's Sons, 1991.

Morf Gustav. *The Polish Shades and Ghosts of Joseph Conrad*. New York: Astra Books, 1976.

Moser Thomas. *Joseph Conrad. Achievement and Decline*. Cambridge, Mass.: Harvard U. P., 1957.

Najder Zdzisław. *Joseph Conrad. A Chronicle*, trans. Halina Carroll--Najder. New Brunswick, N.J.: Rutgers, U. P., 1983.

Nettels Elsa "'Amy Foster' and Stephen Crane's 'The Monster'," *Conradiana*, 15: 3 (1983), 181-90.

Perłowski Jan. "O Conradzie i Kiplingu," in *Wspomnienia i studia o Conradzie*, ed. Barbara Kocówna. Warszawa: Państwowy Instytut Wydawniczy, 1963, 110-31.

Pinsker Sanford. "'Amy Foster': A Reconsideration," *Conradiana*, 9: 2 (1977), 179-86.

Purdy Dwight H. *Joseph Conrad's Bible*. Norman: U. of Oklahoma P., 1984.

Retinger Joseph H. *Conrad and His Contemporaries*. New York: Roy, 1943.

Ruppel Richard. "Yanko Goorall in the Heart of Darkness: 'Amy Foster' as Colonialist Text," *Conradiana*, 28: 2 (1996), 126-32.

Schwarz Daniel R. *Conrad: "Almayer's Folly" to "Under Western Eyes."* Ithaca, N.Y.: Cornell U. P., 1980.

Turno Witold [Tarnawski Wit]. "Conrad a Janko Góral," *Wiadomości Literackie* (Warszawa), 1934: 47 (574), 7.
Urbisz Krystyna. "The Theme of Isolation in Joseph Conrad," *Zeszyty Naukowe Uniwersytetu Jagiellońskiego. Prace Historycznoliterackie*, 29 (1974), 291-305.
Yim Sung-Kyun. "Distancing and Mystifying: Conrad's Narrative Technique in 'Amy Foster' and 'The Lagoon'," *English Language and Literature*, 42: 4 (1996), 827-38.
Wasiolek Edward. "Yanko Goorall, A Note on Name Symbolism in Conrad's 'Amy Foster'," *Modern Language Notes*, 71 (1956), 418-19.

Anna Brzozowska-Krajka,
Maria Curie-Skłodowska University,
Lublin, Poland

Yanko Goorall: A Waxwork from the Wax Museum of Polish Romanticism

Why was a highlander from East Carpathians, and not an inhabitant of any other region of Poland, selected by Conrad to become the protagonist of his short story "Amy Foster?" This apparently plain question provides a key to the interpretation of this short story as well as to some fundamental aspects of Joseph Conrad's creative personality. The present attempt at answering this question is meant to penetrate through his mask and to shed some light upon the hidden dialogue between his first and second homelands, permanently taking place in his psyche. The two determinants of the protagonist's identity – *genius loci* (East Carpathian borderland) and race (the ethnonym "Goorall") – indicate romantic, and not later, roots of his creative intention. These two categories point explicitly to the vitality of the romantic mythologization of the East Carpathians and their culture: they penetrate to the very heart of the romantic ideology. My thesis opposes that of Busza who argues for the Young Poland (modernist) "Tatromania" as inspiring and influencing the creation of "Amy Foster."[1] This fascination concerned primarily West Carpathian (Tatra) highlanders and not East Carpathian ones (*huculi*) which make the homeland of the protagonist of "Amy Foster."[2] This definite location was rather inspired by the *romantic cult of Polish eastern borderland* – the cult of a native home.[3] Conrad, too, identified himself with such "family nest" by regarding himself as a nobleman (*szlachcic*) from the Ukraine.[4]

An East Carpathian highlander belonged to the pantheon of romantic "saints"[5] – idealized and worshipped figures. A romantic rendering of this geographical-cultural region, especially between 1825-1865, became a matter of literary fashion. It resulted from the ideology of romanticism which promoted regionalism, comprising visions of Polish landscapes with relics of their past, and was almost obsessed with region and its sociology. The cult of the historical, the folkloric and the exotic constituted other basic components of this ideology. It amounted to cultural and social nobilitation of the milieu and social strata underappreciated or despised before by the rigorous doctrine of classicism, and it regarded peasants as the uncontaminated foundation of the indigenous element, the only canon of romantic faith.

For Poles, East Carpathians constituted the exotic East, like Siberia and Caucasus. These mountainous eastern fringe areas of the former Polish Commonwealth were associated with the elemental force of an archaic Slavic race. This region was regarded as preserving such features in pure form, untainted by civilization. East Carpathians were a part of Ukraine whose romantic image and cultural identity permanently existed in Polish spiritual culture. In idealistic imagination of Polish romantics this was a region of dialogue and friendship, of reciprocal responsibility and union. For many eminent Polish romantic writers (e.g. S. Goszczyński, J. B. Zaleski, K. Rzewuski, A. Malczewski, J. Słowacki) and also for Conrad's father, Apollo Korzeniowski, and for the Korzeniowski and Bobrowski families – Ukraine was native land, the Edenic land of childhood and youth.

In the XIXth century and earlier Ukraine was regarded as belonging to the sphere of Polish cultural-political influence, as a region of Poland, an integral component of the realm of Polish culture, a part of the Polish Commonwealth, legally and historically – and not as a separate country. The history of this land was co-created by the Polish nobility (*szlachta*) guarding the south-eastern and eastern borders of the Polish state. It was in Ukraine where the myth of Polish borderland chivalry as a bulwark of Christianity (*Antemurale Christianitatis*) was born, where ideals of the noble knight were cultivated and practised the longest. Thus, Ukraine was a mythical treasury of Polish chivalric past. Scattered in this land were graves of Poles' ancestors who had performed feats of valor by guarding the greatness of the state.[6] According to M. Mochnacki, Ukraine was the true "Scotland of Poland"[7] – the fascinating exotic land located so close to ethnic Poland and yet so different from her. Another Polish romantic writer, K. W. Wójcicki, expressed a typical opinion that no region of Poland (except for the Cracow area) surpassed the beauty of Ukraine – the paradise of Poland.[8] And East Carpathians (the land of *huculi*) were advertized (until well into the XXth century) as a fringe area of exquisite beauty, grandiose mountains, murmuring brooks – as one of the most interesting regions in the geographical atlas of Poland.[9]

Polish romantic writers, born mostly in the eastern areas of the Polish Commonwealth, deeply felt this uniqueness and charm of Ukraine and her past, as well as her resultant privileged position, providing a more "poetic" status than that of other regions of Poland.[10] This fascinating country, and especially its two principal figures – cossack and highlander – supplied material for literary creations. Not only were they attractive anthropologically, but they personified romantic yearning for strangeness and liberty, nonexistent in the partitioned Polish Commonwealth; they combined a drive for freedom with the instinct of self-preservation. This vision was clearly formulated by M. Janion:

> Cossacks and highlanders? Yes, gifted with a particularly strong instinct for independence, these two social groups fused into a free folk in Polish romantic imagination. These two types of characters functioned as principal impersonations of ideals of the folk, natural way of life (past or present), of the sense of freedom, independence and pride cherished by lower strata of the society. Mostly cossacks appeared in this role in works of the "Ukrainian School" of Polish romantic literature; but later also highlanders.[11]

Cossacks and highlanders constituted the free folk of Polish romantics – both owing to their historical past, to their freedom from feudal serfdom, and to the landscape in which they lived. The key value of freedom pervaded all elements of Polish Carpathian highlander culture: images of the land, of *polonina* (mountain pasture), the collective way of living, the dress, and even the appearance of a man's head – long wavy hair falling on broad shoulders.[12] Nature and History determined the rich spirituality of these people: they became a symbol of dormant power and the hope of Poland, permanently associated with ideals of liberty, independence and heroism. Under the circumstances of national and political thraldom, Polish romanticism took for its manifesto J. J. Rousseau's maxim: a man is born free. Thus, romantic heroes were fashioned as "apostles of freedom."[13]

Such was the romantic outfit of the protagonist of Joseph Conrad's "Amy Foster": "a mountaineer of the eastern range of the Carpathians" ("Amy Foster," *TS*, 121). He perfectly fits the stereotype of the romantic hero who strives for independence and happiness, gifted with a syndrome of features constituting these two crucial values. The subsequent comparative analysis is intended to prove Yanko Goorall's affinity with this romantic model (*genotyp*) – through distancing and evaluating reflection of this "picture in the head" (in terms of W. Lippmann, the originator of the theory of stereotype).[14] It could have been created by the following set of factors: the cult of freedom derived from family traditions, the cultural-political atmosphere in Lvov and Cracow, young Conrad's stay with his father in Topolnica (south of Sambor),[15] young Conrad's summer holidays in Krynica,[16] a possible excursion in the direction of the Tatra mountains,[17] the education given by Izydor Kopernicki (Apollo Korzeniowski's and Tadeusz Bobrowski's friend, a physician, anthropologist and ethnographer),[18] possible personal contacts with or reading works by Lucjan Malinowski (a collector and lover of folklore),[19] and Wincenty Pol (a poet, geographer and ethnographer).[20] This image could have also been created by young Conrad's reading of geographic-ethnographic magazines (which he found particularly interesting)[21] and of the play *Karpaccy górale* (Carpathian highlanders) by Józef Korzeniowski (also of the Nałęcz coat of arms), included in the secondary school curriculum in Galicia; it is also highly possible he could see this play on stage in Lvov or Cracow.[22]

Such image could have been stimulated by Conrad's probable hiking trip during the Easter of 1874 with Pulman from Lvov to East Carpathians, reported by Najder.[23]

Like his romantic antecedents, the protagonist of Conrad's "Amy Foster" is a strong, unique individuality, of provincial descent. Romantic writers regarded provinces, especially the south-eastern and eastern borderland, as a sanctuary of tradition,[24] as a region which produced noncommonplace people of marked individuality and elevated them to the status of a romantic hero. For being "other," they had to pay a high price of suffering and of eventual failure of their mission. These distinctive qualities are very strongly marked in Conrad's creation of Yanko Goorall. He is portrayed by Dr. Kennedy, who assumes the role of a guide explaining this peculiar specimen, as "Quite a curiosity, isn't he?" (126) – later "domesticated" by old Swaffer who is very fond of various kinds of outlandish curiosities. Such presentation of the protagonist largely arises from application of typical devices of stylization, which pertain to romantic care for local color – a key attribute in romantic delineation of provinces, corresponding to romantic presentation and appreciation of the peasant folk. According to the classical principle of synthesizing (typifying), this decorum was meant not to lead to detailed description of a different social-cultural reality, but rather to function as a sign of identification of an exotic hero.[25] Conrad developed this principle of relative verisimilitude in order to stronger articulate his ideological stance.

The very exotic name of this character – Yanko, i.e. little John – served as such signal of identification. It was the most popular patronymic among Polish highlanders, almost a tribal denomination: according to a XIXth century manuscript describing customs practised in this region, six out of ten young male highlanders were named so. This manuscript follows to argue that *Jan* (John) was the hero of all folk tales of this region, personifying all supreme virtues and feats and that this name was regarded superior to all others. Baptizing by other Christian male names was unwillingly accepted in this milieu. A loving, exemplary Christian couple was expected to christen their

                                    Anna Brzozowska-Krajka

children by their own names: intergenerational transmission made them inherited.[26] Thus, in the name of Conrad's protagonist, the suffix "*ko*" is particularly significant. Linguistic investigations have proven this suffix appeared in all proper names in the Polish language spoken by inhabitants of Lvov and of Poland's south-eastern territory until 1939. It performed a patronymic and diminutive-hypocoristic function.[27] The name Yanko, i.e. *Jan*'s (John's) son, pointed to the area of borderland of cultures: it both identified the hero with this exotic province and was the first signal of Polishness.

Exactly the same geographical-cultural location is implied by Yanko Goorall's speech: "at first in a sort of anxious baby-talk, then, as he acquired the language, with great fluency, but always with that singing, soft, and at the same time vibrating intonation that instilled a strangely penetrating power into the sound of the most familiar English words, as if they had been the words of an unearthly language" (117). The dialect of the south-eastern part of the Polish Commonwealth was interspersed with Ukrainian influences. The grammar and phonetics of Poles inhabiting these areas was distinguished by profuse use of diminutives, and melodious, soft, sing-song manner of speech.[28]

Romantic Polonophilism, enriched with overtones of romantic Messianism, determined the portrait of the protagonist of "Amy Foster." Here Conrad made use of the stereotype of the Pole-Catholic which functioned in Polish tradition since the XVIIth century (evocation of biographical context and of autobiographical *The Arrow of Gold* proves it to be deeply rooted in the writer's mind). It denoted a man of intense faith, who sensed God in the surrounding space, and who followed God's unwritten, eternal laws through prayers and good deeds, aimed at gaining Divine grace.

Ironically enough, the seal of God's approval was put on Yanko Goorall's journey into the unknown: "before he left his home, he drove his mother in a wooden cart [to "the miraculous Holy Image in the yard of the Carmelite Convent"]: – a pious old woman who wanted to offer prayers and make a vow for his safety" (115). However, Conrad was not true to historical facts in the construction of this fictional image. Most East Carpathian highlanders belonged to the Orthodox Church. No historical sources testify to the existence of a carmelite convent in the specific geographical location evoked by Conrad in "Amy Foster" (the East Carpathian area).[29] Most probably the Marian sanctuary in Berdyczów is the empirical prototype of the Carmelite Convent mentioned in the text of Conrad's "Amy Foster." Since the XVIIIth century it was the principal center of Catholic cult in Ukraine – analogous to Częstochowa in Poland and Wilno (Ostra Brama) in Lithuania. The image of Madonna of the Carmelite Convent in Berdyczów was the pride of Ukraine, Volhynia and Podolia, the protection for inhabitants of these areas. It was painted in the XVIth century on a canvass stuck to a cypress board. It was a copy of the archetypal *Salus Populi Romani* from the Santa Maria Maggiore Basilica in Rome. It was famous for many graces. In 1752 it was announced as miraculous by the Church. On approval of Pope Benedict XIV, it was crowned with papal golden crowns. The sanctuary was the destination of numerous pilgrimages from the entire Ukraine, Volhynia and Podolia.[30]

The transferrence of the Marian sanctuary from Berdyczów into Yanko Goorall's East Carpathian milieu enhances Conrad's strong intentional polonization of his protagonist. He is clearly shaped according to the principle of triple identity: an East Carpathian highlander, a Carpathian highlander (see his ethnonym "Goorall"), a Pole. This tendency prevailed in Poland since the time of S. Staszic (the end of the XVIIIth century), through romantic fascinations of S. Goszczyński, Ż. Pauli, L. Pietrusiński, Delaveaux, A. Wrześniowski and W. Pol, and continued until researchers active in the time of Conrad's Polish youth who attributed purely Polish or pan-Carpathian features to the Carpathian region and its culture (e.g. Izydor Kopernicki). These views were more a matter of wishful thinking, dreams and ideals, than of cool appreciation of reality. A Carpathian community was perceived by Polish romantics as Polish. In the delineation of his protagonist, Conrad yielded to this principle as well: he combined East Carpathian exotic ethnographic local color and culture with appropriate ideology and romantic techniques of stereotypical presentation.

Conrad emphasized Yanko Goorall's religious ardor (his family heritage) by means of magico-cultic images: "the string with a couple of brass medals the size of a sixpence, a tiny metal cross, and a square sort of scapulary which he wore round his neck" (131). According to folk beliefs, multiplication of such objects was intended to strengthen their protective power. The same function was performed by cultic ways of sacralization of time and place: making the sign of cross before a meal, saying the morning prayers, evening kneeling in prayer: "he was still to be heard every evening reciting the Lord's Prayer, in incomprehensible words and in a slow, fervent tone, as he had heard his old father do at the head of all the kneeling family, big and little, on every evening of his life" (131; see also 128). Highlighting essential elements of the home ritual (typical especially of folk religion) points to the communal, protective function of religion in Polish customs. The paradigm of a good Pole-Catholic (as distinct from members of other religions), included a set of features that implied his moral superiority. How strongly they are set against the English provincial mentality depicted in "Amy Foster":

> he remembered the pain of his wretchedness and misery, his heart-broken astonishment that it was neither seen nor understood, his dismay at finding all the men angry and all the women fierce. He had approached them as a beggar, it is true, he said; but in his country, even if they gave nothing, they spoke gently to beggars. The children in his country were not taught to throw stones at those who asked for compassion. (124)

Polish romantics logically and self-consciously argued for a need for faith. Therefore, religion and morality constituted the basis of their political programme, literature and activities. For them, God and all His manifestations were the foundation of complete systems of philosophy of history, as well as of human attitudes and social psychology.[31] According to the doctrine of romantic pantheism, they also attempted to find God's thoughts in "books of Nature." Divine harmony was reflected in an individual's moral sense of world order. Hence, those living close to nature were regarded as morally perfect, and Polish folk, and consequently Polish nation, were the people of "naturally pure hearts": Polish romantics, after J. G. Herder, identified folk with nation,[32] which led to viewing folk as the exclusive embodiment of nationality, and folk culture as the only national culture.[33] The Rousseauan conception of man as a child of nature fulfilled this ideal; it was also accomplished in Conrad's delineation of Yanko Goorall. He made this character representative of romantic vitality, an integral part of the organism of Nature, the universe. The protagonist's dialogue with nature, conducted in symbolic language, combines the conscious with the unconscious in a typically romantic way. These ties, resulting from regarding man as an offspring of nature, were incomprehensible to the English villagers in "Amy Foster," a substantial component of the "otherness" and queerness of this stranger, viewed by them as a visitor from another world. Yanko Goorall knows the meaning of rain, wind, of bleating of sheep (124). He treats as brothers three Norwegian pine-trees growing in front of Swaffer's house: they remind him of his East Carpathian homeland and are the confidantes of his grief and tragedy. Yanko's spirituality, sensitivity and nostalgia constitute essential features of the romantic image of East Carpathian highlander. The latter characteristic has become almost a cliché: according to the popular song "Czerwony pas" (red belt) based on Maksym's song in Józef Korzeniowski's play *Karpaccy górale* (Carpathian highlanders),[34] for an East Carpathian highlander the best place to live is his mountain pasture ("*Dla Hucuła nie ma życia, jak na połoninie, | gdy go losy w doły, doły rzucą, wnet z tęsknoty zginie*" – when taken out of this environment, he soon dies of homesickness).

The image of child of nature is manifest even in Yanko's outward appearance: he is a handsome young highlander, "designed" by lofty mountains according to the principle of romantic historical-geographical determinism. His upright stature reflects the romantic tendency to vertical perception of highlanders.[35] This verticalism is clearly visible in his presentation against the indigenous Kentish community inscribed in horizontal space:

> But here on this same road you might have seen amongst these heavy men a being lithe, supple and long-limbed, straight like a pine, with something striving upwards in his appearance as though the heart within him had been buoyant. Perhaps it was only the force of the contrast, but when he was passing one of these villagers here, the soles of his feet did not seem to me to touch the dust of the road. (111)

Parallelism of man and nature appears also in the metaphorical image of Yanko as "a woodland creature" (111) and "a wild bird caught in a snare" (126). The latter stereotypical symbol denotes a set of meanings connected with the archetype of freedom, following the sequence of associations: man – bird – freedom. They were inherent both in Carpathian highlander folk songs (see e.g. the one starting with the words: "***Hej, wolny jo, chłopiec wolny / wolny jako ptosek polny" – I am a free young highlander, like a bird in the field) and in their literary prototype, the poem "Huculska ptaszyna" (an East Carpathian bird) by K. B. Antoniewicz (1847), a sentimental romantic author.[36] This poem was widespread in the artistic milieu in Lvov and largely determined the character of East Carpathian tradition in Polish literature. Conrad's application of such folk song imagery stressed the dissonance between the role of Nature, its immanent divinity (romantic pantheism), and the plight of the protagonist who lives according to her rules; though socially degraded, he is morally pure and spiritually superior to the indigenous provincial English community. Yanko Goorall's strong individuality, inherent in his role and tragic fate, constitutes a barrier that effectively prevents his assimilation. His peregrination illustrates the pattern of the romantic, XIXth century journey, which most often was not concluded with return to one's family nest – unlike journeys in the XVIIth and XVIIIth centuries which were terminated by the return home with some trophy: wealth, wisdom, fame, or experience.[37] The social motivation of the protagonist's behavior was determined by his sense of uncertain future: his migration was hopeful but also entailed homelessness and strong alienation. The principal character of "Amy Foster" (the writer's partial alter ego), too, was imprinted with the romantic pattern of biography: he could not change his nature and was the same man in his new milieu, since he came from outside, from "there." This otherness, a typical feature of the European and Polish romantic hero, assumed in "Amy Foster" the literary form of otherness as Polishness.

Conrad's realization of the character paradigm of the East Carpathian highlander also makes use of another element of a typically romantic model (*genotyp*): the motif of undeserved suffering in portraying the hero as living "in a painful way." Yanko Goorall's life story represents the supremely cruel and tragic predicament of a romantic "pilgrim." He is a typical romantic outstanding individuality, a "queer" stranger placed in the milieu of English province, an apostle of freedom without freedom, a man of cultural borderland who lacks proxemic distance and builds his personal space and space of social interaction on principles of cultural pluralism and respect for other human beings. Yanko's perception of the world follows the distinction between the familiar and the alien – the principle of composition characteristic of genres of popular literature. Such delineation of the protagonist reveals the writer's de-mythologizing stance, which consists in shaking the native system of values cherished by romantics and in an implied polemic against the divine order of the world. The divine harmony turns out not to be the harmony of love. The fictional world of "Amy Foster" is created as godless, or governed by a malicious demiurge (reflecting Conrad's profound, pessimistic conviction about the senseless and unethical world). According to this principle, the angel of love, Amy – who "appeared to his [Yanko's] eyes with the aureole of an angel of light" (124), i.e. a man's good guide and protector, a divine messenger – turns out to be the angel of death.[38] This justifies the central place of its protagonist in the structure of this short story – the giver of life and death, imprinted with ambivalence of the sacred, with divine attributes. The divine lover betrayed Goorall; his striving for freedom led to disaster. The imperfect world produced the supreme tragedy which could befall a Christian: a lonely death with indispensable rites of passage unfulfilled, i.e. an "evil" death. According to Polish folk beliefs, it prevents the moribund from entering God's Kingdom in the Other World, from joining the community of dead ancestors. Such "evil" death left the deceased in a state of permanent liminality,[39] of "betwixt and between," beyond the communities of both the living (which ensured a sense of safety and realization of individual ambitions) and the dead.[40] This constitutes the heart of the deep semantic structure of "Amy Foster." Conrad's choice of the protagonist of folk origin (following the literary doctrine of Polish romanticism) emphasized the immensity of Yanko's tragedy, crucial for comprehending his plight. Through the lack of dialogue, through communication based on the application of incompatible codes, he was deprived of the possibility of change in status, of aggregation to the new community.

"Amy Foster" has a strong imprint of its author's ideological polemic – most clearly manifest in its conclusion, where the religious principle of retribution (one's death determined by the nature of his/her life)[41] is undermined. This text reveals a total bankruptcy of the ideology and axiology greatly appreciated by the author – beliefs in the triumph of freedom, in the happy termination of the romantic journey, in the value of ethical attitude to the world. Yanko Goorall, Dr. Kennedy's exhibit, a figure from the wax museum of Polish romanticism, becomes an anti-pattern, illustrating the incompatibility of romantic ideals with the new reality, the crisis of these ideals and resultant disillusionment. Thus, the Conradian realization (*fenotyp*) of the conventions of Polish romanticism (*genotyp*) assumes the form of a metaphor, or rather allegory, a moral parable, exemplum. In fact, it becomes the writer's own polemic against his inherited tradition, which was shaping him and which could have possibly limited the field of his activity and cramped his individuality. It seems "Amy Foster," like *Lord Jim* (completed just before the writing of "Amy Foster"), portrays Conrad's polemical stance on his romantic heritage – the same crisis of romantic ideology and axiology which might have possibly determined his emigration from Poland, motivated perhaps by a desire to get rid of the burden of his past, to become a new man, symbolically reborn, like a *tabula rasa* which can be filled with completely new experiences, feelings, ideas and values. Conrad's presentation of Yanko Goorall's romantic biography is intentionally entrusted with Dr. Kennedy – an intelligent and ambitious physician of insatiable curiosity, scientific bent and penetrating mind, who "believes that there is a particle of a general truth in every mystery" (106). He resembles his likely Polish prototype, Dr. Izydor Kopernicki, who was one of young Conrad's initiatory fathers in Cracow, implanting in his mind ideas and beliefs of his (Apollo Korzeniowski's and Tadeusz Bobrowski's) generation.

Explanation of Yanko Goorall's mystery sheds light on the personality and life choice of Joseph Conrad who, like the protagonist of "Amy Foster," was himself an alienated superior individual, a romantic pilgrim (the Polish word for pilgrim – *wędrowiec* – denotes the title of the magazine which young Conrad liked to read). In his short story masterpiece "Amy Foster" Conrad admirably managed, by means of romantic techniques of shaping a stereotype, to convey a part of the truth about himself into the creation of the protagonist, an unfortunate adventurer from East Carpathians endowed with romantic features of character and experiences: an elevated conception of individual morality, dignity and honesty, a chivalric spirit, an acute sense of social justice. The typically romantic convention of using an exotic costume to convey patriotism was transformed by Conrad into a largely autobiographical image, an expression of his own ideas.[42] Following the romantic principles of the national spirit of literature, of the creative transformation of elements of folklore, Conrad reinterpreted his earlier views in terms of irony (another key category of romantic aesthetic).[43] Thus, by applying the conceptual framework of romanticism and the romantic "vocabulary" of patriotic lyrical poetry, Conrad's "Amy Foster" echoes the romantic thesis about a distinct and specific nature of Polish national mentality – a recurrent idea in Polish nonfictional writings at the end of the XIXth and the beginning of the XXth century.

NOTES

1. Andrzej Busza, "Conrad's Polish Literary Background and Some Illustrations of the Influence of Polish Literature on His Work," *Antemurale* (Romae – Londini: 1966; Institutum Historicum Polonicum Romae; Societas Polonica Scientiarum et Litterarum in Exteris Londini), 10, 228-30.

2. Jan Majda, *Młodopolskie Tatry literackie* (Kraków: Wydawnictwo Literackie, 1989).

3. Jacek Kolbuszewski, "Romantyczne Tatry, romantyczni górale," in *Tatry i górale w literaturze polskiej. Antologia,* ed. Jacek Kolbuszewski (Wrocław: Ossolineum, 1992), xxxvii-xlii.

4. Joseph Conrad, "To Józef Korzeniowski," 14th February 1901, in *CL,* II, 322-3.

5. Janina Kamionkowa, "Obyczaj romantyczny. Rekonesans," in *Problemy polskiego romantyzmu,* vol. 1, ed. Maria Żmigrodzka, Zofia Lewinówna (Wrocław: Ossolineum, 1971), 371.

6. George G. Grabowicz, "Ukraina," in *Słownik literatury polskiej XIX wieku,* ed. Józef Bachórz, Alina Kowalczykowa (Wrocław: Ossolineum, 1991), 977.

7. Maurycy Mochnacki, *Pisma po raz pierwszy edycją książkową objęte,* ed., Intro. Artur Śliwiński (Lwów: 1910), 200.

8. Kazimierz Władysław Wójcicki, "Nad-Prucie. Wyjątek z opisu Pokucia," *Kwartalnik Naukowy,* 2 (1835), 94; see also a similar opinion by Mieczysław Romanowski, "Kilka dni w górach Pokucia," *Dziennik Literacki,* 1857: 138, 1235.

9. Jan A. Choroszy, *Huculszczyzna w literaturze polskiej* (Wrocław: Uniwersytet Wrocławski, 1991), 179; Renata Hołda, "Galicja, Arkadia, Utopia," *Literatura Ludowa,* 1995: 4/5, 27-42.

10. George G. Grabowicz, op. cit., 977.

11. Maria Janion, "Kozacy i górale," in *Z dziejów stosunków literackich polsko-ukraińskich,* ed. Stefan Kozak, Marian Jakóbiec (Wrocław: Ossolineum, 1974), 135.

12. Józef Korzeniowski, *Karpaccy górale. Dramat w trzech aktach,* ed. Stefan Kawyn (Wrocław: Ossolineum, 1969), 5.

13. Janina Kamionkowa, op. cit., 372.

14. Walter Lippmann, *Public Opinion,* 1922, quoted after Andrzej Kapiszewski, *Stereotyp Amerykanów polskiego pochodzenia* (Wrocław: Ossolineum, 1977), 11.

15. According to Ludwik Krzyżanowski ("Tatrzański góral i artystyczna telewizja Conrada," *Wiadomości Literackie* «Warszawa», 1934: 43 «570», 6), between March and October 1868 Conrad stayed with his father in Topolnica – south of Sambor, on the border of the Lvov and Stanisławów administrative regions, in the area inhabited by Ruthenian

highlanders. See also "Apollo Korzeniowski to Kazimierz Kaszewski," Biblioteka Jagiellońska, Cracow, MS 3057 [24 June 1868], in *Conrad under Familial Eyes,* ed. Zdzisław Najder, trans. Halina Carroll-Najder (Cambridge: Cambride U.P., 1983), 118-20.

16. He spent there the summer vacations of 1870-72. According to Adam Gillon, *Joseph Conrad* (Boston: Twayne, 1982), 56, and Barbara Kocówna, *Polskość Conrada* (Warszawa: Ludowa Spółdzielnia Wydawnicza, 1967), 40, he spent them with his grandmother, and according to Zdzisław Najder, *Joseph Conrad. A Chronicle,* trans. Halina Carroll-Najder (New Brunswick N.J.: Rutgers U.P., 1983), 31, he was accompanied there by Adam Pulman.

17. It might be implied by Conrad's letter "To Gustaw Sobotkiewicz" of 17/29 March 1890 written from Kazimierówka – see *CL*, I, 4-5, reminiscing his trip on a highlander cart somewhere close to the Polish-Hungarian border in the company of Sobotkiewicz, his daughter Maria (her marriage surname: Dembowska) and Adam Pulman. Especially in the 1860s and 1870s (before the opening of the Cracow – Chabówka railway in 1884 and the Chabówka – Zakopane railway in 1899), such excursions from Cracow in the direction of the Tatra mountains were a very popular tourist attraction. They were a fashionable social pastime of rich townsfolk and landed gentry – see *Tatrami urzeczeni. Dawna turystyka w słowie i obrazie,* ed. Roman Hennel (Warszawa: "Sport i Turystyka," 1979). They made strong impressions on their participants, reflected also in the mentioned letter by Conrad who confesses in his correspondence with Sobotkiewicz that "those earlier impressions, feelings and memories have in no way been erased. And now, reading your letter they are revived more clearly than ever" ("To Gustaw Sobotkiewicz," *CL*, I, 44).

18. According to Zdzisław Najder, *Joseph Conrad. A Chronicle*, 31, "From 1871 on Konrad received additional educational assistance from an eminent anthropologist Izydor Kopernicki, who had been a close friend of Konrad's father and a 'Red' conspirator from the Ukraine as well as a veteran of the 1863 insurrection." See "Tadeusz Bobrowski's Letters to Conrad [Konrad Korzeniowski]," in *Conrad's Polish Background. Letters to and from Polish Friends,* ed. Zdzisław Najder, trans. Halina Carroll (London: Oxford U.P., 1964), no. 18 (3rd/15th August, 1881), 72-5; no. 19 (22 August, 1881), 75-6; no. 20 (30/VIII/10/IX, 1881), 77-8; no. 27 (12th/24th June, 1883), 90-1; no. 28 (27 June/9 July, 1883), 91-2; no. 37 (28 August/9 September, 1886), 109-10. On Izydor Kopernicki's friendship with Apollo Korzeniowski and Tadeusz Bobrowski see Andrzej Busza, 142-6. It seems that Kopernicki's folkloric-ethnographic fascinations which developed after his return to Poland in 1871 and were connected with his active membership in the Anthropological Commission of the Cracow Academy of Sciences (Akademia Umiejętności), could have shaped similar interests of young Conrad. On Kopernicki's contribution to ethnography

and folkloristics see *Dzieje folklorystyki polskiej 1864-1918*, ed. Helena Kapełuś, Julian Krzyżanowski (Warszawa: Państwowe Wydawnictwo Naukowe, 1982), 172-81; Medard Tarko, "I. Kopernicki jako folklorysta," in *Z zagadnień twórczości ludowej. Studia folklorystyczne*, ed. Ryszard Górski, Julian Krzyżanowski (Wrocław: Ossolineum, 1972), 322-32.

19. Lucjan Malinowski was an outstanding dialectologist, collector of folk texts and the father of Bronisław Malinowski – Conrad's later friend (Zdzisław Najder, *Joseph Conrad. A Chronicle*, 483). Between 1870-72 Lucjan Malinowski was a teacher at St. Anne's Gymnasium in Cracow – it is possible that there and then young Conrad could have been exposed to his views and fascinations. In 1872 Lucjan Malinowski published in Cracow his *Listy z podróży etnograficznej po Szląsku* (Letters from ethnographic peregrinations in Silesia). On Lucjan Malinowski's folkloric interests see *Dzieje folklorystyki polskiej...*, 181-9.

20. He spent the last few years of his life in Cracow, where he died in December 1872. He represented "patriotic geography," combining geographic, ethnographic and literary interests. His "poetic" journeys were made mostly in eastern borderlands of the former Polish Commonwealth. See also Wincenty Pol, *Obrazy z życia i natury*, vols. 1-2 (Lwów: 1869-1870).

21. Especially of *Wędrowiec*, a weekly published in Warsaw between 1863-1906. See Zdzisław Najder, *Joseph Conrad. A Chronicle*, 33. See also Bobrowski's letter in which he induces Conrad to write reports from his journeys to *Wędrowiec*: "Tadeusz Bobrowski's Letters to Conrad [Konrad Korzeniowski]," in *Conrad's Polish Background...*, no. 17 (16/28 June, 1881), 71-2.

22. On popularity of Józef Korzeniowski's play *Karpaccy górale* in Galicia in the second half of the XIXth century see Stefan Kawyn, *Józef Korzeniowski. Studia i szkice* (Łódź: Wydawnictwo Łódzkie, 1978), 129 et al.

23. Zdzisław Najder, *Joseph Conrad. A Chronicle*, 35.

24. Marta Piwińska, "Człowiek i bohater," in *Problemy polskiego romantyzmu*, vol. 2, ed. Maria Żmigrodzka (Wrocław: Ossolineum, 1974), 48.

25. Józef Bachórz, "O polskim egzotyzmie romantycznym," in *Problemy polskiego romantyzmu*, vol. 2, 302.

26. Ludwik Kamiński (vel. Kamieński), *O mieszkańcach gór tatrzańskich. Najdawniejsza monografia etnograficzna Podhala*, ed. Jacek Kolbuszewski (Kraków: Oficyna Podhalańska, 1992), 85-6.

27. Zofia Kurzowa, *Polszczyzna Lwowa i kresów południowo-wschodnich do 1939 roku* (Warszawa: Państwowe Wydawnictwo Naukowe, 1985), 116. According to Stefan Warchoł, the suffix *"ko"* performed a diminutive function in Polish proper names already before the XIIIth century – Stefan Warchoł, *Geneza i rozwój słowiańskich formacji ekspresywnych z sufiksem -k, i -c* (Warszawa: Państwowe Wydawnictwo Naukowe, 1984), 186-7; see

also *Słownik staropolski*, ed. Stanisław Urbańczyk, vol. 4 (Wrocław: Ossolineum, 1953), 195-6. Ewa Wolnicz-Pawłowska's investigations in archives showed the suffix *"ko"* to be most productive in the area of the East Carpathian highlands located between the rivers Stryj and San – Ewa Wolnicz-Pawłowska, *Osiemnastowieczne imiennictwo ukraińskie w dawnym województwie ruskim* (Wrocław: Państwowe Wydawnictwo Naukowe, 1978), 38-9; see also Feliks Czyżewski, "Wpływy ukraińskie w gwarze osady Łomazy powiat Biała Podlaska," in *Studia z Filologii Polskiej i Słowiańskiej*, vol. 15 (Warszawa: 1976), 111; Stefan Warchoł, "Elementy wschodniosłowiańskie w nazwach mieszkańców Przemyśla," *Slavica Lublinensia et Olomucensia*, (Lublin: 1977), 177-97.

28. On the speech of *huculi* in East Carpathians see Wincenty Pol, *Prace z etnografii północnych stoków Karpat*, ed. J. Babinicz, Intro. Julian Zborowski (Wrocław: Polskie Towarzystwo Ludoznawcze, 1966), 148-9.

29. *Zakony męskie w Polsce w 1772*, ed. Ludomir Bieńkowski et al. (Lublin: Towarzystwo Naukowe Katolickiego Uniwersytetu Lubelskiego, 1972); Piotr Paweł Gach, *Kasaty zakonów na ziemiach dawnej Rzeczypospolitej i Śląska 1773-1914* (Lublin: Katolicki Uniwersytet Lubelski, 1984); Władysław Chotkowski, *Historia polityczna Kościoła w Galicji*, vol. 2 (Kraków: 1909).

30. X. Witold [Nowakowski], *O cudownym obrazie Najświętszej Maryi P. Berdyczowskiej* (Kraków: 1897), 5; Józef Wanat, "Kult Matki Bożej w Zakonie Karmelitów Bosych w XIX wieku," in *Niepokalana. Kult Matki Bożej na ziemiach polskich w XIX wieku,* ed. Bolesław Pylak, Czesław Krakowiak (Lublin: Katolicki Uniwersytet Lubelski, 1988), 411-12.

31. Marta Piwińska, "Bóg utracony i Bóg odnaleziony," in *Problemy polskiego romantyzmu*, vol. 1, 290.

32. Symbiosis of the concepts of "folk" and "nation" resulted from political ideas of the romantic generation. See Julian Maślanka, "Folklorystyka polska w latach 1831-1863," in *Literatura krajowa w okresie romantyzmu 1831-1863*, vol. 2, ed. Maria Janion et al. (Kraków: 1988), 47-86; Krystyna Poklewska, *Galicja romantyczna (1816-1840)* (Warszawa: Państwowy Instytut Wydawniczy, 1976), 185.

33. Wanda Paprocka, *Kultura i tradycja ludowa w polskiej myśli humanistycznej XIX i XX wieku* (Wrocław: Ossolineum, 1986), 34.

34. Józef Korzeniowski, *Karpaccy górale....*, 7-8; on this feature of the East Carpathian (*hucuł*) spirit see also: Włodzimierz Szuchiewicz, *Huculszczyzna*, vol. 1 (Kraków: 1902), 55.

35. It does not reflect, as Claude Maisonnat maintains ("Exile, Betrayal and the Foreclosure of the Name-of-the-Father in 'Amy Foster'," *L'Epoque Conradienne*, 18 «1992», 123), his struggle into the symbolic order.

36. Jan A. Choroszy, op. cit., 63-4.

37. Marta Piwińska, "Człowiek i bohater...," 53.

38. See a complementary interpretation by Claude Maisonnat, op. cit., 112, in which she is also treated as the angel of death.

39. Anna Brzozowska-Krajka, *Polish Traditional Folklore. The Magic of Time*, trans. Wiesław Krajka (Boulder – Lublin – New York: East European Monographs – Maria Curie-Skłodowska University – Columbia U. P., 1998), 42 ff.

40. On various determinants of liminality see: Victor Turner, "Betwixt and Between: The Liminal Period in Rites de Passage," in Victor Turner, *The Forest of Symbols. Aspects of Ndembu Ritual* (Ithaca N. Y.: Cornell U. P., 1967), 93-111.

41. Marian Filipiak, *Aksjologiczne treści antropologii biblijnej* (Lublin: Uniwersytet Marii Curie-Skłodowskiej, 1991), 16; Anna Brzozowska--Krajka, op. cit., 51.

42. See also Bertrand Russell's intuitive statement that "Amy Foster" constitutes a key to Conrad's psyche: Bertrand Russell, *Portraits from Memory and Other Essays* (New York: Simon and Schuster, 1956), 88-9. See also Zdzisław Najder, *Joseph Conrad. A Chronicle*, 273.

43. On irony as an aesthetic category see Piotr Łaguna, *Ironia jako postawa i jako wyraz (Z zagadnień teoretycznych ironii)* (Kraków: Wydawnictwo Literackie, 1984), 52 et al.; Włodzimierz Szturc, *Ironia romantyczna, pojęcie, granice i poetyka* (Warszawa: Państwowe Wydawnictwo Naukowe, 1992); Włodzimierz Szturc, *Osiem szkiców o ironii* (Kraków: Universitas, 1994).

translated by Wiesław Krajka

Part II

...and Worldwide

Wojciech Kozak,
Maria Curie-Skłodowska University,
Lublin, Poland

Spatial Axiology of the Sea, the Land and Ships in Conrad's Sea Fiction

To understand the problem of spatial axiology in Conrad's marine fiction, one not only needs to locate it in the reality of sailing of the day or to place it in the context of widely-discussed ethos of life at sea.[1] If we assume that no writer remains unaffected by the philosophical and artistic tendencies of his time, it also seems well-founded to relate the question of space in Conrad to the modernist quest for myth.

The crisis of the Western civilization in the late 19th and the early 20th century, brought about by great historical changes, along with revolutionary discoveries in science, to mention but theories of Freud and Einstein, had contributed to a general feeling of despondency, uncertainty about the present and distrust of the future – a feeling that was shared by many writers of the time, who felt a burning need for new principles of artistic creation. As some critics put it, "at the heart of the modernist aesthetic lay the conviction that the previously sustaining structures of human life, whether social, political, religious, or artistic, had been either destroyed or shown up as falsehoods or fantasies."[2] One of the ways to overcome the feeling of all-embracing "catastrophe" was to turn to the past in general and to myth in particular, as expressive of order and cohesion lost in those times. In his essay "Ulysses, Order and Myth" T. S. Eliot argued:

> In using myth, in manipulating a continuous parallel between contemporaneity and antiquity, Mr Joyce is pursuing a method which others must pursue after him.... It is simply a way of controlling, of ordering, of giving shape and significance to the immense panorama of futility and anarchy which is contemporary history....
>
> It is...a step toward making the modern world possible for art...toward order and form.[3]

185

The modernist revival of interest in myth was well-exemplified by the widespread popularity of J. Frazer's *The Golden Bough*, an outstanding and comprehensive study in mythical beliefs and rituals, which many of the writers, Eliot, Joyce, Lawrence and Yeats among them, read and professed to have drawn upon.[4]

Another appreciation of myth as an undying source of literary practice came from N. Frye, who defined the symbolism of The Bible and classical mythology as a grammar of literary archetypes.[5] In a similar manner he wrote that "the structural principles of literature...are to be derived from archetypal and anagogic criticism, the only kinds that assume a larger context of literature as a whole."[6]

It would be a far-fetched statement to say that the author of "Heart of Darkness" was an apologist of myth to the same extent as other modernist writers, such as Eliot or Joyce, were. Critics have relatively rarely pointed to Conrad's reliance on the mythical. More often it has been his innovations in narrative techniques, in the use of symbolism and his investigation into complexity of the human psyche that have been placed among the greatest literary achievements of the writer. It, nonetheless, seems justifiable to the author of this paper to assume that even though Conrad did not explicitly claim affinity with the literary practice of mythopoeia, he was not entirely detached from the spirit of his epoch, for which myth became one of the most fruitful sources of artistic imagery. Critical findings of L. Feder, A. Guerard, J. Darras or V. Young, which point to the presence of the mythical and the mythological in the writer's fiction, and which have been widely recognized among critics, appear to validate this assumption.[7] The sea, ships and the land have been chosen for the foregoing discussion, as they stay in close interrelation and, besides men, are generally agreed to be the major elements of Conrad's fictional world.

The notion of space is crucial for understanding mythical axiology. In mythical worldview space is never homogeneous. There is always a distinction between the friendly, sacred, "our" world, and the hostile, profane and dark domain of demons malevolent to man – a distinction between Cosmos and Chaos, to refer to the terms coined and often used by M. Eliade.[8] The ontological sources of the mentioned dichotomy should be traced back to the group of myths usually referred to as myths of creation. Stories of this sort can be found almost in every mythology. Whatever is the original cause of the world coming into being (its emergence as a result of a verbal act of gods or the work of a demiurge, its physical birth from a deity or by means of magical transformation of objects and creatures, etc.),[9] the essential meaning remains the same: it was through the act of creation, which happened at the beginning of time, that the ultimate separation of Cosmos from Chaos took place. Chaos is most often presented as darkness or night, vacuum, a yawning abyss, and, most importantly, as water. The emergence of the world is therefore seen as a transition from darkness to light, from vacuum to objects, from shapelessness to shape, that is – from destruction to creation.[10]

Generally speaking, the water element is *fons et orgio* – it stands for the source of all existence. Water was present at the beginning of time and has returned at the end of every cosmic cycle to give rise to a new one. It precedes and supports every creation.[11] Such functions of water are to be found in the Judeo-Christian depiction of the rise of the world taken from the Book of Genesis, where water preceded the act of creation. It was also through water, that is the Flood which God sent on earth, that humanity was annihilated and then regenerated into a new cycle, with Noah as its progenitor. The biblical waters, opposed to "the dry land," are accompanied by darkness, which, in turn, stays in contrast to light:

> 2. And the earth was without form, and void: and darkness was upon the face of the deep. And the Spirit of God moved upon the face of the waters.
> 3. And God said, Let there be light: and there was light.
> 4. And God saw the light, that it was good: and God divided the light from the darkness. (Genesis, I)[12]

In Conrad's marine fiction and essays upon life at sea the briny is frequently mythicized as the dark waters of Chaos. In *The*

Mirror of the Sea, for instance, one finds the following description:

> If you would know the age of the earth, look upon the sea in a storm. The greyness of the whole immense surface...the great masses of foam...give to the sea in a gale an appearance of hoary age, lustress, dull, without gleams, as though it had been created before the light itself. (*MS*, 71)

To know the sea in a storm, to understand its might and ruthlessness, one needs to retrace one's imagination back to the primordial time of creation. The parallel between the briny and the waters of Chaos is clearly drawn through use of the phrase "know the age of the earth," qualifying adjectives describing the water element as "lustress," "dull," "without gleams," and, most importantly, through a call to perceive the sea as "created before the light itself." The image of the raging sea is based on the dichotomy of light and darkness, crucial for Conrad's marine imagery. It is especially noticeable in two of his works: *The Nigger of the "Narcissus"* and "Typhoon." Both the texts make use of hyperbole – a means to present the storm as a global disaster. In *The Nigger...*, for example, during the storm "nothing seems left of the whole universe but darkness, clamour, fury – and the ship" (*NN*, 53). Both the narrator and the characters are gripped by an apocalyptic fear that "the sun would never rise upon a freezing world" (82). In "Typhoon" it is the whole universe that recedes to its nascent form, with stars dissolving into clouds of gas and darkness taking over:

> The last star, blurred, enlarged, as if returning to the fiery mist of its beginning, struggled with the colossal depth of blackness hanging over the ship – and went out. ("Typhoon," *TS*, 88)
> The gale howled and scuffed about gigantically in the darkness, as though the entire world were one black gully. (43)

In both the texts one finds accumulation and reiteration of words and expressions like "abyssal darkness," "wild night," "great darkness," "void," "dim," "blackness" or "gloom" – to give but a few.

In mythical beliefs worldwide, creation of Cosmos out of Chaos entails the initial conflict between two antagonizing powers – that is a god and a devil, whatever names they are assigned in a particular myth. This original dichotomy is the source of any classification of reality made by the primitive mind, which rests on binary oppositions expressive of the "positive" and the "negative" meaning. In his discussion of the Slavic cosmogonic myth R. Tomicki sees the antagonism between God and Devil as the basic and most elementary structure of the cosmogonic myth.[13] He also writes that "the opposition of the two creators is an instrument of semantic differentiation of the various levels of reality, and thus the whole process of creation rests essentially on setting up this dichotomic classification."[14] Among the most common semantic oppositions Tomicki enumerates those concerning the elements (heavenly fire vs cosmic waters), space (up, east, right vs down, west, left), time (day, morning, summer vs night, evening, winter), colors (white, light vs black, dark), numbers (odd vs even), qualities (fertility, arable land vs barrenness, waste land), and anthropology and sociology (humans, insiders, man vs demons, outsiders, woman).[15] The process of creation is connected with the original combat between two powers. It is often the fight with the serpent or the dragon, which, defeated, is cast somewhere into the depths of the ocean or the underworld.[16] Devil, subjugated and humiliated as he is, is still active in the world through his agents, mythical demons and tricksters of all kind.[17]

Conrad's briny is not empty. In *The Mirror of the Sea* it is full of malignant spirits of essentially fiendish character. Through the writer's use of pathetic fallacy, which is much like the mythical interpretation of natural phenomena,[18] the wind, the gale and the ocean are stylized as living creatures, agents of evil:

> gales have their physiognomy...some cling to you in woebegone misery, others come back fiercely and weirdly, like ghouls bent upon sucking your strength away...some are unvenerated recollections, as of spiteful wild-cats, chewing at your agonized vitals; others are severe, like a visitation; and one or two rise up draped and mysterious, with an aspect of ominous menace. (*MS*, 76; see also 71, 98-100, 137)

Setting out to sea, therefore, becomes a mythical journey into the kingdom of darkness, inhabited by malignant tricksters, with perils lurking in wait for the sailors. Consequently, the return of the ship to its port after a long and dangerous voyage means coming back from darkness into light. Such is the case of the *Narcissus* approaching the shore:

> The coast to welcome her stepped out of space into the sunshine...the wide bays smiled in the light, the shadows of homeless clouds ran along the sunny planes...and the sunshine pursued them with patches of running brightness. (*NN*, 162)[19]

As it has already been mentioned, the crucial distinction into the sacred and the profane space has its origin in cosmogony. For a primeval man, life, if it is to have any order and meaning, is inseparably connected with his mythology. Since he needs to live in accordance with myth, or rather re-live it in all aspects of his existence, he is bound to repeat the acts of gods that happened *ab initio*, in the beginning of time.[20] If creating the world God separated Cosmos from Chaos, the primeval man needs to do the same. Hence, every building of a house, as well as starting a camp or a village is re-living cosmogony. The first step is to locate it in the very center of the universe. The "center," of course, does not refer to geography or astronomy, but to the axiology of the sacred space. Consequently, any space that is sacred is in the center or, in other words, there are many centers of the world and the world is always in the center.[21] A house, a camp, a village or a town is always the *imago mundi*, located around the center of the universe. In many primitive communities this center is symbolized by a pole or a tree – the *axis mundi*, which is believed to support the world. Whenever the pole or the tree are destroyed, the community sees it as a macrocosmic disaster, a sign of the end of its world.[22] What follows is that for man it is not possible to live outside the sacred space.

In Conrad's marine fiction it is ships that are assigned the axiological meaning of the *imago mundi*. Among the waters of Chaos the ship constitutes an enclave meaningful and ordered, a hermetic microcosm.[23] This function is highlighted in *The*

Nigger of the "Narcissus," where the ship takes on a planetary dimension of the earth floating about in the universe: "The passage had begun, and the ship, a fragment detached from the earth, went on lonely and swift like a small planet" (29). Ships are repeatedly referred to as a home, and the loss of a ship is often presented as a dire calamity in the lives of the characters. For old Captain Whalley from "The End of the Tether" it is not possible to have any other kind of life: "What to other parties was merely the sale of a ship was to him a momentous event involving a radically new view of existence" ("The End of the Tether," *YS*, 57). Whalley, who has now "no ship and no home" (54), lands himself in a severe predicament. In "Youth" Marlow recalls the *Judea* as a kind of sanctuary in which the sailors acquire sea-life experience ("Youth," *YS*, 20). The ship sometimes becomes a footing for family life. Such is the case in "Freya of the Seven Isles," where Jasper Allen and Freya imagine their life together aboard the brig, and when it has been wrecked on a reef Jasper sinks in utter despair: "He had waited for two years...for a day that would never come to a man disarmed for life by the loss of the brig, and it seemed to him, made unfit for love to which he had no foothold to offer" ("Freya of the Seven Isles," *TLS*, 229).[24]

However, the space of the ship, like the mythical one, is not free from potential dangers coming from outside and en-croaching on the existence of its inhabitants.[25] A danger already mentioned is the one posed to the ship by the sea raging in storm. Another comes from people who do not fit this sacred space, that is the characters who are ignorant of rules of life at sea, who do not share the affection for Conrad's *imago mundi*, who selfishly cherish their own weaknesses and dilemmas threatening to disintegrate the social structure of the group.[26] It is perhaps James Wait from *The Nigger of the "Narcissus"* who most fully embodies the qualities of a mythical intruder, a misfit among the crew, a messenger of evil and darkness. In his disdain for the other sailors, in shunning his duty to work, in constant complaints about his declining health, this highly selfish charac-ter becomes a symbolic embodiment of death and destruction, exerting sinister impact on the crew and the ship. Wait's appearance on deck is depicted as accompanied by sudden dying of light, followed by darkness:

> He seemed to hasten the retreat of departing light by his very presence; the setting sun dipped sharply, as though fleeing before our nigger, a black mist emanated from him; a subtle and dismal influence; a something cold and gloomy that floated out and settled on all the faces like a mourning veil. The circle broke up. The joy of laughter died on stiffened lips. There was not a smile left among all the ship's company. Not a word was spoken. (*NN*, 34)

The black man's presence starts to impinge on the thoughts and feelings of the seamen. His selfishness, contemptuous treatment of the shipmates and their duties, make the crew doubt the meaningfulness of work and weaken the sense of group solidarity. Although Wait claims to belong to the ship, he obviously does not. His cabin is separated from the rest of the *Narcissus*. Heat and drought of the room make it clearly the residence of a fiend:

> It was very hot in the cabin, and it seemed to turn slowly round, detach itself from the ship, and swing out smoothly into a luminous arid space where a black sun shone, spinning very fast. A place without any water! No water! (113)

The demonic aspect of the character is rightly stressed by W. Krajka, who points to Wait's presentation at the end of the novel as having no connections with the world: "James Wait – deceased – found no papers of any kind – no relations – no trace..." (169).[27] Nature turns against the *Narcissus* carrying on board the agent of evil. The sea is unnaturally still, there is no sign of the wind which would bring the ship and its people back home. It becomes apparent that in order to continue the voyage the crew has to get rid of Wait.

Semantic tensions resulting in spatial dichotomy arise also from the opposition between the ship and the land, the two frequently interacting on the principle of repulsion.[28] The writer often introduces the metaphor of the ship as a living creature when far away from the shore and as a dead one when brought to the land. Thus, the opposition is between movement usually associated with life (the ship at sea) and inertness commonly connected with lifelessness (the ship as caged by the land). In *The Nigger of the "Narcissus"* the land, that is the port, is described as a cemetery, a modern inferno produced by civilization:

> Brick walls rose high above the water – soulless walls, staring through hundreds of windows as troubled and dull as the eyes of over-fed brutes. At their base monstrous iron cranes crouched, with chains hanging from their long necks, balancing cruel-looking hooks over the decks of lifeless ships...and a penetrating smell of perfumes and dirt, of spices and hides, of things costly and of things filthy, pervaded the space.... The "Narcissus" came gently into her birth; the shadows of soulless walls fell upon her, the dust of all the continents leaped upon her deck, and a swarm of strange men, clambering up her sides, took possession of her in the name of the sordid earth. She had ceased to live. (164-5)

In the above quotation the port is enslaved – another characteristic feature of the land, which is often presented as a space caging and limiting in contrast to the free and independent ship. As Conrad writes in *The Mirror of the Sea*, "[a] ship in dock...has the appearance of a prisoner meditating upon freedom in the sadness of a free spirit put under restraint.... There never seem chains and ropes enough [for] the safe binding of free ships to the strong, muddy, enslaved earth" (*MS*, 101).

If the sea is assigned a negative axiological status when compared to the ship, it becomes the opposite in relation to the land. In this relation the briny functions in the broad meaning of marine universe, embracing not only the notion of the water element (chaotic itself, as has been previously argued) but also the ships, the sailors and ethos of life at sea as opposed to existence on land. While the latter stands for civilization, the former embodies the world of nature; while the land is very much subject to history, the briny is presented as more timeless; finally, there is an unbridgeable gap between people of the land and people of the sea.

If we were, for example, to approach the 19th century sailing from a historical point of view of developing commerce, it would be difficult to accept Conrad's seamen as detached from this historical reality, wholly devoted to sailing they called "craft" rather than "job" and not associating it with any commercial profit. It is interesting to notice that money, lacking in a mythical source and nonexistent in an archaic society, is made a disintegrating factor in many of the writer's stories. It is almost never mentioned in connection with life at sea, and often presented as a product of civilization developed on land. In *The Nigger of the "Narcissus"* it is in the port, only after the voyage has been completed, that the sailors get their pay. The place is portrayed as drab, cold, and again, bearing signs of enslavement:

> The room was large, white-washed, and bare...behind the grating a pasty-faced clerk had...jerky movements of a caged bird. Poor Captain Allistoun also in there, and sitting before a little table with piles of gold and notes on it, appeared subdued by his captivity. (*NN*, 167-8)[29]

People of the sea, following the principles of marine ethos and called by the writer "the ancient and honourable sea-folk" are opposed to those belonging to the land, disdainfully referred to as "landlubbers" or "a vain people of landsmen." Among other Conrad's works this opposition is well-exemplified in "The End of the Tether," with Massy, the owner of the *Sofala,* and its captain, Whalley, standing on the opposite poles. Massy cannot and does not want to understand sea ethos. His physical repulsiveness is to render his highly inaccurate treatment of the crew and the steamer, based on ruthless exploitation. The man soon starts to detest the *Sofala,* which cannot provide him with money frittered away on the local lottery. The first meeting of Captain Whalley with Massy is symbolically portrayed in the story as that of a God's messenger sent from above onto the ship and a demon emerging from the depths and darkness of hell:

> He [Whalley] seemed to have fallen on board from the sky. His footsteps echoed on the empty steamer, and the strange deep-toned

> voice on deck repeating interrogatively the words, "Mr Massy, Mr
> Massy there?" had been startling like a wonder. And coming up from
> the depths of the cold engine-room, where he had been pottering
> dismally with a candle amongst the enormous shadows...Massy had
> been struck dumb by astonishment in the presence of that imposing
> old man with a beard like a silver plate, towering in the dusk rendered
> lurid by the expiring flames of sunset. ("The End of the Tether," *YS*,
> 120)

To recapitulate, in Conrad's marine fiction, the sea, the land and ships stay in close semantic interrelations that to a large extent are determined by their axiological significance, both to the narrator and the characters. It has been argued here that these aspects of space are frequently assigned a positive or negative value through the writer's reliance on some paradigms of judgment made by the primitive mind, determined by mythical thinking. The axiological tensions discussed above are those between the sea and the ship, the ship and the land, and, finally, between the sea and the land. Of the three it is only ships that can be called the real center of the world, the real *imago mundi*.[30] The sea becomes Chaos while opposed to the ship, but in the broader meaning of marine reality it is contrasted to the land. If we were to outline an axiologically-oriented model of the fictional world discussed here, it would have the ship in its very center, the land on some distant periphery and the sea somewhere in between.

Conrad was aware that the marine world depicted in his fiction was rapidly changing. The progress of civilization was affecting life at sea, and the reality of his writings was passing away. In *The Mirror of the Sea* he wrote:

> History repeats itself, but the special call of an art which has passed
> away is never reproduced. It is as utterly gone out of the world as the
> song of a destroyed wild bird.... And the sailing of any vessel afloat is
> an art whose fine form seems already receding from us on its way to
> the overshadowed Valley of Oblivion. (*MS*, 30)

Clearly, there is a nostalgia for the old world which is on its wane. The writer's fiction and essays may be read as an attempt at holding back this world, at giving it some meaningful, timeless structure, which might be a counterbalance to the fear of history. In this sense it seems not important whether Conrad the man believed in any God, myth or religion. There is fair evidence he did not.[31] What seems important, though, is that Conrad the writer tried to assign a certain axiological hopeful meaning to human existence, a bit of consolation to a mind perplexed at the chaotic world around. It is in a vision of some ordered and meaningful reality that myth and Conrad's writings converge.

NOTES

1. The problem of Conrad's sea ethos has, e.g., been exhaustively discussed by Wiesław Krajka, *Isolation and Ethos: A Study of Joseph Conrad* (Boulder – New York: East European Monographs – Columbia U.P., 1992).

2. *The Norton Anthology of American Literature*, 3rd ed., ed. Nina Baym et al. (New York: Norton, 1989), vol. 2, 942.

3. Thomas S. Eliot, "Ulysses, Order and Myth," *The Dial*, 75 (1923), 480-3. This ordering function has, likewise, been accentuated by twentieth--century students in myth and religion: see, e.g., Mircea Eliade, who writes that through myth "the world is no longer an opaque mass of objects arbitrarily thrown together, it is a living Cosmos, articulated and meaning-ful," – Mircea Eliade, *Myth and Reality*, trans. Willard R. Trask (New York: Harper Torchbooks, 1968), 145; see also Mark Schorer: "A myth is a large controlling image that gives philosophical meaning to the facts of ordinary life; that is which has organizing value for experience" – Mark Schorer, "The Necessity of Myth," in *Myth and Mythmaking*, ed. Henry A. Murray (New York: George Braziller, 1960), 355.

4. For a discussion of the influence of Frazer on these writers see John B. Vickery, *The Literary Impact of "The Golden Bough"* (Princeton: Princeton U.P., 1973).

5. Northrop Frye, *Anatomy of Criticism* (Princeton: Princeton U.P., 1957), 135.

6. Ibid., 134.

7. Jacques Darras, *Joseph Conrad and the West. Signs of Empire*, trans. Anne Luyat, Jacques Darras (London: Macmillan, 1982), 42-3, 47-52; Lilian Feder, "Marlow's Descent into Hell," in *The Art of Joseph Conrad*, ed. Robert Stallman (East Lansing: Michigan State U.P., 1960), 162-70; Albert Guerard, "*The Nigger of the 'Narcissus'*," in ibid., 121-39; Vernon Young, "Trial by Water: Joseph Conrad's *The Nigger of the 'Narcissus'*,"

ibid., 109-20. The word "mythological" is understood here as "drawing on stories and characters from mythology" whereas "mythical" carries a broader meaning of "typical of the worldview of archaic communities" – a distinction similar to the one made by John White in his *Mythology in the Modern Novel* (Princeton: Princeton U.P., 1971), 7-8. In the present paper "mythical" has been given priority over "mythological" for the reason that we do not aim at tracing parallels between particular characters or stories taken from mythology but rather focus on investigating some paradigms of archaic or "primitive" thought recurrent in Conrad's writings.

8. The sacred/the profane dichotomy has surfaced in a great number of Eliade's essays, space being only one aspect of the opposition. For an overview of the subject and an annotated bibliography of major works dealing with it see Mircea Eliade, et al., *The Encyclopedia of Religion*, ed. Mircea Eliade, 15 vols (New York: Macmillan, 1987): Joel P. Brereton, "Sacred Space," 12, 526-35. See also N. J. Girardot, "Chaos," 3, 213-18; Carsten Colpe, "The Sacred and the Profane," trans. Russell M. Stockman, 12, 511-26. Eliade devotes a separate chapter to the discussion of space in his *The Sacred and the Profane: The Nature of Religion,* trans. Willard R. Trask (New York – Evanston: Harper Torchbooks, 1961), 20-65.

9. The basic types of creation in myth are discussed by Clyde Kluckhohn, "Recurrent Themes in Myth and Mythmaking," in *Myth and Mythmaking,* 48 ff. See also Charles H. Long, "Cosmogony," in *The Encyclopedia of Religion,* 4, 94-100.

10. See "Chaos," in *The Encyclopedia of Religion,* esp. 214-15.

11. Mircea Eliade, *The Sacred and the Profane...,* 130.

12. The biblical quotation comes from Authorized King James Version.

13. Ryszard Tomicki, "Religious Dualism in the Slavic Cosmogonic Myth," in *Poland at the Tenth International Congress of Anthropological and Ethnological Sciences,* ed. Maria Frankowska, trans. James Sehnert (Wrocław: Ossolineum, 1978), 60.

14. Ibid., 61.

15. Ibid.

16. Eleazar Mieletinski, *Poetyka mitu,* trans. Józef Dancygier (Warszawa: Państwowy Instytut Wydawniczy, 1981), 40; Tomicki, op. cit., 81.

17. Ibid., 81.

18. The primeval man did not perceive himself as different from the world of nature. Accordingly, he attributed human features to natural phenomena. See Mieletinski, op. cit., 203.

19. Of course, it would be a gross simplification to perceive Conrad's sea only as gloomy, soulless and inimical to man. For all his awareness of the power and ruthlessness of the briny, the writer felt a deep affection for it, which was most strongly articulated in *The Mirror of the Sea.* Therefore, his attitude towards the water element would be best rendered as that of *odi et amo.* Whenever in this paper the sea is understood as Chaos, it concerns the

semantic tension arising from the axiological opposition between the briny and ships, the latter exhibiting features of space that is ordered and sacred. It does not hold true, e.g., when the sea is contrasted to the land.

20. The problem of re-living cosmogony as crucial to a primitive man's existence has been discussed in a number of works by Mircea Eliade: e.g. *Myth and Reality*, 6-8, 11-12 ff.; *Myths, Dreams and Mysteries*, trans. Philip Mairet (London – Glasgow: Collins, 1968), 18, 23.

21. Mircea Eliade, *The Sacred and the Profane...*, 22, 57.

22. Ibid., 33.

23. Similar conclusions have been reached by C. F. Burgess, *The Fellowship of the Craft: Conrad on Ships and Seamen and the Sea* (London: Kennikat Press, 1976), 132; Herman M. Daleski, *Joseph Conrad. The Way of Dispossession* (London: Faber and Faber, 1977), 32; Albert Guerard, op. cit., 123, 125, 134.

24. It should be borne in mind, however, that the protagonists' family links are often presented as a potential threat to the fulfilment of their marine duties. In general, the sea world, portrayed by Conrad as essentially masculine, allows place neither for women nor for a family (see ironic descriptions of the idyllic life of the captain's family on board the *Diana* in "Falk"). Hence, the writer's references to the ship as a home should be read as generally expressive of affection he feels for it, and not as a eulogy of family life thriving at sea.

25. Primitive societies try to identify any strangers, potential invaders of their microcosm, with mythical demons defeated by God in the beginning of time: see Mircea Eliade, *The Sacred and the Profane...*, 47-8; see also Ryszard Tomicki, op. cit., 81, who emphasises the idea that the primordial demon is active in the world through his agents.

26. Some parallels between a primitive mythical tribe and the community of sailors as presented by Conrad have been discussed by the author of this paper: Wojciech Kozak, "'Ancient Sea-Folk' – Some Tribal Aspects of the Community of Sailors in Conrad's Fiction," *Kwartalnik Neofilologiczny*, 43: 4 (1996), 359-68.

27. Wiesław Krajka, op. cit., 180. The symbolic function of the character is, likewise, stressed by Albert Guerard, op. cit., 124, 127.

28. The contrast between the two aspects of space has been, e.g., accentuated by Jacques Berthoud, *Joseph Conrad: The Major Phase* (Cambridge: Cambridge U.P., 1978), 41-2; C. F. Burgess, op. cit., 3-28.

29. The motif of money or treasures as essentially connected with the profane land and sharply opposed to the principles of marine ethos appears in a number of works by Conrad: see, e.g., "The End of the Tether," "Typhoon," or *The Rover*.

30. C. F. Burgess, op. cit., 52: "The land...may be presumed to be deceitful; the sea may be expected to be deceitful; but a ship, never."

31. It is generally agreed among critics that the writer shared with his contemporaries a sense of crisis of values and pessimism about human life, derived from and strengthened by his personal experience of an exile drifting about in foreign cultures. His worldview has been usually referred to as catastrophic, sceptical and nihilistic: Charles B. Cox, *Joseph Conrad: The Modern Imagination* (London: Dent and Sons, 1974), chap. "The Question of Suicide"; Michał Komar, *Piekło Conrada* (Warszawa: "Czytelnik," 1978), esp. chaps "Proste prawdy Conrada" and "Człowiek jako zwierzę złośliwe"; Zdzisław Najder, *Nad Conradem* (Warszawa: Państwowy Instytut Wydawniczy, 1965), chap. "O 'filozofii' Conrada." See also Conrad's letters, esp. "To Aniela Zagórska," 6 Feb. 1898, *CL*, III, 276; "To R. B. Cunninghame Graham," 14 Jan. 1898, ibid., II, 37.

Carl Schaffer,
University of Scranton,
Scranton, USA

Conrad's Leggatt and the Jewish Golem:
Where Parallel Lines Meet

Conrad's novella "The Secret Sharer" has been widely recognized as an allegory of a descent into the self, a remarkable story so resonant that Albert Guerard places it "among the first – one is tempted to say only – symbolist masterpieces in English fiction" (Guerard, 14-15). Whatever the final evaluation may be, certainly the strongest symbolic component is the compelling and elemental figure of Leggatt himself – a luminescent stranger who emerges, almost as if invoked, from the depths of the sea, an outlaw befriended by a young captain on his first command and given secret refuge in the captain's quarters. It is there, of course, that the two become the "secret sharers" of the story's title, cabin-mates in an oneiric world that lies between dream and wakefulness, reason and madness, law and barbarism. For the young captain narrating the story, the figure is a strange and secret "double," as he calls him, of some inner wellspring within his own soul, a dark and instinctual self that resonates to the core of what is innermost in himself and, by extension, in everyone. It is, as Guerard says, the "archetypal myth dramatized...in great literature since the Book of Jonah: the story of an essentially solitary journey involving profound spiritual change in the voyager. In its classic form the journey is a descent into the earth, followed by a return to light" (15).

That description, with its dark echoes from Hebraic literature, suggests parallels with yet another archetypal figure who, in contrast to Leggatt, ascends from the earth into light and returns, when his duties are done, to the elements from which he arose. I am speaking of the golem in Jewish legend, a fantastic creature formed from virgin earth and imbued with life through cabalistic ritual mirroring the act of divine creation through which man was created by God. Indeed, the connection between Leggatt and the golem-figure is especially relevant when we remember the golem's role as a precursor to the modern psychological double. R. Tymms, in his study *Doubles in Literary Psychology*, points out that

> The roots of the theme will be found in the ordinary phenomenon of family likeness and chance resemblance; but they will also be seen to be firmly embedded in magic and in the earliest speculations on the nature of the soul. In keeping with these various origins, the development of the theme will prove to be correspondingly various, as the magic of the soul (in folk-lore) gives place to the magic of the personality, with its often dissociated substrata of consciousness (in romantic and modern psychological thought). (Tymms, 15-16)

Tymms believes, in fact, that the very concept of the double began in primitive societies where it was believed that one's soul appeared just at the point of death, a borderline between two abutting worlds, one solid and knowable, the other insubstantial and incomprehensible. Viewed as a spiritual landscape, it could be painted much like Conrad's opening scene, with "the straight line of the flat shore joined to the stable sea, edge to edge, with a perfect and unmarked closeness" ("The Secret Sharer," *TLS*, 91). The cabalist who creates the golem explores an even more esoteric coastline, the frontiers of the region where the soul is first formed. He must, like the captain-narrator, leave behind the secure and established edifices of civilized and traditional belief, as it is emblemized by the Paknam pagoda on its "mitre-shaped hill," and risk navigating into the uncertain and dangerous mysteries of the unknown. And he knows, too, that in the process of sharing the secrets of a single soul one may come to know the scope of a greater, cosmic consciousness. It is written, after all, that when God created Adam He made him as a huge golem, stretching across the ends of the world, and while, in this as yet unanimated state, God showed him all the generations of mankind that were to come. Indeed, as Erich Neumann has put it in his *The Origins and History of Consciousness*, "the original question about the origin of the world is at the same time the question about the origin of man, the origin of the consciousness and of the ego" (Neumann, 7).

Small wonder, then, that the concept of the golem has fascinated so many writers in European literature, including Mary Shelley, Gustav Meyrink, Achim von Arnim, E. T. A. Hoffman, and A. v. Chamisso, among others, and there is much folklore to draw on from biblical and aggadic stories. In one tale, for example, Abraham and his teacher Shem are said to have pored over the *Book of Formation* and, after three years, were able to create a world. In another, Rabbi Abraham ibn Ezra is said to have created a man, after which he commanded it, "Go back!" and it returned to what it had been before (Berdichevsky, 752). We are told, too, of a rabbi named Rava who created a man and sent him to a Rabbi Zera, who, it is said, recognized it as a golem when it was unable to speak and commanded it to turn back to its dust. Still another account of a golem tells us that "Rav Hanina and Rav Oshaya busied themselves on the eve of every Sabbath with the Book of Creation...." After three years of study "they made a calf one-third the natural size and ate it" (Scholem, 166). Yet another tells of Ben Sira, who, with his father Jeremiah, created a man on whose forehead they wrote *emeth*, the Hebrew word for *truth*; they afterward destroyed it by reversing the combinations of letters by which he was created and erasing the first letter, aleph, from *emeth* so that it read *meth*, or *he is dead* (179). And one sage named Ibn Gabirol even created a woman golem to serve him – although for chaste purposes, for we're told, "When he was denounced to the authorities, he showed them that she was not a full or complete creature. And he restored her to the [hinges] and rounds of wood of which she had been constructed" (Berdichevsky, 752; Scholem, 199). A story closer to our time tells of a French sage named Rabbi Samuel who created, at the time of the Crusades, a golem that served him both as a servant and bodyguard (Ausubel, 604). And, in a well-known version recounted by J. Grimm, a golem grew so tall that the rabbi who created him had to trick him into leaning over so that he could erase the *aleph* – a stratagem which worked to his disadvantage, as the crumbling golem fell on top of him and crushed him. That version may well have been based on the story of the famous Polish golem of Chelm created by a Rabbi Elijah, who imbued his creation with life by inscribing on its forehead the tetragrammaton. That golem, too, grew to tremendous size, and the Rabbi, terrified of both its sheer bulk as well as its destructive temperament, managed to turn it to dust by erasing the Divine Name from its forehead (604).

But the most famous golem in folklore, one which incorporates many facets of the earlier stories and which is perhaps most relevant to Conrad's Leggatt, is the one created by the renowned Rabbi Yehudah Loew of Prague, known also as the Maharal. In that version, the Jews of Prague are about to be accused by a priest named Thaddeus of the blood-libel – the charge that they used the blood of Christian children for ritual purposes. The Maharal, with two adepts, creates a golem in order to protect the Jewish community as well as to root out the perpetrators of this insidious slander. This golem is large, but otherwise looks human, and is called Joseph. It has no voice – a common flaw of the golem, attributed, some say, to an inherent flaw of the less than divine creator. It follows orders with an almost robotic mindlessness, so that he who controls it must maintain absolute command: for example, when the rabbi's wife tells it to fetch water from the well and then forgets about him, she returns home to find the house filled with water, and the golem returning with another two buckets. As it patrols the ghetto, the golem is capable of becoming invisible by means of an amulet the Maharal has given it, acquiring a ubiquitous and ferocious presence that inspires fear and dread on the part of the enemies of the Jews, while some in the Jewish community wonder if the golem is not really a ghostly double of the rabbi himself (Bloch, 76). When its mission is done – when it has unearthed the plot of Thaddeus and saved the Prague Jews from annihilation, the golem is returned via another ritual to the elements from which it sprang.

Already we can see emerging from the pattern of this story parallels to the tale of the captain and Leggatt, not least of which is the perception of the golem as the Maharal's doppelgänger. The traditional reading of "The Secret Sharer" has of course focused on Leggatt as a symbolic manifestation of a dark aspect of the narrator, what Guerard calls the "embodiment of a more instinctive, more primitive, less rational self" (Guerard, 11). The insecure captain, on his first command, feels somewhat inadequate to the task and must find within himself the strength to command a crew that seems to share those doubts. As he admits, "[W]hat I felt most was my being a stranger to the ship; and, if all the truth must be told, I was somewhat of a stranger to myself" ("The Secret Sharer," *TLS*, 93). The emergence of Leggatt from the depths of the sea, a symbol perhaps of the unconscious, marks his encounter with what he perceives to be an eerie, mirror image of his own self. The captain's dilemma brings out the universal predicament of the civilized man who has lost touch with, or perhaps we should say has repressed, the darker, primordial aspect of his character. He shuns it, is revulsed by it, much as the eminently accountable chief mate is surprised and somewhat repulsed by the scorpion he finds drowned in his inkwell. Leggatt, too, is a figure of blackness, a "legate" of the captain's own dark underworld. Despite the luminescent glow in which he is first seen, he is a creature of darkness, as he admits himself when he is about to leave: "As I came at night, so shall I go" (132). We recall that he commits his crime in a fit of rage so overwhelming that his victim is left "black in the face" (102). And despite the fact that Leggatt insists he is no "murdering brute" (106), that he is, after all, a parson's son, the captain is held in thrall by the confidence, strength, and poise of this man who seems born to lead. If the literary double functions, as R. Tymms defines it, as a representive of some moral, spiritual, or psychological aspect of the protagonist's character (Tymms, 16), certainly Leggatt represents to the captain a much-looked-for and as yet untapped inner strength. He is, indeed, what Jung calls the "'shadow archetype'...of the dangerous aspect of the unrecognized dark half of the personality." He is the "'magic demon' with mysterious powers." And, Jung adds, "A good example [of this 'magic demon'] is G. Meyrink's *Golem*" (Jung, *Two Essays...*, 96).

The Prague golem of the Maharal, too, interestingly enough, has a like function. His role as guardian of the ghetto also emphasizes a primordial, even brutal side that must be drawn upon by the Maharal to safeguard the Prague Jews. It is an element that has, as in the captain's case, been repressed, or subsumed, by the powerless Jewish community, and the golem seems to express one aspect of its communal soul that has not dared to reveal itself – a role somewhat similar, perhaps, to that of James Wait in *The Nigger of the "Narcissus,"* who Conrad has said serves as "the centre of the ship's collective psychology" (*NN*, ix). Indeed, much cabalistic discussion has focused on the nature of the golem's soul. The thirteenth-century work of Moses de Leon, *The Zohar*, perhaps the most important cabalistic work, asserts that the soul itself consists of three aspects: *nefesh*, which controls the most basic biological functions; *ruach*, which governs our moral sense and defines what is right and wrong; and *neshamah*, which is the highest element and binds the spiritual communicant with his Maker (*The Zohar*, II, 281). Meir ibn Gabbai maintained that a golem possessed only *nefesh*, the animalistic aspect of the soul, while Moses Cordovero insisted that it possessed none of the three, but rather, a vital spirit called *hiyyuth*, which exists on a higher level (Scholem, 194-5). Whatever its name, the soul of the golem is recognized to be a force which, as in "The Secret Sharer," emerges at a time of intense crisis, a force which must be drawn upon to resolve that crisis by going beyond the accepted laws of the land. The golem, a creature which can be destroyed without its creator being held accountable by religious law for its murder, can, by the same reasoning, exact its own vengeance with impunity.

In that sense, we see still another interesting parallel between the golem and Conrad's Leggatt: both, as outlaws as well as saviors, follow imperatives outside the accepted moral order in order to accomplish a greater good. Indeed, Leggatt's own dual role is underscored by the fact that, as L. H. Leiter and P. Bidwell have discussed, he is the chief mate of the *Sephora*, a name which is a variant of the Hebrew Tzipporah, the wife of Moses, who, as we know, was forced to flee Egypt after murdering a cruel overseer. The dual role is consistent with the double motif, where, as R. Jackson has pointed out, "the narrative center, often the protagonist himself, is divided into two sides, one subverting and one upholding the dominant social order" (Jackson, 45). The distinction isn't so clear in "The Secret Sharer," of course: Leggatt, the fugitive from justice, has killed his shipmate, but that action saves the ship (or so he says); while the captain, who is supposed to impose justice, actually obstructs it by hiding Leggatt from the pursuing captain of the *Sephora*, and it is understandable that he has been "frequently described as an apostate from maritime law" (Davis, 67). Indeed D. Curley has insisted that Leggatt "represents the higher nature of the captain, his ideal self in fact, and that everything in the story points in that direction" (Curley, 179); while M. Murphy is just as insistent that nothing is certain in the story, and that the captain must be viewed as an unreliable narrator. And it seems inevitable that the character of the charismatic murderer Leggatt will continue to invite contradictory interpretations.

As cloudy as the answers seem in Conrad's story, neither are the moral imperatives so clear in various versions of the golem legend. For example, in the Yiddish playwright H. Leivick's verse-drama *The Golem*, we are led to understand that the root of the golem's own violent nature is derived from the Maharal's own rage against those who are seeking to bring harm to his people, a primordial fury which is transferred to – or perhaps simply mirrored by – the golem. Although golems traditionally are unable to speak, Leivick's golem can, and, in the process of creation the incipient form looms over the Maharal and tells him, "The whole night through you kneaded me; / With coldness and cruelty you shaped me" (Leivick, 124). By the end of the play, the golem, revulsed by his recognition of the violence within him, runs amok and murders two members of the synagogue – the very congregation he was created to protect. In both Conrad's and Leivick's stories, the protagonist works outside of the law in order to follow what is considered to be a higher moral imperative, even if it may lead to disaster. And in both cases, the "appointed task" to be "carried out, far from all human eyes," with only the elements for "spectators and for judges," effects a balance of the scales: between internal and external systems of justice, as well as between two opposing elements of the psyche.

That inner division is one that the captain recognizes, of course, from the start of his story. Insecure in his new command, he looks for a source of strength from far below and, as we know, finds it. As Guerard has noted, when the captain allows – even if unintentionally – the ladder to remain overboard, he "has in a sense summoned Leggatt, who later remarks that 'it was as if you had expected me'" (Guerard, 22). The captain has, in his own way, ritualistically invoked Leggatt to arise, just as the mystical communicant does with the golem; and it seems fitting that, in the case of both Leggatt and the golem, they should first appear in an incomplete, inchoate state. The captain tells us, "With a gasp I saw revealed to my stare a pair of feet, the long legs, a broad livid back immersed right up to the neck in a greenish cadaverous glow. One hand, awash, clutched the bottom rung of the ladder. He was complete but for the head" ("The Secret Sharer," *TLS*, 97). Appropriately, that picture is completed by the captain himself, who has just "put my head over the rail" (97) so that, seen from the water, it might well be perceived as the disembodied head of the corpse, as if sense and sensibility were each regarding the other. Only when the captain's cigar falls into the sea with a hiss "quite audible in the absolute stillness of all things under heaven" (98), when fire and water give voice to a serpentine, uroboric susurrus, does the figure of Leggatt emerge completely and the story of the mirror-doubles begin. It is, in its own way, a reenactment of the cabalistic ritual through which the mystic, with his two communicants, invokes the golem, even as the original Creator had enclosed the tripartite souls of *nefesh, ruach,* and *neshamah,* represented by fire, water, and air, in its original vessel of earth.

And indeed, once Leggatt is seen in his entirety, he displays the most salient characteristic of the golem – voicelessness, remaining, as the captain describes him, "mute as a fish" (98). Just why the golem is, in most versions of the story, unable to speak is not entirely clear. One explanation is, as we have said, that this flaw stems from the imperfection of its mortal creator. For example, in the incident related above, where Rabbi Zera recognized Rava's golem for what it was because of its muteness, we are told, "But if not for his sins, he would have answered." Even more appropriate for the purpose of this discussion is Bahya ben Asher's opinion that Rava's golem was mute because it had no rational soul, which is the source of speech. Another opinion states that it is possible to give a golem the power to speak, but not to procreate or reason, because, again, as one medieval cabalist writes, "this is beyond the power of any created being and rests with God alone" (Scholem, 193-4). In all cases, the golem's muteness, or inability to shape language, or to reason, is connected with his role as a creature from the depths who arises from the irrational, or perhaps we should say prerational, sphere of existence. So it is with the golem of Prague: formed of earth blown across water in the predawn light, sent forth into the ghetto in the dead of night, sometimes with Yehudah Loew's amulet of invisibility, the golem, believed by many to be the ghost of the Maharal stalking the streets, embodies within his silence the unseen elemental forces that sleep within all of us.

The same pattern exists in the evolving figure of the now recapitated Leggatt, who has emerged, as the captain puts it, "as if he had risen from the bottom of the sea." He tells us, "As he hung by the side-ladder, like a resting swimmer, the sea-lightning played about his limbs at every stir; and he appeared in it ghastly, silvery, fish-like." And, the captain adds, if we may repeat the image, "He remained as mute as a fish, too." For the remainder of his stay on ship, Leggatt will exist on an almost subliminal level. He will be clothed in the captain's own "sleeping-suit" – in fact, he even remarks he will "freeze on to it" until the Day of Judgement; he will remain, of course, in the captain's sleeping quarters, which are shaped, appropriately enough, like the capital letter "L," Leggatt's own initial, as if he were the primary key to the captain's identity; he will continue to speak only in whispers so low that the captain, as he puts it, has "to strain my hearing, near as we were to each other, shoulder touching shoulder almost" ("The Secret Sharer," *TLS*, 106); and he will obey the captain who has concocted what he calls his "scheme for keeping my second self invisible" (115). Indeed, Conrad seems constantly to underscore the point that, as C. B. Cox has put it, Leggatt "inhabits an area of consciousness that borders on dreams" (quoted in Abdoo, 71).

When his "appointed task" is done, Leggatt, like the golem, must return to the elements from which he has been summoned. It seems fitting that Leggatt should be exiled to a land described at one point as the "gate of Erebus," as if it led to the very bowels of the earth. The captain gives him half his hoard of gold – three sovereigns – perhaps a mythical allusion to the Stygian fare, perhaps a token of their shared selves. More telling, in the utter blackness of the cabin the captain, in a moment of empathy and impulse, rams his hat onto his resisting "other self." The captain tells us that he does so to provide Leggatt protection from the sun, but the action is rich in symbolic suggestion. As Guerard has noted, "We know that in Jungian psychology a hat, in dreams, represents the personality, which can be transferred symbolically to another" (Guerard, 25). And certainly we see, in the dramatic closing scene, a newfound strength and decisiveness on the part of the captain that Leggatt seems to have imparted to him. He brings his ship precariously close to land, despite the objections of his crew. With an action strikingly parallel to the one Leggatt described on the *Sephora*, he shakes his "thunder-struck" mate – although with a control Leggatt was incapable of – and forces him to perform the proper maneuvers. And of course, as Leggatt slips back into the depths from which he came, the captain notes the hat floating in the water and, judging its direction, is able to order the helm shift that saves the ship. It seems that Leggatt has indeed shown the captain the right way to strike out toward his own destiny.

In the sense, then, that Leggatt gives the captain the capability to take on risks that the ironically named Captain Archbold of the *Sephora* is unable to do, he performs much the same role as the Golem, as he is called, in G. Meyrink's novel, whose narrator is told by a cabalist, "Hear and understand. The man who sought you out, and whom you call the Golem, signifies the awakening soul through the innermost life of the spirit. Each thing that earth contains is nothing more than an everlasting symbol clothed in dust.... Nothing that takes shape unto itself but was once a spirit" (Meyrink, 71-2). That golem story in fact shows some striking parallels with Conrad's, not least of which is the bizarre plot device where the narrator loses his identity when he dons the hat, and assumes the persona, of a man named Athanasius Pernath. Even more interesting for the purposes of our comparison is a scene where the narrator meets a man named Amadeus Laponder, jailed for murder and rape, whom we recognize as the Golem of the story. The narrator tells Laponder that he has in a phantasmagoric vision seen a "headless apparition" which offered him a handful of red and black seed pods, colors Meyrink associates with death. It is a dire gift, a gift which holds within it the potential for destruction, a gift which, like the captain's coins in Conrad's story, implies the acceptance of a shared existence. Taking them would be an acceptance of death; denying them, an affirmation of life – on certain terms. The narrator chooses a third alternative: he knocks them out of the apparition's hand, thereby creating yet another alternative by which the individual asserts his own control over his own destiny. Strangely enough, the Golem reveals that he had had the same vision but, in contrast, had accepted the offer, assuring his own fate as a creature of violence. He tells the narrator, "Never would I have believed that a third way could have been found" (253). In short, although the Golem has sought out the narrator, as the cabalist Hillel explains, to awaken him, it is the narrator who has, with predictable irony, effected that realization within the golem. Similarly, although Leggatt appears to unleash the forces within the captain's shadow-self, it is the captain who enables him, through his daring maneuver, to become a "free man, a proud swimmer striking out for a new destiny" ("The Secret Sharer," *TLS*, 280).

Of course, in Meyrink's story, the narrator redeems himself by denying the Golem, and by extension, his primordial nature; in Conrad's, the narrator accepts his other self. But in the end, we see that Leggatt and the golem in Jewish folklore occupy strikingly similar places in the cosmogony of our shared consciousness. It doesn't matter if either or any of the authors of the golem stories were aware of the common ground they shared. Indeed Jung himself said once of Meyrink's archetypes, "Meyrink does not know anything of my theories. He deals with it in an entirely literary fashion one could say, with all the advantages and disadvantages of that method, yet the figures are perfectly recognizable" (Jung, *Dream Analysis...*, 501). And so they are to us too, Leggatt and the golem: creations from a matrix of violent elemental forces, sharers of the darkest mysteries of the soul, they wander with branded foreheads within the deepest recesses of our world, waiting for the incantation that will summon our most secret strengths.

WORKS CITED

Abdoo Sherlyn. "Ego Formation and the Land/Sea Metaphor in Conrad's *Secret Sharer*," in *Poetics of the Elements of the Human Condition: The Sea*, ed. Anna-Teresa Tymieniecka. Hingham, Mass.: Kluwer, 1985, 67-76.

Ausubel Nathan, ed. *A Treasury of Jewish Folklore*. New York: Crown, 1948.

Berdichevsky Micah Joseph [Micha bin Gorion], comp. *Mimekor Yisroel: Classical Jewish Folktales*, ed. Emanual bin Gorion, trans. J. M. Lask. Bloomington: Indiana U.P., 1976.

Bidwell Paul. "Leggatt and the Promised Land: A New Reading of 'The Secret Sharer'," *Conradiana*, 3: 2 (1971-72), 26-34.

Bloch Chayim. *The Golem: Mystical Tales from the Ghetto at Prague*, trans. Harry Schneiderman. Blauvelt, N.Y.: Rudolf Steiner, 1975.

Curley Daniel. "The Writer and His Use of Material," *Modern Fiction Studies*, 13: 2 (1967), 179-94.

Davis W. Eugene. "The Structure of Justice in 'The Secret Sharer'," *Conradiana*, 27: 1 (1995), 64-73.

Guerard Albert J. *Conrad the Novelist*. Cambridge, Mass.: Harvard U.P., 1958.

Jackson Rosemary. "Narcissism and Beyond: A Psychoanalytic Reading of *Frankenstein* and Fantasies of the Double," in *Aspects of Fantasy: Selected Essays from the Second International Conference on the Fantastic in the Arts,* ed. William Coyle. Westport, Conn.: Greenwood, 1984, 43-55.

Jung Carl Gustav. *Dream Analysis: Notes of the Seminar Given in 1928-1930 by C. G. Jung,* ed. William McGuire. Princeton: Princeton U.P., 1982; Bollingen Series, 96.

Jung Carl Gustav. *Two Essays on Analytical Psychology,* trans. R. F. C. Hull. Princeton, N.J.: Princeton U.P., 1972.

Leivick H. *The Golem,* in *Three Great Jewish Plays,* ed. Joseph C. Landis.New York: Applause, 1986, 115-254.

Meyrink Gustav. *The Golem,* trans. Madge Pemberton. New York: Farrar, 1928.

Murphy Michael. "'The Secret Sharer': Conrad's Turn of the Winch," *Conradiana,* 18: 3 (1986), 193-201.

Neumann Erich. *The Origins and History of Consciousness.* Princeton: Princeton U.P., 1970.

Scholem Gershom. *On the Kabbalah and Its Symbolism.* New York: Schocken, 1965.

Steiner Joan E. "Conrad's 'The Secret Sharer': Complexities of the Doubling Relationship," *Conradiana,* 12: 3 (1980), 173-86.

The Zohar, trans. Harry Sperling and Maurice Simon. 5 vols. London: Soncino, 1934.

Tymms Ralph. *Doubles in Literary Psychology.* Cambridge: Bowes & Bowes, 1949.

Hans Ulrich Seeber,
University of Stuttgart,
Stuttgart, Germany

Surface as Suggestive Energy.
Fascination and Voice in Conrad's "Heart of Darkness"

Conrad's verbal art of arranging suggestive images and words, incidents and characters cannot, although by no means entirely foggy and impenetrable, be rendered adequately by discursive paraphrase and analysis. The poverty of reduction is the inevitable result. Still, the dialogue with such a text is equally inevitable, and if it is to yield results, it is probably best to explore, with the help of relevant contexts, the semantic and aesthetic implications, including the contradictions, of key-words such as, for example, "fascination" and "voice." It is precisely that which I propose to do in my paper. In "Heart of Darkness" there is, in fact, a chain of fascinations linking Europeans and Africans, Marlow, Kurtz and the listeners, fictional and nonfictional, through the medium of voices and sounds. Despite his emphasis on "seeing" in his famous "Preface" (1897) to *The Nigger of the "Narcissus"* ("to make you *see*"), which is in itself ambivalent, since "see" obviously refers to both sensual and intellectual cognition, Conrad's art of making an "appeal through the senses" relies just as much on hearing and listening. In his comment on Henry James, Conrad emphasizes the need of the novelist to speak out heroically on the eve of ultimate destruction, "to interpret the ultimate experience of mankind in terms of his temperament":

> He is so much of a voice that, for him, silence is like death; and the postulate was, that there is a group alive, clustered on his threshold to watch the last flicker of light on a black sky, to hear the last word uttered in the stilled workshop of the earth. It is safe to affirm that, if anybody, it will be the imaginative man who would be moved to speak on the eve of that day without to-morrow.... ("Henry James: An Appreciation," *NLL*, 14)

Novels like *Lord Jim*, *The Nigger of the "Narcissus,"* "Heart of Darkness" and *Nostromo* are narrative studies in fascination and vocal effects. As we ponder on the specific quality they convey, as we ponder on our own fascination in the reading of these texts, we might well start from the insight that Conrad presents us a communicative act, in which we are invited to share in the fascination of observers, participants and oral narrators who seem to be in the thrall of a charismatic or rather pseudo-charismatic protagonist. Now fascination cannot be explained in terms of moral abstractions. The text of "Heart of Darkness" thus contains, among many others, two major tensions and contradictions, the second of which I propose to explore in my paper. First, in verbal art written at the turn of the century, the poetics of fascination depends for its effect on speech which lacks the unquestioned authority it used to have in religion and elsewhere. Second, rhetorically and ideologically, Marlow never quite abandons the traditional moral framework of good vs evil, culture vs nature; yet the fascination his language tries so hard to express and to convey is an irrational, quasi-
-religious experience which operates beyond the domain of the moral and the rational scheme of interpretation prevalent in the culture of nineteenth-century England.

Fascination

Fascination seems to be one of those terms which have as yet eluded the attention of the critics. In everyday language it denotes an unusual degree of attention which we give, for whatever reason, to an object of our experience. The intensity of the experience may be such as to freeze the experiencing subject into immobility or to release an explosion of emotional rhetoric trying to speak the unspeakable, i.e. the sort of strained language typical of Marlow. The experience is profoundly contingent, since it seems impossible to account for the huge variety of preferences and tastes that one encounters. Why is one person fascinated by butterflies, another one by a map of Africa? In a modern democratic culture, with its striking dissolution of belief systems and values, interest and fascination, in a sense fashion and style, are pretty much the only factors left to produce new relevancies and distinctions.

The interaction between subject and object called fascination operates beyond the domain of good and evil. What is involved is not a moral, but an aesthetic and, particularly in the context of archaic culture, a religious experience. Romantic literature has always known this. The seductive power of a *femme fatale* is, very much like that of a work of art or of a political Messiah, not due to her being the agent of the devil, but to properties like beauty, sexual attraction, energy and language. Pre-modern cultures endow the object of fascinated observation, or even awe, with magical properties. The fetish or the idol gain power over us, in a sense overwhelm our faculties, because they partake of supernatural energies. The quality of the experience is not affected by the fact that gods can be good or evil. Faced with what R. Otto calls the invisible presence of *"Das Numinose"* (*fascinans*, the holy) the mind of the religious person is filled with a mixture of happiness and fear, attraction and repulsion. Being both immeasurably powerful and deeply mysterious, the *mysterium tremendum* of the divine informs true religious experience with profound ambivalence. For ancient man, fascination is linked to the experience of a supernatural power existing beyond the boundaries of the familiar and the normal in life. In a sense, this is true even today. It is only the strikingly unusual, be it a charismatic person, an artistic achievement or a natural occurrence which is capable of producing fascination proper.

One might deem it superfluous to salvage possibly outmoded forms of consciousness from the ashes of oblivion. However, at the turn of the century philosophers, linguists, anthropologists and historians of culture developed an intense interest in pre-historic forms of thought and experience of which Conrad was not unaware. When scientific positivism and European culture reached in a sense an unprecedented height, a deep epistemological and cultural uneasiness concerning language in particular made itself felt. If the scientific paradigm of positivism does no longer suffice to explain the mystery of life, if abstract language in particular more and more appears to be futile rhetoric unable to express the bewildering complexity of life, then a writer could not but take recourse to the language of sensory experience, of myth and of parody. This is precisely what Conrad does in *The Nigger of the "Narcissus"* and "Heart of Darkness." He exploits the suggestive power and semantic richness of modern and ancient images and symbols for the purpose of making an effective aesthetic appeal. As they blend, interact and cancel out each other, a host of suggestions is produced which cannot be adequately paraphrased. (On this complexity see, for example, Fothergill, Burden). However, it seems to me that the negotiation between prehistoric and modern culture, sometimes translated by the text into a clash between nature vs corrupt civilization, sometimes into a clash between the disciplines ("work") of cultured life and the unrestrained play of wild, instinctual life, demonstrates, despite the frequent racist stereotyping of the natives, the superiority of the vital, irrational, physical, "natural" dimension of life over culture and morality as a source of fascination. Whether Marlow's moral rationalization of his final experience of Kurtz is to be taken at face value is at least doubtful. One could argue that Marlow's moral interpretation of Kurtz's "The horror! The horror!" is an illusion necessary for the preservation of his self-respect, just as his lie concerning Kurtz's last cry is necessary to keep the Intended's self-respect intact. The question is, of course, undecidable.

In Conrad's text, fascination is the effect on us of three media: image, voice and charismatic power, all of which belong both to premodern and to modern consciousness, to the age of idols, fetishes and prophet speaking to us out of the wilderness just as much as to the age of operas, gramophones, films, electronic media and dictators. In a sense, then, Kurtz's relapse into atavism is accompanied, on the level of novelistic discourse, by a reversion to modes of communication which are simultaneously modern and archaic. Thus the word "fascination" itself is thoroughly modern, insofar as it refers, like "love," to the contingency of individual experience, and yet it also reminds us of its origins in the premodern, magical thinking of ancient man. In Latin the verb *fascinare* means "to bewitch," "to enchant." It is no coincidence, therefore, that the skeptical Marlow is paradoxically likened to an idol and Buddha and that, like God, he is speaking to his listeners out of the dark, his body remaining unseen. By simulating Marlow's oral narrative, the novelist wishes to accomplish the required effect of "magic suggestiveness" ("Preface" to *The Nigger of the "Narcissus"*) which is identified by R. Otto in his famous study *Das Heilige...* (Otto, 80) as a major artistic mode in the representation of *das Numinose*. *Das Numinose* defines the specific irrational feeling of religious awe and fear, which is most powerfully present when the artist presents a "mixture of terrible fearfulness and most sublime holiness."[1] True, Kurtz must be called a profane and sinister, in short a modern travesty of Otto's *das Numinose,* but there is enough of the *Energie* (27) of the *Fascinans* (42) left in him to attract Marlow. Furthermore, Marlow himself is fascinated by the suggestive, awe-inspiring and incomprehensible silence of the wilderness, which, pregnant with undecoded meanings and menacing power, reminds one of the silence and the mysterious power of the god of mysticism. Otto links the experience of *das Numinose* with representations of Buddha in Chinese art (86).

It seems to me that the representation of Kurtz's voice also incorporates or at least alludes to elements of Christian discourse. The "gift" (see Corinthians I: 12) of speech proves Kurtz to be a creature of God. However, since he uses this gift without true "charity" (13: 1) he merely produces sounds without meaning, somewhat in the manner of a "sounding brass" (13: 1), and becomes "nothing" (13: 2). Yet, by a modern revaluation of values the absence of truth or meaning does not prevent the sounds, which prove the presence of an exceptional energy, from becoming the focus of an intense fascination. Again, the ambivalence of Kurtz's voice is reflected in Biblical language. The voice of the charismatic person reminds one both of a bodiless "voice from heaven" (Mark 1: 13) and, with a new complexity of meaning, of "the voice of one crying in the wilderness" (1: 3), who is both a prophet and a lost soul. For unlike Jesus, who resisted the temptations of the devil in the wilderness (1: 3), Kurtz yields to them. In other words, Kurtz radiates the fascination of a fallen god, and Marlow, being equally modern, feels attracted to him somewhat in the manner the romantics were attracted by the energy of Milton's Satan.

Conrad dramatizes and conceptualizes the experience of fascination. The word itself appears at crucial points in the unfolding of the story. Marlow ends his analogy of the Romans venturing into the wildernes of untamed Britain, which foreshadows his own report, on a sombre note of sympathetic speculation:

> He has to live in the midst of the incomprehensible, which is also detestable. And it has a fascination, too, that goes to work upon him. The fascination of the abomination – you know, imagine the growing regrets, the longing to escape, the powerless disgust, the surrender, the hate."
> He paused. ("Heart of Darkness," *YS*, 50)

Pauses are rare in Marlow's speech, and they invariably indicate profound significance and profound emotional involvement on the part of the speaker. The civilized explorer is both attracted and repelled by the call of the wild. If the "abomination" were so utterly alien and incomprehensible, it could hardly exert such a fascination. In *psychological* terms, the traveller and artist in fact responds to what Freud would call the "repressed" in himself, which is immediately censored by conscience. Does Conrad vacillate between moral and psychological models of interpretation? Or is the need to explore the psychological truth of wilderness without (the "savages") and within (Marlow) contaminated by the artistic need to find an appropriate rhetorical and ideological medium of communication? If the latter is true, words like "abomination," "fiend-like," "devil," "darkness" and the like are merely used to reach the audience rather than to camouflage a psychological insight. *In terms of literary history* Conrad rewrites the romantic fascination for the energy of the satanic. *In terms of colonialist discourse* Conrad wavers between subversive fascination and traditional contempt for the natives, understanding appreciation and conventional stereotyping of the barbaric other as utterly alien and incomprehensible.

There is apparently no rhetorical substitute for the connotative power of language and images charged with traditional meanings. Since scientific discourses cannot be scrapped, this frequently leads to a highly suggestive coexistence of scientific and mythical meanings. As a young man and romantic dreamer, Marlow is charmed by maps of far-off countries, the Congo in particular. As artist and narrator, he interprets his fascination with the river Congo in the following manner: "And as I looked at the map of it in a shop-window, it fascinated me as a snake would a bird – a silly little bird" (52). As a grown-up person, he decides to let his early fascination determine the course of his life: "The snake had charmed me" (53). The most fascinating object he meets on his travels is, however, not wilderness in its purity, but a contorted, even pathological blending of wilderness and refined culture, Mr. Kurtz. If one reads, as one surely must, the word "snake" as a deliberate reference to Biblical language, Marlow's confession is a profoundly disconcerting and romantic one: he becomes attracted to evil itself. If one takes up the clue offered by the interpretive comparison, Marlow is simply the victim of a biological and psychological affinity, a human animal which in a sense cannot help being devoured by another one. In the latter case the source of the fascination is predominantly to be found in vital energy operating under the conditions of modern culture.

I shall now make an attempt to substantiate this claim by exploring the semantic layers which seem to be suggested by the text when one reads the term "voice" in the light of medical discourse (Miethe, Hermann-Röttgen), sociological theories of the charismatic person (Weber) and the contemporary critique of language (Mauthner). According to medical discourse, the voice is shaped by three factors: the body, the psyche and the culture in which the speaking individual happens to live. The semantics of this grid provided by medical discourse do not exhaust the meaning, let alone the procedures, of a near-poetic text like "Heart of Darkness." What I have to do, therefore, is to explore a complex suggestiveness which is engendered by the interaction of scientific and symbolic meanings.

A Voice! a Voice!

exclaims Marlow. Clearly the fascination Kurtz induces in him is focussed upon Kurtz's voice. A voice cannot be reduced any further. It expresses the very individuality and the very temperament of a person. Yet, judging from the voice, Kurtz's individuality seems to be curiously limited. There is no attempt to specify the quality of his voice. We only learn that it is deep and strong. Thus Kurtz appears to be a "remarkable person," as witnessed by his remarkable effects on other persons, but the very quality which accounts for his individuality in particular and its extraordinary effect on others is comparatively unspecific as far as the words of the text are concerned. If one assumes, as I do, that Conrad's novel fascinates the reader by a combination of charismatic person and charismatic text, the seeming contradiction indicated above makes sense. The charismatic person is essentially a type maintaining its identity best when viewed from a distance. Not surprisingly, we never get an inside view of the mind of Kurtz. It relies for his or her power over others on vocal and suggestive communication rather than the written word. The voice of the charismatic person is, like the voice of God, the law itself; but, unlike the voice of God, it is also the expression of his psychophysical identity. It is therefore extremely abstract and extremely individual at the same time. The voice expresses individuality and yet partakes of the universality of a social and psychological type. The "magic suggestiveness," required of the speech of the charismatic speaker, is not brought about by the precision of quasi-scientific or quasi-historical language. It presupposes a language which is indefinite and full of blank spaces, thus inviting the imaginative participation of the reader. Again, not surprisingly, there is no scene showing Marlow and Kurtz speaking to each other at length.

Before pursuing this point further, a brief look at the history of voice in novelistic discourse before Conrad is necessary. Unlike Bakhtin, for whom the term "voice" is a metaphoric substitute for "social heteroglossia" (Bakhtin, 263), i.e. the combination of socially determined styles to be found in a novel, I use the term "voice" in the strict semiotic and linguistic meaning of "vocal communication." In the history of English novel before Conrad the quality of vocal communication was never paid much attention, neither in theory, where the term is hardly ever used, nor in the fictional texts themselves simulating oral speech to characterize individuals and tellers of tales like Marlow. In order to acknowledge the act of speaking, Jane Austen usually confines herself to using the verbs "said," "replied" or "cried." The huge variety of meaningful tones or, as linguists say, "vocal stereotypes," was largely ignored as the individual's identity was supposed to unfold itself in his acts and the content of his speeches. However, Gothic novels, focussing on the spectacular delineation of passions, used a wider spectrum of verbal possibilities and generally the development towards psychological realism in Eliot and others meant that the representation of subjectivity implied giving greater attention to nuances of tone. Still, voice continued to play a subsidiary role in characterization and the separation of voice from content which we find in Conrad was unthinkable.

I suggest three possible reasons for the striking importance attributed to voice at the turn of the century. First of all, Nietzsche's critique of idealism and metaphysics and his praise of the body turned the assumptions of occidental philosophy upside down. Psychologists like Wilhelm Wundt regarded man as a psychophysical unity and medical researchers like Barth contributed classic studies of the physiology and pathology of the voice. Second, the recent invention of the gramophone separated enunciating body and voice and made the preservation of a huge variety of voices possible for future use and enjoyment. Joyce makes Bloom explicitly meditate on this phenomenon in the Hades chapter of *Ulysses*. In fact, in the year 1887, well before the publication of "Heart of Darkness," the

Deutsche Grammophon-Gesellschaft offered the first gramophones for sale. Third, Immanuel Kant's critique of pure reason
was transformed, in the course of the nineteenth century into
a critique of language, the most influential work being F.
Mauthner's *Beiträge zu einer Kritik der Sprache*.[2] For Mauthner
the modern languages of culturally advanced societies are not
neutral and effective tools necessary for human communication
and cognition. On the contrary, they exert a "tyranny" (Mauthner, 1) over us, defining the range of our ideas. Language cannot
be reduced to a function of logic and grammar. As an act and as
a power (47), it has a suggestive energy like someone subjecting
us to a "hypnosis" (43). This is particularly the case when words
become, in the course of time, divorced from their roots in
sensory experience and metaphor and acquire the status of
empty discursive husks, of "dead word symbols" (66). Theology,
philosophy, science and political theory are endlessly producing
abstractions of this kind, words like "progress" and "evolution"
(25), whose very emptiness gives room for endless speculations
and associations for those users who have not lost their belief in
them. According to Mauthner, the most striking symptom of the
decadence of modern culture is the theatrical quality of its
language (230). In his seminal work, cultural criticism thus
becomes a criticism of language. The languages of modern
culture are degenerate playthings (51), unable to express feelings
or to enable real communication or to increase our knowledge.
Instead, they produce endless misunderstandings (56).

The relevance of all this for the language of Kurtz and Marlow
is obvious. Marlow dismisses Kurtz's political and humanitarian
rhetoric as fundamentally false and obsolete. The official
discourse of progressive philantropic colonialism, endlessly
repeated by the newspapers, is for him simply "rot" and
"humbug" ("Heart of Darkness," *YS*, 59). Examples are
highlighted for the sake of ironic distancing. If Kurtz still
impresses Marlow, it is therefore not by virtue of the meanings
transported, but by virtue of the suggestive power of something
physical and psychological, i.e. the voice itself. The text seems to
be completely or perhaps strategically silent on the question

whether a physical, homoerotic attraction is implied. Whatever the answer to this question, the relationship between depth and surface becomes inverted. It is the vocal surface itself, the materiality of the sign, which causes an effect. It appears as if the deep structure of meaning were replaced or at least rivalled by effects emanating from the suggestive energy of the surface.

Mauthner does not quite envisage the radical possibility and logical consequences of his thought sketched here. Yet his description of the properties of literary language, which partly recovers the sensuous saturation of archaic language, to some extent explains Marlow's stylistic procedure. Words are essentially imprecise, particularly when they are positioned in a literary organization. Since they have blurred, moving edges (*flimmernd und zitternd* – Mauthner, 109) every recipient is expected to flesh out, with the help of memory and imagination, the suggestions of the text in his own way.

Conrad, like Mauthner, realizes that abstract terms such as "voice" offer a particularly wide range of interpretive possibilities, especially when rhetorical emphasis and context invite the reader to activate their semantic potential. I distinguish six meanings of the sign "voice" in Conrad's text, the first three of which are all related to its psychophysical properties:

(a) Kurtz's deep, ringing voice is emphatically *male*. The fact has causal and symbolic implications. Only a male and only an exceptionally big male – the text mentions seven feet – possesses the required size of the chest and of the vocal chords to do this. On the symbolic level, the huge male conforms to the notion of the romantic hero who is of course deconstructed by the ironic naming device.

(b) The second and less obvious cause of Kurtz's voice might be, very much like that of Wait in *The Nigger of the "Narcissus,"* the *pathological* state of his body, which again suggests connotations of psychological, ethical and cultural breakdown.

(c) What Marlow responds to is primarily not Kurtz's moral depravity or the poignancy of the protagonist's thwarted utopian ambitions, but the sheer presence of *energy*: "The volume of tone he emitted without effort, almost without the trouble of moving his lips, amazed me. A voice! a voice!" ("Heart of Darkness," *YS*, 135). "Though he could hardly stand, there was still plenty of vigour in his voice" (143). Since Kurtz's voice is the manifest sign of a vital force, the emptiness of his rhetoric is paradoxically able to enthrall the listener like magic. The fictional listeners are carried away by "a magic current of phrases" (118). For Marlow, Kurtz's voice, i.e. an aesthetic impression, is far more memorable than his actions. Representing a natural force, Kurtz is really a Darwinian and Nietzschean character, a superman and a Shavian life-force. In that respect he resembles another obsessive talker of contemporary literature, Shaw's Tanner in *Man and Superman*, who is also a would-be philantropist and reformer, and whose rhetoric persuades not because it reveals the truth but because it epitomizes energy (Seeber).

(d) Numerous references to the powers of the dark, read in conjunction with Kurtz's utopian aspirations, suggest that Kurtz is interpreted by Marlow as a fallen God or a false prophet. The unique qualities of his charcter and his voice, far from having to be attributed to contingency, are in fact typical features of the charismatic personality.

As Levenson pointed out, Weber's analysis of charisma as a mode of rule is important for an understanding of "Heart of Darkness." Two points, however, need to be added to his reading. Weber is aware of the ambivalence of charisma, its roots in primitive consciousness and its persistence in modern guises, and he is also aware of the function of orality and voice in the practice of charismatic rule.

Weber's scientific, objective, value-free method of sociology does not distinguish between good and bad, god-like or devil--like charismatic leaders or a mixture of the two. Theologians apparently think otherwise, but from the point of view of Weber's sociology of rule, Kurtz is a charismatic person and also a parody of such a person. To have success with people, the charismatic leader needs personal qualities lifting him far above the domain of common humanity. He is, therefore, a god-like hero equipped with essentially magic powers. The charismatic leader is not subject to rules and rational procedures (not surprisingly the Manager complains of Kurtz's "unsound method" – "Heart of Darkness," *YS*, 137); his rule is, on the contrary, irrational, realized from moment to moment by creative actions. Not being bound to the rules of tradition and bureaucratic order, charismatic rule is decidedly revolutionary and unpredictable. Archaic warrior-leaders or religious prophets win recognition among devoted followers or disciples by spectacular deeds and words apparently inspired by supernatural powers. These words and deeds may get recorded in historical or holy texts to ensure an integrating effect on the followers of the charismatic person after his death. His chief weapon, however, is the power of the spoken word, the conjunction of body and voice, the *viva vox*, as Otto (80) calls it, which, as Jesus emphasizes, is not bound by written traditions.

The parallels between Weber's characterization of charismatic rule and Conrad's characterization of Kurtz are striking. Kurtz, assuming the role of a deity, establishes his charismatic leadership over the natives to such an extent that they even follow him when he, ill and emaciated, has to command them from a stretcher. The intriguing aspect of Weber's analysis, however, is his claim that charisma is also the essence of modern revolutionary leaders like Napoleon or the literary demagogue Kurt Eisner. Napoleon's rule is the "rule of genius" (Weber, 141) and it is precisely the demagogic genius (140) in the journalist and political speaker Kurtz who casts a spell over his audience. With uncanny premonition Conrad senses the conjunction between political and artistic genius in the ruthless political leaders of modernity. Kurtz, the prophet, succeeds in winning devoted "disciple(s)" ("Heart of Darkness," *YS*, 132) like the Russian, or devoted friends like Marlow. In each case it is the voice which does the trick. Kurtz is incapable of dialogue; he utters his judgements and commands in "splendid monologues" (132), forcing his environment – with the great exception of

Marlow – to act as listeners. "He had the power to charm or to frighten rudimentary souls into an aggravated witch-dance in his honour" (119).

Clearly Marlow and Kurtz share many characteristics. Theirs is the charisma of artists who enthrall their audiences by the power of a voice which, divorced from the body, seems to act like an independent agent. Whereas Kurtz succumbs to the wilderness entirely, Marlow at least acknowledges the power of the call of the wild epitomized by the drums, realizing that culture is only a thin veneer concealing the reality of "primitive emotions" (147). The force of the latter forms a bond and a *chain of fascinations* between the exotic other, Marlow, Kurtz and the reader, the "grunting" natives and the "grunting" listeners on board the yacht.

(e) The fifth connotation associated with "voice" in "Heart of Darkness" concerns cultural and personal reduction. A person merely consisting of voice does no longer meet the criteria of a full human being: "The man presented himself as a voice"(113). "The voice was gone. What else had been there?" (150). Since the voice forms sounds deprived of real meaning, Marlow's memory is filled with an "immense jabber" (115), a bewildering pandemonium of various voices and noises. A voice divorced from the body and from meaning seems to float in the air like something unreal and absurd, ghostly and eerie. Thus voice is linked to the concepts of "unreality," "absurdity" and "dream" which are constantly used by Marlow to interpret his bewildering experience of colonialism's "fantastic invasion" of Africa (131). By metaphoric transfer Kurtz, "this eloquent phantom" (160) thus becomes a hollow man whose lack of inner, cultural substance causes the tremendous reverberation of his voice in an empty chest: "But the wilderness had found him out early, and had taken on him a terrible vengeance for the fantastic invasion. I think it had whispered to him things about himself which he did not know, things of which he had no conception till he took counsel with this great solitude – and the whisper had proved irresistibly fascinating. It echoed loudly within him because he was hollow at the core" (131).

Given all these contexts, "voice" suggests, in a highly complex fashion, contradictory meanings cancelling out each other: the voice of the hero, the voice of the dummy, the voice of the charismatic leader, the voice of absurdity and unreality. Divorced from the body, it is the meeting-point of modernity and primitive culture, the gramophone and God's or the prophet's *viva vox* (Otto, 79). Still, we must not forget that the reduction of language to voice discussed here is often viewed positively by contemporary poetics. Robert Frost, for example, emphatically bases his poetics of lyrical poetry on "sentence sounds" and "tones" (Scully, 50) which are not entirely subordinated to the meaning of the sentence. Mistrust of the emptiness of the written word, newspaper language in particular, is the critical impulse motivating Frost's preference for the vocal materiality of the sign. Artificial words without meaning, i.e. pure sounds form the materials of provocative sound poems by the Dadaist Hugo Ball as for example "Karawane" which can be made to represent something exclusively by the choice of intonation and stress. However, Conrad's prose text does not and cannot aim at such radicalism despite its use of pauses, elliptic sentence patterns and the like. It primarily invites us to explore its polyvalent, often contradictory meanings.

(f) This brings me to my sixth and last point. I believe one of the connotations suggested and teased out by the very blankness and repetitive weight of the term "voice" is related to the poetics of fascination. Conrad's well-known statements on his own art make this reading likely. The voice of Marlow, of Kurtz and of Conrad himself, are artistic voices speaking to us in a seemingly apocalyptic situation. Voice in this sense hints at the suggestive energy of the artist's utterance and the energy of the suggestive surface of visual and acoustic images. After all, the natives are largely a vocal presence who, as described by Darwin and Barth, express their elementary emotions of grief and anger through gestures and sounds ("howling" etc.).

My emphasis on *surface* needs to be justified. Throughout his narrative Marlow employs, when adopting the role of a cultural

                                                    Hans Ulrich Seeber

critic, the binary opposition reality vs appearance, depth vs surface. Like cultural critics of the nineteenth century, he appropriates a semantic opposition rooted deep in occidental epistemology for purposes of cultural criticism. Invariably the critics, analyzing modern man's specific alienation, diagnose a lack of inner substance and worth. So does Marlow. According to him, the irresponsible and greedy "pilgrims" chasing after the modern idol ivory in the Congo have "nothing inside but a little loose dirt" ("Heart of Darkness," *YS*, 81). Clothes hide no longer, as they do in Carlyle, the spirit of the absolute, but the "darkness" of "primitive emotions": "Kurtz discoursed. A voice! a voice! It rang deep to the very last. It survived his strength to hide in the magnificent *folds* (my emphasis) of eloquence the barren darkness of his heart" (147). However, since the truth of verbal signs and the reality of life can no longer be ascertained, all we seem to be left with is the suggestive energy of surfaces and styles. Conrad's text cannot be reduced to a mere attempt at rhetorical and opera-like effects, the sort of effect that is clearly evident on the occasion of Wait's first spectacular appearance in *The Nigger of the "Narcissus,"* when his ringing voice silences and enthralls the crowd of sailors, but it certainly inverts and thereby deconstructs the classical dichotomy of story and meaning, surface and depth. There is some truth in the anonymous narrator's claim that the suggestive surface of Marlow's story radiates meanings rather than encapsules them for the reader to uncover. This is indeed one of the characteristic tensions and paradoxes of Conrad's art: whereas Conrad, the moralist and cultural critic, denounces the surfaces of theatrical, operatic and rhetorical effects as hollow and empty lies, the artist Conrad very much relies on voice and image and rhetoric and the musical genre which makes the best use of them at the expense of meaning, i.e. the opera. Does the almost random production of incompatible meanings in "Heart of Darkness" "really" mean that both Marlow and we as readers are seduced by sounds and sights, by appearances and surfaces, including verbal surfaces, rather in the manner Baudrillard analyzes the effects of modern media? Such a thinking would certainly be compatible with Nietzsche's thinking in "Nietzsche contra Wagner":

> Oh those Greeks! they knew how to live. For that, it is necessary to
> stay bravely with the surface, the wrinkle, the skin, to worship
> appearance, to believe in forms, sounds, words, in the whole Olympus
> of appearance.... And are we not returning to this, we daring spirits
> who have climbed to the most elevated and dangerous top of
> contemporary thought and have looked around from there?[2]

Clearly, the relevance of Conrad's poetics of fascination is not
confined to "Heart of Darkness." Whenever political dema-
gogues like Donkin (*The Nigger of the "Narcissus"*), Gamacho,
the Montero brothers (*Nostromo*) or other pseudo-charismatic
characters as, for example, Wait (*The Nigger of the "Narcissus"*)
appear on the scene, they seem to cast a magic spell over their
audience by the sheer power of their voice and the theatrical
quality of their gestures, actions and physical appearance. I have
already pointed out the magic effect of Wait's voice on the crew.
For the majority of the crowd listening to a speech by the
revolutionary Pedrito Montero in *Nostromo*, the effect of
fascination is created by merely watching the gestures of the
speaker and listening to his voice, very much as if they were
enjoying an operatic performance:

> What he began was a speech. He began it with the shouted word
> "Citizens!" which reached even those in the middle of the Plaza.
> Afterwards the greater part of the citizens remained *fascinated* [italics
> mine] by the orator's action alone, his tip-toeing, the arms flung above
> his head with the fists clenched, a hand laid flat upon the heart, the
> silver gleam of rolling eyes, the sweeping, pointing, embracing
> gestures, a hand laid familiarly on Gamacho's shoulder;.... (*N*, 389-90)

Conrad's caricature of political rhetoric emphasizes its histri-
onic, operatic quality. Rather than communicating "deep"
thoughts and arguments, its "phrases" ("[T]he happiness of the
people," "[S]ons of the country" – 390), which are usually
inaudible anyway, convey emotive suggestions, an attitude of
passionate involvement, which is even better communicated by
the political actor's quasi-theatrical performance. In this performance (primitive, animal-like) the quality of the voice plays
a major role. It is chiefly due to its powerful presence that the

trick of emotional persuasion is accomplished. Thus the "crowd" responds to "the howling voice of Gamacho" (391) by producing "vast, deep muttering" (391).

The discovery of atavism by medical science (Cesare Lombroso) at the turn of the century helps to undermine the stability of the classical binary opposition culture vs nature. According to a widely held notion shared, for example, by John Davidson and Aldous Huxley and fitting perfectly into their and Conrad's notion of cultural criticism, modern crowds in a sense behave like savages. Their unthinking devotion to a charismatic leader is, therefore, paralleled by the charismatic quality of Karain's rule over his followers in "Karain: A Memory." However, the reader of "Karain: A Memory" experiences the haunting voice in at least three functions and meanings. (1) The mere physical and vocal presence of Karain, the native chief, among his followers, induces in them acts of devotion and of respect. Karain has the effect of a magnet on the rest of the community. (2) As he tells his story of revenge, which ends in the catastrophe of Karain shooting his friend Matara rather than the Dutch lover of Matara's sister, the white listeners are enthralled both by the content and the oral style of Karain's tale, Karain's seemingly free-floating voice in particular. Similarly, the readers of Conrad's tale are meant to be enthralled by the artist's impressionistic evocation of the exotic setting. (3) The unbearable, haunting voice of Matara's ghost urging Karain to complete the revenge can only be neutralized by the intervention of a magic spell. After the death of Karain's sword-bearer and protector a spell is provided by Hollis, a white man, whose incantatory words and voice transform a ribbon and a jubilee sixpence representing Queen Victoria into a powerful amulet and fetish which restores Karain's self-confidence. What appears to be a mere hoax exploiting Karain's superstitions turns out to be an event which in fact calls into question the validity of binaries like West vs. East, rationalism vs. irrationalism, culture vs. nature, reality vs. fiction/illusion. After all the Western people have their ghosts, too, who suddenly return during the magic ritual performed by Hollis. Furthermore, the end of the text, raising the question of reality, contrasts Jackson's seeming preference for Karain's world with the narrator's insistence upon the superior status of "home," i.e. London. The question whether the sight of alienated urban crowds is more real than Karain's strange experience remains undecided. It would appear, following the argument of this paper, that the suggestive energy of surfaces is potent in both cultures (one of which used to be subsumed under the category "nature" at the time), presumably because seeing images and hearing voices are also – explicitly so in the case of Karain – acts of believing. Such acts of believing turn mere surfaces, appearances or images, including verbal/vocal surfaces, into veritable truths, while lack of belief transforms truths into illusions. It seems to me correct to speak of the "real/illusory world" (Krajka, 255; see also Griem, 110 f.) created by Conrad. Due to belief, a deceptive imitation or fictional act acquires the status of a truth. The transgression of seemingly clear borderlines by Kurtz and by Hollis, and also by Marlow, the reader and, last but not least, the author himself, is a logical step implied in Conrad's epistemological, anthropological and aesthetic views. This step also reflects the nihilistic, Nietzschean episteme of the time. In *Götzen-Dämmerung* Nietzsche attacks the occidental notion and search for truth and pointedly gives one of his sections the title "Wie die 'wahre Welt' endlich zur Fabel wurde" (How the "true world" finally became a fiction) (Nietzsche, II, 963).

NOTES

1. "Mischung entsetzlicher Fürchterlichkeit und höchster Heiligkeit" (Otto, 81).

2. *"O diese Griechen! sie verstanden sich darauf, zu **leben**! dazu tut not, tapfer bei der Oberfläche, der Falte, der Haut stehnzubleiben, den Schein anzubeten, an Formen, an Töne, an Worte, an den ganzen **Olymp des Scheins** zu glauben! Diese Griechen waren oberflächlich, – aus **Tiefe**.... Und kommen wir nicht eben darauf zurück, wir Wagehalse des Geistes. die wir die höchste und gefährlichste Spitze des gegenwärtigen Gedankens erklettert und von da aus uns umgesehn haben"* (Nietzsche, II, 1061; quoted after Pfeiffer, 23).

WORKS CITED

Bakhtin M. M. *The Dialogic Imagination: Four Essays*, ed. Michael Holquist. Austin: U. of Texas P., 1985.

Barth Ernst. *Einführung in die Physiologie, Pathologie und Hygiene der menschlichen Stimme*. Leipzig: Thieme, 1911.

Burden Robert. *"Heart of Darkness": An Introduction to the Variety of Criticism*. Basingstoke: Macmillan, 1991.

Crystal David. *The Cambridge Encyclopedia of Language*. Cambridge: Cambridge U.P., 1987.

Ellis James. "Kurtz's Voice: The Intended as 'The Horror'," *English Literature in Transition* (1880-1920), 19 (1976), 105-10.

Fothergill Anthony. *"Heart of Darkness."* Milton Keynes: Open University Press, 1989.

Griem Julika. *Brüchiges Seemannsgarn: Mündlichkeit und Schriftlichkeit im Werk Joseph Conrads*. Tübingen: Narr, 1995; Script Oralia 81.

Krajka Wiesław. "Making Magic as Cross-cultural Encounter: The Case of Conrad's 'Karain: A Memory'," *Conrad, James, and Other Relations*, eds. Keith Carabine and Owen Knowles with Paul Armstrong. Boulder – Lublin – New York: East European Monographs – Maria Curie-Skłodowska University – Columbia U.P., 1998, 245-59; *Conrad: Eastern and Western Perspectives*, ed. Wiesław Krajka, vol. 6.

Levenson Michael. "The Value of Fact in 'Heart of Darkness'," in Joseph Conrad. *"Heart of Darkness."* A Norton Critical Edition, ed. Robert Kimbrough, Third Edition. New York – London: Norton, 1988, 391-405.

Mauthner Fritz. *Beiträge zu einer Kritik der Spache*. Erster Band: *Zur Sprache und zur Psychologie*. 2 Auflage. Stuttgart – Berlin: Cotta, 1906. Translations from this text are mine.

Miethe Erhard, Hermann-Röttgen Marion. *Wenn die Stimme nicht stimmt...Symptome, Ursachen, Therapie*. Stuttgart: Thieme, 1993.

Nietzsche Friedrich. *Werke in drei Bänden*, ed. Karl Schlechta. Darmstadt: Wissenschaftliche Buchgesellschaft, 1994.

Otto Rudolf. *Das Heilige: Über das Irrationale in der Idee des Göttlichen und sein Verhältnis zum Rationalen* (1917). München: Beck, 1987.

Pecora Vincent. "'Heart of Darkness' and the Phenomenology of Voice," *English Literary History*, 52: 4 (1985), 993-1015.

Pfeiffer K. Ludwig. "Suggestiveness or Interpretation: On the Vitality of Appearances," in *Reflecting Senses: Perception and Appearance in Literature, Culture and the Arts*, ed. Walter Pape and Frederick Burwick. Berlin – New York: Walter de Gruyter, 1995, 15-32.

Scully James, ed. *Modern Poets on Modern Poetry*. London: Fontana, 1971.

Seeber Hans Ulrich. "The 'Hero' Speaks. Energy and Verbal Power in Dramas of the Turn of the Century (Shaw, Synge)," in *Word and Action in Drama: Studies in Honour of Hans-Jürgen Diller on the Occasion of his 60th Birthday*, ed. Günter Ahrends et al. Trier: Wissenschaftlicher Verlag, 1994, 119-35.
Weber Max. *Wirtschaft und Gesellschaft: Grundriss der verstehenden Sociologie*. 5 Auflage. Tübingen: Mohr, 1976.

James N. Brown,
Macquarie University,
Sydney, Australia
Patricia M. Sant,
Macquarie University,
Sydney, Australia

Empire Looks East: Spectatorship and Subjectivity in "Karain: A Memory"

"Am I a woman, to forget long years before an eyelid has had the time to beat twice?" he exclaimed, with bitter resentment. He startled me. It was amazing. To him his life – that cruel mirage of love and peace – seemed as real, as undeniable, as theirs would be to any saint, philosopher, or fool of us all. ("Karain: A Memory," *TU*, 43-4)

It would appear to us, the readers of Conrad's short story, as it seems to appear to Karain's listeners (the three English gun-runners who comprise his audience) that the only conceivable response to the Malayan chieftain's rhetorical question, "Am I a woman...?," is a resounding, astonished "No!" – especially following as it does the narrator's lengthy and lingering early descriptions of Karain's dignity and "luxuriant strength" (7). Karain's exclamation serves, however, to place under interrogation the problematics of the sexualization and gender identification of raced bodies. This paper explores the construction, by Western culture (by and in the person of the narrator and his companions), of the identities of Karain (and his people), and of the Orient, as an exotic "Other" by the West.[1]

We situate "Karain: A Memory" in the "network of 'knowledge'" specific to Lacanian theory, especially his theory of "the gaze,"[2] and the refinements of that theory in contemporary analysis as explicated particularly by L. Mulvey and H. K. Bhabha.[3] Mulvey's concern is primarily (and now famously) with the visual pleasure afforded the male viewer of narrative cinema by the camera's privileging of his voyeuristic positionality, Bhabha's with race and class; both, however, are concerned with white male constructions of othered subjectivities – based on race, sex, class, color, sexual preference – in order to control and silence their voices. Working from these post-Lacanian analysts, we will argue that Conrad prefigures developments in twentieth-century cinematic and visual representation in his foregrounding of the look, in "Karain: A Memory," to emphasize the constructedness of the Other and of (European, male) subjectivity in terms of the Lacanian gaze.

Mulvey's now-famous argument that popular narrative film is primarily addressed to the male protagonist in the diegesis – and by extension to the male spectator in the audience – is relevant to "Karain: A Memory." Mulvey held that, in narrative film, woman is represented as the passive object of the male gaze, thus playing to male desire but, conversely, that the image of woman as icon threatens to awaken man's unconscious castration anxieties, from which the man can escape only by either voyeurism or fetishistic scopophilia. Thus for Mulvey woman in narrative film functions as image, and man as the bearer of the look;[4] and this interpretation of film fuelled debates concerning subjectivity and representation throughout the late 1970s and the first half of the 1980s.

The controversy pursuant to Mulvey's article was significantly enriched by the appearance, in the Winter 1983 number of *Screen* (a leading international journal of film and television theory) of Bhabha's article, "The Other Question: The Stereotype and Colonial Discourse." Bhabha, like Mulvey, uses psychoanalytic theory, but applies it to an examination of representations of racial difference as otherness in the discourse of colonialism. Like Mulvey,[5] Bhabha posits the nature of the stereotype (here created in colonial discourse) as *ambivalent*, and argues that this ambivalence in discourses of racism (as in sexism) is one of their most insidious aspects; he emphasizes (anticipating S. Zizek's ideological reading of Lacan), the importance of socio-cultural structures – class, gender, ideology – in the construction of the colonial subject. Barbara Creed says of this essay that it demonstrates that differences

> are repressed in favour of a generalized image of the colonized subject
> as "other,"...a "degenerate" who must be controlled by and subjected
> to the colonizer. Like the discourse of narrative realism in the cinema,
> the colonial discourse renders invisible its codes of construction and
> presents the colonized subject as transparently and immutably
> "other."[6]

Bhabha argues that the racial stereotype of colonial discourse can be understood as a *fetish* in its masking of the difference of color and its consequent affirmation of wholeness – the sameness of skin and color, the fantasy of a pure origin. "The fetishized stereotype functions to reactivate, in the colonial subject, the Imaginary fantasy of 'an ideal ego that is white and whole'."[7] Fetishism and the play of Imaginary desires are the means through which colonial discourse is constructed; a consequence is that his analysis of the workings of racial discrimination "ensures that the subject positions available to both colonizer and colonized are seen as multiple and shifting, occupying a number of positions rather than as fixed and contained, as is usually implied by the stereotype."[8]

Bhabha's account of subject positions illuminates the strategic narrative manoeuvres to be found in "Karain: A Memory," particularly in relation to colonial discourse and his theory of ambivalence, "as one of the most significant discursive and psychical strategies of discriminatory power – whether racist or sexist, peripheral or metropolitan."[9] The ambivalence of the colonizers' constructions of Karain vividly bear out Freud's comment that "affection and hostility in the treatment of the fetish – which run parallel with the disavowal and acknow-ledgement of castration – are mixed in unequal proportions in different cases, so that the one or the other is more clearly recognisable."[10] Contradictory, conflictual, and oppositional constructions of Karain by the narrator and his white shipmates "function...[ultimately] to reactivate in the colonial subject the Imaginary fantasy of 'an ideal ego that is white and whole'."

In "Karain: A Memory" the narrative emphasis is on the gaze, the visual register by which Karain is both known and estranged, on the white men's imperializing look as an object of late nineteenth-century reification and rationalization.[11] Karain is an object to be looked at, looked through, dissected, wondered at, admired, dismissed; and these contradictions are presented as the products of memory, but of memory as *méconnaissance*.[12] The narrative's retrospectivity is emphasized from the first: "We knew him in those unprotected days when we were content to hold in our hands our lives and our property";[13] that he is recalling "the good old days" is insisted upon by the second sentence of the narrative: "None of us, I believe, has any property now, and I hear that many, negligently, have lost their lives" ("Karain: A Memory," *TU*, 3). The "knowledge" of Karain upon which the gun-runners insist is revealed almost immediately to be a scopic economy, a possession of the chieftain's person which simultaneously insists on the immediately accessible "knowability" of Karain and on the unknowability, the theatricality, of his self-representation. Of the bay on which Karain commands three villages, the narrator states: "It was the stage where, dressed splendidly for his part, he strutted, incomparably dignified, made important by the power he had to awaken an absurd expectation of something heroic going to take place – a burst of action or song – upon the vibrating tone of a wonderful sunshine." But this theatricality is interrupted at this point by the narrator's retrospective musing: "He was *ornate* and *disturbing*, for one could not imagine what depth of *horrible void* such an elaborate front could be *worthy to hide*" (6; emphases ours).

This admission of failure of the imagination serves to establish the narrator's sense of Karain's mysteriousness, his awareness in Karain of *das Ding*,[14] the Lacanian thing precisely described by Zizek as that strange interior body which is "in me more than me," both interior and simultaneously exterior, nominated by the Lacanian term *extime* – external intimacy.[15] Zizek explicates Lacan as follows:

> The Lacanian formula for this object is of course *objet petit a*, this point of Real in the very heart of the subject which cannot be symbolized, which is produced as a residue, a remnant, a leftover of

> every signifying operation, a hard core embodying horrifying *jouis-sance*, enjoyment, and as such an object which simultaneously attracts and repels us – which *divides* our desire and thus provokes shame.[16]

These contradictions in the Europeans' comprehension of Karain set the scene for their incomprehension of him and their attempt to possess him.

This ominous hint of horror is, if anything, intensified by the narrator's insistence that the "essential nature" of Karain is *to act*, in the sense of theatrical self-(re)presentation, an anti-essentialism which, when analyzed, becomes a superfluity:

> He was not masked...but he presented himself *essentially* as an actor, as a human being *aggressively disguised*.... He seemed too effective, too necessary there, too much of an *essential condition* for the existence of his land and his people, to be destroyed by anything short of an earthquake. He summed up his race, his country, the elemental force of ardent life, of tropical nature. He had its luxuriant strength, its fascination; and like it, he carried the seed of peril within. ("Karain: A Memory," *TU*, 6-7; emphases ours)[17]

The narrator's inability to grasp an essence in Karain may be signified by his oxymoronic "barbarous dignity" (8) and by his identification of Karain with "the elemental force of ardent life, of tropical nature" (7) in obvious antithesis to the faithfulness to the illusions of the stage by which his "staginess" is also and contradictorily described. Adding to the reader's sense of the narrator's incomprehension of Karain is his contradictory description of his person: Karain is at once an aggressive "burly bareheaded figure" (11) *and* a narcissist "spotlessly neat...[his hair dyed] a light shade of brown" (13). In Bhabha's words, "[t]he construction of colonial discourse is...a complex articulation of the tropes of fetishism – metaphor and metonymy – and the forms of narcissistic and aggressive identification available to the [Lacanian] schema of the Imaginary."[18]

This construction of colonial discourse is strikingly embodied in Karain:

> Some ten years ago...[he] had led his people...to the conquest of the bay.... He gave them wisdom, advice, reward, punishment, life or

> death, with the same serenity of attitude and voice.... He could conceal his heart; had more endurance; he could swim longer, and steer a canoe better than any of his people; he could shoot straighter, and negotiate more tortuously *than any man of his race I knew*.... ("Karain: A Memory," *TU*, 8; emphasis ours)

Until this (early) point in the narrative, it is the difference of Karain's *people* to which the reader has been exposed and in contrast to which Karain has seemed superior and acknowledgeable as "my very good friend" (8). But here we have a statement of overt difference, in a racist discourse in which "[s]kin, as the key signifier of cultural and racial difference in the stereotype, is the most visible of fetishes, recognized as 'common knowledge'...and plays a public part in *the racial drama that is enacted every day* in colonial societies" (our emphasis).[19] And in contrast to his unidentified people, Karain is here fetishized as the "good object," "the prop that makes the whole object desirable and lovable, facilitates sexual relations and can even promote a form of happiness," as he is "that particular 'fixated' form of the colonial subject which *facilitates* colonial relations, and sets up a discursive form of racial and cultural opposition in terms of which colonial power is exercised."[20] Karain as the representative of the colonized is a fetish to the Europeans in Freud's sense that "affection and hostility in the treatment of the fetish – which run parallel with the disavowal and acknowledgement of castration – are mixed in unequal proportions in different cases, so that the one or the other is more clearly recognisable."[21] It is this simultaneous "mixing" of Karain as an object of affection and hostility which this paper will now endeavor to delineate.

The narrator's description of Karain contrasts with the depiction of his people, who are presented synecdochically as "faces dark, truculent, and smiling; the frank audacious faces of men barefooted, well armed and noiseless [which] thronged the narrow length of our schooner's decks with their ornamented and barbarous crowd, with the variegated colours of checkered sarongs, red turbans, white jackets, embroideries" ("Karain: A Memory," *TU*, 3-4). These people are remembered only as "faces, the eyes, the [soft] voices...the gleam of silk and metal; the murmuring stir of that crowd, brilliant, festive, and martial; and...the touch of friendly brown hands that, after one short grasp, return to rest on a chased hilt" (4). In contrast, as we have indicated, Karain is viewed as "dressed splendidly for his part...incomparably dignified...ornate and disturbing. He summed up his race, his country, the elemental force of ardent life, of tropical nature. He had its luxuriant strength, its fascination" (6-7). He had, in short, for the European men who observe him, the fascination of a fetish.

Only after dark, when he comes to the schooner, is Karain's costume described in detail, and then only in terms of its non-adornment, its self-effacement which, the narrator implies, is affected for his performance on *their* stage, where "[he was] simplicity itself then; all in white, muffled about his head; for arms only a kriss with a plain buffalo-horn handle, which he would politely conceal within a fold of his sarong" (11). And here Karain is presented in terms of his interiority, his difference-
-in-sameness; as he converses with the Europeans, "[t]he quiet dignity of his bearing transform[ing] the dim-lit cuddy of the schooner into an audience-hall" (13). Discussion ranges from Queen Victoria to Karain's experiences, "his native country," his mother, "his wanderings" and "the conquest of the bay" on which he rules three small villages (12-14). He is an object of mystery, fascination and fixation, even envy to the Europeans, as they subject him to their surveillance, seemingly compelled to observe him and, if possible, to comprehend him. Their gaze and attention is in the early part of the narrative compelled by the spectacle of Karain's exercise of power over his people when, among them, "armed men stood out of the way, submissive and erect, others approached from the side, bending their backs to address him humbly.... He dispensed justice in the shade; from a high seat he gave orders, advice, reproof" (15).

This then is one register by which Karain's subject-position is delineated in the regimes of visibility and discursivity – fetish-istic, scopic, Imaginary – within the racial stereotype; but as Bhabha has argued, it cannot – and does not – remain unitary.

The quotation from Freud above recognizes the wide *range* of the stereotype, from the loved to the hated; "a shifting of subject positions in the circulation of colonial power which [Bhabha] tried to account for through the motility of the metaphoric/narcissistic and metonymic/aggressive system of colonial discourse."[22] These powerless, European capitalists seem as nearly in awe of the power of Karain over his people as those people seem themselves to be. Where Karain's "lack" can be located is precisely what to their Western eyes and consciousnesses is inscrutable, Karain's other "side," the register that stops the Europeans short of admiration despite their recognition within him of "a fidelity to his purpose and with a steadfastness of which I would have thought him *racially incapable*" ("Karain: A Memory," *TU*, 18; emphasis ours). Ironically, after two years of short visitations to Karain, the narrator is confident in announcing Karain's "profound ignorance of the rest of the world," about which the Europeans "tried to enlighten him, but our attempts to make clear the irresistible nature of the forces which he desired to arrest failed to discourage his eagerness to strike a blow for *his own primitive ideas*.... He was absurd and unanswerable"; and "[s]ometimes we caught glimpses of a sombre, glowing fury within him – a brooding and vague sense of wrong, and a concentrated lust of violence *which is dangerous in a native*" (18; emphases ours). This "realm of the Imaginary" is that within which the Europeans seek to place him. F. Fanon's reading of the problematic of representation (which he suggests is specific to the colonial situation) is relevant here: "the originality of the colonial context is that the economic substructure is also a superstructure...you are rich because you are white, you are white because you are rich. This is why Marxist analysis should always be slightly stretched every time we have to do with the colonial problem."[23] This seems to us to represent precisely the Europeans' attitude toward Karain, *if*, that is, "rich" is modified to mean "rich in wisdom, knowledge, rational understanding." And if we read Fanon as taking an "anti-representationist" position "attacking the notion that ideology as misrecognition, or misrepresentation, is the repression of the real,"[24] then we can better comprehend the argument that skin, as a signifier of discrimination, must continually be produced or processed as *visible*. To quote P. Abbott:

> [W]hereas repression banishes its object into the unconscious, forgets and attempts to forget the forgetting, discrimination must constantly invite its representations into consciousness, reinforcing the crucial recognition of difference which they embody and revitalising them for the perception on which its effectivity depends.... It must sustain itself on the presence of the very difference which is also its object.[25]

What "authorizes" discrimination is the occlusion of the preconstruction or working-up of difference: "this repression of production entails that the recognition of difference is procured in an innocence, as a 'nature'; recognition is contrived as primary cognition, spontaneous effect of the 'evidence of the visible'."[26] This kind of recognition is precisely the kind attributed to the stereotype which, like Karain, "carrie[s] the seed of peril within" ("Karain: A Memory," *TU*, 7). It is the rooting out of this "seed" to which the remainder of "Karain: A Memory" is devoted.

In the ontologies of the self, European man arrogates to himself the properties of reason and bestows on the "Other" emotion, often neuroticized as hysteria, schizophrenia, madness, incoherence, superstition: irrationality. And as the fetish is (according to Freud) most commonly sexual, so colonial representation has commonly conflated the registers of gender and racial difference, sometimes (as here) producing a "good object," the source of scopic and Imaginary fixation and of compulsive scopophilia and incomprehension. After three of Karain's chief men have left the schooner, to which they have come to pay for the guns they've bought, Karain appears before the gun-running British bedraggled, wet and wearing, uniquely, only a red kerchief and a sarong, provocatively "soaked, [which] clung to his legs" as though summoned not only by nature but in response to European desire: "Our lamps burned low. Hollis, stripped to the waist, lay...motionless like a despoiled corpse; at his head Jackson twanged the guitar, and gasped out in sighs a mournful dirge about hopeless loves and eyes like stars" (21). In contrast to the Malay seamen and watchmen, who are "alarmed" and "scared out of their wits by the glimpse of a shadowy figure leaping over the rail, right out of the night as it were," the Europeans appear unsurprised by the unexpected and unusual appearance of Karain. They strip him further, treat him as they would an hysterical woman, and culturally "cross-dress" him. "Hollis, who, being the youngest of us, assumed an indolent *superiority*, said *without stirring*, 'Give him a dry sarong – *give him mine*; it's hanging up in the bathroom'" (22; emphases ours). The implication that all the Europeans wear sarongs is happily ignored in favor of a description of Karain's laying his kriss on the table, "hilt inwards," of his apology "for coming in with a weapon in his hand," and of his stripping: "Karain slipped the dry sarong over his head, dropped the wet one at his feet, and stepped out of it" (22). This metonymic genital and verbal de-masculinization of Karain, occurring as it does at the climax of the narrative, serves to sanction the Europeans' subsequent treatment of him: believing Karain to be now bereft of power and a feminized hysteric, they play priest to him,[27] first hearing his "confession" and then seeking to exorcize him of the ghost of the kinsman whom he had betrayed.

Karain's narration to the Europeans of the cause of his extreme terror is an eloquent account of homosocial bonding over the body of a woman (the sister of Karain's friend with whom he had travelled for years to avenge the friend's family's dishonor) and of Karain's current possession by the spirit of this friend, whom he had inexplicably killed. Karain's guilt and shame are subsumed in his fear of the friend's spirit, and his distraught state upon arrival on board ship, a state resulting from Karain's feeling of exposure to the spirit of his friend since the death of Karain's old spiritual protector. Karain's anxiety is immediately interpreted by the Europeans as hysteria. His condition, as described by the narrator, is paradigmatic of the Lacanian split subject, divided as to the object himself, as to the Thing, which simultaneously attracts and repels him: $ \lozenge$ a. In Karain, the narrator and his shipmates intuit the "secret" of

Karain, as they learn about the extimate kernel which hystericizes and divides him, and now threatens to kill him – the Real which haunts him beyond endurance.[28]

We speak here, obviously, of Lacan's "discourse of the Other," and of the famous *objet petit a*, the surplus or leftover designated by the small *a*. In the late 1960s, Lacan gave definitive form to his theory of discourse by means of the four discourses (master, university, hysteric, analyst), "i.e., the four possible types of social bond or four possible articulations of the network regarding intersubjective relations."[29] Within this paradigm, we may see the narrator of "Karain: A Memory" articulating the *discourse of the master*, in which a certain signifier (S_1), represents the subject for another signifier or, more precisely, for all signifiers (S_2). But as Zizek has pointed out, "the problem is, of course, that this operation of signifying representation never comes off without producing some disturbing surplus, some leftover or 'excrement,' designated by a small *a*."[30] The other discourses are simply three different attempts to "come to terms" with this remnant, and among them can be located both Karain's and the narrator's discursive positions and, indeed, dilemmas. The narrator's representation of Karain places him, to the degree to which he is inexplicable by Western knowledges, in "the discourse of the hysteric," the basic constituent of which is "the question addressed to the master, 'Why am I what you are saying that I am?'"

> In other words, the hysterical question articulates the experience of a fissure, of an irreducible gap between the signifier that represents me (the symbolic mandate that determines my place in the social network) and the nonsymbolized surplus of my being-there.... [T]he symbolic mandate can never be founded in, accounted for by my "effective properties" insofar as its status is by definition that of a "performative."[31]

The Europeans' rationalistic frame of mind renders Karain's plight inexplicable and unintelligible to his auditors: "I looked," the narrator tells us, "at that man, loyal to a vision, betrayed by his dream, spurned by his illusion, and coming to us unbelievers for help – against a thought" ("Karain: A Memory," *TU*, 40). The narrator's response is to rationalize Karain's narrative, to reduce it precisely to something comprehensible and encompassable by the Western mind, an "obscure Odyssey of revenge," the product of "illusions." And indeed, all the narrator is capable of perceiving in Karain's narrative is illusion: in his existential malaise all illusions are of equal magnitude, equal power. Having cross-dressed Karain, Hollis proceeds to further appropriate and disempower him by devising a "Protection...Charm" (46) to ward off the spirit of the man with whom Karain had bonded, in the form of a doubly fetishized and doubly feminized image: a Jubilee sixpence, coin of Victoria's Empire, encased in leather from the palm of a woman's glove and tied with a keepsake ribbon. It is, says Hollis, "a thing like those Italian peasants wear" (50), thus conflating antagonistic belief systems, one (Roman Catholic) which wears images, one (Islamic) which forbids "a likeness – an engraved image" (48). In the space of the "cuddy hole," Karain is thus disempowered by the Europeans' perception of his "hysteria" and the feminized "charm" they give him to "cure" him of it. At the moment in the narrative in which Hollis bestows upon Karain the charm of Empire, Karain is for the narrator essentially feminized, immobilized, powerless: Hollis and Karain

> looked close into one another's eyes. Those of Karain stared in *a lost glance*, but Hollis's seemed to grow darker and looked out *masterful and compelling*. They were in violent contrast together – one motionless and the colour of bronze, the other dazzling white and lifting his arms, where the powerful muscles rolled slightly under a skin that gleamed like satin. (50; emphases ours)[32]

As Jackson "moved near with the air of a man closing up to a chum in a tight place" (50), the sensuality of the scene is palpable, as are the power reversals, as white men exert power over a hitherto awesome man of color. Hollis's gaze is "masterful and compelling," while that of Karain is merely "a lost glance"; the European now has attributed to him "powerful muscles."[33] "This is [to quote Bhabha] precisely the kind of recognition, as spontaneous and visible, that is attributed to the stereotype. The difference of the object of discrimination is at once visible and natural – color as the cultural/political *sign* of inferiority or degeneracy, skin as its natural *'identity'*."[34] The last sight we have of Karain, now ashore, is (as we have come to anticipate) remote and spectacular: "With our glasses we could see the blue ribbon on his neck and a patch of white on his *brown* chest...and at the same instant Karain passed out of our life forever" ("Karain: A Memory," *TU*, 53; our emphasis).

But despite the narrator's need to believe that this sixpence, this charm of Empire, has done its work in restoring Karain to power among his own people, doubts remain. Although he is glimpsed through the European telescope as "erect...in a martial pose...his head high" among his people, the Malays are described as "very much puzzled and impressed," and the narrator records that "I wondered what they thought; what he thought...what the reader thinks?" (52). And in this deconstructionist movement, Conrad's narrator points out of the story and directly at the reader, and requires her/him to assess the infallibility of the charm and the reasons and consequences of its working, to interrogate easy assumptions about racist and sexist discursive registers and the ways in which they record and inscribe difference as "identity." K. Abraham's comments on "'skin' in racial discourse [as] the visibility of darkness, and a prime signifier of the body and its social and cultural correlates," are relevant to the scopic drive in this "Memory":

> [T]he pleasure-value of darkness is a withdrawal in order to know nothing of the external world. Its symbolic meaning, however, is thoroughly ambivalent. Darkness signifies at once both birth and death; it is in all cases a desire to return to the fullness of the mother, a desire for an unbroken and undifferentiated line of vision and origin.[35]

Meeting the narrator in London some time after their Mindanao (ad)venture, Jackson articulates the lack of clarity with which he remembers Karain and Karain's effect upon him. That the Europeans' construction of Karain as fetish leaves him no subjectivity other than that which they bestow upon him in response to their own needs for self-aggrandizement and self--deceit is emphasized by the narrator's mirrored view of Jackson in the window of the gunshop, ironically named Bland's. Karain has been brought to Jackson's mind by the "row of weapons, perfect and severe, drawn up in a line behind the black-framed panes" ("Karain: A Memory," *TU*, 53); and the narrator, looking into the window, "could see another man, powerful and bearded, peering at him intently from amongst the dark and polished tubes that can cure so many illusions" (53-4). This doubling of Jackson, occurring immediately following Jackson's question, "Do you remember Karain?" may bring to mind the powerful Karain reconstructed by memory; this reflected image of himself in the gunshop window elicits from Jackson an ambiguous admission: "Yes; it made me think of him." Without specifying the referent of "it," he continues talking, stating that he had seen in the morning's paper a report of "fighting over there again. He's sure to be in it. He will make it hot for the caballeros. Well, good luck to him, poor devil! He was perfectly stunning" (54). The antepenultimate sentiment registers an oxymoronic (even if commonly used) wish for good fortune, the penultimate assertion a contamination in terms of darkness and evil. The final assertion – "he was perfectly stunning" – is a comment usually applied to a woman's rather than to a man's effect on a man, and functions to remind the reader of the homoerotic quality of the "cuddy hole" scene. Jackson's comments also function to (re)assert European power over and superiority to Karain, a power bestowed upon Jackson by the narrator's description of Jackson in London as "magnificent as ever. His head was high above the crowd.... He was inspiring" (53). And "[w]hat this statement recognizes is the wide *range* of the stereotype, from the loyal servant to Satan, from the loved to the hated; a shifting of subject positions in the circulation of colonial power."[36]

The narrator, needing to believe that he is a "man of the world" who "knew" Karain, has revealed little about Karain and a great deal about his own requirements of self-deception;

even as he applies a veneer of romantic irony to his memory of Karain and his own memory of Karain's retrospective memory, he succeeds in revealing his own continuing need for self--delusion and his continuing belief that (as "Karain: A Memory" begins) "[w]e knew him...." Doubts that Karain was either possessed or "cured" of that possession by white man's magic charm voiced by Jackson – "Yes.... I mean, whether the thing was so, you know...whether it really happened to him.... What do you think?"– are immediately contextualized by the narrator's response: "My dear chap...you have been too long away from home. What a question to ask! Only look at all this" ("Karain: A Memory," *TU*, 54).

"All this" is a lengthy depiction of urban London in gruesome detail; and observing this ghastly scene, Jackson vivifies it – "it pants, it runs, it rolls; it is strong and alive; it would smash you if you didn't look out" – only to deny its comparative reality for him to another fantastic animation: "it would smash you if you didn't look out; but I'll be hanged if it is yet as real to me as...as the other thing...say, Karain's story" (55). Symbolic and Imaginary, with a hint of the (unspeakable) Real are here conjured up for a moment, for the reader to contemplate their relative degrees of relevance to Jackson's (and the reader's) consciousness. The narrator's final ironic assertion – "I think that, decidedly, he had been too long away from home" (55) – offers no closure except, perhaps, to suggest that the construction of colonial experience – and its inevitable Karains – produces exotic interludes which alleviate the intolerability of the Symbolic unalleviated by "the other thing."

NOTES

1. Particularly relevant are: Edward W. Said, *Orientalism: Western Constructions of the Orient* (London: Routledge and Kegan Paul, 1978); Michele Drouart, "'Gunrunning,' Theatre, and Cultural Attitude in Conrad's 'Karain'," *SPAN: Journal of the South Pacific for Commonwealth Literature and Languages*, 33 (1992), 134-49; Wiesław Krajka, "Betrayal, Self-Exile and Language Registers. The Case of 'Karain: A Memory'," *L'Epoque Conradienne*, 19 (1993), 47-69; Wiesław Krajka, "Making Magic

as Cross-cultural Encounter: The Case of Conrad's 'Karain: A Memory'," in *Conrad, James and Other Relations,* eds. Keith Carabine and Owen Knowles with Paul Armstrong (Boulder – Lublin – New York: East European Monographs – Maria Curie-Skłodowska University – Columbia U.P., 1998, 245-59 (*Conrad: Eastern and Western Perspectives,* ed. Wiesław Krajka, vol. VI); and especially Christopher Gogwilt, *The Invention of the West: Joseph Conrad and the Double-Mapping of Europe and Empire* (Stanford: Stanford U.P., 1995), esp. Chapter 2, "The Charm of Empire: 'Karain: A Memory'," 43-63 (an early version of which was published in *Mosaic: A Journal for the Inter-disciplinary Study of Literature,* 24:1 «Winter 1991», 77-91).

2. See especially Jacques Lacan, "Of the Gaze as *Objet Petit a,*" in *The Four Fundamental Concepts of Psychoanalysis,* ed. Jacques-Alain Miller, trans. Alan Sheridan (Harmondsworth: Penguin Books, 1994), 67-119.

3. Laura Mulvey, "Visual Pleasure and Narrative Cinema," *Screen,* 16: 3 (Autumn 1975), 6-18, rpt. in *The Sexual Subject: A Screen Reader in Sexuality,* ed. Mandy Merck (London – New York: Routledge, 1992), 22-34; Homi K. Bhabha, "The Other Question: The Stereotype and Colonial Discourse," *The Politics of Theory,* ed. Francis Barker (Colchester: U. of Essex, 1983), rpt. in *Screen,* 24:6 (1983), 18-36, and in *The Sexual Subject...,* 312-31 (from which the citations in this article are taken).

4. Mulvey, 27-8.

5. "But in psychoanalytic terms, the female figure poses a deeper problem [for the male spectator than identification with the main male protagonist whose property the woman as object becomes in the course of the film narrative]. She also connotes something that the look continually circles around but disavows: her lack of a penis, implying a threat of castration and hence unpleasure. Ultimately, the meaning of woman is sexual difference, the absence of the penis is visually ascertainable, the material evidence on which is based the castration complex essential for the organization of entrance to the Symbolic Order and the Law of the Father. Thus the woman as icon, displayed for the gaze and enjoyment of men, the active controllers of the look, always threatens to evoke the anxiety it originally signified (ibid., 29).

6. Barbara Creed, "Introduction" to "Part V: The Social Subject," in *The Sexual Subject...,* 293.

7. Ibid., 293-4.

8. Ibid., 294.

9. Homi K. Bhabha, "The Other Question...," op. cit., 312.

10. Sigmund Freud, "Fetishism" (1927), in Sigmund Freud, *On Sexuality* (Harmondsworth: Penguin Books, 1981; Pelican Freud Library, vol. 7), 345 ff., cited in ibid., 324.

11. For a reading of the Marxian notion of commodity fetishism as a prefiguration of the Lacanian "mirror stage," see especially Slavoj Zizek,

"Commodity Fetishism," in his *The Sublime Object of Ideology* (London and New York: Verso, 1989), 23-6. Zizek here explores Lacan's location of the discovery of symptom to Marx, "in the way Marx conceived the *passage* from feudalism to capitalism: 'One has to look for the origins of the notion of symptom not in Hippocrates but in Marx, in the connection he was first to establish between capitalism and what? – the good old times, what we call the feudal times'.... [I]n societies in which there is fetishism in 'relations between men' – in pre-capitalist societies – commodity fetishism is not yet developed." Relations between colonizer and colonized can thus be understood, Marx pointed out, as "relations of domination and servitude" (ibid., 25-6). See Karl Marx, *Capital*, vol. 1 (London: 1974), 59-82; and Jacques Lacan, "R. S. I.," *Ornicar?*, 4 (1975), 106. See also M. Drouart: "Karain and his world are brought within the focus of a telescope that only 'we' are able or permitted to see. They are cut off from the ordinary world (as the Europeans see it), and reconstructed as 'extraordinary,' by the gaze of the European visitors" (M. Drouart, "'Gunrunning'...," 141).

12. Lacan argues that the operation of *méconnaissance* is what establishes the relationship of the self to the self: "It should be noted that a clue may be found in the clear alienation that leaves to the subject the favour of stumbling upon the question of its essence, in that he cannot fail to recognize that what he desires presents itself to him as what he does not want, the form assumed by the negation in which the *méconnaissance* of which he himself is unaware is inserted in a very strange way – a *méconnaissance* by which he transfers the permanence of his desire to an ego that is nevertheless intermittent, and, inversely, protects himself from his desire by attributing to it these very intermittences" (Jacques Lacan, *Écrits: A Selection*, trans. Alan Sheridan «New York – London: W. W. Norton, 1977»), 312-13).

13. See Frantz Fanon: "[T]his behaviour [of the colonizer] betrays a determination to objectify, to confine, to imprison, to harden. Phrases such as 'I know them,' 'that's the way they are,' show this maximum identification successfully achieved.... There is on the one hand a culture in which qualities of dynamism, of growth, of depth can be recognised. As against this, [in colonial cultures] we find characteristics, curiosities, things, never a structure" (Frantz Fanon, "Racism and Culture," in his *Toward the African Revolution* «London: Penguin Books, 1970», 44), quoted in Homi K. Bhabha, 329.

14. Jacques Lacan, *Le Séminaire, livre VII: L'Ethique de la psychanalyse* (Paris: Editions du Seuil, 1986), 133.

15. Jacques-Alain Miller, "Extimité," *Prose Studies*, 11: 3 (December 1988), 121-31.

16. Slavoj Zizek, *The Sublime Object of Ideology*, 180.

17. See M. Drouart: "Theatre imagery joins forces with that of Romantic exoticism to appropriate that which appears as Other, by

naturalising it through cultural convention, which nonetheless allows it to remain 'different' and even exaggerates that difference. As Said puts it, what is 'circulated' by and within culture is 'not "truth" but representations' that 'rely upon institutions, traditions, conventions, agreed-upon codes of understanding for their effects [Said, *Orientalism*..., 22]. The narrator's use of theatre imagery translates into that same 'will' that Said finds in Orientalism, that '*intention* to understand, in some cases to control, manipulate, even to incorporate, what is a manifestly different (or alternative and novel) world' [12]" (142).

On *teatrum mundi* as "a crucial organizing principle of this short story," see Wiesław Krajka, "Making Magic as Cross-cultural Encounter...."

18. Homi K. Bhabha, "The Other Question...," 323. Bhabha's description of the Lacanian schema of the Imaginary is worth quoting at length: the Imaginary is "the transformation that takes place in the subject at the formative mirror phase, when it assumes a *discrete* image which allows it to postulate a series of equivalences, samenesses, identities, between the objects of the surrounding world. However, this positioning is itself *problematic*, for the subject finds or recognizes itself through an image which is simultaneously alienating and hence potentially confrontational. This is the basis of the close relation between the two forms of identification complicit with the Imaginary – narcissism and aggressivity. It is precisely these two forms of 'identification' that constitute the dominant strategy of colonial power exercised in relation to the stereotype.... Like the mirror phase 'the fulness' of the stereotype – its image *as* identity – is always threatened by 'lack'" (ibid., 322-3).

19. Ibid., 324.

20. Ibid.

21. Sigmund Freud, "Fetishism," (1927), in his *On Sexuality*..., 345 ff., quoted in Homi K. Bhabha, 324. See also Christian Metz, *Psychoanalysis and Cinema: the Imaginary Signifier* (London: Macmillan, 1982), 67-78; Steve Neale, "The Same Old Story: Stereotypes and Differences," *Screen Education*, 32-3 (Autumn-Winter 1979-80), 32-7.

22. Homi K. Bhabha, op. cit., 324.

23. Ibid., 325.

24. Frantz Fanon, *The Wretched of the Earth* (Harmondsworth: Penguin Books, 1969), quoted in Homi K. Bhabha, op. cit., 325.

25. Paul Abbott, "Authority," *Screen,* 20: 2 (Summer 1979), 15-16, quoted in Homi K. Bhabha, ibid., 325.

26. Ibid., 325.

27. We are here indebted to Michel Foucault's analyses of sexuality, madness, incarceration and scopophilia. See especially his *Madness and Civilization: A History of Insanity in the Age of Reason*, (1965), trans. Richard Howard (New York: Vintage Books, 1988); *Discipline and Punish: The Birth of the Prison*, (1975), trans. Alan Sheridan (Harmondsworth:

Penguin Books, 1977); *The History of Sexuality*, vol. I, *An Introduction*, (1978), trans. Robert Hurley (New York: Vintage Books, 1990). For Freud the hysteric and the feminine were, notoriously, identical. See, for example, his "A Note on the Unconscious in Psychoanalysis," in his *On Metapsychology*, trans. James Strachey (Harmondsworth: Penguin, 1984), 52.

28. See S. Zizek: "the subject is an answer of the Real (of the object, of the traumatic kernel) to the question of the Other. The question as such produces in its addressee an effect of shame and guilt, it divides, it hystericizes him, and this hystericization is the constitution of the subject: the status of the subject as such is hysterical. The subject is constituted through his own division, splitting, as to the object in him; this object, this traumatic kernel, is the...'death drive,'...a traumatic imbalance, a rooting out" (S. Zizek, *The Sublime Object of Ideology*, 180-1).

29. Jacques Lacan, *Encore: Le séminaire, livre XX*, 1972-3 (Paris: Editions du Seuil, 1975).

30. Slavoj Zizek, *Looking Awry: An Introduction to Jacques Lacan through Popular Culture*, An October Book (Cambridge, Mass. - London: Massachusetts Institute of Technology P., 1992), 130.

31. "In contrast to *perversion*, which is defined precisely by the lack of a question. The pervert possesses an immediate certainty that his activity serves the enjoyment of the Other. Hysteria and obsessional neurosis, its 'dialect,' differ concerning the way the subject attempts to justify his existence: the hysteric by offering himself to the Other as the object of its love, the obsessional by striving to comply with the demand of the Other via his frenetic activity. The answer of the hysteric is thus love, while that of the obsessional is work" (ibid., 181, note 10). It should be pointed out here that, in Lacanian terms, we articulate "The *discourse of the university* [which] immediately takes this leftover [the *objet petit a*] for its object, its 'other,' and tries to transform it into a 'subject' by applying to it the network of 'knowledge' (S_2). This is the elementary logic of the pedagogical process: out of an 'untamed' object (the 'unsocialized' child), we produce a subject by means of an implantation of knowledge. The 'repressed' truth of the discourse is that behind the semblance of the neutral 'knowledge' that we try to impart to the other, we can always locate the gesture of the master" (ibid., 130-1).

32. On the homosocial structuring of patriarchal society, and on the triangular erotic relations which structure nineteenth-century fiction, see especially the following: René Girard, *Deceit, Desire, and the Novel: Self and Other in Literary Structure*, trans. Yvonne Freccero (Baltimore: Johns Hopkins U.P., 1972); Gayle Rubin, "The Traffic in Women: Notes Toward a Political Economy of Sex," in *Toward an Anthropology of Women*, ed. Rayna Reiter (New York: Monthly Review Press, 1975), 157-210; Luce Irigaray, "When the Goods Get Together," in *New French Feminisms*, ed. Elaine Marks and Isabelle de Courtivron (New York:

Avon-Discus, 1976); Richard Klein, "Review of *Homosexualities in French Literature*," *Modern Language Notes*, 95: 4 (May 1980), 1070-80; Eve Kosofsky Sedgwick, *Between Men: English Literature and Male Homosocial Desire* (New York: Columbia U. P., 1985).

33. That the feminization of raced bodies is a standard trope of European views and fictions of "the Oriental" is argued convincingly in a large body of work, most convincingly, in our view, in Marjorie Garber, "The Chic of Araby: Transvestism and the Erotics of Cultural Appropriation," in her *Vested Interests: Cross-Dressing & Cultural Anxiety* (New York: Harper Perennial, 1993), 301-52. On the problematics of homoerotic desire for the body of the raced other, see Jonathan Dollimore, "Desiring the Other," in his *Sexual Dissidence: Augustine to Wilde, Freud to Foucault* (Oxford: Clarendon Press, 1991), 332-56.

34. Homi K. Bhabha, op. cit., 325.

35. Ibid., 328. See Karl Abraham, "Transformations of Scopophilia," in his *Selected Papers* (London: Hogarth Press, 1978).

36. Homi K. Bhabha, op. cit., 324.

Solange Ribeiro de Oliveira,
Federal University of Ouro Preto,
Mariana, Brasil

The Woman in White and the Man in Motley:
Aspects of Hybridism in Conrad's *Almayer's Folly* and "Heart of Darkness"

> Caliban:
> Thou didst prevent me; I had peopled else
> This isle with Calibans. (Shakespeare, *The Tempest*, I,
> ii, ll. 350-1)

The Congo Journey: "Heart of Darkness" and *Almayer's Folly*

In 1890 Joseph Conrad went up the Congo, "to his highest point of navigation," on one of his last and most audacious journeys. In those days, Conrad was still Józef Teodor Konrad Korzeniowski, the young expatriate Polish seaman, a Russian citizen in name only: since the end of the eighteenth century Poland, then part of the Russian empire, had been no more than a tenuous fiction of collective identity. The journey would provide material for the writing, almost ten years later, of Conrad's first masterpiece, "Heart of Darkness." As he went up the river, Conrad also carried in his luggage the initial chapters of *Almayer's Folly*, his first novel.

At the time, forced by personal and political circumstances into a condition of displacement and off-centeredness, Conrad struggled with a cosmopolitanism which found literal and metaphorical expression in what we may call a process of constant translation or, as J. Clifford puts it, of "maximal linguistic complexity" (Clifford, 101).The young traveller was in fact constructing his world in three languages. His mother tongue had been revived by a recent visit to Poland. His second, the French of Imperial Belgian Congo and of his youth in Marseille, recurred in his letters to Marguerite Poradowska, a cousin by marriage, with whom he was involved in something

Clifford calls "largely a literary entanglement." At the time, Conrad also kept a diary in English, the language of his African friendship with the Irishman Roger Casement, of his future marriage and writing career, as well as of the British nationality he would adopt just before the composition of "Heart of Darkness" in 1898-99. No better preparation than this continuous involvement with translation between languages and cultures could be devised for the development of a profound awareness of transcultural relationships, which was to evolve into one of Conrad's central themes. More, perhaps, than any contemporary writer, he was able to realize the problematic construction of cultural selves, constantly entangled in the diverging "webs of meaning" woven by different peoples in distant places and changing times.The biographical coincidences between *Almayer's Folly* and "Heart of Darkness" signal another coalescence. Both novels crucially reveal Conrad's obsession with themes recurring in present-day cultural criticism, such as the impossibility to discover the right and pure culture and the connection between discourse and the wielding of power. The two novels also project a set of all-important related matters, which may be summed up under the central question of hybridism.

The Quest for Original Purity in *Almayer's Folly*

The plot of *Almayer's Folly* turns on the failure of Kaspar Almayer's imperialist dream. A second-generation Dutch colonial living in Indonesia, symptomatically placed at a crossroads of cultures – European, Arab, Philippino, Malay – Almayer curbs his white man's pride and marries an imperfectly acculturated Malay girl. The daughter of Sulu (Philippino) pirates, captured in the course of a bloody encounter, the young woman has become the adoptive daughter of her captor, the trader Lingard. In exchange for the alliance, Lingard promises the ambitious but confused young man the key to commercial success and the revelation of the secret route to a fabulous gold mine. Time turns these dreams into dust. Almayer gradually finds himself stranded in an obscure native settlement by a virtually unknown equatorial river. Besides, he is enmeshed in a network of disparate political relationships, involving conflicting religious and commercial interests. He vainly hopes to mend his fortunes with the settlement of a British trading post. So he builds the large house which gradually comes to be known as *Almayer's Folly*. But the British presence never materializes; Borneo remains under Dutch rule, and the house becomes a local joke, the visible reminder of the character's misjudgement.

The representation of the protagonist as a loser in the tough imperialist game is impressive for this first novel, competently constructed on the model of a traditional realist nineteenth--century narrative. However, the text seems even more centrally concerned with another futile hope, entertained by Almayer's daughter Nina. A beautiful half-caste, the offspring of his interracial marriage, the young woman nurses a secret dream: to recapture the mythical purity of her native ancestors' culture. Under the spell of her mother's tales about her race's warlike past, Nina tries to discard her white heritage and chooses her dark half. She runs away with Dain Maroola, a Balinese Rajah's son. The success of her attempt to eliminate her white heritage may, however, be called into question. An analysis of the novel, in spite of its seemingly happy end, will reveal the ineradicable character of racial and cultural hybridism, the syncretic nature of all culture.

Hybridism and the Harlequin in "Heart of Darkness"

The theme of hybridity recurs in "Heart of Darkness," in the figure of the "harlequin," a label for Kurtz's young associate in the heart of Africa. The harlequin owes this designation to the fact that, with the limited resources of a remote trading outpost, he has been forced to cover his originally brown holland clothes with bright patches. Initially believed to be English, he is also alluded to as a twenty-five-year old Russian, differently per-

ceived by the several characters who make the *foci* of narrative
consciousness. For the first narrator, the sailor retelling Marlow's story, the harlequin's mere existence seems inexplicable
and altogether bewildering. Marlow sees him quite differently:
a fine fellow who stuck to his work for its own sake ("Heart of
Darkness," *YS*, 90), a living embodiment of the efficiency
celebrated by the character as the hallmark of enlightened
English imperialism, in contrast with those old invaders of
England, the Romans: who were "no colonists," but "mere
conquerors" (50). Otherwise, the manager of the post where
Marlow waits for his ship to be repaired angrily refers to the
"be-patched youth" as "that scoundrel," a "wandering trader,"
"a pestilential fellow" (90-1). These contradictory assessments
are matched by the conflicting references to the young man's
ancestry. In the passage reporting a dialogue overheard by
Marlow between the manager and his nephew, he is first alluded
to as "an English half-caste," then simply as "the half-caste."
This explicit identification, added to the several references to his
clearly emblematic motley clothes, proves more than enough to
establish the character's hybrid condition in the reader's mind.

The harlequin plays a key role in the novel. Marlow's trip to
the heart of Africa is partly a quest for Kurtz, whom the man in
motley's reverently serves. A first-class trader from a distant
outpost, Kurtz seems to embody Marlow's ideal of efficiency: he
has been sending in as much ivory as all the others put together.
The youth in motley is the only white man who helps the trader
collect his ivory treasure and nurses him in his terminal illness. In
fact, the harlequin is the one who finally ends Marlow's search
by taking him to the dying Kurtz. Yet this devoted helper, an
indispensable prop for Marlow's whole enterprise, is referred to
by the English manager as "a wandering trader," "a pestilential
fellow," "that scoundrel," "an example of unfair competition"
(90-1). Such strong language can at least partly be explained by
prejudices against half-castes: they provide visible evidence of
the unsavoury sexual entanglements involved in the colonial
enterprise. The reader may react quite differently. Varying
interpretations, attesting the interest aroused by the puzzling

character, have been attributed to the harlequin, as in studies by J. W. Canario ("The Harlequin in 'Heart of Darkness'," 225), E. K. Yoder ("The Demon Harlequin in Conrad's Hell," 90), J. Verleun ("Marlow and the Harlequin," 219), and J. Helder ("The Fool Convention and Conrad's Hollow Harlequin," 368). The four scholars see him, respectively, as a modern representation of the European aborigine, a representative of the chthonian spirit of the underworld, an idealistic dupe, and a deformed simpleton devoid of moral sense (368). The first view agrees best with the line adopted in this essay. In the light of recent cultural studies, the harlequin, with his mixed ancestry and his motley appearance, may indeed be taken as a figure not only of European, but of modern culture in general – a fictional anticipation of Michel Serres' allegorical harlequin in *Le Tiers-Instruit*, emblematic of the contemporary, inevitably hybrid, cultural subject.

In the earlier novel, *Almayer's Folly*, hybridity, embodied in Nina Almayer, stays put where Western ethnocentric thought will usually have it – in a far off place, safely away from the hegemonic cultures. Much more interestingly, "Heart of Darkness" places hybridity, represented by the harlequin, where colonial ideology would hardly see it – in the very heart of the Empire. The half-caste in fact proves close to three Conradian characters: first to Nina Almayer, in *Almayer's Folly*, and ultimately to Marlow, the main narrator, and to Kurtz himself in "Heart of Darkness." In this connection, Conrad's first novel and his first masterpiece nod to each other in mutually illuminating references, as fictional premonitions of the key postcolonial category of hybridity.

Hybridity and the Theory of Culture

The importance of the concept can hardly be exaggerated. In *Culture and Imperialism*, Said has called it "*the* essential idea for the revolutionary realities of today"(Said, 317). As a matter of fact, hybridity has long loomed as one of the central subjects for anthropologists and scientists in general, as studied in R. J. C. Young's "Hybridity and Diaspora." Briefly summed up, Young's long scholarly discussion implies a definition of the hybrid as the product of cultural interaction through language and sex (Young, 6). Scarcely used till the nineteenth century, the term then referred to a physiological phenomenon. In our own time, it has been reactivated to describe a cultural category, prompting questionings about the ways in which contemporary thought has broken with the racialized formulations of the past.

Among several others – the supposed infertility and alleged degeneration of the hybrid, for instance – Young mentions a problem for the supporters of the arguments in favor of "pure" "superior" races. Did not Europe provide examples of hybridism? Britain herself was made up of a mixture of Belgian, Kymraig, Teutons, Danes and Normans. Young likewise cites Carl Vogt's statement of 1863: "the Anglo-Saxon race is itself a mongrel race, produced by Celts, Saxons, Normans and Danes, a raceless chaos without any fixed type."Young adds John Crawfurd's observation of 1861: "At best we [English] are but hybrids, yet, probably, not the worse for that" (17). This was answered with the argument that the races remain distinct, in spite of being intermingled. "They do not fuse, but live on separately, in a kind of natural apartheid."

Young also recalls the ideal of a living racial mixture that remains distinct, developed by Matthew Arnold into a theory of English culture as multicultural. Young adds that today, "as the rival notion of the imperial bulldog breed ebbs away, commentators are again invoking hybridity to characterize contemporary culture" (18). In this regard, Young's stance is extremely cautious. Rejecting possible implications of a supposed fusion, which would favor the dominant race,Young mentions Bakhtin's idea of the undoing of authority in language through linguistic hybridization. He also recalls Homi Bhabha's "astute move," which shifts "this subversion of authority through hybridization to the dialogical situation of colonialism" and defines hybridity as "a problematic of colonial representation... that reverses the effects of the colonialist disavowal, so that other 'denied' knowledges enter upon the dominant discourse and estrange the basis of authority." Young also comments on Bhabha's extension of the notion of hybridity to include forms of counter-authority, a "Third Space"which intervenes to effect the "hybrid moment of political change." Thus, while hybridity denotes a fusion, it also describes a dialectical articulation, as in Risjdoe's "mongrelization." Young finally mentions H. L. Gates Jr's theory of the ironizing double-voiced "trickster"discourse of the black literary tradition. Here one point of view is self-consciously layered palimpsestically on – and against – another: the "Signifying Monkey" exploits what Voloshinov called the "inner dialectical quality of the sign" to produce a hybridized, critical speech (24).

The Racial Question in *Almayer's Folly*

The several questions discussed by Young provide a conceptual framework for the discussion of the interlocked categories of race and gender indispensable for a reading of *Almayer's Folly*. Predictably, the racial question proves central.The novel invokes a dense social mosaic, made up of Europeans from different countries, Arabs, Malays, inland Dyaks (allegedly head-hunters).This brings up their respective cultures and religions – the Balinese prince's Brahminism, two forms of Islam, two forms of Christianity, totemism – all throwing their hostile, panoptic gazes upon one another. Successive rings of imaginary inferiority explain the way the Dutch colonial rulers make a joke of Almayer, who laughs at the Malay Lakamba, who derides his Arab rivals. The same principle operates at a personal level. Almayer despises his Indonesian wife, who, in turn, despises what she sees as his white man's weakness. The pattern tediously repeats itself in the criss-cross of mutually demeaning voices.

The racial question also provides the key to plot solutions. Almayer helps his daughter to run away with Dain only to escape the humiliation of letting the Dutch officers realize her union with a native. As he tearfully puts it: "I am a white man, and of good family.... It would be a disgrace...white men finding my daughter with this Malay" (*AF*, 184). Almayer's complaint is countered by Nina's resentment at the isolation to which her condition as a half-breed had condemned her at school. Because of this rejection, Nina, like her mother, resists being europeanized by her convent education. She rejects her upbriging, "returns scorn for scorn, contempt for contempt, hate for hate" (179).

The shadow of race falls even between mother and daughter, as it does between man and wife. "You speak like a fool of a white woman," the Malay mother once tells Nina (147). Race likewise stands between the lovers, partly explaining their mutual attraction, especially the Balinese prince's fascination for "that woman that half belonged to his enemies" (172). Dain hardly ever thinks of his beloved without associating her with the emblematic white dress she always seems to wear. One of the basic ideas in Young's study comes out here: theories of race are also covert theories of desire (Young, 9). Culture is always lacking; there is no efacing the desire for the cultural Other (3).

Conrad's Ideological Ambivalence

Colonial desire, the ancestral longing for the eroticized other, underlies Nina Almayer's love story, as it does the attraction she exerts over her father's Dutch guests and over Reshid, her Arab suitor. In this respect, Conrad's ideological ambivalence is notorious. Often praised by his non-racist representations of alterity – as in J. McClure's *Kipling and Conrad: The Colonial Fiction* – he has also been accused of racism, by Chinua Achebe, for instance. A perusal of *Almayer's Folly* supports both views. Twenty-one occurrences of the adjective "savage" attributed to non-white characters can be traced to the narrator's voice – a piece of narrative *naiveté* absent, it must be said, from the infinitely subtler strategies of "Heart of Darkness." This equates Conrad's Indonesians with European representations of cultural others as untutored, backward creatures – *analphabetiques*, in

Montaigne's famous phrase – virgin pages to be written upon by the colonizer's history. In *Almayer's Folly*, the implied narrator's prejudice likewise appears in his countless, comically contemptuous references to Babalatchi, the Rajah's omnipresent go-between. The same might be said of the frequent allusions to Nina's Malay mother as a witch, both in the narrator and in the other characters' voices. The figure of the witch brings to mind the multiform monsters constructed by European discourse as validating devices for violent conquest. Pre-adamic natives, kindred to Montaigne's cannibal, they would have been condemned to monstrosity, had it not been for the redeeming intervention of the European conqueror – or so the colonizer's discourse goes. Again, the infinitely more complex fabric of "Heart of Darkness'"s disallows this representation, partly redeeming Conrad's fiction from accusations of racism. The terrifying cannibal figure is undermined, for instance, by Marlow's native carriers. Assumedly cannibals, they outnumber their white masters thirty to five. However, even as they suffer the pangs of lingering starvation, Marlow's "hungry and forbearing friends" ("Heart of Darkness," *YS*, 108) refrain from eating the whites. They anticipate modern doubts about the actual existence of cannibal tribes, voiced by W. Arens and P. Hulme, among others. For Arens and Hulme, theories about cannibals lack the necessary scientific rigor, having always relied on indirect sources and hearsay reports.

The Collusion of Race and Gender in *Almayer's Folly*

Conrad's first novel bears witness to the old collusion of race, gender and social group, as a triple strategy of oppression articulating colonial discourse. There is no ignoring the implied narrator's misogynistic voice, referring, for instance, to a supposedly "unscrupulous greediness of women who cling desperately to the very scraps and rags of love" (*AF*, 193). Male resentment against women's attempts to reach for power through seduction is equally obvious. On the double grounds of race and gender, the seemingly ridiculous, but in fact politically sophisticated, Babalatchi disapproves of Nina, as a "woman who, being half white, is ungovernable" (129). The Rajah's *factotum* argues how "unsatisfactory it was to have women mixed up in state affairs. Young women, of course. For Mrs. Almayer's mature wisdom and for the easy aptitude in intrigue that comes with years to the feminine mind, he felt the most sincere respect" (133). That is, to Babalatchi's mind, women's traffic in a man's world can be tolerated only after age has, so to speak, deprived them of their sexual power, compensating that by the acquisiton of political cunning, otherwise seen as man's own exclusive gift.

Nina's mother is no stranger to this kind of reasoning. Only, seeing it from the other side of the sexual fence, she fully endorses seduction as woman's legitimate weapon. The Malay mother turns her last meeting with her daughter into a lesson in sexual politics. Recalling her subjection, on grounds of race and gender, to a white "man who had no courage and no wisdom" (148), the old woman teaches her daughter how to become her future master's mistress. She thus hopes to make up for the fact that she had been unable to marry her captor Lingard, the great "Rajah Laut": she had nourished a hope of finding favor in his eyes and ultimately becoming his "wife, counsellor, and guide" (22). That dream failed, the mother tries to teach her daughter how to win and keep power through love and cunning: "there will be other women" in later years, the mother warns Nina, for Dain "is a great chief" and "such things must be" (153). Mrs Almayer's uncritical acceptance of the local brand of patriarchy initially meets with Nina's resistance, which the mother attributes to the daughter's half-whiteness. But the seemingly innocent and docile young woman learns her lesson quickly, as the unfolding of the plot reveals. Dutiful daughter of her revengeful mother, Nina begins to shape her lover Dain into "a god for others to worship"; meanwhile, she smiles her mysterious "smile of triumph, or of conscious power, or of tender pity, or, perhaps, of love" (172).

Nina appears equally adept at assimilating her mother's more ambitious plans: to turn Dain's love into a weapon against the white conquerors' well-known formula of conquest, "prayers on their lips and loaded guns in their hands" (153). She learns her mother's lesson so quickly that even the distracted Almayer can not fail to discern her half-conscious plans to use Dain "as a tool of some incomprehensible ambition" (180). Nina's engagement in a simultaneously sexual, racial and political war comes out in her words to her father: "I have been rejected with scorn by the white people and now I am a Malay. [Dain] took me in his arms, he laid his life at my feet. He is brave; he will be powerful, and I hold his bravery and his strength in my hand, and I shall make him great" (180). At this stage, the girl in white has fully embraced her mother's plans for the expulsion of whites from Indonesia.

In this connection, the fact that Dain comes from Bali is instructive. As C. Geertz comments in *Negara*, the island south of Borneo and east of Java remained remarkably independent of the rest of Indonesia. Largely because of its commercial isolation, Bali evaded Dutch rule into 1849.The Balinese were regarded as among the proudest and most graceful people of the Archipelago. This helps explain why Nina sees her Balinese prince as the ideal Malay chief of her mother's tradition – "reckless, ferocious, ready with a flashing kriss for his enemies" (64). He proves most suitable to father her child. By brave deeds, she hopes their child will restore the splendor of their people's past. Dain's son will fulfil Nina's mother's revenge, so that the old woman can live to see "the white men driven from the islands" (152).

Caliban's Children: Malinche's Revenge

Differently put, Conrad's first novel looks back to *The Tempest*. As Prospero accuses him of having attempted to rape Miranda, Caliban does not refute the charge. He admits he would have liked to consummate the rape in order to people the island with little Calibans.Together with their father, they would have driven the white people away, as in Nina's mother's dream. No doubt shared by all subjected people, this dream reverts legends associating the founding of nations with the rape of women, like the Sabines, mothers of Rome and Lucrece, whose sacrifice leads to the expulsion of the Etruscan kings. In "Interpretações da América Latina," Augusto Tamayo Vargas cites Otávio Paz's equivalent notion of a Latin American "Malinche complex" – an allusion to Malinche, Cortez's Indian mistress and translator (Vargas, 461). Malinche symbolizes the "violated mother," inseparable from the conquest of the Americas. According to Paz what she recalls is not a mere historical process, but a violation perpetrated on the very flesh of Indian women.

Nina Almayer's double subversion – against both sexual and racial colonial discourse – represents Malinche's revenge. Having found her Caliban, Nina is ready to bear his children, future avengers of conquered lands and violated native women. She can herself be seen as a female projection of the Caliban figure, who variously subverts the traditional pattern. She belies the alleged sterility of the hybrid. Unlike so many barren mulatto heroines in fiction (studied by Teófilo de Queroz Júnior in *Preconceito de Cor e a Mulata na Literatura Brasileira*, and by Heloisa Toller Gomes in *As Marcas da Escravidão*), she bears a healthy son. She is also revolutionary in another respect: she contradicts the unilateral process of conquest, which couples men of the dominating group with women of the dominated one. Reversing this pattern, Nina stands for the weaker gender but the stronger race.

She becomes the mother of Caliban's children, who will hopefully chase the white people from the islands.This explains Nina's mother's wild joy – contrasted with her father's murderous fury – when the news of a grandson's birth reaches their village. The Malay heir will vindicate his race against the white invader. Original purity, warlike greatness, will be restored to the race of "giants who had lost faith in their strength" (*AF*, 165) – or so the youthful parents believe.Yet the question remains: will Nina's son really drive the invaders away? And will she, a half-breed brought up as a Christian, totally erase her white inheritance to become the Malay Ranee? Does the implied narrator unreservedly endorse the happy end of the novel ? The critical reader may wonder. For, however much she may choose to present herself as a Malay, Nina remains white in many respects. The novel leaves no doubt that this alterity – symbolized by the white dress she invariably wears – largely explains her attraction for Dain.

That Nina cannot totally obliterate her white inheritance is made clear in the scene where she first expresses her love by kissing Dain in the mouth.To do this, she searches her "reminiscence of that despised and almost forgotten civilization," looking for a "sign of love, the fitting expression of the boundless felicity of the present, the pledge of a bright and splendid future" (72). Nina's caress, the text implies, is unknown in the Malay lovemaking tradition. Dain is "surprised and frightened at the storm raised in his breast by the strange and to him hitherto unknown contact" (72). Thus her kiss, which carries the mark of the culture Nina consciously rejects, bears the germ of the white man's infectious culture. It bodes both happiness and danger. As it announces the birth of her people's avenger, it is the kiss of life. But it is also the kiss of death, taking the virus of a hated civilization to infect Dain's comparatively untainted culture. It partly warrants the fulfilling of the witch-like mother's dream, the white man's expulsion. But it also keeps the stamp of his indelible seal. Emblematically, the ambiguity of Nina's kiss signals the fact that colonial exploitation does not come to an end. It goes on, under the shape of new dependencies and asymetries.

The Futility of the Quest for Mythical Original Purity

The question persists. Is Nina's double rebellion really feasible? Can she erase what has been written upon her by her Western education? Is her conscious adoption of a freely chosen racial and cultural identity so easily achieved as her symptomatic rejection of the English language? In other words, is the retrieval of lost, archaic forms, possible? The answer is not so positive as the happily ending love story seems to imply. Nina's partial whiteness seems ineradicable.This emerges again in the final scene of her departure. When her puzzled lover turns to Almayer for an explanation of her tears, the father answers: "you will see them more than once" (188). Nina's tears betray the white woman she cannot completely tear away from herself. Dain realizes that. He is "conscious of something in her he could not understand..., something invisible that stood between them.... She was his, and yet she was like a woman from another world.... No desire, no longing, no effort of will or length of life could destroy this vague feeling of their difference" (187).

Nor can the traces of his half-caste daughter fade from Almayer's heart. Having followed "his skin" and not "his heart" in disavowing her, he is determined to forget her (192). He can in fact "erase all traces of Nina's footsteps" from the sand (195), as he watches the lovers' canoe disappear in the distance. But forget he cannot, at least not until opium turns him into a shadow of himself, "an immense man-doll broken and flung there out of the way" (204). Almayer's inability to forget his half-caste daughter, as hers to discard her white self, argues for the impossibility, in an irrecoverably hybridized world, to do away with the Other, both within and without oneself. As Clifford puts it: "there is no going back, no essence to redeem" (Clifford, 4). The birth of Nina and Dain's child may, however, point to another, hopeful way. It may signal the instauration of what Bhabha calls "an agonic process, in which the seeming authority and certainties of colonial discourse are subverted, questioned and destabilized."

The notion of the impossibility of a return to mythical unity and purity pervades the first chapter of "Heart of Darkness." About to start the tale of his attempted voyage to the center, Marlow projects a visible image of hybridity. This image, almost of a symbolic meeting of East and West, shows the character-narrator sitting on a cruising yawl on the Thames, at the centre of hegemonic Europe, in the highday of colonialism: "with his legs folded before him, he had the pose of a Buddha preaching in European clothes and without a lotus-flower" ("Heart of

Darkness," *YS*, 50). Confronted with this image, the reader is reminded that, when he goes to Africa, Marlow finds his double in another hybrid figure, the ambiguous harlequin. So, ironically, his voyage proves cyclical. He seems to have travelled to another continent only to meet the hybrid that already existed in himself. His experience seems to anticipate Grewal and Kaplan's reflections in *Scattered Hegemonies*:

> Western culture is itself, as is every cultural formation, a hybrid of something. Yet the dominant Western attitude towards hybridity is that it is always elsewhere or it is infiltrating an identity or location that is assumed to be, to have always been, pure and unchanging. (Grewal, Kaplan, 7-8)

The Threefold Image of Hybridity in "Heart of Darkness"

At the end of his journey, speaking from his boat on the Thames, Marlow has learned his lesson. Like "all men who have 'followed the sea' with reverence and affection," he is able to evoke "the great spirit of the past" ("Heart of Darkness," *YS*, 47), with its succession of invading peoples. Buddha-like, he deals the death blow on Nina's ingenuous belief in archaic survival; he nods his approval at the ongoing process of hybridization which has always presided at the meeting of cultures. Not unexpectedly for the modern reader, Marlow's search reveals something he has always had, inseparable from himself: the hybridity exhibited by his pose and dress. They seem to cry out that collective identities are all hybrid, always relational and inventive, to be continuously re-imagined and re-invented as intercultures. This realization may be the centre actually reached by Marlow, the only approachable heart in an otherwise impenetrable darkness. And this is what Marlow finds when he meets his double, the man in motley.

We have already discussed this puzzling figure, the pejorative light in which the "be-patched youth" is seen by other characters, as well as his key role in the plot. Without him, Marlow would have been unable to fulfil his several missions, to find

Kurtz, or to meet his Intended in London, with all the perplexing questions raised by the visit. The man in motley also recalls another figure, the Shakespearean clown, a frequent vehicle for reflection, like Touchstone or Lear's fool. So also the man in motley may prefigure new perceptions of truth: hybrid, subversive forms of culture representation, certainly more in tune with our own times than with Conrad's day. This makes Conrad's fiction somehow prophetic of a vision tantalizingly beckoning between his lines. There, perhaps, lies one of the possible answers to the interpretative challenge of "Heart of Darkness," which after the lapse of a century, keeps on intriguing its readers. The imaginative projection of all cultures as inescapably mongrel, doubly represented by the harlequin and by the "Buddha in European clothes," may largely contribute to the intriguing effect of the novel and to its cryptically subversive representation of Western culture. Conrad hints at an awareness of hybridization as the effect of colonialism. This awareness, as Bhabha points out in *The Location of Culture*, may lead to important changes in perspective, to a "disturbing questioning of the images and presences of authority" (Bhabha, 114). In *Almayer's Folly*'s Nina, Conrad embodies the rebellion of the historically muted subject, as well as the quest for essentialist memories of a nostalgic past. In "Heart of Darkness" Marlow's awareness of the impossibility to reach the center nods to a more positive, even if hardly less elusive, movement: towards a narrative that, in Bhabha's words, will let no culture "look at itself narcissistically in the eye." Modern cultural discourses will have to face "an irretrievably plural space," "from which to speak both of, and as, the minoric, the exilic, the marginal and the emergent" (149). Nothing more precise need be said of the English Marlow, or of the ambivalently pictured harlequin, than what is revealed of Kurtz himself – the mysterious object of so much love, hatred, admiration and repulsion: "all Europe contributed to [his] making" ("Heart of Darkness," *YS*, 117). It would still be possible to connect the half-caste harlequin, as Clifford does, with "the young wanderer, Korzeniowski, "who was shedding his official nationality to become Conrad" (Clifford, 108).

Recurring in Marlow, the seeker, as well as in Kurtz, the sought one, the harlequin also ultimately connects them with their creator. This multiple, unsettling representation, evades stereotyped images of the conqueror as carrier of knowledge as well as that of any one culture as the holder of purity and truth. Sameness appears inseparable from otherness, announcing "a world where syncretism and parodic invention are becoming the rule rather than the exception...a multinational world of institutional transience" (94). Moving all the time, definable by the tendency to move rather than by their precise direction, cultures and their representations keep on arousing "profound perplexity in the living" (Bhabha, 167). It is this perplexity towards representational truth, that, in contrast with Conrad's comparatively naive first novel, makes "Heart of Darkness" so fascinating. With its Chinese box narrative structure, within the multiple frame of its several narrators and its perpetually decentering movement the novel exhibits what Douglas Brown has called Conrad's "structural scepticism." In this context, the harlequin figure proves, in Wilson Harris's apt phrase, "the central clown," who brings together heterogeneous elements in creative cross-fertilization (Harris, 113).The clown inaugurates a kind of presage for "the multivocal exchanges occurring in the politically charged situations" (Clifford, 10), a "restless, uneasy, interstitial hybridity: a radical heterogeneity, discontinuity, the permanent revolution of forms" (Young, 25).

Predictably, "Heart of Darkness" has provoked creative responses from postcolonial writers, re-writings like Ngugi wa Thiongo's *The River Between* and Tayeb Salih's *Season of Migration to the North*. In *Journey through Darkness* Peggy Nightingale argues that Conrad also preceded Naipaul's fictionalization of the converse effect of colonialism, pictured in Kurtz's turning from idealism to materialism, from humanity to brutality. By associating Kurtz, the harlequin, and the narrator Marlow with hybridism, Conrad also proves a pioneer of the cultural theorist's preoccupation with this crucial topic. "Heart of Darkness" remains a tantalizingly provoking text, as well as a uniquely proto-postcolonial and modernist novel.

WORKS CITED

Achebe Chinua. "An Image of Africa: Racism in Conrad's 'Heart of Darkness'," in Achebe Chinua. *Hopes and Impediments: Selected Essays.* New York: Doubleday, Anchor, 1989, 1-20.

Arens W. *The Man-Eating Myth: Anthropology and Anthropophagy.* Oxford: Oxford U. P., 1980.

Bhabha Homi K. *The Location of Culture.* London – New York: Routledge, 1994.

Brown Douglas. "From 'Heart of Darkness' to *Nostromo*: An Approach to Conrad," in *The New Pelican Guide to English Literature,* vol. 7. *From James to Eliot,* ed. Boris Ford. Harmondsworth: Penguin, 1983, 131-49.

Canario John W. "The Harlequin in 'Heart of Darkness'," *Studies in Short Fiction,* 4: 3 (1967), 225-33.

Clifford James. "On Ethnographic Self-Fashioning: Conrad and Malinowski," in Clifford James. *The Predicament of Culture. Twentieth-Century Ethnography, Literature and Art.* Cambridge, Mass.: Harvard U. P., 1988, 92-113.

Geertz Clifford. *Negara.* Princeton: Princeton U. P., 1980.

Gomes Heloisa Toller. *As Marcas da Escravidão.* Rio de Janeiro: Editora da UFRJ, 1994.

Grewal Inderpal, Kaplan Caren, eds. *Scattered Hegemonies. Postmodernity and Transnational Feminist Practices.* Minneapolis: U. of Minnesota P., 1994.

Harris Wilson. *The Womb of Space. The Cross-Cultural Imagination.* Westport, Conn. – London: Greenwood, 1983.

Helder Jack. "Fool Convention and Conrad's Hollow Harlequin," *Studies in Short Fiction,* 12: 4 (1975), 363-8.

Hulme Peter. "Columbus and the Cannibals," in Hulme Peter. *Colonial Encounters. Europe and the Native Caribbean, 1492-1797.* London – New York: Methuen, 1986, 13-43.

McClure John A. *Kipling and Conrad: The Colonial Fiction.* Cambridge, Mass.: Harvard U. P., 1981.

Mix Miguel Rojas. "Los Monstros: Mitos de Legitimatión de la Conquista?," in *América Latina. Palavra, literatura e cultura,* vol. 1, ed. Ana Pizarro. Campinas: Editora da Unicamp, 1993, 123-50.

Phillips Jerry. "Educating Savages. Melville, Bloom and the Rhethoric of Imperialist Instruction," in *Recasting the World. Writing after Colonialism,* ed. Jonathan White. Baltimore – London: The Johns Hopkins U. P., 1993.

Said Edward. *Culture and Imperialism.* New York: Alfred A. Knopf, 1994.

Serres Michel. *Le Tiers-Instruit.* Paris: François Bourin, 1991.

Vargas Augusto Tamayo. "Interpretações da América Latina," in *América Latina em sua Literatura*, ed. César Fernández Moreno. Sào Paulo: Editora Perspectiva, 1972, 455-77.
Verleun Jan. "Marlow and the Harlequin," *Conradiana*, 13: 3 (1981), 195-220.
Yoder Emily K. "The Demon Harlequin in Conrad's Hell," *Conradiana*, 12: 2 (1980), 88-92.
Young Robert J. C. "Hybridity and Diaspora," in Young Robert J. C. *Colonial Desire: Hybridity in Theory, Culture and Race*. New York: Routledge, 1995, 1-28.

Steven Trout,
Fort Hays State University,
Hays, USA

The Imperial Editor: Language, Race,
and Conrad's *Lord Jim*

Lord Jim is a novel filled with remarkable voices, with characters who appear briefly, perhaps only for a page or two, yet whose eccentric spoken language, like that of Dickens' characters, fixes them permanently in the reader's mind. Indeed, no less remarkable than Conrad's visual artistry, his ability to make us *see*, is the sheer energy of his dialogue – or, rather, the monologues through which his typically loquacious characters display their personalities. Consider, in this regard, the resident surgeon whom Marlow encounters while leaving the hospital where the alcoholic chief engineer of the *Patna* has been confined. "He's been drinking hard at that Greek's or Italian's grog shop for three days," remarks the surgeon as he describes the engineer's delirium tremens,

> What can you expect? Four bottles of that kind of brandy a day, I am told. Wonderful, if true. Sheeted with boiler-iron inside, I should think. The head, ah! the head, of course, gone, but the curious part is there's some sort of method in his raving. I am trying to find out.... Traditionally he ought to see snakes, but he doesn't. Good old tradition's at a discount nowadays. Eh! His – er – visions are batrachian. Ha! Ha! No, seriously, I never remember being so interested in a case of the jim-jams before. (*LJ*, 54-5)

The surgeon emerges from this monologue not as a mere background character, but as a vital – perhaps too vital –personality, whose high spirits and heartless jokes are anything but insignificant. He is, in fact, a striking example both of Conrad's delineation of imperialist attitudes, within the people who form Jim's cultural environment in the first half of the novel, and the allusive, intertextual richness of *Lord Jim* as a whole. The surgeon's uncertainty regarding the origins of the grog-shop owner – who might just as easily be a "Greek" as an "Italian" – suggests a kind of imperialist xenophobia, a view of the world in which only two parties are recognizable: Englishmen and everyone else. Moreover, since this scene appears immediately after Marlow's interview with the chief engineer, whose terrifying "howl pursues [him] like a vengeance," the surgeon's incongruous good humor and dispassionate scientific curiosity are more than a little disturbing (54). Through his insensitive response to the engineer's agony, the surgeon – though described by one critic as "robustly sane" (Verleun, 27) – seems a mild descendant of the numerous mad physicians and deranged researchers featured in the fiction of the 1880s and '90s, including H. G. Wells's Dr. Moreau and the Invisible Man, R. L. Stevenson's Dr. Jekyll, and the (again, incongruously jovial) Belgian physician who measures Marlow's skull, prior to his departure for the Congo, in Conrad's "Heart of Darkness."

No less significant are Marlow's reactions to the various voices that speak so garrulously amid his own oral narrative. This essay considers Marlow's encounter with the idiosyncratic language of two especially irrepressible characters – the "half--caste" sea captain who delivers Jim to Patusan and the "third-class deputy-assistant," also "of mixed descent," who perpetuates the myth of Jim's possession of a priceless treasure (in reality, Jewel). In contrast with the surgeon, who speaks with such disconcerting fluency and ease, these two characters express themselves through less polished idioms that reflect both their marginal status, as half-castes, and their ambition to be admitted into the white colonial elite. Both are comic figures, whose mimicry of "civilized" language and manners, characterized by hilarious malapropisms and unctuous assertions of familiarity, belongs to a well-established tradition in colonial fiction. Yet despite their facetious treatment in the text (a treatment made possible by the narrator's complacent sense of superiority) these characters reveal the essential instability of Marlow's world view. Occupying a gray area – racially, culturally, and linguistically – between the colonizer and the colonized, between self and Other, both half-castes raise questions that Marlow, an upholder of European supremacy, does not address or even recognize; thus, both characters elude their imperial editor, an editor who transcribes assertions of equality, when made by non-Europeans, into dismissive comedy.

The first of these half-castes, the captain of the brigantine, provides one of the reader's earliest glimpses into the potentially lethal situation awaiting Jim in Patusan. But he does not tell his story directly. So filled with bizarre diction errors is the captain's English, which "seemed to be derived from the dictionary of a lunatic," that his narrative of capture by the Rajah, one of several leaders vying for control of the region, is filtered through Marlow, who provides commentary and translations for comic effect. For example:

> He told me further, gnashing his teeth, that the Rajah was a "laughable hyaena" (can't imagine how he got hold of hyaenas); while somebody else was many times falser than the "weapons of a crocodile." Keeping one eye on the movements of his crew forward, he let loose with volubility – comparing the place [Patusan] to a "cage of beasts made ravenous by long impenitence." I fancy he meant impunity. (*LJ*, 239)

This passage illustrates, among other things, the sheer density of Conrad's narrative technique, which simultaneously establishes the captain as a memorable minor character (by allowing us to hear just enough of his confused vocabulary), translates his garbled discourse into idiomatic English, and ominously juxtaposes his violent account with the preparations for Jim's own imminent journey (hence the reference to the "movements of the crew"). Like everything in *Lord Jim*, the captain's information reaches Marlow in a cryptic jumble, which must then be translated into a coherent order; thus, though not exactly "delayed," the "decoding" that must take place in this passage points to the epistemological difficulties faced throughout the novel by Marlow and the reader alike.[1]

What interests me even more about this scene, however, is the way in which the captain himself is "decoded" – or perhaps it would be more accurate to say "encoded" – by his observer.

Through his facetious treatment of the captain's language, Marlow distances this character from himself, despite their shared devotion to the craft of seafaring, and quickly relegates him to a subordinate position in the colonial hierarchy. His interjections and corrections – "can't imagine how he got hold of hyaenas," "I fancy he meant impunity" – are assertions of power and control, since this commentary implies a set of linguistic absolutes, of authoritative usages, by which the captain may be judged not only absurd, but inferior. Language and political power are thus conjoined. The physical description of the half-caste, which presents him as a stunted, almost simian, caricature of the European mariner, further reflects Marlow's immediate assumption of superiority. The "master" of the brigantine, we are told, is a "dapper little half-caste, in a blue flannel suit, with lively eyes, his round face the colour of lemon peel, and with a thin little black moustache drooping on each side of his thick, dark lips" (238). At the end of the scene, Marlow likens the "little wretch's face" to "the shape and colour of a ripe pumpkin" (241). As is often the case with Conrad's *male* Eurasian characters, the results of miscegenation are here presented as less than physically attractive, as degenerative. Moreover, the image of the captain "gnashing his teeth" (239) suggests an atavistic bestiality lurking beneath the comical imitation of "civilized" manners, while his "dapper" dress and apparent love of language for its own sake establish him as a remote, Asian cousin of the European decadent aesthete, a figure largely associated in 1900 – just five years after the Wilde trials – with degeneration.[2]

This entire scene is a powerful reminder, then, of the extent to which racial and political assumptions shape the *impressions* described in Marlow's narrative. Nothing in Marlow's presentation of the captain is – or arguably could be – impartial or ideologically innocent; indeed, his (re)construction of the captain's oddity and strangeness is consistent with the observation made by a modern critic of colonial novels in general: "in [this] fiction differentness was not neutral; rather it became a trope that worked against the possibility of reading 'different' as 'equal'" (White, 64). In Conrad's work, the reader's confrontation with "differentness" is far more complex than in the adventure narratives of G. A. Henty, Rider Haggard, or even R. L. Stevenson, whose subversive portraits of dissolute colonialists prefigure, and even rival, Conrad's. Nevertheless, Marlow's automatic denigration of the half-caste suggests that for him as well "different" cannot mean "equal" – a significant conclusion, considering that *Lord Jim* depicts its protagonist's pursuit of his romantic aspirations within two different realms (that of the British maritime versus the almost exclusively non-white region of Patusan) and invites the reader to judge, along with Marlow, the respective value of these two environments. As evidence of Marlow's deprecation of the non-white sphere to which Jim pledges himself, critics have typically pointed to the claustrophobic descriptions of the "primeval" jungle that encloses Jim and his followers, and the contrasting sense of release that Marlow feels when leaving Patusan for the outside world (*LJ*, 287).[3] Yet Marlow's responses to racially mixed characters such as the captain perhaps represent additional, overlooked evidence of his inability to apprehend "differentness" without instantly setting what he sees in opposition to himself.

Unlike Doramin, Dain Waris, or Tamb' Itam, "full-blooded" Malay characters whom Marlow portrays sympathetically, half-castes are subversive, potentially anarchistic figures since they are, by definition, neither entirely one nor the other, neither Occidental nor Oriental; they are familiar but at the same time different. Their very existence destabilizes the binary oppositions – such as civilization vs savagery and enlightenment vs ignorance – upon which European expansion and settlement are based. Rather than the Malay characters, who are tucked away in Patusan, and thus pose little threat to the political or ideological foundations of colonialism, it is the half-castes, then, these characters who operate at the point of contact between Asian and European cultures, who most directly reveal Marlow's otherwise subtle investiture in colonial ideology.[4]

This becomes clear when we return to the half-caste master of the brigantine, and try to consider the character *outside of*

Marlow's commentary. Several interesting points emerge. First of all, one wonders why the captain has adopted such elaborate and unintentionally humorous diction. That he speaks English is not surprising, given the historical realities of the Malay Archipelago, which, by the end of the 19th century, had already seen its share of English adventurers, especially Sir James Brooke, known as the "White Rajah," who established a succession of English rulers in Sarawak that endured into the 1940s, and Jim Lingard (or "Tuan Jim") who successfully traded on the Berau river in east Borneo, the model, many critics have argued, for the waterway that leads into Patusan (Watts, 25). Yet commercial necessity hardly explains such inflated discourse. A solution, perhaps, is suggested when Marlow notes the captain's simultaneous expression of indignation – over the events that he narrates – and pride in the language used to describe them: "He scowled and beamed at me, and watched with satisfaction the undeniable effect of his phraseology" (*LJ*, 239). Ironically, then, the captain's eccentric language is intended to impress and, presumably, to raise its speaker onto an even footing with his audience. Of course, the full measure of his failure in this attempt comes when, near the end of their conversation, Marlow's commentary dips from dismissive witticisms into full-fledged contempt, when he notes that the captain has "the insufferably conceited air of *his kind* after what they imagine a display of cleverness" (240, emphasis mine).

So repugnant, indeed, does Marlow find the half-caste's subtle assertion of equality that he never refers to him by his rightful title as captain – no "fellowship of the craft" here – and, through his droll interjections, calls the other mariner's abilities into doubt. Several details point to the perversity of allowing vessels to be commanded by *his kind*.[5] Marlow states, for example, that after brooding on the "horrid memory" of being tortured by the Rajah the captain "address[es] in a quarrelsome tone the man coming aft to the helm." And, later in the scene, Marlow has us visualize the captain "bursting with importance" as he "shout[s] his orders" to the crew (240). Such details paint the master of the brigantine as a bullying, arrogant clown. Again, however, if we take into account Marlow's prejudices, and attempt to look around them, a different picture emerges. Beyond the simple fact that Stein, a shrewd businessman, would hardly leave one of his trading vessels under the command of an incompetent, there is nothing in the scene, aside from Marlow's disdainful gloss on what he sees, to suggest inferior seamanship on the part of the half-caste or his crew. On the contrary, the captain "keep[s] one eye on the movements of the crew forward" while talking with Marlow, thus displaying a conscientiousness at variance with his otherwise grotesque description, and issues commands, however inelegantly, that result in the successful launching of the ship amid sporadic "cat's-paws" (239).

So why Marlow's hostility? An answer partly lies, as I have suggested, in the subtle political struggle enacted in this scene – as the disturbingly indeterminate half-caste, whom Marlow defensively conceptualizes as *one of them*, as one of a certain *kind* of inferior, strives through his language and dress to be accepted as "one of us." Thus, Marlow presents the captain's language and demeanor as humorous not because they are innately so – for nothing is *innately* comic – but because he sees them within an ideological framework that defuses threatening ambiguities with laughter. The half-caste's presentation as a comic character is comforting in two ways: by aping the "dapper" dress and supposedly sophisticated diction of an English gentleman, the captain reveals his eagerness to accept Western role-models, thus supporting the notion of English imperialism as a beneficent process of education and enlightenment; his absurd inadequacy in this role, however, validates the sense of superiority felt by his audience. It is one thing, after all, for a native or half-caste to model himself after Westerners and to fall comically short of the mark, quite another for him to achieve a complete fluency within the imperialists' culture. The latter would raise too many questions about supposedly intrinsic differences between the races.

This paradoxical perspective, which looks approvingly on the spread of European culture among non-whites while simultaneously distancing the natives from their models, is not limited to *Lord Jim*; the work of Conrad's contemporaries, especially Kipling and Stevenson, suggests that the half-caste captain's eccentric language – and, more importantly, his deprecating treatment by the narrator – follows a set of conventions consistently upheld in turn-of-the-century colonial fiction. Characterizations quite similar to the captain's appear repeatedly, for example, in R. Kipling's *Kim* (1901), a depiction of the British Raj that stresses the cooperation between English-speaking, Anglicized Indians and their white superiors; the two work together, within an espionage network known as the "Great Game," to defeat Russian expansionism and, by inference, Indian home-rule agitation. Again, the reader can take comfort in the fact that loyal and trustworthy natives such as Babu Hurree Chander, a Bengali agent who has been educated in England, have been partially assimilated into the white culture, while chuckling over the failure of these characters to match the sophistication – particularly the linguistic sophistication – of the Sahibs. Though more coherent than the half-caste captain's English, Hurree's discourse, for example, is a blend of British colloquialisms, inflated diction, and generally erroneous snippets of Latin. Consider, for instance, the scene in which Hurree describes to Kim, whom he deferentially addresses as "Mister O'Hara," his infiltration of a camp commanded by villainous Russian operatives:

> "Of course [I said to myself] I shall affeeliate myself to their camp in supernumerary capacity as perhaps interpreter, or person mentally impotent and hungree, or some such thing. And then I must pick up what I can, I suppose.... Onlee – onlee – you see, Mister O'Hara, I am unfortunately Asiatic, which is serious detriment in some respects. And *allso* I am Bengali – a fearful man."
> "God made the Hare and the Bengali. What shame?" said Kim, quoting the proverb.
> "It was process of Evolution, *I* think, from Primal Necessity, but the fact remains in all its *cui bono*. I am, oh, awfully fearful!... I sat down and cried, Mister O'Hara, anticipating Chinese tortures. I do not suppose these two gentlemen will torture me, but I like to provide for possible contingency with European assistance in emergency." (Kipling, 223)

Despite his familiarity with Darwinian theory – elsewhere Hurree refers to himself as a "Herbert Spencerian" – the agent's inconsistent tense (which arbitrarily switches between past and present), missing articles (as in "which is serious detriment"), and opaque bureaucratese ("supernumerary capacity," "possible contingency with European assistance in emergency") reassure the reader that "educated" Indians can, at best, only mimic their colonial betters (and poorly at that), never truly understanding or mastering the Englishman's language or culture. In other words, Kipling presents Hurree, a potentially problematic character, in a way that upholds the distinction between the colonizer and colonized: he may work for *us*, loyally and perhaps even admirably, but he is still *one of them*.

Another passage in *Kim* parallels, almost exactly, Marlow's derisive editorial commentary on the half-caste's language. After Kim is adopted by his father's regiment, Father Victor, one of the regimental chaplains, receives a letter from the Lama, who has agreed to pay for Kim's education. Since the Tibetan monk knows little English, the letter, which the chaplain finds almost incomprehensible, is "[w]ritten by Sobrao Satai, Failed Entrance Allahabad University" (104). As suggested by the correspondent's eagerness to flourish his title as a *failed* would-be student, the humor here derives, just as it does in *Lord Jim*, from the gap between the Asian character's pride in his discourse and the way that his words actually come across to the European audience. The chaplain reads the letter out loud to Kim, supplying a comical gloss quite similar to Marlow's:

> "If your Honour condescending giving my boy best educations Xavier" (I suppose that's St. Xavier in Partibus) "in terms of our conversation dated in your tent 15th instant" (a business-like touch there!) "then Almighty God blessing your Honour's succeedings to third an' fourth generation." (104)

The letter goes on in this vein, piling one malapropism and non-idiomatic construction onto another, until the chaplain turns to Kim for an explanation: "Now, is that ravin' lunacy or a business proposition?" (104), he asks – a remark reminiscent of

Marlow's quip that the captain's vocabulary comes from "the dictionary of a lunatic" (*LJ*, 238). In both instances, language at variance with authoritative models exported from the West is associated, through metaphor, with madness, with a breakdown in the presumably straightforward, ideologically neutral process through which language – or, more specifically, the English language – describes reality. Thus, the imperialist is confident (as modern linguists are not) of the referential stability of "proper" language, assured that its signs *do* lead back to referents, while automatically defining non-idiomatic expression as a collapse in this seemingly straightforward relationship. To use English "incorrectly" is to see the world "incorrectly," as a "lunatic" would. Again, we see how the assertion of linguistic authority spills into racialist assumptions of political power.

Significantly, Father Victor also omits a section of the letter from his reading – "We'll skip the first part," he tells Kim – presumably because he deems the content incomprehensible or irrelevant. Thus, the voice of the colonized "inferior" can be drained of its significance in two ways: by inviting the reader to interpret this voice humorously, a matter of comic conventions, and by *silencing* it – the prerogative of the imperial editor, who is, after all, in charge. The latter strategy, common in turn-of-the--century narratives set in Africa or Asia, appears even in Stevenson's prophetically Conradian tale of colonial riffraff, *The Ebb-Tide* (1893), a book which, in other respects, under-mines the very assertions of racial superiority that we have considered in *Lord Jim* and *Kim*. The subversiveness of Steven-son's novella becomes apparent in even the briefest description: set in the South Pacific, the tale focuses on three white expatriates – Davis, an American sea captain who has lost his certificate due to drunkenness; Herrick, a disgraced university man; and Huish, a feral, avaricious Cockney – who agree to command a schooner whose previous officers have died of disease; the trio subsequently attempt to steal and then to scuttle this vessel, while helping themselves to its cargo of California champagne.

Throughout, Stevenson contrasts these grotesque adventurers with their dignified and *temperate* Polynesian crew, especially an elderly sailor named Taveeta (or "Uncle Ned," as he is dubbed by Captain Davis), who describes for Herrick the fate of the original captain and first mate. Significantly, Taveeta illustrates through his story the dangers of ignoring or automatically deprecating unfamiliar language, a considerable irony since, as we will see in a moment, his own discourse is condescendingly edited by Stevenson's third-person narrator. Grimly amusing, the tale recounts how the captain and mate unknowingly landed upon a small-pox infested island, where they "rollicked along unconcerned, [and] embraced the girls who had scarce energy to repel them" – while remaining oblivious to the death wails that came from "the back parts of the settlement." Though warned by Taveeta ("I no savvy *talk* that island...I savvy hear um *cly*") the two ultimately blundered into a house, where, to their horror, they discovered the cause of the "barbaric keening" which they had ignored. A week later, both officers died. As a tale of cultural miscommunication, this section of *The Ebb-Tide* is matched only by the similarly miserable history of Kayerts and Carlier in Conrad's "An Outpost of Progress." Yet the same attitudes that prevent the white officers from perceiving any significance in "barbaric keening" prompt the narrator to "clean up" Taveeta's language, effectively *silencing* his idiosyncratic voice. "The reader shall be spared Uncle Ned's unwieldy dialect," writes the narrator before recounting the seaman's tale, "and learn in less embarrassing English the sum of what he now communicated" (Stevenson, 219). Thus, Stevenson's text gives in to the very assumptions of racial and linguistic authority that it so deeply subverts.

The moment of silencing – or, rather, of attempted silencing – in Marlow's conversation with the half-caste comes when the captain mimics "to perfection the act of stabbing from behind" and remarks that Jim is "[a]lready like the body of one deported" (*LJ*, 240). Angered, as we will see, by the unflattering aptness of the word "deported," Marlow's immediate impulse is to cut the half-caste off. But then he takes his cue from Jim: "Behind him [the captain] I perceived Jim smiling silently at me, and with a raised hand checking the exclamation on my lips" (240). The scene forms a revealing triangle, as the two whites, whose sense of superiority is all the more powerful because they seldom express it openly, silently agree between themselves to suffer the captain's ridiculous babbling. Moreover, Marlow's irritation at this particular moment in the conversation – here the contemptuous reference to "his kind" appears – points to an additional reason for his animosity toward the half-caste, one that goes beyond the subtle political tension that we have examined. As at least one critic has suggested,[6] the captain's words accidentally describe Jim's true condition. Thus, Marlow finds the half-caste repugnant precisely because his "lunatic" language has a perverse accuracy. Extracted by Stein from the white realm where he is too proud and sensitive to survive, and shuffled off to Patusan, Jim is like "one deported." By the same token, the captain's pronouncement that his passenger already bears "the similitude of a corpse" has a sinister significance in two respects. First of all, Jim is driven, as the French ethnographer O. Mannoni claimed all colonialists were,[7] to seek a "world without men," a place where he can reduce human beings to objects that serve his egocentric fantasies of heroism and redemption (Hawkins, 71). For this reason, Jim *is* corpse-like, his quest for mastery (however beneficial to Patusan in the short term) a retreat from life. Secondly, the comment foreshadows Jim's actual demise, adding to the foreboding atmosphere created by the captain's other remarks, which culminate in the declaration that he has had "plenty too much Patusan" (*LJ*, 239).

This reading suggests that Marlow's reaction to the "master of the brigantine" has less to do with the reality of the man in question, than with Marlow's needs as an observer – needs that derive, in part, from the imperialist culture to which he belongs. As we have seen, Marlow uses humor to ward off the half-caste's encroachment into the territory – political, cultural, and linguistic – of "pure" whites, a strategy shared by Kipling's narrator in *Kim* when distancing Anglicized Indians from Sahibs. In addition, the humor reflects Marlow's efforts to combat the uncanny accuracy of the captain's language, which describes more of Jim's past history and failings than intended.

To consider further the way in which such unacknowledged needs shape the narrator's "editing" of non-European voices, I will turn, briefly, to a similar scene – Marlow's encounter, "at a little place on the coast about 230 miles south of Patusan," with a corrupt colonial official. Presumably representing the interests of the Dutch government, this "third-class deputy-assistant" takes shape through details that again stress the degenerative results of miscegenation: he is "a big, fat, greasy, blinking fellow of mixed descent, with turned-out shiny lips," a shirt "odiously unbuttoned," and "a large leaf of some sort on top of his head" (278). Just as the half-caste captain resembles a chimpanzee, the "deputy-assistant" is presented as a pig, almost as one of the swinish Beast People from H. G. Wells' *The Island of Doctor Moreau* (1896).[8] In accord with his repellent appearance, the official offers to fence stolen property – namely a priceless emerald that Jim (a "sort of white vagabond") has supposedly plundered:

> "Tell him to come to me if they let him get alive out of the country. He had better look out for himself. Eh? I promise to ask no questions. On the quiet – you understand? You too – you shall get something from me. Small commission for the trouble. Don't interrupt. I am a Government official, and make no report. That's business. Understand? I know some good people that will buy anything worth having, and can give him more money than the scoundrel ever saw in his life. I know his sort." (279)

Though richly comic, because of his deluded belief in the fictitious emerald (what Marlow sardonically refers to as a "Jim-myth"), the official's comments reflect the lawless underside of imperialism – or, rather, the instability of any distinction between "legitimate" and "criminal" imperialist ventures. Note, for example, the curious contradictions that the character takes for granted: since he is a "Government official," he will, of course, "make no report"; "good people...will buy anything worth having," including items seized by force from their rightful owners. Not surprisingly, the doctrines of Victorian political economy and social Darwinism pervade these remarks. The terse statement, "[t]hat's business," justifies everything. Everyone is engaged in a scramble for wealth, so why not make a deal?

Marlow's repeated – and doubtless emphatic – attempts to curtail this overture (twice, the "deputy-assistant" asks him not to "interrupt") reflect an understandable impatience. Yet the comments that he wishes to silence also have, once again, implications best ignored. After all, just how inaccurate is the official's interpretation of Jim as a lawless marauder or "vagabond?" How much legitimacy does Stein's trading company truly have in Patusan, where so many different ethnic groups compete for economic and political dominance? And what of Marlow's own familiarity with the unsavory intrigues, coups, and acts of plunder by which imperialist expansion is achieved? Here, we should recall that Marlow's interview with the "deputy-assistant" is not the first instance in which he receives a sordid business proposition. During Jim's hearing, Marlow visits his "agent's office," where he is "fastened upon by a fellow fresh from Madagascar with a little scheme for a wonderful piece of business. It had something to do with cattle and cartridges and a Prince Ravonalo something." Marlow presents himself as a victim in this situation, implying – somewhat contradictorily – that he was forced to buy the entrepreneur a meal, thus allowing his own tiffin to be "spoiled," in order to "shak[e] him off." But the scene is perhaps more complex than that. Like the two half-castes, the "fellow fresh from Madagascar" manifests the physical characteristics of the degenerate or criminal *type*, as defined by the 19th-century pseudo-sciences of physiognomy and phrenology: "globular eyes starting out of his head in a fishy glitter" and "bumps on his forehead." Yet his motto – "[t]he minimum of risk with the maximum of profit" – might have come from a far more respectable imperialist such as Cecil Rhodes, whose expansionist machinations in southern Africa often reflected the need to satisfy investors lured by similar promises (170). Again, Conrad's novel blurs the line between criminal adventurism and "legal" empire building – between degenerative lawlessness and progressive expansion. Moreover, though Marlow presumably forgoes this ambiguous investment opportunity, his willingness at least to *listen* to the salesman's pitch, however uncomfortably, is a revealing admission. Such, then, is the instability of Marlow's "editing": though he would like to push the "deputy-assistant's" insinuations as far from himself – and Jim – as possible, because of this earlier scene, the official's words slip beyond their editor's control.

The two episodes that I have considered in detail, each involving Marlow's encounter with an ambiguously situated but verbally irrepressible character, point to a number of conclusions. I opened this essay by asserting that a large, though perhaps overshadowed, portion of Conrad's genius in *Lord Jim* is his creation of memorable voices, voices whose Dickensian idiosyncrasies stay with us forever. Yet, obviously, we do not hear these voices within a vacuum. They are mediated – edited – through Marlow's rhetoric, which inevitably imposes upon them the ideological constructs that order his vision of the world. So, as we have seen, when Marlow invites us to laugh at the captain's language, ideological assumptions come into play. From what standpoint are the captain's words "wrong" – and thus comical? At the same time, however, the constructs of superiority/inferiority that Marlow superimposes on the half--castes' language, through his derisive commentary or attempts at suppression, ultimately fail to silence the significance of this language. The reader cannot overlook the grim felicity of "deported," substituted for "departed," nor fail to see a correspondence between "business," as defined by the brazenly exploitative "deputy-assistant," and the "legitimate" economic opportunities opened by imperialism. Thus, Marlow's authority over the non-European voices in his narrative, an extension of the political authority that he enjoys as a "pure" Englishman in Asia, breaks down, and, in this collapse, it becomes possible to see *Lord Jim* as both a colonial *and* prophetically postcolonial narrative.

Moreover, the kind of analysis that I have engaged in – examining the way in which characters produce one meaning when we view them comically, and quite another when we consider the assumptions behind our laughter – could easily be applied to other Conrad narratives. Indeed, the number of Asian or African characters who, like the half-caste captain or Kipling's Hurree Chander, imitate European customs, dress, or aspirations for a presumably comic effect, is quite large. In *Almayer's Folly*, for example, we are invited to laugh at Jim Eng, whose pretense to be an Englishman nevertheless carries an ominous significance by mirroring Almayer's own false ties to a homeland he has never seen. The actions of Makola in "An Outpost of Progress" also produce Conradian irony at its most devastating: presented initially as a comic flunky, Makola ultimately imitates his masters to the point of matter-of-factly trading human lives for irony – an action that the hypocritical Kayerts and Carlier condemn. As these examples, together with those that I have considered in *Lord Jim*, suggest, perhaps humor in Conrad's fiction serves, more than anything else, both to mask and, paradoxically, to signal the moments when that fiction becomes most subversive and threatening.

NOTES

1. For more on the technique of "delayed decoding," see Ian Watt, *Conrad in the Nineteenth Century* (Berkeley – Los Angeles: U. of California P., 1979), 169-80, and Bruce Johnson, "Conrad's Impressionism and Watt's Delayed Decoding," in *Conrad Revisited: Essays for the Eighties,* ed. Ross C. Murfin (University: U. of Alabama P., 1985), 51-70.

2. The attributes of the "half-breed" or "half-caste" as a stock figure in Victorian adventure narratives are concisely described by Robert H. MacDonald, *The Language of Empire: Myths and Metaphors of Popular Imperialism, 1880-1918* (Manchester: Manchester U. P., 1994). "The fear of the other [writes MacDonald] may be expressed at its deepest in things sexual, for the most violent language is reserved to describe the products of miscegenation.... The 'half breed,' 'breed,' or 'mulatto' was invariably the villain of the adventure story.... The 'mulatto' combined the worst of both races, never the best. As Edgar Wallace put it, 'black is black and white is white, and all that is between is foul and horrible.'...to a culture in which

East and West, light and dark, were polarized, the reward of cohabitation was loss of caste, or, for the other, something much worse. And Kipling's famous words insisted, 'never the twain shall meet'" (MacDonald, 35).

3. See, for example, Leo Gurko, *Joseph Conrad: Giant in Exile* (New York: Collier, 1979), 117.

4. Conrad's fascination with the interpretive dilemmas posed by miscegenation can be traced to his earliest fiction. In *Almayer's Folly*, for example, Nina's bi-racial background serves both as an essential plot element (it is her refusal to conform to her father's cultural definitions that leads to his catatonic demise) and as a focal point for the novel's deconstruction of the distinction between civilization and savagery. For an astute treatment of "miscegenation as an ironic metaphor for racial misunderstanding" (130) in Conrad's second novel, see Gail Fraser, "Empire of the Senses: Miscegenation in *An Outcast of the Islands*," in *Contexts for Conrad*, eds. Keith Carabine, Owen Knowles, and Wiesław Krajka (Boulder – Lublin – New York: East European Monographs – Maria Curie-Skłodowska University – Columbia U.P., 1993; *Conrad: Eastern and Western Perspectives*, ed. Wiesław Krajka, vol. 2), 121-34.

5. In its portrayal of non-white seamen, Conrad's fiction is generally equivocal. In *Lord Jim*, for example, the two Malays who remain at their posts on board the *Patna* provide a yard stick – like Bob Stanton's heroic death or the conduct of the French lieutenant – by which to measure Jim's disgrace. Yet the text also presents these characters as automatons; without directions from their white superiors, they are incapable of action (or, in this case, experiencing panic or anxiety). Their calm in the face of disaster, however robotic, stands in grotesque juxtaposition with the cowardly behavior of the white officers, but the narrative simultaneously defuses much of the irony. Likewise, the presentation of the Congolese helmsman in "Heart of Darkness" suggests that the "fellowship of the craft" is restricted to whites. Yet another comic character (here, again, the humor derives from the native's pantomime of a "civilized" function), the helmsman regards the river boat's engine as a deity who must be constantly placated and apparently understands nothing of the technology that he oversees. Though Conrad's fiction often grants a high level of dignity and competence to non-white seamen, such characters remain – by virtue of their limitations – beyond the realm of trial and initiation inhabited by white sailors.

6. See Jan Verleun, *Patna and Patusan Perspectives: A Study of the Function of the Minor Characters in Joseph Conrad's "Lord Jim"* (Groningen: Boekhuis, 1979), 91-3. Verleun claims convincingly that "[t]he Captain's curious English seems symbolically interpretable throughout" (Verleun, 92).

7. See Mannoni's classic study of the colonial mind set: O. Mannoni, *Prospero and Caliban: The Psychology of Colonialization*, trans. Pamela Powesland (New York: Frederick A. Praeger, 1956), 108. The relevance of

Mannoni's work to Conrad's fiction is argued by Hunt Hawkins, "Conrad and the Psychology of Colonialism," in *Conrad Revisited: Essays for the Eighties*, ed. Ross C. Murfin (University: U. of Alabama P., 1985), 71-88.

8. Since Wells' novella concerns, among other things, the impossibility of artificially translating lower life-forms into their evolutionary superiors, it is not surprising that Conrad's racially-mixed characters, themselves the products of "unnatural" or "perverse" acts, echo the monstrosities of Moreau's island.

WORKS CITED

Fraser Gail. "Empire of the Senses: Miscegenation in *An Outcast of the Islands*," in *Contexts for Conrad*, eds. Keith Carabine, Owen Knowles, Wiesław Krajka. Boulder – Lublin – New York: East European Monographs – Maria Curie-Skłodowska University – Columbia U.P., 1993, 121-33; *Conrad: Eastern and Western Perspectives*, ed. Wiesław Krajka, vol. 2.

Gurko Leo. *Joseph Conrad: Giant in Exile*. New York: Collier, 1979.

Hawkins Hunt. "Conrad and the Psychology of Colonialism," in *Conrad Revisited: Essays for the Eighties*, ed. Ross C. Murfin. University: U. of Alabama P., 1985, 71-87.

Johnson Bruce. "Conrad's Impressionism and Watt's 'Delayed Decoding'," in *Conrad Revisited: Essays for the Eighties*, ed. Ross C. Murfin. University: U. of Alabama P., 1985, 51-70.

Kipling Rudyard. *Kim*. Oxford: Oxford U.P., 1987.

MacDonald Robert H. *The Language of Empire: Myths and Metaphors of Popular Imperialism, 1880-1918*. Manchester: Manchester U.P., 1994.

Mannoni O. *Prospero and Caliban: The Psychology of Colonialization*, trans. Pamela Powesland. New York: Frederick A. Praeger, 1956.

Stevenson Robert Louis. *The Ebb-Tide*, in Stevenson Robert Louis. *The Ebb-Tide. Doctor Jekyll and Mr. Hyde and Other Stories*. Harmondsworth: Penguin, 1979.

Verleun Jan. *Patna and Patusan Perspectives: A Study of the Function of the Minor Characters in Joseph Conrad's "Lord Jim."* Groningen: Bouma's Boekhuis, 1979.

Watt Ian. *Conrad in the Nineteenth Century*. Berkeley: U. of California P., 1979.

Watts Cedric. "Introduction," in Joseph Conrad. *Lord Jim*. Harmondsworth: Penguin, 1986.

Wells Herbert George. *The Island of Doctor Moreau*. London: Everyman, 1993.

White Andrea. *Joseph Conrad and the Adventure Tradition: Constructing and Deconstructing the Imperial Subject*. Cambridge: Cambridge U.P., 1993.

Patrycja Poniatowska,
University of Wrocław,
Wrocław, Poland

Beb Vuyk's "Full of Sound and Fury":
A Journey into "Heart of Darkness"

"Full of Sound and Fury," a short story by Beb Vuyk, one of the three published in 1959 in a collection entitled *Gerucht en geweld* (which can be roughly translated into English as "The sound and the fury"), by its very title draws the reader's attention to the author's conscious use of existing literary texts. Moreover, because it consists of a phrase originally appearing in Shakespeare's *Macbeth* but already employed by William Faulkner as the title for his famous novel, it implies Beb Vuyk's awareness of some intertextual practices. The title itself, the additional layers of meanings it generates at the reading of the story in the context of both *Macbeth* and *Sound and Fury* and the author's strategies involved in constructing a strongly autobiographically loaded story around the phrase so well-known to a relatively broad reading public would be on their own an intriguing subject of research (which, to my knowledge, has not been undertaken yet). In my paper, however, which focuses on the use Beb Vuyk makes of Joseph Conrad's "Heart of Darkness," the overt intertextuality of the title, so consciously and intricately used by the author, serves only as an indicator of the fact that some motifs, words, and circumstances a reader comes across in Beb Vuyk's "Full of Sound and Fury" are not purely "innocent," that they are overcoded and beside their "face value" (i.e. their primary referentiality to real events and the author's authentic experiences in postwar Indonesia) they generate also other meanings resulting from the relationship the story has not with the outer, historical reality, but with a pre-text, Joseph Conrad's novella.

"Full of Sound and Fury" could be easily read on its own and even then for a reader not acquainted with "Heart of Darkness" it would supply enough stimulus for reflecting upon issues of identity, power, language, colonial and postcolonial discourses, etc., and additionally provide aesthetic pleasure of an excellently constructed story with carefully built-up suspense and an astonishing ending. The influential Dutch literature historian and critic, the author of the so far most comprehensive history of Dutch-Indonesian literature[1] calls *Gerucht en geweld* "a magnificent collection, the best piece of writing she [Beb Vuyk] has created" (Nieuwenhuys, 476). He maintains as well that Beb Vuyk's books are always autobiographically marked ("Beb Vuyk always writes autobiographically or semi-autobiographically" – 478), he warns, nevertheless, that a reader should not interpret them as a precise recreation of the real sequence of events in their unchanged form, but rather perceive them as an artistic, fictionalized rewriting of personal experiences of the author as well as of other people she came in contact with (485).

In press interviews, Beb Vuyk stresses herself the autobiographical quality of her writings. Said Beb Vuyk: "I am a story-teller and because I cannot invent anything myself, I write about everything that is going on around me" (Vuyk, "Het laatste...") and "I describe what I see, what my eyes see and what moves my heart" (Roggeman, 4). She acknowledged, however, the fact that except her own experiences gained while living in Indonesia, the factors exerting influence upon her works must be looked for also in literature. Her youthful fascination with the Gentlemen Adventurers has become a commonplace repeated by almost all critics discussing her books.[2] Extraordinary life of travelers, discoveries at the remote corners of the world, exotic landscapes and active existence full of passion and exciting adventures so different from the conventions restricting her energy and strong individuality at her parental home inspired initially her desire to travel far and settle in Indonesia (her father was half-Indonesian) and then were the examples she followed creating her first novels.

Yet, her attitude to literature as a factor affecting her own work evolved and began gradually to take on more profound forms than pure enchantment with action and otherness of setting. As her own writing progressed, and maybe more importantly, as the alien world she had entered became more and more her own,[3] she became more aware of processes going on in a text and practices involved in the creation of it. When trying to define the influences she had been exposed to in the later stages of her literary career, she pointed to Joseph Conrad and identified him (and especially his narrative techniques) as the source of several elements appearing in her works (in particular in the collection *Gerucht en geweld*): "Following the example of Conrad, I work with a 'narrator,' a story-teller who creates a tale of what he has seen or heard more or less as a spectator, not more in the centre, but on the periphery" (11).

The shaping power of Conrad can be relatively easily detected in "Full of Sound and Fury," a short story written in 1959. The structure of it strongly resembles "Heart of Darkness" as the story is constructed as a narrative within another narrative. The main, frame narrative recounts a journey up the river Kapuas undertaken by a journalist in search of material for articles (although the circumstances and the aim are not very clear at the beginning) shortly after Indonesia gained independence. The inner narrative consists of one of the stories the frame narrator listens to aboard the boat, the story "full of sound and fury," retelling one of episodes from the Indonesian independence war in which the second narrator actively participated as a resist-ance-movement member. A short summary, I believe, would be helpful at this point.

The first-person frame narrator (actually unnamed anywhere in the text) sets out on a thousand-kilometer-long journey from Pontianak to Putussibau, on the island of Borneo. Only at the end of the story do we learn that the aim of the enterprise was collecting the material for a series of travel reports. One of the men accompanying the frame narrator is Tjondro, sent with her[4] for rather unclear reasons (uncertainties, silences and under-statements are almost endlessly multiplied in the story): accord-ing to one version of explanation he is to protect her, according to another his task is to watch her incessantly. Almost im-mediately Tjondro becomes the main focus of the narrator's attention. He is an anguished man who saw and contributed to the atrocities of the independence war. Now haunted by his past, trying to free himself from the unbearable burden of memories, he is compelled to keep retelling his experiences in stories full of blood, violence and sufferings. One evening, having got drunk during a visit in one of settlements of the Dajaks living along the river, he begins a shooting party without any discernible reason and then sinks in tears and despair on his knees. At that climactic point, the narrator hears him whisper "*Sial, sial!,*" the word combining the meanings of evil, calamity and catastrophe.

This is the moment when the inner narrative begins, as on the following day the frame narrator notices that Tjondro's back is covered with awful scars and inquires after the cause. Tjondro's narrative is an account of a failed plot that was to have resulted in the blowing up of one of the colonial government buildings. It turned out, however, that one of the members of the resistance--movement group responsible for the execution of the action was a traitor. The whole group were taken prisoner and interrogated by the Dutch. Tjondro recounts the horrors of the night he spent listening to the cries of his tortured friends and then tells about the interrogation and beating he himself was subjected to. Accidentally shot in his arm by one of the Dutch soldiers, he was transported to a hospital, where he met a Dutch nurse who helped him escape.

Together with those members of his group who avoided having been captured, he decided to avenge their betrayed and killed friends. At this point, the frame narrator begins to interfere more and more frequently as Tjondro overwhelmed with emotions and anguish speaks less and less clearly collapsing into incomprehensible murmur and stammering. Significantly, although the inner narration is conducted in the first person singular, it does not take much time to realize that a reader does not have a direct access to Tjondro's story. His "broken Dutch" interspersed with frequent passages in local languages is polished by the frame narrator, who, having pretended at the beginning to transmit Tjondro's account as accurately and objectively as possible, in fact presents her own reconstruction of it adjusted to the needs of a literary text as perceived from the "high culture" perspective. This editorial work transgresses mere translation (problematic as it even could be for the authenticity of the narration), the demand of making the story intelligible in its verbal stratum to a reader from a different national group. It also obscures Tjondro's emotional involvement in his story (a reader does not know when exactly Tjondro "stammers and murmurs," when he resorts to his native language, or how his pitch changes), filters it as a far-going interpretation on the part of the frame narrator (the frame narrator admits, for example, not having grasped the particulars of Tjondro's story because of linguistic difficulties), and transforms a presumably varied, faltering account into a smooth flow of full, compound sentences that on their own would not reflect Tjondro's hesitations, pauses, or growing unease.

The resistance movement members tracked down the traitor, caught him, and sentenced to death. While the sentenced was digging his own grave, the group debated over the manner of execution and who was to perform it. At a moment of total confusion and nervous agitation to the utmost, Tjondro hit the traitor with a sword and one of his friends finished the work shooting the wounded.

The frame narrator takes over and finishes the first narration in a couple of short sentences: having come back to Djakarta, she meets Achmad – previously one of the most important members of the resistance movement, now a prominent official – who tells her "the story that Tjondro told me, but differently. Because Tjondro was the traitor" (Vuyk, "Full of Sound...," 32). These are the last words in the story.

From this rough outline it is visible that whereas Conrad's "Heart of Darkness" dramatizes "the struggle between incompatible epistemologies, different knowledges" rather than "a political struggle between coloniser and the colonised" and "blacks are only figures in a landscape" (Parry, 36), the political questions receive greater prominence in Vuyk's "Full of Sound and Fury" and are more directly probed into, although, obviously, other issues such as identity, responsibility and ethics are explored as well. Also the majority of main characters are

                                    Patrycja Poniatowska

natives of Indonesia and no European,[5] or better – no representative of European establishment, is heard to speak in the story. The undifferentiated "savages," who, for all the complexity of the debate on the racial controversy voiced by Conrad's novella, seem to constitute a homogeneous entity pushed on the peripheries of the world, the order or the self, are replaced by a multilingual multitude defying one obvious classification. The discourse of the colonizer, who perceived the colored from his own ethnocentric perspective as unfalteringly identical among them and different, the Other, in relation to himself, and so denied the representatives of the subordinated group any separate identity, must withdraw under the pressure of multiple cultures with the tensions among their peculiar customs, rituals and interests, as well as under the massive attack of a variety of individual histories, lives, and motivations.

Vuyk's short story actually commences where Conrad's novella ends. The ultimate assessment of the human soul and European culture presented by Conrad, reverberating in the final scene of Marlow's narrative in the words the dying colonizer Kurtz whispered: "The horror! The horror!" serves as a starting point for the narrative of the downfall of colonialism and foundation of the postcolonial world as perceived by the colonized. Tjondro's "*Sial, sial*" overheard by the frame narrator makes her alert to a possible deeper, concealed meaning of his violent behavior: "'He is not used to drinking,' said Pat Amat shaking his head, but I knew that it was much more serious" (Vuyk, "Full of Sound...," 21). Similarly, at the same time, the repeated words of a tormented man struggling with himself, the words associated with fear and despair, evoke in a reader's mind not merely an image of a personal tragedy, but also another layer of meanings conveyed by a broader, literary context. Beb Vuyk leaves it for the reader to fill up with the knowledge he/she has of "Heart of Darkness" some empty spaces of her text, namely the colonial pre-history of her narrative. Having referred the reader to the complexities of the moral debate on colonialism proceeding in "Heart of Darkness" with its simultaneous "denouncement of infamous assumptions of imperialism's ideology" and "production for its canon of the vindication of idealistic intent" (Parry, 23) and with its "duplicity of reasons" (Daleski, 70), "Full of Sound and Fury" can carry on the analysis into the time of the twilight of the colonial era and further on. It can also make use of "dialogic possibilities," and continue being "a site of struggle between disparate languages and outlooks" (White) whose centre of gravity is relocated in the direction of politics, without running the risk of leaving other relevant issues undiscussed.

When compared to "Heart of Darkness," "Full of Sound and Fury" manifests a significant degree of condensation. Leaving aside the radical difference between the very size of the novella and the short story, the time-span of the frame narration of "Full of Sound and Fury" is much shorter: it covers a couple of days, though there is a greater time-lapse between the described voyage up the Kapuas River and the frame narrator's return to Djakarta. The language is very concise and the narrators restrain themselves from interpreting their experiences, commenting on them or attempting to generalize their meaning. Simultaneously the narrative structure is simplified: the multiplicity of inter-twined stories and competing discourses is hinted at rather than elaborately presented. We are not supposed to look for the precise equivalents of Marlow or Kurtz among the narrators of "Full of Sound and Fury," the story after all by no means strives to be an exact replica of "Heart of Darkness." It comprises, nevertheless, numerous elements so strongly reminiscent of Conrad's novella, that in their totality they reinforce the sense of purposeful parallelisms.

The most striking are some foregrounded aspects of the figure of Tjondro that make him resemble Kurtz. Tjondro could be Kurtz, deprived of his no matter how dubious yet engrossing power and grandeur, Kurtz reduced to the misery of his essential loneliness in the struggle against himself, against his abhorred past and present, against powers haunting him from inside. The young Russian accompanying Kurtz defines his existential situation in terms of excessive, unbearable suffering and ines-capable entanglement in the things and circumstances loathed.

Tjondro is also a prey to the memories of the horrors he underwent and contributed to during the Indonesian independence war. He is guilt-ridden, obsessed by fear, torn between the attempts to soothe his pain in drunken forgetfulness, fishing (which a doctor recommended him to calm his nerves) or blind, uncontrolled violence ("When I don't know how to cope any more, I go shooting, just so, somewhere in the wild, without a target" – Vuyk, "Full of Sound...," 23) on the one hand, and – on the other – imperative necessity to re-live his experiences and relieve himself by retelling the stories of war: "He told stories, because he had to tell them in order to free himself" (14).

As Kurtz is identified with excess, which in the terms of "Heart of Darkness" is a factor dooming to failure, Tjondro is similarly incapable of self-possession. His lack of restraint reaches nearly monstrous dimensions when having drunk himself almost into unconsciousness, he seizes his gun and totally unprovoked begins to shoot in the direction of the Dajaks whose hospitality he and his companions have just witnessed and experienced. There is no stopping him until finally exhausted he falls on his knees in hysterical sobbing, shouting incomprehensibly. The scene renders him most vulnerable and least human (or least fully human), as he cannot move on his own, must be almost dragged aboard the boat and then his speech disintegrates into inarticulate cries. Tjondro is also a man who has personally experienced the extremities of human existence on the "dark" pole of it. The frame narrator mentions also another man – Arif – accompanying her on the boat and the stories of his childhood he told her, but comparing the two she points to the basic difference between them: "Arif suffered from remorse because he did not fight and Tjondro's remorse was caused just by his participation in the struggle for independence. Arif did too little and Tjondro *too much*, and his guilt was inscribed in blood" (15; my italics).

Both Kurtz and Tjondro let ungovernable impulses of human nature go rampant to the point where it is impossible to wring oneself loose from the clutches of the unleashed anarchy. The discrepancy between their alleged motivations, as they strive to present them in their narratives, fictions they create of their achievements and vocation, and the real urges pushing them grows more and more visible. And for all their individuality and uniqueness of their experiences, both "Heart of Darkness" and "Full of Sound and Fury" employ strategies which imbue the two characters with a more universal meaning, and grant them a symbolic status. Kurtz, to the making of whom "the whole Europe contributed," indicates that all colonizers are complicit in his enormities, and the whole European culture is responsible for the atrocities committed by the colonizers. Tjondro, whose origin is not conclusively established ("His name was Javanese, but he hardly looked like a Javanese" – 5) and whose war experiences are almost monumentally hyperbolized, is presented as an "all Indonesian man": "Blood always flowed in his stories which conjured up the vision of distress and anxiety, bitterness and confusion of a whole generation" (15). Consequently, when in his narrative he juxtaposes his own ethos of a martyr for the just cause (liberating his country from foreign oppressors) and the mean motivation of the traitor (who betrayed their plot in order to take revenge on a hated member of the resistance--movement group), but then it turns out that he was the traitor himself, the phenomenon, the shift in the hierarchy of values becomes applicable not only to him exclusively; it turns out impossible to discriminate when and what takes over: heroism or pursuit of private ends. What remains from idealistic motives are greed, desire of power and personal revenge, the laudable impulses inscribed in and propagated by the discourses of the dominant ideology are reduced to the lowest promptings and the discourses themselves exposed as purely fictional constructs.

Like Kurtz who always is associated with darkness, surrounded by impenetrable mystery and shadows of the night in their literal and symbolic meanings, Tjondro is presented as a nocturnal creature avoiding the light of a day. Though during the day he feels secure, his nerves calm down and the anxiety loses its grip on him, the night with all the dread it brings activates him. Night and darkness are also the governing element of his stories and the scenery in which he retells them and they mesmerize and perturb the frame narrator like Kurtz's captivating eloquence enthralled Marlow. His experience of darkness is always bound up with unspeakable sufferings and a forfeit of identity by plunging either in dehumanizing brutality or in fear that strips one from one's individuality. His narrative is preceded by the frame narrator's suggestive evocation of darkness which bears overtones of the quality approaching a religious incantation or magical chant: "the background of the dark forest and the dark night [seemed] a dark sea" (19). In the night he hears terrible cries of his tortured friends and gains the insight into the elemental forces governing a human being: primal instincts: "I was lying on the ground, hands over my ears; I realised that I cried with him, but I knew then that it was not because I pitied him, only because I was terrified" (25).

Significantly, in the story the experience serves to blur the clear-cut distinctions and unsettle categories reinforced by the discourse of colonization. The human condition finds its common denominator in suffering that can be borne or inflicted on others – this becomes for a moment a basis for defining relations of power. The positions of a victim and of a persecutor, however, can be by no means considered to be immutably fixed and taken for granted. The fluidity of the extremes of this polarization questions the existence of any permanent and "natural" attributes or prerogatives of certain groups and/or individuals other than the "darkness" of fear and pain. The Japanese who occupied the islands spreading terror and death were captured, tortured and killed by the Dajaks who led their own war and, in their turn, used to be oppressed by the white colonizers. Victimized Tjondro quickly moves (at least in his story) to the position of a willy-nilly executor. Even, as the narrative takes us further back into history, the Dutch colonizers – the arch-oppressors – turn out to have been exposed to the same lot they have prepared for the natives of Indonesia fighting for independence. The nurse who helped Tjondro escape from captivity was namely a member of the Dutch resistance movement during the

Second World War and, arrested by the Nazis, was tortured and faced a death sentence.

"Full of Sound and Fury" penetrates the unfathomable depths of the heart of darkness of human nature and colonial and postcolonial relationships as well as it explores "Heart of Darkness": the field of battle of discourses contesting for the ultimate meaning, with the white, European ethnocentric discourse emerging relatively triumphant in spite of its being severely undermined by the constant presence of powerful opponents and self-contradictions. As the final scene of "Heart of Darkness" transports us back to London which was once "a dark place of the earth," yet now is the centre of "cultivation" where official institutionalized meanings are constructed and then spread over the world, the last scene of "Full of Sound and Fury" takes place at a new location: Djakarta on the island of Java. From the grandeur of the tropical jungle, "primitive" houses of head-hunters, and violent, tormented, hardly intelligible stories of Tjondro, the narrator moves to the city which used to be a "savage" place – an old Javanese port, until Batavia was founded there by the Dutch – a center of trade and the local headquarters of colonial authorities, for all its importance, still situated on the periphery of the world and looking up to the polished urban metropolies of the Low Countries (Balicki, Bogucka, 228-44). Now it has become the center itself, the capital of a newly created state, the seat of official institutions producing and produced by the official discourse.

The narrator meets there major Achmad, formerly one of the leaders of the resistance movement, now – an officer of Intelligence Service, a representative of military and governmental powers. One would hardly be able to create a greater contrast between two characters than the gap separating Achmad from Tjondro. The former has it all. His sophisticated articulateness hinted at by the narrator counterparts gradual deterioration of Tjondro's narrative abilities and his "broken Dutch," his elegant, nuanced behavior exposes even more drastically Tjondro's incapability of self-control balancing on the verge of insanity, his aristocratic parentage and appearance highlight the fact that Tjondro comes essentially from nowhere and does not look trustworthy. Most importantly, Achmad is Western-educated and his degree form Leiden University secures for him a highly respected position in society. He clearly belongs to the ruling elite and demonstrates his consciousness of the privileged place he occupies.

Paradoxically enough, the polar opposition of the two figures renews the pattern of dichotomies on the basis of which Beb Vuyk tried to grasp the effects colonization and decolonization had on various groups of Indonesian population: "And so it appears that the colonisers cherish the sense of superiority, at the same time, however, their knowledge is deficient: they do not want and are not able to understand the colonised people. On the other hand, Vuyk describes the process in which revenge, distrust and inferiority complex emerge among the colonised" (Pattynama, 210). The pattern, however, is now implanted in the description of the postcolonial reality. The hegemony of colonial oppositions of white and colored, civilized and primitive is supposed to have been challenged and eradicated. What used to be defined as a margin is vested with authority and gains an autonomous, central status. Nevertheless, it appears that the center when deprived of the periphery would lose its central position because its centrality relies on the existence of the other relegated to the margin. So the colonial margin, now constituting the center, continues to divide and differentiate within itself: a new margin is constructed where individuals like Tjondro or groups like the Dajaks are positioned, and the notion of centrality is established by the perpetuation of concepts and principles of the discourse which is the legacy of colonialism. The same system (only slightly adapted) of generating and legitimization of meanings is still maintained as valid, in spite of all the attempts and endeavors "Full of Sound and Fury" undertakes to blur sharp distinctions and redefine contradictions.

Whereas the mixture of original customs of the Dajaks and European influences is portrayed with grotesque, almost ridiculous overtones, Achmad's cultural and ethnic complexity is presented in highly appreciative terms. When in houses of the

Dajaks, still decorated with heads of killed enemies, the traditional meal is served in "yellow and green plastic mugs" (Vuyk, "Full of Sound...," 17), the effect is that of a cultural clash exposing "primitiveness" of the inhabitants of remote islands, readily and indiscriminately absorbing the discards of a typical mass production. This resembles in a way the effect of Marlow's characterization of a black fireman, when after ironical words expressing estimation for work well done, the explanation of the fireman's eagerness follows, which reveals that it results from the fear of demons who are said to get angry if not fed properly and on time. In both cases the indigenous people are identified as naive and unsophisticated, accepting ingredients out of context served to them by those who wield power. How drastically different is the level of Achmad's intercultural achievements. He is characterized as the one who "has become very western but has remained very Javanese" (31), he moves with graceful ease across cultural barriers reading European theologians and Javanese mystics, commenting expertly on the narrator's journalistic accomplishments and leading a polite conversation tinted with slight irony.

As Marlow in the final scene of his narrative is unable to contradict the Intended, again a "superior creature," to break the chivalric code demanding from a man that he protect the weaker vessel, to acknowledge before her what he has learned about the nothingness and darkness of human nature and colonial enterprise, and finally to resist confirming her version of cultural discourse she is created by but simultaneously co-creates maintaining that "she knew, she knew," similarly the narrator of "Full of Sound and Fury," for all her compassionate good will toward Tjondro and striving after objectivity, dismisses his narrative when faced with another version of the same story comprised, however, in the official discourse epitomized by rational and self-possessed Achmad. At this point the disconcerting remark occurring earlier in her narrative: "But then I did not doubt a second in his [Tjondro's] words, because he could tell stories so magnificently" (14), can be deciphered in the new light of information obtained in the final scene: now she does not believe in what Tjondro has told her, now she knows the truth, no matter how enigmatic and fragmentary it could be. Achmad, with his reputation of heroic past and the present authority voices the governing discourse and "knows better." There are no arguments provided why his version should be given credit to, but the position from which he speaks. He is additionally a representative of the so-called high culture, while it is interesting to notice that although Tjondro is not illiterate, he confesses that he is unable to express himself in writing: "I cannot write...as soon as I see paper in front of me, the sentences slip away" (14). Tjondro belongs to the oral culture of Indonesia, of stories passed down from generation to generation, and although this phenomenon is potentially subversive in relation to and liberating from the dominant, codified, written culture brought by the colonizers, we realize that this quality does not gain recognition in new circumstances and the discourse of Leiden University graduates speaking idiomatic Dutch still prevails.

Although the absolute status of the capital and Achmad's version of the conspiracy story are partially unsettled by the fact that this narrative does not clarify the existing uncertainties or solve any doubts, but on the contrary, it creates even broader, unabridged gaps and defers the meaning almost into infinity (again a journey to the heart of darkness and back to "the centre of civilisation" does not provide all the answers, rather it poses new questions), it remains the fact that his (and metropolitan) variant of the story goes unobjected to by the narrator. The outcome of Achmad's story is presented as *the* truth: the last sentence, "Because Tjondro was the traitor" does not receive any qualification or restriction. No addition in the sort of "he maintained," or "according to him" modifies the irrevocability of the statement. After all, as Foucault wrote: "We cannot exercise power except through the production of truth" (Foucault, 12).

As "Full of Sound and Fury" repeats and recreates narrative situations of its pre-text, the structures of colonial discourse are endlessly readapted and reduplicated when the colonialism itself is apparently eradicated. A process of constant differentiation and reproduction continues without a pause.

NOTES

1. The term originally sounds *"Indisch-Nederlandse literatuur"* and although much debated on, it refers by a more or less common consensus to writings in Dutch which describe or whose action takes place in Indonesia.

2. See for example Joop van den Berg et al., "Of course, Beb Vuyk remains a writer who was initially strongly influenced by gentlemen--adventurers Kipling, Stevenson and Conrad" (Berg, 112).

3. The terms *"eigen"* (own) and *"ander"* (other) are often used in discussions of Dutch-Indonesian literature since much of it revolves around the differences between the worlds and cultures of Dutch colonizers (own) and of native population (other) and their separateness. Beb Vuyk's (whose father, as well as her husband, was half-Indonesian) undermines the strict dichotomies of those two worlds as, rebelling against conventions restricting her in the Netherlands, she chose to live among the native inhabitants of the Moluccas, spoke like *totok* (a white person) but looked like an Indian girl (Vuyk, "Het Laatste...," 1991), remained in Indonesia after it gained independence as a citizen of the new country, but left for the Netherlands in 1958 because of political reasons, where she lived till her death in 1991.

4. Although in the text there is only one slight hint that the narrator is female, I am going to call the frame narrator "she," because of very clear autobiographical references: Beb Vuyk did actually undertake such a trip at that time and wrote travel reports for one of Indonesian magazines. Nevertheless, equating the narrator's sex with that of the author, on the basis of similarities to Beb Vuyk's actual life, must always be very tentative, since the writer herself warns that she "is sometimes present in her stories in the disguise of a man" (Roggeman, 11).

5. The question of national identity of the frame narrator is problematic.

WORKS CITED

Balicki Jan, Bogucka Maria. *Historia Holandii,* wyd. drugie, poprawione i uzupełnione. Wrocław: Zakład Narodowy im. Ossolińskich, 1989.

Berg Joop Van den et al. *In Indie geweest. Maria Dermout, H. J. Friedericy, Beb Vuyk.* Amsterdam: EM. Querido's Uitgeverij B.V., 1990.

Daleski Herman M. *Joseph Conrad. The Way of Dispossession.* London: Faber and Faber, 1977.

Foucault Michel. "The Political Function of the Intellectual," *Radical Philosophy,* 17 (1977), 12-14.

Nieuwenhuys Rob. *Oost-Indische Spiegel. Wat Nederlandse schrijvers en dichters over Indonesie hebben geschreven, vanaf de eerste jaren den compagnie tot op heden.* Amsterdam: EM. Querido's Uitgeverij B.V., 1972.

Pattynama Pamela. "Etnocentrisme en waarheid," in *Vrouwenstudies in de jaren negentig, een kennismaking vanuit verschillende perspectieven*, ed. M. Brouns et al. Bussum: Dick Countinko, 1995, 211-31.

Parry Benita. *Conrad and Imperialism. Ideological Boundaries and Visionary Frontiers*. London: Macmillan Press, 1983.

Roggeman Willem. "Gesprek met Beb Vuyk," *De Vlaamse Gids*, 69ste jaargang, mei/juni 1985: 3, 2-13.

Vuyk Beb. "Full of Sound and Fury," in her *Gerucht en geweld*. 2nd ed. Amsterdam: Contact, 1992, 5-32.

Vuyk Beb. "Het laatste vraaggesprek met Beb Vuyk. Ik wilde een leven snel en hijgend van daden," *Nieuwe Rotterdamse Courant*, 10.08.1991, interviewer: Caroline van den Heuvel.

White Andrea. *Joseph Conrad and the Adventure Tradition. Constructing and Deconstructing the Imperial Subject*. Cambridge: Cambridge U.P., 1993.

Anita Mathew,
University of Goa,
Goa, India

An Eastern Appreciation of Joseph Conrad: His Treatment of Evil in "Heart of Darkness" and *Under Western Eyes*

The Ultimate Reality

The significance of Conrad's message is as extraordinary today as it was at the turn of the century. In fact it is prophetic. The "truth" his fiction seeks to convey deserves to be cherished and preserved particularly in this postmodern era of fragmented consciousness. This is so because it is inextricably related as much to the basic nature of all beings as to the magnificent mystery of the human mind and the mystical link which binds everything together in the universe. It also reveals that we happen to be in this world primarily for the sake of Existence, Consciousness and Bliss, with the evolutionary obligation to move our consciousness further along planes of the physical, vital, mental and psychic, in order to arrive at a holistic realization of why pain, suffering and death are an integral aspect of human existence.

W. B. Yeats said, "Art is the vision of reality." With the passage of time it has become evident that Conrad's art traced multiple aspects of reality to arrive at the truth. His unique treatment of evil shows that he seems to have grasped the concept of ultimate reality as understood by Sri Aurobindo, the great Indian mystical seer and thinker.[1] Conrad's idea of evil, couched within the larger concept of consciousness, is very similar to what Sri Aurobindo presented in his Integral Philosophy.[2]

The last decade of this century has witnessed a drastically transformed world order. Rapid strides in science and techno-logy seem to have brought about exploitative material plenitude – a culture which Sri Aurobindo termed "economic barbarism."

Fortunately scientists have begun to realize that there are certain eternal questions which defy rational explanation, particularly in the field of ethics. One of these is the ever intriguing and enigmatic question of the origin of evil. The unbridled growth of materialism has begun to show one of the many facets of evil, the deterioration and depletion of the earth's natural resources, apart from the sense of alienation in human beings which has resulted in the dichotomy of mind and matter, the outcome being a sense of fragmented consciousness. The only redeeming consequence of this catastrophe is our increasing realization of the need to shift back to the importance of spiritual resurgence or recreation and a complete respect for Nature. There is still time. As his works amply testify, Conrad envisioned at the start of the century what would happen if we followed just one path, viz, that of materialistic progress. He indirectly warned that we should stem the tide of this rank materialism to be able to foster our conscience to recognize the evil besetting us and lurking in us, and instead we should choose to live in harmony with nature and our fellow beings. Now at the end of the twentieth century we should understand what Conrad discovered and revealed as a "new reality" (the ultimate reality as different from phenomenal reality) which would be the solution to all human problems, including the one of evil.

Conrad's novels make a vivid impression that he had epiphanically glimpsed the ultimate reality. His comprehensive treatment of evil in his entire literary output proves this. However, it is essential to bear in mind that this kind of reality is based on the philosophy of Sri Aurobindo's "adventure of consciousness,"[3] where the evil is a powerful and necessary catalyst to allow human consciousness to evolve further so that in due course of time we realize the undeniable divine in all creation.

Conrad insisted that we have first to learn to "see" more, to "hear" more and to "feel" more to delve into and to understand mystical meanings of reality. He obviously believed that the reality had mystical meanings as indeed the ultimate reality does have. Various critics who have interpreted ambiguity, paradox and duality appearing in Conrad's works, have attributed them to his being a modern writer, influenced by radical thinking of the age. He has been described by most merely as a "realist," "romantic" or "existentialist," since he was concerned with consciousness, human motives and forces like the evil which governed life. In fact, Conrad falls in line more with contemporary philosophers such as H. Bergson and G. B. Shaw who propounded the philosophy of the Life-Force and, above all, with Sri Aurobindo's attitude to evil in life and with his treatment of it. Conrad even comes closer to Sri Aurobindo than to Bergson or Shaw. He was not aware of Sri Aurobindo and his philosophy, but like the mystical poets Blake, Shelley and Yeats, and due to his innate mystical bent of mind, he seems to have independently hit upon Sri Aurobindo's idea of consciousness as the ultimate truth of reality.

In Conrad's novels good and evil are dealt with as part of natural phenomena. They are not mutually exclusive. On the contrary, when they are rent apart, as is shown in most of his works, they cause atrophy which leads to anarchy and destruction. Conrad assigns an elemental status to good and evil. Death is generally dealt with little fanfare by him, including decisions by human beings to commit suicide, if they found life on earth intolerable due to isolation and alienation. It is similar to the "cosmic *moksha*" (salvation) which Sri Aurobindo describes as a scheme of the evolution of consciousness formulated by a greater spiritual power. Death is simply a release of one's soul from life or body. It is not a terrible end to one's whole being which would comprise the spiritual essence within every form of life. It is evident in Conrad's writings that he wanted his readers to understand what leads to "fragmented consciousness" in human life. He also expected to anticipate what would happen if we remained "conscienceless." He no doubt wanted to demonstrate that if we forgot "the heart of darkness" and chose the luminous core of sanitized good alone, we would miss the mystical and basic truth of reality as well as what is needed for a complete and genuine progress of man's mind to higher consciousness.

Definition of Evil

From both a simplistic dictionary meaning of evil and from a broader explanation of evil in *Encyclopedia of Religion* it is clear that Conrad's treatment of it is not limited merely to a religious interpretation. It is important to note that in Conrad's view there is no absolute evil as there is no absolute good. Good and evil are comingled or "coeval." His theory of the development of evil, using mythical symbolism to express its mental manifestation and its role in leading to an evolution of consciousness, comes closest to Sri Aurobindo's concept of evil.[4] Sri Aurobindo demonstrates that all suffering results from narrowness of consciousness at all levels. Nowhere, on any plane, is it a question of severing evil from the rest, but of convincing it of its own "light" – the "heart" of darkness. Otherwise, no sooner is evil healed in one place or exterminated in another than it revives instantly elsewhere – in some other place, in some other form. Evil is not just outside, it is within and below. As a matter of fact, we really do not know anything of the good of the world or its evil, as it originates in ignorance within the mind of man, due to his limited consciousness.

Just as Sri Aurobindo emphasizes the need of pain and suffering as an integral part of life on earth, Conrad, too, in all his major works, stresses the ambivalent nature of evil. For Conrad, evil helps to solve man's eternal dilemmas in his mortal existence. It is present within every being. It can neither be repelled by laws of dogmatic religion or deterministic philosophies, nor can it be contained by the thin crust of morality framed by the modern civilization. It has to be accepted as a necessary part of creation and existence. In his efforts to harness evil to advantage, man cannot afford to forget his past or his link with his fellow beings, Nature or the universe. Using his acute insight, Conrad brought out the elusiveness and contrast in the qualities of both good and evil, embedding them in an overall concept of consciousness. He disclosed the effect of evil by couching his tales in symbolism and a mythical ambience, which lent them an air of mystery as well as a deep mystical significance. He revealed the power of evil as elemental in its scope and corrosive in its content. It is the "heart of darkness" that can afflict from without and from within. It cannot be resisted by good. The contrast has to be recognized first. It should then be followed by an awareness of the conflict (which arises in the mind) between what we understand as being good and what we choose to establish as evil. It is merely a distortion of the mind that creates suffering, causes harm and injury which then becomes the origin of evil. This realization helps the mind to make choices. The commencement of the "adventure of consciousness" at all levels of the mind appears when we realize that there is good in evil as well. According to Sri Aurobindo, such "gnostical" understanding of the nature of evil can make existence worthwhile, living a joy, and death simply a release. Conrad also glimpsed this truth about evil, which enables us to arrive at an Aurobindonian-Conradian framework of evil within a concept of consciousness.

Conrad's Quest for Truth

The reason for choosing "Heart of Darkness" and *Under Western Eyes* to show the applicability of the framework and to appreciate Conrad's quest for truth, is mainly because both these novels fall on either end of the spectrum of the years he was meant to have written his masterpieces – between 1899 and 1911. From the time he started writing "Heart of Darkness," followed by *Lord Jim, Nostromo* and *The Secret Agent*, we find his treatment of evil leading towards his attempt to understand the potential of human beings to use its force in order to evolve their consciousness.

In "Heart of Darkness" Conrad instinctively understood the dominant and dormant qualities of evil. He also knew that primeval evil overcomes the mind of man. He did not, however, limit it to an individual's experience of its elemental, atavistic control over nature and all beings, as is explained by most of his critics. He went further. The evolution of his characters as well as the shaping of his themes and plots show that various facets of evil caused by man's mind play a vital part in the development of human consciousness.

Conrad examined the whole idea of "traditional" conscience forcibly nurtured by external checks laid down by religion and social obligations. This kind of conscience crumbles under the impact of uncontrolled evil desires that take root in the human mind due to its ignorance. It leads to growth of a false self or a selfish ego. The mind then absorbs evil qualities from their mythical to their conceptual manifestations. The human mind's capacity to make conscious choices, using its clear light of reason, is insufficient to overcome these attractive, adverse forces of evil.

When participating in the "adventure of consciousness" along the right lines, a man endowed with free will can fathom the divine in him. It is this spiritual manifestation which gives him the strength to nurture a good conscience. In "Heart of Darkness" Conrad presents this as a solution to withstand evil in order to let consciousness evolve to higher planes. In his opinion, the best way to save the deteriorating humanity lies in man's understanding of his hidden potential which is "the light of consciousness" to grasp ways to overcome evil. In "Heart of Darkness" Marlow represents the rational consciousness, while Kurtz, who is consumed by evil, stands for the wrong movements of vital consciousness. Marlow realizes that his level of ordinary mental consciousness can distort reality. He discovers that reality is what Sri Aurobindo explains in terms of a ray of white light.[5] Marlow first begins to see a different facet of what he believed was reality when he reaches Africa and starts noticing how the "white" men show up their hollow inner selves in the alien and hostile environment.

He discovers by degrees the strong subtle power evil can exercise and the effects it can generate in the human mind as symbolized by Kurtz who has reached the "black rock at the bottom."[6] A human being has the divine potential to tide over such feeling that drives him to the bottom – which Conrad reveals through Marlow. With the passage of time Marlow gains faith by realizing the importance of the true meaning of "deliberate belief" and "innate strength." His trip to Africa was merely to fulfil a childish dream of exotic adventure, unlike all the other white men, agents or workmen, whose primary motive was exploitation, accumulation of ivory – to fill their own coffers and assuage their greed. As he travels within Africa from one station to another, he is shocked by the harshness, cruelty and wanton destruction of the land by his fellow men. He gets increasingly disillusioned as he becomes aware of the evil he sees perpetrated by those in charge of each station which were meant to be outposts of advanced Western civilization. When faced with the basic question of survival, these men become soulless. As Marlow becomes enlightened, he feels a growing sense of oppression as he proceeds into the heart of darkness. Finally he faces the cataclysmic central encounter with Kurtz. The experience shatters his mental equanimity. He realizes what Sri Aurobindo lucidly states about the being hit by the revelation of the power of pure evil. It was as if he "had turned for years and years for lifetimes around the same Problem without ever truly touching it – all of a sudden it is there caught at the bottom of the hole – struggling under the light – all the world's evil within one point." Marlow watches Kurtz as he struggles with his soul and lies dying. He sees how evil can begin to perceive its own light within. When Kurtz realizes in the end that he chose the wrong path emerging from the infrarational elements of his vital consciousness leading his soul to self-destruction, he sees the "horror" of the "black rock at the bottom." Thereby he makes Marlow understand the "secret" of what Sri Aurobindo calls the "Law of Descent."[7] For Marlow, Kurtz becomes the central point of close scrutiny. After he experiences the power of evil embodied in Kurtz, he knows that it was just his indomitable will, the rational state of his mind and his well-tried "true conscience" which saved him from going Kurtz's way. The forces of evil act on both Kurtz and Marlow in the story. Kurtz has surrendered to them consciously. He has given himself up to economic barbarism, even though he is known as a very talented, cultured being. Kurtz has indulged in unhealthy emotions to gorge his falsely nurtured ego. Since all he does is without any conflict of consciences, he becomes evil incarnate.

Through Marlow's experience of reacting to Kurtz we begin to understand Conrad's quest for the truth of reality. We see Marlow as a sensitive observer of both nature and human life. He is an expert seaman widely travelled. He views all that he sees with no narrow prejudices or preconceived notions. He goes to Africa with no selfish motives like to garner wealth, to achieve fame or to bring so-called civilization to the natives. Strong feelings and immediate reactions come unhindered to him. They finally prompt him to make his "choice of nightmares." He chooses to be loyal to Kurtz.

Marlow's consciousness is jolted into a new awakening when he realizes that Kurtz is beyond redemption. Marlow's personality undergoes a traumatic change after the incident. This is so because Conrad did not believe that man could resist the forces of evil with deterministic and dogmatic aspects of religion, without a conflict of consciences to nurture his own growth of consciousness. Therefore he wrote to Garnett while voicing his dislike of Tolstoy: "[t]he base from which he starts – Christianity – is distasteful to me. I am not blind to its services...great, improving, softening, compassionate it may be, but it has lent itself with amazing facility to cruel distortion and is the only religion which with its impossible standards, has brought an infinity of anguish to innumerable souls on the earth."[8]

This in turn led Conrad to believe: "Skepticism was the tonic of minds, the tonic of life, the agent of truth, the way of art and salvation."[9] To overcome evil human beings must not set up impossible standards by getting conditioned by a purely religious idea of conscience.

Kurtz had thought he would bring civilization to "savages," but instead he was reduced to a "shadow" of awe inspiring evil. This was so because he did not discover his own true self. His mission failed because he had not followed what Conrad calls "the ability to be scrupulously faithful to your conception of life." He had not undertaken what Sri Aurobindo calls the "adventure of consciousness." To do this, human beings must become aware of the difference between intellectual knowledge and the knowledge of what Sri Aurobindo calls Truth Consciousness.[10] To counter the forces of evil and to start the ascent to truth consciousness we have to first understand what is meant by "Ignorance" as represented by Kurtz. According to Sri Aurobindo, "Ignorance" is "the limited, separative consciousness of the ego, striving to become integral with the universal 'I'." It has also to be understood as the counterpart of true knowledge or "Gnosis."[11] Kurtz was ignorant since he was under the illusion of *avidya*. Therefore he became the incarnation of evil. But he had the ability of the rational mind to choose what pleased him. His total involvement in his emotions and ambition created a monstrous ego which finally destroyed him. It was *avidya* that Marlow discovered when he finally met the "universal genius."

Soon afterwards Kurtz died, uttering the words "The horror! The horror!" At this point Kurtz glimpsed the "heart of darkness" – the upward movement of the subconscious emerging from the black rock at the bottom. Kurtz's last cry seems to be the protest of "the divine in man." It is this separation of the human spirit from the divine within man, caused by ignorance, which leads to the forces of evil growing within the mind of man.

Marlow got transformed as he watched Kurtz die. He got enlightened. In Sri Aurobindo's terms this was replacement of the ego by a new consciousness. Marlow gained this insight about truth through his encounter with Kurtz. He is thereafter willing to guard Kurtz's reputation as he begins to believe, having gone through an extremely unusual experience, that Kurtz was indeed "a remarkable man."

Evil exists in the mind of man and to combat evil man needs to test his strength, as Marlow did in the dark forests of Africa untouched by modern civilization. Evil cannot be thwarted or accepted fatalistically. Its energy has to be channelled along the right path. The birth of consciousness which takes place in Marlow is due to the positive aspect of evil. Kurtz died and was buried. Marlow remains to dream the nightmare out to the end. He too "peeped over the edge" but unlike Kurtz, was able to resist the temptation of succumbing to evil of the vital consciousness. Evil then is ephemeral in the overall riddle of life.

Marlow adopts the pose of Buddha at the start of his narration and also at the end of it. This is significant as Conrad had decided to treat evil not as a mythical enigma in the way most religions explain it, but as conceptual in the manner clearly defined by Buddhism. Buddha is the symbol and incarnation of wisdom. Marlow underwent a radical transformation of rational consciousness. The human mind, spiritually inspired, uses innate wisdom to answer through experience the amorphous questions related to evil. Therefore, the story of "Heart of Darkness" has a very deep meaning, as it began Conrad's quest for the truth of reality.

In *Under Western Eyes* Conrad provides an added dimension to his quest for the truth of reality, using evil as the foundation of his theory of consciousness. In "Heart of Darkness" evil is the pivotal point from which he examines the human beings' capacity to understand its forces within the mind and outside it, when it is a part of all creation. In *Under Western Eyes* he clearly offers a solution to the question of how an individual can evolve his consciousness along the rational and mental plane in order to live within and rise above the powers of evil. He brings out the fact that the reason should not consider itself supreme. The reason, too, has to aspire towards enlightenment by combining its clear light with the intuitive knowledge instilled in every human being. Once the reason acquires this wisdom, it can discover the truth about evil and help propel rational consciousness towards Truth Consciousness.

We see that each of the characters in *Under Western Eyes* exhibits some facet of the rational in the human mind. Razumov, an untested scholar, as the protagonist, is pitted against the vast autocratic Russian system. The State becomes repressive, killing the capacity of human beings to choose the path to develop their consciousness. Conrad's belief in the right of the individual to prevail against the collective is exactly similar to the idea of Sri

Aurobindo that "[t]he primal law and the purpose of the individual life is to seek its own self development to find itself, to discover within itself, the law and power of its own being and to fulfil it." If a State resorts to methods that do not encourage an individual to develop his own unique consciousness along the right path, then it becomes what Sri Aurobindo calls "a conventional and typical society." In such a society a human being is considered an insignificant part of a large mindless machine. The individual's conscience is controlled by conventions of the State. Soon there arise human beings who are able to perceive that this type of society killed the Truth and that they are being forced to live a lie.

The autocratic regime of Russia that Conrad presents in *Under Western Eyes* is a typical society. This is what makes it evil. The authorities who control the lives of the people are despots. Their sole function is to arbitrarily judge and pronounce verdicts without allowing an individual to make any choice of his own, based on freedom or reason. This compels individuals to revolt against the stifling system. In *Under Western Eyes* General T– the military man and Counsellor Mikulin the bureaucrat represent the evils of authoritarianism. Both these men, along with Prince K–, believe that everyone must stay prisoner of the system, be used by it despite its being valueless. The main job of these custodians of power is to nip in the bud any sign of individuality. They annihilate anyone who they suspect as "rebel."

Victor Haldin, on the contrary, believes in quick and violent ways of uprooting such evil, but his revolutionary act of murdering the statesman Mr. de P– only causes anarchy and ends in his being executed. For Conrad, revolutions and anarchy do not change any evil system but create more evil and can not end it. Haldin's act finally leads to a series of events which bring only unhappiness and suffering to many innocent people, while the evil despotic system remains unscathed. But his blundering into Razumov's secluded and isolated life catapults Razumov into the path of self-realization. The stirring of conscience in him before he decides to betray Haldin shows the imperative need for every individual to question any conventional system that becomes an obstacle to achieve his unique consciousness. Razumov is led into a situation in which he has to resort to continuous deceit. He thought himself intellectually superior to all around him, but is really supercilious. He cannot understand such people as Ziemianitch and Haldin whom he regards as traitors. On the other hand, he is willing to trust the autocratic system, since he has never questioned its credibility. Since he has never known parental love, he does not consider faith or emotions as an integral part of the human being. This is shown clearly when he beats Ziemianitch mercilessly and encourages Kostia to steal his father's money. This shows the extent to which a human being who lives an isolated existence is made ignorant of evil in a system which leads him to betrayal and makes him sink into a web of his own falsehood. He has succumbed to *avidya* as he has never undergone any conflict of consciences and does not know what it is to have one's own true identity.

On the other hand, Haldin is enlightened about the short-comings of the system, but the destructive passion of anarchy overcomes his rational consciousness, which leads him to death. His act of violence lays waste not only what is harmful but also what is good. He is fooled by Razumov's cool exterior and trusts him to his own detriment. Yet, unlike Razumov, he has made his choice and is ready to face its consequences. Razumov has no ideals, so far he has never faced any situation requiring a significant moral choice. Haldin, therefore, acts as a catalyst for Razumov's consciousness to awaken and develop. Unfortunately, the realization occurs too late for him to forge a meaningful relationship with Nathalie Haldin. As a result, ironically, she becomes the second instrument to jolt him into "Truth" by exposing his ineptitude.

Nathalie Haldin comes closest to having the "subjective mind" which Sri Aurobindo believes is the most capable of understanding adverse forces present within and outside human psyche. It gives the correct perspective to reason and grows in strength to combat evil at all levels of consciousness. The "subjective mind" combines "spiritual reason" and "soul intuition." This makes it different from the Western idea of critical reason which is represented in *Under Western Eyes* by the professor of English.

Conrad makes it clear that if man does not understand the limits of reason, he will be overtaken by evil. This is shown by all the characters of the novel, especially by Mikulin, Peter Ivanovitch, Haldin and Razumov. It is obvious that Conrad wanted to show the need for reason alone should be replaced by higher knowledge. This knowledge is reflected in all the women characters in the novel: in Mrs Haldin's selfless love for her children, Sophia Antonovna's resolve to change the oppressive system, Tekla's compassion and courage, and finally in Nathalie Haldin's combination of strength, fortitude, quiet intelligence and devotion with her steadfast belief in "concord." She is deeply affected by all that happens. Yet when tragedy strikes, each time she recovers to become a better person. She acquires the "subjectivism" which Sri Aurobindo describes as the ability "to gaze deeper, to see and feel what is behind the outside and below the surface and therefore to live from within."

The other characters remain striking examples of *avidya* which develops the false ego of the "separative consciousness." This is at the level of mental consciousness rather than vital, as was the case of Kurtz. Hence they become the target of what Sri Aurobindo describes as perverted consciousness or *"Rakshasic Maya"* created by false or evil "asuric powers" to seem like true knowledge. Nathalie Haldin defers from them by seeking to fulfil her destiny for peace and harmony through work. She begins to believe in what Sri Aurobindo describes as follows:

> the fulfilment of the individual is not the utmost development of his egoistic intellect, vital force, physical well being and the utmost satisfaction of his mental, emotional, physical cravings but the flowering of the divine in him to its utmost capacity, of wisdom, power, love and universality and through this flowering his utmost realisation of all the possible beauty and delight of existence.

Her thinking shows the capacity of enlightened reason to work towards a fundamental change of the collective of a typical society. Such evolved consciousness alone can enable mankind to overcome the powerful effects of ephemeral evil. Once a human being understands the limits of reason and substitutes it with this intuitive knowledge, he is on the way to *vidya*, a combination of what Sri Aurobindo calls "*Tapas*" (meditation) and "*Ananda*" (utmost peace and tranquility).

Conrad creates in Nathalie Haldin a representative of such knowledge capable of laying bare all falsehood. Her evolved consciousness exposes evil and allows Razumov to live what remains of his broken life in some peace with himself.

With *Under Western Eyes* Conrad completes his understanding of evil as an ephemeral part of existence, but necessary for the human mind to make choices leading to action using reason and intuitive knowledge. This leads human beings to evolve to higher planes of consciousness. Conrad, therefore, like Sri Aurobindo, believes in the truth that there is in all life "a larger intimate power" which is, as Sri Aurobindo states, "more one with the depth and source of existence and more able to give us indivisible truths of life, its root realities and to work them out, not in an artificial and mechanical spirit but with the divination of the Secret Will in existence and in free harmony with its large, subtle and infinite methods."

Conclusion

Conrad wrote that "[e]veryone must walk in the light of his own heart's gospel. No man's light is good to any of his fellows. My view of life rejects all formulas, dogmas and principles of other people's making. We are too varied. Another man's truth is only a dismal lie to me." The search for his own original truth obliged him to claim a different idea of reality itself. He founded the idea on importance of a holistic way of life. He was aware that every human being has the potential to evolve his consciousness to higher planes. Through conflict of consciences, as a prelude to self-realization, every human being can understand that the truth of human existence lies beyond the realm of ordinary senses or intellectual will. In fact, it lies deep within himself, in the intuitive knowledge of his identity with the divine or the soul present in all the matter. Lack of self-knowledge prompts an individual to resort to falsehood, betrayal, anarchy and destruction. When this happens, he cannot reconcile the good and evil within him. As a result, he falls prey to alienation and despair.

It is clear that for Conrad evil was due to an individual's inability to rise above his ignorant ego to seek higher levels of consciousness by exercising self-restraint and self-mastery. Conrad attaches utmost importance to the idea of fellowship. All his works reflect the crying need for solidarity and fidelity among human beings – to resist the forces of evil that lead to the fragmentation of consciousness.

The end of the millennium has proved Conrad's fears. It shows that he was prophetically aware of what would happen if human beings concentrated on material progress alone. It is evident that in Conrad's view, the rational mind of man must be balanced with his ethical values and spiritual ideas nurtured by evolving his own conscience, together with his aesthetic beliefs, so that he grows to the stature of the complete individual, the cultured being, civilized to the very depths of his psyche.

NOTES

1. Aurobindo Ghosh, also spelled Aravinda, (b. August 15, 1872, Calcutta, India; d. December 5, 1950, Pondicherry), was an Indian seer, poet and nationalist who originated the philosophy of cosmic salvation through spiritual evolution. He was educated in a Christian convent school in Darjeeling, and then, still a boy, he was sent to England for further schooling. He entered Cambridge University where he became proficient in two classical and three modern European languages. After returning to India in 1893, he took various administrative and professorial posts. He turned to his native culture and began serious study of Yoga and Indian languages, including classical Sanskrit.

According to Sri Aurobindo's theory of cosmic salvation, the paths to union with Brahman are two way streets or channels: enlightenment comes from above (thesis), while the spiritual mind (super mind) strives through yogic illumination to reach upward from below (antithesis). When these two forces blend, a gnostic individual is created (synthesis). This yogic illumination transcends both reason and intuition, and eventually leads to freeing an individual from bonds of individuality.

2. According to Sri Aurobindo's mystical system, the whole universe, including all life on earth, came into being through the involvement (or involution) of the Supreme Divine consciousness into nescience, inconscience and subconscience. After effecting its own involution (or state of Ignorance), the divine consciousness has been retracing its steps back to its primordial divinity through the process of evolution. So far it has come up to the level of mental consciousness in the rational man of today. On its return to its original divinity, the divine consciousness has evolved from subconscience into matter, from matter into life, and from life into mind. Now onwards, the consciousness will evolve from the level of the mind into higher mind, then into illumined mind, intuition. From intuition it will become the overmind and finally culminate into the supermind. At the level of supermind, involving the divine consciousness which began as inconscience, it will be all superconscience. All elaborations of the philosophical categories used by Sri Aurobindo have been made after *Sri Aurobindo's Writings – Glossary of Terms* (Pondicherry: Sri Aurobindo Ashram, 1978).

3. According to Sri Aurobindo, the evolutionary process in Nature is but a part of the adventure of consciousness. On its return to its original and primal condition after the divine consciousness, it affected its own devolution (fall or descent), and involution (into inconscience) and then initiated its own evolution from Ignorance. As such, evil, suffering and pain appear in the evolution of consciousness on the level of the mind. They can be eradicated only by evolving the mind into its higher planes, until the supermind is repossessed.

4. Sri Aurobindo describes the concept of evil to comprise grief, pain, suffering, error, falsehood, ignorance, wickedness, incapacity, nondoing of what should be done, and wrongdoing, deviation of will and denial of will, egoism, limitation, separation from other beings – all these make up the effective figure of what we call "evil," are facts of the world consciousness...they are facts whose complete sense or true value is not that which we assign to them in our ignorance.

A limited consciousness growing out of nescience is the source of error, a personal attachment to the limitation. The error born of it is the source of falsity, of wrong consciousness governed by the life-ego, the source of evil. But it is evident that their relative existence is only a phenomenon thrown by the cosmic Force in its drive towards evolutionary self-expression. What we call "sin" or "evil," is merely excess and defect, wrong placement, inharmonious actions and reactions.

5. The ray of white light can be broken by a prism into a multiplicity of colors, though it remains the same light at its source. Our conditioned responses understand only the multiplicity. We repeatedly tend to forget that beyond our ordinary mental consciousness other levels of conscious-

ness exist, just as the white light does, in spite of the spectrum of colors it can be split into by a prism.

6. According to Sri Aurobindo, evil is like the black rock at the bottom when it operates on all levels of consciousness, whether physical, vital, mental or psychic. Evil can be correctly interpreted by the mind, if it is first recognized and then accepted without giving in to its powerful destructive potency. For this, man has to rely on the growth of his consciousness and fight the urges of false identity and base instincts. He will then understand that evil is only "[t]he subconscious line which recedes downward.... Everything is broadened and illumined but everything closes in and becomes concentrated on a single sharp dark point increasingly exact and pressing."

7. The law of oppression or descent is actually a golden law that draws us both downwards and upwards into the depths of the subconscient and inconscient to the central point from where it starts the evolution towards the higher planes of consciousness.

8. Allan Ingram, *Joseph Conrad: Selected Literary Criticism* (New York: Methuen, 1986), 83.

9. Ibid.

10. Sri Aurobindo's explanation of the universe is that of a spiritual evolution as the meaning of our existence. It is a series of ascents, from the physical being and consciousness to the vital, the being dominated by the life self. The mental being is realized in the fully developed man, and thence into the perfect consciousness which is beyond the mental into the supramental Consciousness, and the supramental is the *Truth Conscious-ness* which is the integral consciousness of the spiritual being.

11. There are two kinds of knowledge: *vidya* and *avidya*. *Vidya* is the knowledge of the self, the identity with our real being with One that is the world, with the supreme. *Avidya* means ignorance which includes all branches of intellectual knowledge. The latter leads to divisiveness and the duality perceived by mental consciousness.

Daniel Fraustino,
University of Scranton,
Scranton, USA

"Heart of Darkness" and Walt Whitman's "Passage to India"

Romantic influences in "Heart of Darkness," especially English and American, have been documented over the years in a number of publications. These influences include Poe's "The Fall of the House of Usher," Coleridge's "The Rime of the Ancient Mariner," and several Hawthorne novels and short stories.[1] It has been suggested with probable accuracy that the title of the novella itself is taken from Hawthorne's "Young Goodman Brown," in which N. Hawthorne describes the young hero's mad, despondent rush into the wilderness to discover his identity with the forces of evil (Goldwyn, 75). Apparently Conrad was greatly enamored with English and American romantics, with what they thought and what they valued. He even uses as the narrative structure of "Heart of Darkness," a motif popular among these writers: the self-discovering journey into Nature central to many romantic works including Keats's "Endymion," Shelley's "Alastor," Wordsworth's "Tintern Abbey," Thoreau's "Walden," and Irving's "Rip Van Winkle," to name just a few. In a recent article, I discussed the numerous parallels between Conrad's novella and R. W. Emerson's well-known essay "Self-Reliance." I argued Conrad's fidelity to many traditional romantic values and ideas as expressed by Emerson, such as the corrupt nature of Western material values; the nobility of aboriginals; and their superiority, physically and psychologically, to Western Europeans. Both writers express their extreme hatred of lies and hypocrisy, and the importance of work as a builder and barometer of character (Fraustino).

I would like to discuss the many parallels between "Heart of Darkness" and still another romantic work, Walt Whitman's

"Passage to India," written in 1871 and published in 1881. Like his literary mentor R. W. Emerson, Whitman seems uncompanionable to Joseph Conrad, the former's jubilant idealism contrasting with the latter's dim views. In fact, it would be difficult to find another romantic writer more optimistic about human nature and contemporary civilization than Walt Whitman. "I celebrate myself" are the first three words of "Song of Myself" (Whitman, "Song...," l. 1). Fitting snugly within the tradition of other contemporary idealists like Wordsworth and Emerson, Whitman views the physical world as the "handkerchief of the Lord" (l. 103), a "uniform hieroglyphic" (l. 106) of a clear and present spiritual reality. Deeming himself "deathless" (l. 406), "divine" (l. 524), and a "Kosmos" (l. 497), Whitman celebrates "reality," "materialism" (ll. 483-4), and the accomplishments of modern technology.

Of course, if we were to search for a companionable piece in Whitman to "Heart of Darkness," "Passage to India" would probably not come to mind, for it views civilization as an evolving plan masterminded by a divinely benevolent intelligence for the purpose of mankind's spiritual unification. The conclusion to this plan, Whitman tells us in "Passage...," shall be heralded and made plain to all by the appearance on earth of a poet-Messiah, a secular son of God. Despite its distinctly un-Conradian thesis, "Passage to India" contains much that would have appealed to Conrad, especially given Conrad's interest in the literature of the period. For one thing, next to *Moby Dick* and "The Rime of the Ancient Mariner," "Passage to India" is arguably the most famous work of literature in English written about the sea and navigation to come out of the 19th Century. With Christopher Columbus as its protagonist, "Passage to India" poeticizes the circumnavigation of the earth by sea to emblemize the spiritual unification of humankind. Nevertheless "Passage to India" clearly engages many of the same issues and ideas that inform "Heart of Darkness," such as the impassive, alienating silence of nature; the return to the past for self-discovery, and specifically the return to Africa. Like "Heart of Darkness," "Passage to India" discusses the importance of work in the self-discovery process, and anticipates the appearance of a human being with special intellectual powers, but primarily that of gifted speech, someone who will ultimately speak the truth and resolve life's ambiguities and enigmas. Finally, Conrad may have directly borrowed from Whitman the idea of blank spots on the map.

While Whitman's romanticism fits snugly within the tradition of Wordsworthian and Emersonian idealism, Whitman clearly articulates Western man's growing alienation from nature. And he does so in "Passage to India" in language that Conrad could have directly transcribed into "Heart of Darkness." Little need be said about Conrad's dim views on nature and the wilderness. The title of his novella aptly reveals them: the darkness at the heart of man also permeates the heart of nature. Thus Marlow describes Africa's wilderness as "inscrutable" ("Heart of Darkness," *YS*, 48), "incomprehensible" (62), and "God-forsaken" (60), to quote just a few of the innumerable references that describe Africa in this way. At the end of the novella, summarizing his journey into Africa, Marlow compares his excursion to "a passage through some inconceivable world that had no hope in it and no desire" (152). As L. Feder has made clear, Conrad artistically envisioned the African wilderness as hell[2] – alienating, incomprehensible, and insane. Nature and ultimately reality defy our logic and control.

Whitman suggests the same profound disconnection between Western man and nature in "Passage to India" where he describes physical nature as "impassive" (Whitman, "Passage...," l. 110), "separate" (l. 106), "unnatural," "unloving," and the "cold...place of graves" (ll. 96-8). This, according to Whitman, characterizes the contemporary relationship between industrial, technological man and his physical environment. In language that could be quoted from "Heart of Darkness," Whitman refers to unresponsive physical earth as a "teeming ...darkness" (l. 83), "inscrutable" (l. 86) and "unspeakable" (l. 84), its human inhabitants possessing "never-happy hearts" (l. 91).

While Conrad's views on nature's impassive antagonism toward humans are clear from the beginning of the novella, less clear is the cause of this antagonism, an issue complicated by the natives' apparent lack of discomfort in Africa's uncompromising wilderness. In fact, Conrad's aboriginals thrive in the jungle and on the dead hippo meat they must eat. The causes, according to Conrad, for these very different reactions to the wilderness between native Blacks and European Whites become clear as we examine the differences between the white men themselves, that is, between Marlow's European contemporaries and those ancient whites who colonized the English wilderness nineteen hundred years ago.

Unlike the Europeans at the turn of the last century, the Romans invading England nineteen hundred years ago "were men enough to face the darkness" ("Heart of Darkness," *YS*, 49), while Marlow's white contemporaries in the Congo, who live in words and appearances, immediately discompose in the wilderness when confronted with real danger, as when they are attacked by Kurtz's native followers. The Africans, contrasting with the whites, are "big powerful men...with courage [and] with strength" (104). When attacked their "faces" are "quiet"; some even "grinned," and their "short, grunting phrases" quickly "settle the matter to their satisfaction" (103).

Conrad's point is the same as Whitman's in "Passage to India" and Emerson's before Whitman: in the process of becoming more civilized, intellectual, technological, and material, Western man has lost contact with his inner world and with his subconscious, that is, with the real sources of spiritual strength. This explains why the white men in "Heart of Darkness" cannot survive when that inner strength is sorely tested in the wilderness. A man, Marlow says, "must meet...truth with his own true stuff – with his own inborn strength" (97). According to Conrad, modern civilization has robbed white men of their inner resources. However, in contrast, the blacks in "Heart of Darkness" survive and even thrive in unfettered nature; the Romans, "men enough to face the darkness" (49), survived nineteen hundred years ago though with difficulty; but contemporary Europeans hardly survive at all.

Like Conrad and many English and American romantics, Whitman suggests that something in contemporary Western civilization has robbed us of a reinforcing, vitalizing relationship with nature. We are instead, to quote "Passage to India," "restless," "yearning," "feverish" in spirit and "unsatisfied of soul" (Whitman, "Passage...," ll. 90-2). For Whitman more than Conrad, this is the result of technological advancement. For both writers, and for many English and American romantics, this alienation is the result of an encroaching intellectuality that alienates us from our instincts, our unconscious, and ultimately from our physical environment. While Conrad, unlike Whitman, is not suggesting the possibility of redemption or a reconciliation of man and Nature, Conrad may be suggesting a larger humanism, something like a Laurentian wholeness of self that Westerners have lost, a symptom of which can be seen in our modern disconnection from nature.

While Whitman's view of alienated, technological man is not in itself enough to strongly establish "Passage to India" as a textual source for "Heart of Darkness," Whitman's solution to the problem does strengthen the case, for "Passage to India" has as its shaping metaphor a journey to the past, to the pre-civilized self, to what Emerson and other romantics call instinct, the source of aboriginal selfhood and spiritual strength. Certainly Conrad would have found this appealing, for "Heart of Darkness" has an identical motif: passage down the river as an excursion, in Marlow's words, "to the earliest beginnings of the world" ("Heart of Darkness," *YS*, 92). Only by "travelling [to] the night of first ages" (96) can we discover "our kinship with [the] wild and passionate uproar" (96) that characterizes the human self.

In their two works, Conrad and Whitman describe voyages to discover identity and selfhood, and they achieve this through a journey to the past. "Passage to India" clearly states from the very beginning that the passage intended is chronological: "The Past! the Past! the Past!" (Whitman, "Passage...," l. 9), Whitman cries out in Stanza I. In returning to the past modern man will, according to Whitman, rediscover what science, technology, and materialism have obscured: "primal thought" (l. 165), "reason's early paradise," "wisdom's birth," and "innocent intuition" (ll. 172-3). According to Whitman, the return to ancient mythological wisdom – especially "Africa's fables" (l. 20) – will heal the split between man and his environment created by scientific rationalism and modern technology.

Both "Heart of Darkness" and "Passage to India" also emphasize the importance of work in this journey toward self-discovery. In Whitman, of course, it is the workers who bridge the gaps of oceans and continents and who ultimately unify mankind through these connecting efforts. But the religious worship of which Whitman sings in "Passage to India" emphasizes work in a way that runs deeper than that of merely catalyzing connection. The "captains, voyagers, explorers...engineers...architects, machinists" (ll. 137-8) Whitman catalogs in "Passage to India" surpass in importance "trade or transportation," functioning in "God's name" and "for thy sake O soul" (ll. 39-40). For Whitman work is more than an executor of a divine plan; as in Conrad, it is the means to selfhood and self-understanding.

In "Heart of Darkness," work defines who we are and what is real. "I don't like work," Marlow says, "but I like what is in the work, – the chance to find yourself. Your own reality – for yourself, not for others – what no other man can ever know" ("Heart of Darkness," *YS*, 85). To Conrad, work reliably measures character. The superficial accountant, for instance, who initially appears like "a hairdresser's dummy," ultimately commands Marlow's respect because "he was devoted to his books, which were in apple-pie order" (68). The brickmaker, on the other hand, who makes no bricks and sits around doing nothing, whose "show of work" is merely a "pretense" to his real purpose, appointment to a trading post, is described by Marlow as "unreal...a papier-mache Mephistopheles" (81). While Marlow's fondness for the cannibals aboard ship stems from their being "men one could work with" (94), his respect for Kurtz may originate in his early surmize that Kurtz is a dedicated worker. Hearing the perplexing story of Kurtz's paddling "three hundred miles" and then "suddenly [deciding] to go back," Marlow speculates that Kurtz "was just simply a fine fellow who stuck to his work, for its own sake" (90).

Although the world remains mysterious, illogical and alienating to Marlow at the end of his journey, Marlow does, he says, obtain knowledge of himself, which, regardless of its ultimate value, places him in his own eyes one notch above his money--filching, cookery-devouring, beer-gulping contemporaries in Brussels. Marlow's attainment of selfhood and self-understanding, despite its hopeless cynicism, is romantic; and Marlow qualifies as a romantic hero. Returning to Brussels thoroughly isolated and cynical, Marlow may remind us of Byron's Childe Harold, whose elevated, romantic stature derives from his self-understanding and honesty, despite his thorough disillusionment and self-acknowledged sinfulness. Like Harold and other romantic heros, Marlow affirms a meaningful value system that rejects contemporary self-interest, materialism, lies, and hypocrisy. Marlow's integrity and even wisdom are manifested by his Buddhist appearance at the beginning of the narration, in which he is described as having "sunken cheeks, a yellow complection, a straight back, an ascetic aspect, and with his arms dropped, the palms of hands outwards, [resembles] an idol" (46).

Central to both the poem and the novella is the search or anticipation of a special being, a kind of superman, someone with special intellectual gifts but particularly that of verbal articulation – someone who will resolve the contradictions of life that disrupt our understanding, that unsettle us, and that ultimately antagonize and alienate us. In "Heart of Darkness," of course, this being is Kurtz, of whom "all Europe contributed to the making" (117). Clearly, Kurtz's special appeal to Marlow is that of his giftedness, and "of all his gifts the one that stood out preeminently...was his ability to talk, his words – the gift of expression" (113). Clearly, the central drama and conflict in "Heart of Darkness" concerns Marlow's speaking with Kurtz, who, Marlow leads the reader to believe, can explain and reconcile all of Marlow's insane experiences. Marlow desperately wishes reconciliation to a civilization whose ruthless system of economic exploitation purports to be altruistic, indeed missionary. Marlow seeks Kurtz because of the latter's education, genius, altruism, yet financial success within the existing system of colonial exploitation. He wishes Kurtz to explain to him the white man's wanton killing of blacks under the pretense of their criminality. Marlow seeks explanation for the whole sequence of absurd events that commence upon Marlow's landing in Africa: the "objectless blasting" (64), the "wanton smash-up" of drainage pipes (65-6), the brickmaker who makes no bricks (76-8), the ineffectual leaky pail used to extinguish the fire (76), and the seaman's manual found in the middle of a continent (99), to name just a few of the infernal events that obscure Marlow's grasp of reality and threaten his sanity as they have innumerable white men before him.

For these reasons Marlow seeks Kurtz, a super man, a modern Messiah whose words, Marlow supposes, will illuminate with a "pulsating stream of light" (113-14) the dark flow of events that have challenged Marlow's innocence and understanding. Kurtz, of course, is perfect for the role, for he performs more successfully than any of his contemporaries the company's sordid burglary, while writing eloquently and passionately on civilization and the suppression of savage customs. Kurtz's "magic current of phrases" and "altruistic sentiments" (118) make Marlow tingle with its presupposition of an ultimate divine moral order, its "notion of an exotic Immensity ruled by an august Benevolence" (118). Through his vast understanding and language command, Kurtz, Marlow anticipates, will clear away contradictions and redeem Marlow's failing innocence; Kurtz will restore Marlow's trust in humanity and human nature; finally Kurtz will make clear God's benevolent plan in the dim, enigmatic wilderness.

Kurtz is established early as Marlow's savior, the journey towards Kurtz the central movement in this Modern spiritual drama of a Fall and attempted redemption. And in this way the novella importantly parallels Whitman's "Passage to India," which also includes as its central drama the anticipation of a human being whose special gifts of speech, specifically the mythical, metaphorical speech of poetry, will resolve life's "aged fierce enigmas" and "strangling problems" (Whitman, "Passage...," ll. 230-1). This poet-Messiah will soothe the "hearts" of all us "fretted children" (l. 107). Like Kurtz, who Marlow supposes will resolve the mystery encountered in Africa's wilderness, Whitman's super man will reveal the secrets (l. 108) that riddle our experiences, hook and link the "separations and gaps" and "completely" justify this "cold, impassive, voiceless earth" (ll. 109-10).

Finally, Conrad may have borrowed from Whitman the notion of "blank spaces" (l. 219) on the map, although Conrad's meaning in this reference is quite different from Whitman's. While "Passage to India" refers to the exploration of the globe and of "blanks to be fill'd on a map" (l. 140) as a positive fulfillment of a divine plan, Marlow mentions "blank" spaces four times in discussing the importance of map spaces to him as a boy. He refers to the "many blank spaces on the earth" that he saw on maps when he was a "little chap," and the Congo as "the most blank" but changing by the time Marlow was grown. No longer "a blank space any more" when Marlow reaches adulthood, the Congo has "ceased to be a blank space of delightful mystery...for a boy to dream gloriously over." While Whitman views the exploration of the world's blank spaces as a fulfillment and illumination, Conrad apparently denounces exploration as exploitation, the white spaces on the map now "[places] of darkness" ("Heart of Darkness," *YS*, 219), that is, of plunder and greed. However, it still appears very possible that Conrad borrowed from "Passage..." the idea of blank map spaces, especially in view of the many echoes and parallels noted above.

On the surface, Conrad's attraction to Whitman and other romantics may seem to contradict his own dark view of existence expressed in "Heart of Darkness." In the wilderness, Conrad does not find "reason and faith," as does Emerson (Emerson, 10); nor does Conrad agree with most other generally held notions of romantic idealism expressed in Whitman and elsewhere: that the universe is full of good, that an almighty power rolls through all things, that God is accessible through the contemplation of nature, that man is divine and his instincts incorruptible, that values are universal, and reality ultimately meaningful. On the contrary, in "Heart of Darkness" nature is "inscrutable" ("Heart of Darkness," *YS*, 93), "accursed" (95), and unchanged from the "night of first ages" (96); man is at best "hollow at the core" (131) and probably much worse: a "vast grave full of unspeakable secrets" (138), of "forgotten and brutal instincts" (144). Man's language therefore is a "deceitful flow," our survival depending in "Heart of Darkness" on our ability not to discover and comprehend, but to dig "unostentatious" linguistic "holes" (117) in which to bury the rank truth. In "Heart of Darkness," the universe has no manifest intelligence that communicates intelligible truth; rather, we are "cut off from the comprehension of our surroundings" (96). Life, Marlow states, is a "Droll thing," a "mysterious arrangement of merciless logic for a futile purpose" (150).

What then, we may ask, was the appeal to Conrad of Whitman and other romantics, especially in America and England? The answer, I believe, does not lie in any nostalgia on the part of Conrad for romantic faith and certitude, as one might at first suppose, but rather in romanticism's unremitting social criticism: that society and culture are absolutely corrupt, its institutions hollow, deadened, indeed like whited sepulchers. In Whitman, and specifically "Passage to India," Conrad found frank, insightful criticism of culture and society articulated in a century marked by overwhelming scientific, technological, and industrial success. More to the point perhaps, Conrad found in romantic literature the prolific expression of a system of values compatible with his own, a system which sought selfhood beyond the lies and hypocrisy fostered by material gain.

NOTES

1. G. S. Amur, "'Heart of Darkness' and 'The Fall of the House of Usher': The Tale of Discovery," *Criticism*, 9 (Summer 1971), 59-70; Warren Ober, "'Heart of Darkness': 'The Ancient Mariner' a Hundred Years Later," *Dalhousie Review*, 45 (Autumn 1965), 333-7; Merrill Harvey Goldwyn, "Nathaniel Hawthorne and Conrad's 'Heart of Darkness'," *Conradiana*, 16 (1984), 73-8.

2. Lilian Feder, "Marlow's Descent into Hell," *Nineteenth Century Fiction*, 9 (March 1955), 280-92.

WORKS CITED

Emerson Ralph Waldo. "Nature," in *The Complete Works of Ralph Waldo Emerson,* vol. 1. New York: Houghton Mifflin, 1903.

Fraustino Daniel V. "Self-Reliance in 'Heart of Darkness'," *Conradiana,* 27 (1995), 74-80.

Goldwyn Merrill Harvey. "Nathaniel Hawthorne and Conrad's 'Heart of Darkness'," *Conradiana,* 16 (1984), 73-8.

Whitman Walt. "Passage to India," in Whitman Walt. *Complete Poetry and Selected Prose,* ed. James E. Miller Jr. Cambridge, Mass.: The Riverside Press, 1959.

Whitman Walt. "Song of Myself," in Whitman Walt. *Complete Poetry and Selected Prose,* ed. James E. Miller Jr. Cambridge, Mass.: The Riverside Press, 1959.

Wordsworth William. "Ode: Intimations of Immortality," in *William Wordsworth,* ed. Stephen Gill. Oxford: Oxford U.P., 1984.

Jorge Sacido-Romero,
University of Santiago,
A Coruña, Spain

Reconsidering Conrad's
The Shorter Tales of Joseph Conrad[1]

For my godson Marco Sacido-Lechap

In a luncheon presentation of the Seventh Annual Comparative Literature Symposium (January 1974), D. W. Rude lamented as "unfortunate" the neglect critics and biographers had shown towards a posthumous anthology of Conrad's short fiction titled *The Shorter Tales of Joseph Conrad* (Rude, 189). The situation concerning this selection of Conrad's short pieces has very much been one of oblivion during the twenty two years that have passed since the publication of Rude's essay. Of the small number of authors that go as far as mentioning it, F. R. Karl, for instance, devotes just one dismissive (yet insightful) paragraph of his monumental *Joseph Conrad: The Three Lives* to the description of the special "Preface" that starts the volume saying that it is "a very bland" one (Karl, 905). Likewise, Z. Najder argues that "the writing [of the 'Preface'] emanates weariness and defensiveness" and doubts "if it ever encouraged anyone to read the volume" (Najder, 487). It was not until R. Ambrosini's *Conrad's Fiction as Critical Discourse* that the preface written by Conrad to introduce the tales of this volume received a more positive appreciation. Ambrosini considers it one of the most important documents in studying Conrad's view on the creation of imaginative prose in general and on his activity as a writer in particular: in this "Preface" Conrad "offers a new context for the evolution of his art" (Ambrosini, 13; see also 12, 32, 40-2, 47). Yet Ambrosini's interest is exclusively for the "Preface," not for the anthology itself, for the way it is structured and to what it responds. The purpose of this essay is not to give a fully satisfactory answer to these questions (that would take too long). Ours is a much more humbler aim, namely: to provide the reader of *The Shorter Tales of Joseph Conrad* with some new pieces of information about its making as an addition to D. Rude's essay, so as to throw some more light on Conrad's editorial activity a few months before he died.

The Shorter Tales of Joseph Conrad was published by Doubleday, Page and Company in November of 1924, three months after Conrad's death.[2] It is a 452-page volume to which a "Preface" is attached at the beginning (v-xii). It is divided in two parts that contain four tales each: "Youth," "The Secret Sharer," "The Brute" and "To-morrow" in Part I and "Typhoon," "Because of the Dollars," "The Partner" and "Falk" in Part II.

The story of the publication of *The Shorter Tales...* starts on January 30, 1924, when Conrad wrote to Eric Pinker, who had become his agent after James B. Pinker's death:

> It would be interesting to know what new scheme Doubledays are going to add to this "intensive culture" of Conrad success. I can't imagine what it can be unless broadcasting readings of selected passages.

Forty-eight hours later, February 1, 1924, "the new scheme" Conrad speculated about was described by Frank N. Doubleday and S. A. Everitt in a letter sent by them to Eric Pinker. The second paragraph of that letter offers a good summary of Doubleday's new plan:

> We think that we could make a holiday book of the short stories of Joseph Conrad in one volume for $5.00, and we plan to put in all the stories of less than 20,000 words, which would include about fifteen. We think that we could get a new market for next Christmas, and we made up a dummy that we are putting in the mail to-day. We think this attractive, and hope you will agree with us. The plan of the book is to have no title on the side, exactly as the dummy, and the suggested wording for the back is:
> SHORT STORIES
> By
> JOSEPH CONRAD
> DOUBLEDAY, PAGE AND CO.[3]

They end the letter by opening the plan "to any revision" by Pinker right after suggesting the following alternative: either Conrad asks Muirhead Bone or "somebody else" to write "an introduction," or they "let it go without an introduction, and include a publishing note stating the plan of the book."

Enclosed inside the same envelope there came a list of the stories to be included and those to be left out. The latter group contained: "Gaspar Ruiz," "The Duel," "The Return," "A Smile of Fortune," "Freya of the Seven Isles," "Falk," "The Planter of Malata," "The End of the Tether," and "Typhoon." "Heart of Darkness" was among those to be included in the volume despite the fact of its being 42,000 words long, double the length of all the other stories of less than 20,000 words in a book that was to have 562 pages.[4]

Probably, at the same time Eric Pinker received the letter containing the publisher's plan, Conrad had a letter from Doubleday mentioning (without much detail) his intention to publish a book of short stories. This may have been so because as early as February 7, 1924, Conrad, in a letter to Doubleday, expressed his reserve towards "the scheme for a book of collected short stories," considering it as something "in fact unthinkable" (Jean-Aubry, II, 338). Yet a very different thing would be (he goes on) "a selected volume, a selection of the least significant tales...with a special preface where I could try to express plainly my point of view."

In a similar tone of reticence, two days later (February 9) he wrote to Eric Pinker that in "last mail's letter" F. N. Doubleday mentioned a

> speed dispatch to you (Pinker) of the details of a new publication-
> -scheme, which it seems is something in the nature of a volume of
> collected short stories. I should imagine he really means a volume of
> selected S.S. I have my private views on that subject. But we shall see.

Some time between February 9 and February 12, 1924 Doubleday's letter to Eric Pinker, doubtless, reached Conrad. On the latter date Conrad gave a full account of his "private views on the subject" in a long three-part letter he sent to Pinker.

Of parts 2 (his "answer to Doubleday's scheme") and 3 (his
"counter-scheme"), he sent two "duplicates" and kept "the
triplicate" for himself. In his article on *The Shorter Tales...*,
Rude gave a full account of parts 2 and 3 based on the duplicates
forwarded by Pinker to Doubleday. In part 2 Conrad distances
himself literarily from R. L. Stevenson, objects to the oversize of
the planned selection, shows his bafflement at using length as
a principle of selection, opposes the idea to ask Muirhead Bone
to preface the book and offers to write a five-thousand-word
introduction that would invest the selection of short stories with
the value of "'sanctioned by the author'." In part 3, titled "MR.
CONRAD'S SCHEME," we find the skeleton of the "Preface"
to *The Shorter Tales...* he would submit to Doubleday three
months later.

Part 1 (to which Rude does not refer in his article) is
a manuscript sheet in which Conrad describes to Pinker the
contents of what he is sending and tells him to forward
a duplicate of parts 2 and 3 to Doubleday with a "covering
letter" saying "'this is what C writes me with the request to
transmit this duplicate to you. I think he is right'." But this part
is something more than a set of instructions. It functions as an
authentic "frame" of his more formal business dealings with his
much-respected American publisher as specified in parts 2 and 3.
In it we find Conrad's more direct and informal reaction to
Doubleday's scheme as privately expressed to his agent, Pinker:
his radical opposition to the publisher's plan ("As to the scheme
it is definitely NO"), his reticence to his own counter-scheme
("Even as my own I am reluctant"), the different view he had on
the publication of his works in England ("My idea would be to
have nothing of the sort in England"), his concern about getting
a good profit out of it as he "proposed to give *unpublished text* to
the amount of 5000 w." ("We know that I can get L 250 any time
for that text alone"), and his fear about the harm it may cause the
collected edition of his works in America ("I feel it may be
dangerous for the Concord Ed. But I daresay they thought it
out.") In this short private communication we find explicitly
expressed the two sides of Conrad's involvement in the scheme:

the artistic and the financial. This is a very direct proof that (apart from his open declaration in formal writing: be it the letters to the publisher, or the "Preface" to *The Shorter Tales...* itself) for Conrad this "scheme" was something more than a mere commercial transaction, he reacted as a conscious and ambitious artist, even at the end of his life. (He died on August 3, 1924, six months later.)

On the other hand, the elaborate quality of parts 2 and 3 of the February 12 letter (a well-argued answer to Doubleday's scheme and a thorough outline of the preface) contrasts with the rashness with which it was written, probably on receiving, from Pinker, Doubleday's letter containing his plan. Conrad starts Part 2: "I am writing to you without loss of time on the matter submitted by Garden City in their letter of Feb. 1st. 1924: SHORT STORIES by JOSEPH CONRAD." Judging from this evident contrast, we may conclude that, at that time, Conrad was considering the possibility of a publication of some type of selection of his short works and had in mind a more or less clear idea of its characteristics. Doubleday's had not been the only publication scheme that involved taking stories out of their original places and to which Conrad had shown his disapproval at the beginning of that year. In two unpublished letters he wrote to Pinker in mid-January 1924, he drastically declines, both on artistic and on financial grounds, a proposal from Ernest Rhys to include one of his tales in an anthology of various authors that was to be published in England by J. M. Dent and Sons. In the first letter, dated January, 9, 1924, Conrad argues:

> In regard to that rag-bag of a volume of short stories it seems to me to be purely a publisher's affairs which cannot be justified on any reasonable ground as far as the authors are concerned. Why do they come in?... As an advertisement it is worthless.... The financial side has nothing very fascinating about it.... I seem to remember that last year I declined a similar proposal. Any collection of that sort is apt to convey a false impression because the great public will attach to it the idea of "the best." Altogether a mere piece of book-making....[5]

Four days later, on January 13, 1924 Conrad wrote to Pinker: "I am very glad to know that you share my view on those absurd anthologies thrown out to the market." So, Conrad had "declined" publishers' proposals that implied wrenching material from their proper place two times in the previous ten months or so, right before he became involved with *The Shorter Tales*.... It is not strange he showed a great amount of reluctance when Doubleday's plan reached him. On the other hand, the fact that the idea of publishing stories separately had been presented to him twice in a year (at least) probably made him reflect upon it and build in his mind some "private view on" "a volume of selected S(hort) S(tories)."[6] The main point is that if Conrad ever accepted a plan of this nature, it would be on his terms.[7] So much so that when Doubleday's scheme came along he remodelled it completely and expressed his views both privately (in the February 12 letter to Pinker and Doubleday) and publicly (in the "Preface" to *The Shorter Tales*....)

In tracing the editorial history of *The Shorter Tales of Joseph Conrad* D. Rude jumps from the February 12 letter right to one dated March 27, 1924: "Conrad twice discussed the volume in later letters to Doubleday" (Rude, 193).[8] But Conrad referred to the volume at least three times in his correspondence with Eric Pinker. These three letters provide further information about the editing process and the final shape of *The Shorter Tales*.... On February 14, 1924 for instance, Conrad thanked Eric Pinker "for your letter in which you say you backed up my scheme." Conrad's "counter-scheme" meant too big a reduction in the number of words: from 205,000 to 127,000, according to Doubleday's "word estimates" (which, nevertheless, were "very rough" and "very liberal").[9] Pinker told Conrad he feared Doubleday's negative reaction to his alternative plan. Conrad, in this same letter of February 14, answered Pinker:

> Your remark about reduction of bulk has caused me to write to Everitt and say that should bulk be important *Falk* could be included in my list.
>
> This would bring my scheme well over 170,000 words. Garden City scheme was 205,000, but their list of "under 20,000 word stories" included, perhaps by mistake, *H. of Darkness*....

Conrad added "Falk" to his scheme to make up for the decrease in the number of words. During the next month Conrad had time to think over the whole plan and by the mid-March he made his last change: substituting "Falk" for "The Inn of the Two Witches." He communicated this change to Eric Pinker in the second unpublished letter of this period dated March 10, 1924:

> Just a word to let you know that I've had a letter from G. City agreeing to my scheme for the vol. of Short Stories. You have heard from them too no doubt.
> I cable the suggestion that *The Witches* should be thrown out and Falk substituted; and asked for the latest date they are likely to require the new preface.

The inclusion of "The Inn of the Two Witches" was certainly in accordance with Conrad's initial plan for "a selection of the least significant tales."[10] It seems there is no doubt that he did not like this story very much. Jessie Conrad in *Joseph Conrad as I Knew Him* (1926) refers to "The Inn of the Two Witches" as one of "those stories Conrad could never find a good word for" (Jessie Conrad, 119). In the "rag-bag" letter quoted above (to Eric Pinker, January 9, 1924) Conrad himself commented on the plan for an anthology proposed by Ernest Rhys that included this story and pointed out that: "From a literary point of view I confess that I am not very much in love with 'The Inn of the Two Witches' (which was written to order and it is not a 'representative' story)...." Why did Conrad decide to substitute a story he was not happy about with "Falk," one "of the most highly finished" of his stories?[11] The February 14 letter talks about "including" "Falk" in his list to increase the "bulk" of the volume, without taking out "The Inn of the Two Witches." In the letter dated March 10, on the other hand, Conrad suggests throwing out "The Inn of the Two Witches." Why? We must bear in mind that this was Conrad's suggestion, not the publisher's (the longer the volume, the more valuable it would be in commercial terms). There may be more than one reason why Conrad decided to do this. Probably, for the sake of symmetry: four stories in each part. Or maybe because "Falk" was published in the same collection as "Typhoon"[12] so that it strengthened the unity of Part II of the volume of tales, which starts with the latter story.[13] Certainly because it is a story about seamen, although, on the other hand, it does not fit as well as "The Inn of the Two Witches" in the youth-maturity contrast that structures the volume.[14] Perhaps Conrad wanted to balance the selection of stories by placing two outstanding pieces in each part ("Youth" and "The Secret Sharer" in Part I, and "Typhoon" and "Falk" in Part II) alongside two stories of less importance ("The Brute" and "To-morrow," and "Because of the Dollars" and "The Partner," respectively). Be that what it may, it was clear from his February 12 letter to Eric Pinker that, on the one hand, "a certain if not very obvious unity of purpose" and, on the other, to make the volume "look worth the money" and "to appeal to the taste and even the feeling of the readers" remained Conrad's two main aims and sine qua non conditions for its publication. So, a change such as this was not something made at random, it had some purpose indeed.

The last letter of this period is the one dated March 12, 1924 where Conrad discusses royalties on the volume, says that "*Falk* will be substituted for *Inn of Witches*," tells Pinker that Everitt (from Doubleday, Page and Co.) asked "for the preface middle of May our latest," and points out parenthetically an idea that he will later develop in the March 27 letter quoted by Donald Rude: "Having regard to the new stuff it will contain (which will make it necessary for every Conrad-collector to buy it)..."[15]

Now what remained to be done for Conrad was to write the preface he had volunteered to contribute to the volume and had been asked to submit by the middle of May. In a letter dated May 1, 1924 Conrad told Eric Pinker:

> I am working at the Preface for the vol. of Selected Tales, and expect to have it ready in a few days. I will be delayed by a visit from Sir Hugh Clifford, who is coming on Sat. and will stay till Tuesday morning.[16]

Judging from the three-part letter of February 12 to Pinker and Doubleday (via the former) Conrad had little work left to do. As we pointed out above, by comparing the third part of the letter (the so-called "Mr. Conrad's scheme") with the "Preface" of *The Shorter Tales of Joseph Conrad* we can see that much of the thinking had already been done and that the published "Preface" was thoroughly outlined. Conrad worked really fast in producing the final draft of the "Preface": on May 1 (a Thursday) he told Pinker he was still working on it, a week later (Thursday, May 8) he wrote to Doubleday saying he had already sent the "Preface" to the United States; all this despite the delay caused "by a visit from Sir Hugh Clifford" (from Saturday, May 3 to Tuesday, May 6) Conrad alluded to in the letter quoted above. He was probably done with the "Preface" on Monday 5 and sent it to Doubleday on this very same date, as he told Pinker that "The Preface for the 'Shorter Tales' (about 2,000 w) was posted yesterday to catch the *Majestic* to-morrow (Wed)."[17]

It is a curious fact from a generic point of view that this letter is the first instance in which Conrad called the volume "Shorter Tales," the title under which it was going to be published. Previously, he had called the pieces chosen by him either "short stories,"[18] or "Selected Tales,"[19] despite the fact that the published title was already given by S. A. Everitt (from Doubleday, Page and Co.) in answer to "Mr. Conrad's scheme" dated February 29, 1924 (to Eric Pinker):

> We gladly agree to the alternative plan suggested by Mr. Conrad for
> THE SHORTER TALES
> of
> JOSEPH CONRAD
> [...]
> When Mr. Conrad's new preface (and we are delighted with this idea) comes, we will set the new book.[20]

It is interesting to see that for the American publisher the difference between "short story" and "tale" was fundamental for commercial reasons. If Doubleday planned to use "short stories" for those "of less than 20,000 words,"[21] it was perhaps because the public would relate them to a certain type of fiction. Inclusion of stories like "Falk" or "Typhoon" made it inadmissible for the volume to be called "short stories," and they chose "shorter tales" instead, a more comprehensive and much vaguer label. With reference to Conrad's view on this matter of genre: in spite of the fact that he had a clear idea of what was "not a short story,"[22] he did not pay much attention to the denomination label the pieces included in the volume were going to be given. He did not refer to the selection as "shorter tales" till the very end, when he told Pinker he had sent the "preface" to Doubleday. In the typescript of the "Preface" kept in the Berg Collection of the New York Public Library, the word "stories" of the title had to be crossed out and substituted by "tales."[23]

Although a few other letters from Doubleday, Page, and Co. where a reference is made to *The Shorter Tales...* concerning strict business matters[24] remain, the editorial history of this anthology is traced. Nevertheless an important question remains, a question with no definite answer perhaps: what made Conrad accept the publication of such a volume despite his initial opposition to it and his old concern, expressed in numberless instances, about not being considered "a writer of the sea?"[25]

One could start by arguing that as Conrad, from the beginning of his carrier, had a prejudice against the American public[26] (considering it qualitatively beneath the English), so the publication of a selection meant no offense to the "unity of artistic purpose" of each of the collections of short stories if kept out of England: "My idea would be to have nothing of the sort in England," wrote Conrad in the first part of the February 12 letter to Pinker concerning Doubleday's plan for *The Shorter Tales....* On the other hand, Conrad knew perfectly well that publishing in America meant money and fame: his financial success and growth in readership began with the publication of *Chance* by Doubleday on March 26, 1914. When Conrad sent J. B. Pinker proof of *The Secret Agent* on August 5, 1907 he made a chance observation that time would prove absolutely right:

> Here's the last of the proof. Try to have a corrected set sent to the States. If the money or *the public* ever comes to us it will be from there. (*CL*, III, 463)

He knew that there was "a good deal of curiosity as to my (Conrad's) personality in the *US*,"[27] "that ever since *The Nigger*.... I have had in the U.S. a very good press-invariably,"[28] and that his May 1923 visit to America had been a complete success.[29] Though somehow flattering in tone he told his American friend Elbridge L. Adams on May 31, 1923: "I am going away with a strong impression of American large-heartedness and generosity" (Jean-Aubry, II, 315).

So, after the visit to the United States, it became absolutely evident for Conrad that this country was crucial for his present and future material success.[30] Conrad's usual concern with money continued. His poor health and his waning powers, his expensive way of life, his plan to move to another house, and so on, may account for the business-like attitude Conrad had during the last year or so of his life: "Conrad was 'slipping into an increasing commercial posture'" (Karl, 905). For instance: (1) his letters through the Winter and Spring to Ford Madox Ford concerning their collaborative works are somehow "disturbing" due to "their insistence on financial matters" as "their work together had now become 'properties'" (Karl, 898)[31]; (2) his continuous reference to money matters in the letters of this period, especially to Pinker[32]; (3) in a more humorous tone, the letter quoted above to Eric Pinker dated January 30, 1924 about "broadcasting readings of selected passages":

> If so I should like to know about the machinery for collecting fees. I must be very stupid, but broadcasting always has struck me as a sort of philanthropic undertaking and I don't want to be made a party of any philanthropy.

(4) a letter to Pinker on January 27, 1924 about an offer of 1,000 dollars from an American for signed copies of some his first editions:

> I can't understand that frame of mind, but strictly speaking it is no business of mine, and I will drop him a line to send the vols. along. As to remorse for exploiting human folly I understand that Napoleon and several other great men upon whom I am anxious to model conduct didn't know what remorse was.

(5) his consciousness about the value in pounds per word of his works. About the planned 5000-word preface to *The Shorter Tales...* he said in the letter to Eric Pinker dated February 12, 1924: "I can get L 250 any time for that text alone."

So Conrad wanted money and knew he could get it by exploiting his past work. But this time, the proposed publication scheme meant reshaping. His reluctant artistic side made itself heard. Publishing in America meant less of an artistic risk, but still it was a risk. Had not it been for F. D. Doubleday's insistence, his "old friend and publisher"(Conrad, "Preface," viii), Conrad would probably have rejected the plan. He had great confidence in him. Fame and money had come to Conrad through Doubleday and he was conscious of it. Doubleday's "'intensive culture' of Conrad success" that Conrad seemed to be joking about in the letter of January 30, 1924 was a serious matter that had begun back in 1913:

> The trouble with Conrad is, he is known to only a few people in this country.... Therefore, I (Doubleday) am convinced that there is no way of getting this author before the public except by some unusual and painstaking, as well as persistent effort.
>
> We are anxious to build Mr. Conrad's market in this country.
>
> What we are trying earnestly to do is to get a Conrad interest started.
>
> anything you (J. B. Pinker) can send me (Doubleday) about Conrad...will help just that much to keep our lines fresh and interesting. The American public has an unplumbed capacity for what is known as "human interest stuff" and as long as the supply lasts the propaganda will go on.[33]

Conrad knew from the beginning that an association with such an important publishing house as Doubleday, Page and Co. was a question of major interest for him. As he told Alfred A. Knopf (of Doubleday) on July 20, 1913: "All I can do to help you form a stable connection between me and the firm I am ready to do – even to the sacrifice of my personal tastes" (*CL*, V, 258). The "stable connection" that started at this time was so fruitful that it developed into a real friendship. On December 14, 1922 Conrad wrote to George T. Keating that F. N. Doubleday "is, as you know, my excellent publisher, but what's more he is a good friend to have"(Jean-Aubry, II, 290). Conrad opened his mind to Doubleday in a letter to him dated February 19, 1922:

> I feel that my affairs in America need give me no concern since your invariable kindness, forethought and interest expressed so often in word and deed assure me that they are in the hands of a friend.
>
> This profound conviction, dear Mr. Doubleday, is a source of comfort to me; for it is not "agreements" but the certainty of a friendly appreciation in those closely associated with his work that give confidence and support to a writer. (267)

Conrad, eventually, acceded to "take" some of his "stories out of their appointed places in the group to which they originally belonged" (Conrad, "Preface," viii). He probably did because he needed money, or because he saw no risk in it being read by a public (i.e., the American) he did not think much of in artistic terms, or, maybe, because this scheme came from Doubleday, in whom he had a great amount of trust. Be it as it may, Conrad came up with another scheme (the one that was published) that altered the publisher's original plan completely and ended up being the expression of a very particular view and highly symptomatic production. Conrad did for the first time something he had never done before: consciously select and unify previous work into something new.

NOTES

1. I am greatly indebted to the Trustees of Joseph Conrad Estate for granting me permission to quote from Conrad's unpublished material held at the Berg Collection of English and American Literature, The New York Public Library, Astor, Lenox and Tilden Foundation. I would also like to express my gratitude to the staff of the Berg Collection, without whose collaboration this paper could not have been written. Likewise I wish to thank Mr. Peter Redmon for his suggestions and his helpful revision of the typescript.

2. D. Rude gives December 1924 as the date of publication of the volume. Judging from lists of new books and pieces of advertisement that

appeared in American periodicals, I consider November 1924 as the actual date of the publication. See: "Latest Books," *New York Times*, 9 Nov. 1924, sec. 3, 28; *The Shorter Tales* of Joseph Conrad. Advertisement, *New York Times*, 16 Nov. 1924, sec. 3, 12; *The Shorter Tales* of Joseph Conrad. Advertisement, *New York Times*, 30 Nov. 1924, sec. 3, 10; "The New Books. Fiction," *The Saturday Review of Literature*, 15 Nov. 1924, 291; "The Reader's Guide. Week-End Suggestions," *New York Evening Post Literary Review*, 8 Nov. 1924, 13.

3. This letter is a proof of the inaccuracy of the following affirmation and conclusions in D. Rude's article:

> The scheme for the volume proposed by Doubleday *has not survived*, but we can glean its essential features by examining Conrad's memo responding to it. *To be called Stories of the Sea*, the proposed anthology *would have 16 or 17 stories* selected on the basis of common length, *22,000 words*. Conrad's friend, Muirhead Bone, *was to have been asked to contribute an introduction*. (Rude, 191, emphases mine)

As we can see in the February 1 letter, Doubleday's scheme survived, the volume was not to be called *Stories of the Sea* but *Short Stories (from) by Joseph Conrad* (there is an alternative "from" on the page with Doubleday's suggested list), the exact number of stories the publisher proposed was 15 (not 16 or 17) and their common length was not 22,000 words but just 20,000. Finally, Muirhead Bone's introduction was just an alternative among others.

4. Actually, "Heart of Darkness" is 38,000 words long. For the number of words of Conrad's stories I follow: L. Graver, "Appendix," in his *Conrad's Short Fiction*, (Berkeley: U. of California P., 1969), 201-6.

Besides "Heart of Darkness" the other stories that were to make up the volume were, as ordered in Doubleday's list, the following: "The Secret Sharer," "To-morrow," "The Lagoon," "An Outpost of Progress," "The Brute," "The Inn of the Two Witches," "The Informer," "Because of the Dollars," "The Partner," "Il Conde," "The Idiots," "Karain," "An Anarchist," and "Youth."

5. Shortly after his visit to Oswalds on November 18, 1920 to interview Conrad for *Bookman*, Ernest Rhys wrote to him to ask for "the right to reprint one of his short stories in a collection of such things" (Rhys, "A Night with Joseph Conrad," 300). He sent Conrad, along with the proposal, a Hogarth print to persuade him to agree. Conrad ignored Rhys's offer completely. When both men met again on November 28, 1922, Conrad still did not want to hear a word on the matter: "There [Dent's office] I reminded him how he had evaded my question about the short story and he shook his head" (300). For the exact date of Rhys's visit to Oswalds: Joseph Conrad, "To James B. Pinker," 18 November 1920, Berg Collection, New York Public Lib., New York. (The part referring to Rhys's visit is omitted in Jean-Aubry, II, 250.) For the date of Rhys's meeting with

Conrad in Dent's office see Watts, 135 n15. Rhys was the founder and editor of the famous "Everyman Library" (Dent), "a series of popular reprints on a completely new scale" that started in 1905 (Roberts, 8). Conrad had shown his dislike for an outcome of the "Everyman" project: a cheap periodical bearing the same name. (See: Joseph Conrad, "To Charles Sarolea," 6 August 1912; "To James B. Pinker," 23 January 1913; "To Norman Douglas," late January 1913 «he calls *Everyman* a "rotten rag"»; "To J. B. Pinker," 27 January 1913 «"penny rag"» (*CL*, V, 94, 166-8).

Conrad's letter to Pinker of January 9, 1924 refers to Rhys's project of a second volume, as it is clear in the letter sent by the latter to Pinker in January 7, 1924 discussing the conditions and giving the list of the stories to be included along with their authors. The "similar proposal" Conrad said he had "declined" the year before may be Rhys's project to include "The Lagoon" in the first anthology (of 1923). Perhaps Conrad's reason for not agreeing to the project was pecuniary. See Rhys Ernest, "To Eric Pinker," 19 December (no year): "It would be unfair to the other contributors to the volume to offer a fee of more than L10 for Mr. Conrad's story."

6. Joseph Conrad, "To Eric Pinker," 9 February 1924, Berg Collection, New York Public Lib., New York. At the beginning of April 1922, Conrad received a letter from Joseph Reilly of Ginn and Co. asking for permission to print some of his short stories in a collection to be titled *The Short Story and Its Masters*. The stories to be included were: "An Outpost of Progress," "Karain," "The Lagoon," "Amy Foster," and "To-morrow." Conrad's note to Eric Pinker on verso of Reilly's letter stated that he thought Reilly wanted "too many" stories, that he did not understand "what sort of vol[ume]" he was going to make, yet did not "care very much for it" as "the money can't amount to anything in a publication of that kind." The note Conrad sent Pinker in April 1922 is written on verso of Reilly's letter.

I agree completely with the following commentary made by D. Rude in his essay:

> When Conrad points out (in the "Preface" to *The Shorter Tales*) a second theme in the volume, the contrast between youth and maturity inherent in the volume, his comments echo the pattern which he ascribed to *Youth*, a volume dealing with "the three ages of man" in his letter of 7 February to Doubleday. This fact suggests that Conrad's schemata for the volume may have been generated even before he read and rejected the Doubleday proposal. (Rude, 194)

7. In the same way he had agreed to a school edition of "Youth" and "Gaspar Ruiz" by Dent in 1920 and was willing to agree to a proposal from Eveleigh Nash to publish a volume consisting of "Youth" and "Heart of Darkness" as "'The End of the Tether' could, strictly speaking, make a volume by itself later, should Nash want to do it." Discussed by Conrad in two letters to James B. Pinker on July 13, 1920 and on October 19, 1921, respectively.

8. The other letter referred to by D. Rude: Joseph Conrad, "To Frank N. Doubleday," 8 May 1924, Doubleday Collection, Princeton University Library, Princeton, New Jersey.

9. F. N. Doubleday and S. A. Everitt's letter to Eric Pinker on February 1, 1924. I quote from a note added by hand (probably Everitt's) to the list proposed by Doubleday: "Note – The word estimates are very rough and found to be very liberal." Certainly, these estimates were inexact. According to L. Graver's list the total amount of words would be 180,500 (in Doubleday's scheme) and 107,000 (in Conrad's counter-scheme.) According to Conrad's own estimate the volume proposed by him would be "of about 124,000 words" (127,000 in Doubleday's estimate, and 107,000 according to Graver's word count).

10. Conrad's letter to Frank N. Doubleday on February 7, 1924 (Jean-Aubry, II, 338).

11. Joseph Conrad, "To Alfred A. Knopf," 24 August 1913. *CL*, V, 275. Conrad is actually referring here to two stories, the other being "Amy Foster."

12. Joseph Conrad, *Typhoon and Other Stories*. London: Heinemann, 1903.

13. In the "Preface" to *The Shorter Tales*..., Conrad explains that it is his "desire to give prominence to the stories which begin" each part (i.e., "Youth" and "Typhoon," respectively). There is a third story, that ends the first part, that belongs to the same collection: "To-morrow" (xi).

14. Of "The Inn of the Two Witches" Conrad pointed out in his "counter-scheme" (the third part of the February 12 letter): "the Inn is based subtly on the fidelity of the old seaman Tom to his young officer, which seems even to endure after death."

15. The excerpt of the March 27 letter quoted by D. Rude is:
> I think that in republishing any of my former work it cannot but do good to have some fresh matter included; if only for the reason that it would force every collector of Conrad's items to buy the book, or his collection would not be complete. And of course, it may, I suppose, have some effect also with the general public. (Rude, 193)

16. Najder states in a footnote of his outstanding *Joseph Conrad. A Chronicle* (1983) that the "Preface" was sent on April 30, 1924, a fact that seems very unlikely as Conrad was still working on it on May 1, 1924.

17. Joseph Conrad, "To Eric Pinker," [May 1924], Berg Collection, New York Public Lib., New York. Conrad did not date this letter. Internal evidence makes it obvious it was written in May 1924, and likely on Tuesday, May 6. I have corrected the number of words as the amount given in the typescript is obviously wrong 20,000 words.

Conrad alluded to Doubleday's satisfactory reception of the "Preface" in two letters: "To Richard Curle," May 1924, and "To Frank N. Doubleday," 2 June 1924, published respectively in Curle, 186-7, and Jean-Aubry, II, 344.

18. Letters to Eric Pinker of February 12, March 10, and March 12, 1924.

19. Letter to Eric Pinker of May 1, 1924.

20. Doubleday, Page and Co agreed immediately to Conrad's "counter-scheme" and were willingly open to "any suggestions from you (Pinker) or Mr. Conrad" and "glad, of course, to carry out the necessary changes." So, when Conrad suggested substituting "Falk" for "The Inn of the Two Witches" Doubleday agreed right away, too.

21. Letter from F. N. Doubleday and S. A. Everitt to Eric Pinker, February 1, 1924.

22. Joseph Conrad, "To J. B. Pinker," 28 February 1911, *CL*, IV, 417. Discussing "Freya of the Seven Isles" (26,000 words) Conrad "beg(s) to point out to you (Pinker) that in common fairness a work of that nature cannot come within the definition of short story."

23. Corrections of this eight-page manuscript were made in an unknown hand.

Another proof of Conrad's lack of concern for these subtle matters of genre differentiation is the fact that he called this "a volume of selected stories" in the first line of the preface (Conrad, "Preface," v).

24. S. A. Everitt's letter to Eric Pinker of May 23, 1924, Frank Doubleday's telegram to Eric Pinker on August 14, 1924, and Doubleday's letter to Eric Pinker of November 7, 1924. These letters refer to issues such as royalties, proof sheets, and the contract of the volume.

25. Conrad, "Preface," ix. For Conrad's opposition to being classified as a writer of the sea see, for instance: Joseph Conrad, "To H.-D. Davray," 8 Nov. 1906 and "To J. B. Pinker," 6 May 1907 in *CL*, III, 372-3 and 434-5, respectively. See also: "To Richard Curle," 14 July 1923; "To Richard Curle," 17 July 1923; "To Henley S. Canby," 7 Apr. 1924 in Jean-Aubry, II, 313-18, 320-1, and 341-2, respectively. See the quotation of a letter dated May 19, 1916 to F. N. Doubleday in F. R. Karl's *Joseph Conrad: The Three Lives*, 782 (also quoted in Rude, 194-5).

Despite what these letters said about his rejection of being considered a writer of sea stories, Conrad was going back to the sea theme and discussed maritime matters during the last period of his life. See, for instance, the three letters he wrote Laurence Holt (the Managing Director of the Ocean Steam Ship Co., Ltd., Liverpool) in July 1920 (Jean-Aubry, II, 244-7), or Admiral Goodenough on Sept. 25, 1920 (248-9), or Capt. A. W. Phillips on January 12, 1924 (333-4). On the other hand, of the 19 pieces (written mostly in the 1920s) that constitute *Last Essays* (1926) eleven deal to a greater or lesser extent with the sea.

26. Discussing American rights on a future volume (*Tales of Unrest*) Conrad pointed out to T. Fisher Unwin on April 14, 1897 that his feeling towards the publication of this collection of short stories was:

> That I would like to secure a copyright for the purpose of *not* publishing there. I need not go into the causes of my dislike for that public. They would probably appear absurd. And if you secure the copyright it will be for yourself only. (*CL*, I, 351)

27. Joseph Conrad, "To J. B. Pinker," 18 September 1908, ibid., IV, 125.

28. Joseph Conrad's letter to Alfred A. Knopf on July 20, 1913, ibid., V, 257.

29. See the affectionate letters to his wife, Jessie, of May 1923, Jean-Aubry, II, 307-14. Writing to his wife four days after his arrival:

> I will not attempt to describe to you my landing, because it is indescribable. To be aimed at by forty cameras held by forty men is a nerve-shattering experience. Even D'day looked exhausted after we had escaped from that mob, – and the other mob of journalists.... I went along like a man in a dream.... (Jean-Aubry, II, 307).

30. Conrad did not agree to give F. M. Ford rights to publish *The Nature of the Crime* in the United States arguing that Doubleday was his publisher there. He told Pinker to tell Ford that: "Conrad's affairs in America are too important to be disregarded" – Joseph Conrad, letter to Eric Pinker, 15 February, 1924, Berg Collection, New York Public Lib., New York.

31. Karl also points out how Conrad "had become another man, a plutocrat or a man living on his stock dividends" (Karl, 904).

32. Joseph Conrad, letters to Eric Pinker, 14 May 1923; May 1923 (no day); 11 June 1923 and 14 June 1923, Berg Collection, New York Public Lib., New York. In these letters Conrad refers to some "saving scheme" Doubleday had designed for Conrad. Conrad tries to convince Pinker about the convenience of this scheme to take care of domestic expenses.

33. Frank N. Doubleday's letters to James B. Pinker of July 23, 1913; July 28, 1913; January 12, 1914; March 13, 1914.

WORKS CITED

Ambrosini Richard. *Conrad's Fiction as Critical Discourse*. Cambridge: Cambridge U. P., 1991.

Conrad Jessie. *Joseph Conrad as I Knew Him*. London: Heinemann, 1926.

Conrad Joseph. "Letters to James B. Pinker and Eric Pinker," mss and tss. Berg Collection, New York Public Lib., New York.

Conrad Joseph. *The Shorter Tales of Joseph Conrad*. Garden City, N.Y.: Doubleday, Page, 1924.

Conrad Joseph. "Preface," to *The Shorter Tales of Joseph Conrad*. ts. Doubleday files, Berg Collection, New York Public Lib., New York.

Conrad Joseph. "Preface," to *The Shorter Tales of Joseph Conrad*. New York: Doubleday, Page, 1924, v-xii.

Curle Richard, ed. *Conrad to a Friend. 150 Selected Letters from Joseph Conrad to Richard Curle*. New York: Russell and Russell, 1928.

Doubleday Frank N., Everitt S. A. "Letters to James B. Pinker and Eric Pinker." Berg Collection, New York Public Lib., New York.

Graver Lawrence. "Appendix," in Graver Lawrence. *Conrad's Short Fiction*. Berkeley: U. of California P., 1969, 201-6.

Jean-Aubry Gérard. *Joseph Conrad: Life and Letters,* 2 vols. Garden City, N.Y.: Doubleday, Page, 1927.

Karl Frederick R. *Joseph Conrad: The Three Lives*. New York: Farrar, Straus and Giroux, 1979.

Najder Zdzisław. *Joseph Conrad: A Chronicle*. New Brunswick, N.J.: Rutgers U.P., 1983.

Reilly Joseph. "Letter to Joseph Conrad," 22 March 1922. Berg Collection, New York Public Lib., New York.

Rhys Ernest. "A Night with Joseph Conrad," *Everyman Remembers*. New York, Cosmopolitan, 1931, 291-301.

Rhys Ernest. "Letters to Eric Pinker." Berg Collection, New York Public Lib., New York.

Roberts J. Kimberley. *Ernest Rhys*. Wales: U. of Wales P., 1983.

Rude Donald W. "Conrad as Editor: The Preparation of *The Shorter Tales*," in *Joseph Conrad. Theory and World Fiction*. Proceedings of the Comparative Literature Symposium, January 23-25, 1974, eds. Wolodymyr T. Zyla and Wendell M. Aycock. Lubbock, TX: Texas Tech Press, 1974, 189-96.

Watts Cedric. *Joseph Conrad: A Literary Life*. New York: St. Martin's, 1989.

Index of Names

Index of Conrad's Works

The published volumes of the series
Conrad: Eastern and Western Perspectives